Business Ethics

Foundations of Business Ethics

Series editors: W. Michael Hoffman and Robert E. Frederick

Written by an assembly of the most distinguished figures in business ethics, the *Foundations of Business Ethics* series aims to explain and assess the fundamental issues that motivate interest in each of the main subjects of contemporary research. In addition to a general introduction to business ethics, individual volumes cover key ethical issues in management, marketing, finance, accounting, and computing. The books, which are complementary yet complete in themselves, allow instructors maximum flexibility in the design and presentation of course materials without sacrificing either depth of coverage or the discipline-based focus of many business courses. The volumes can be used separately or in combination with anthologies and case studies, depending on the needs and interests of the instructors and students.

1 John R. Boatright, *Ethics in Finance*, third edition
2 Ronald Duska, Brenda Shay Duska, and Julie Ragatz, *Accounting Ethics*, second edition
3 Richard T. De George, *The Ethics of Information Technology and Business*
4 Patricia H. Werhane and Tara J. Radin with Norman E. Bowie, *Employment and Employee Rights*
5 Norman E. Bowie with Patricia H. Werhane, *Management Ethics*
6 Lisa H. Newton, *Business Ethics and the Natural Environment*
7 Kenneth E. Goodpaster, *Conscience and Corporate Culture*
8 George G. Brenkert, *Marketing Ethics*
9 Al Gini and Ronald M. Green, *Ten Virtues of Outstanding Leaders: Leadership and Character*
10 Mark S. Schwartz, *Business Ethics: An Ethical Decision-Making Approach*

Business Ethics

An Ethical Decision-Making Approach

Mark S. Schwartz

WILEY Blackwell

This edition first published 2017
© 2017 John Wiley & Sons, Inc

Registered Office
John Wiley & Sons Ltd, The Atrium, Southern Gate, Chichester, West Sussex, PO19 8SQ, UK

Editorial Offices
350 Main Street, Malden, MA 02148-5020, USA
9600 Garsington Road, Oxford, OX4 2DQ, UK
The Atrium, Southern Gate, Chichester, West Sussex, PO19 8SQ, UK

For details of our global editorial offices, for customer services, and for information about how to apply for permission to reuse the copyright material in this book please see our website at www.wiley.com/wiley-blackwell.

The right of Mark S. Schwartz to be identified as the author of this work has been asserted in accordance with the UK Copyright, Designs and Patents Act 1988.

All rights reserved. No part of this publication may be reproduced, stored in a retrieval system, or transmitted, in any form or by any means, electronic, mechanical, photocopying, recording or otherwise, except as permitted by the UK Copyright, Designs and Patents Act 1988, without the prior permission of the publisher.

Wiley also publishes its books in a variety of electronic formats. Some content that appears in print may not be available in electronic books.

Designations used by companies to distinguish their products are often claimed as trademarks. All brand names and product names used in this book are trade names, service marks, trademarks or registered trademarks of their respective owners. The publisher is not associated with any product or vendor mentioned in this book.

Limit of Liability/Disclaimer of Warranty: While the publisher and author have used their best efforts in preparing this book, they make no representations or warranties with respect to the accuracy or completeness of the contents of this book and specifically disclaim any implied warranties of merchantability or fitness for a particular purpose. It is sold on the understanding that the publisher is not engaged in rendering professional services and neither the publisher nor the author shall be liable for damages arising herefrom. If professional advice or other expert assistance is required, the services of a competent professional should be sought.

Library of Congress Cataloging-in-Publication Data applied for.

Hardback ISBN: 9781118393444
Paperback ISBN: 9781118393437

A catalogue record for this book is available from the British Library.

Cover image: Jules Correa / EyeEm/Gettyimages

Set in 10.5/12.5pt MinionPro by Aptara Inc., New Delhi, India
Printed and bound in Malaysia by Vivar Printing Sdn Bhd

10 9 8 7 6 5 4 3 2 1

To my parents, Albert and Eileen Schwartz

Contents

Acknowledgments

First, I want to thank my wife Iris, for her continued support through all of my endeavors.

I want to thank the Wiley-Blackwell production team including Liam Cooper, Allison Kostka, Marissa Koors, Manish Luthra, Aileen Castell, Jane Grisdale, and Anula Griffiths for their greatly appreciated editorial support. Thanks to Elaine Silverstein for her valuable comments on an earlier version of the manuscript, along with the other anonymous reviewers. Thanks to my sister Lisa Bonen for her editing suggestions.

I want to especially thank Professor W. Michael Hoffman, and not just for his careful reviews and very helpful comments on various drafts of the book manuscript. It was Professor Hoffman, who, along with Professor Robert Frederick as the editors of the *Foundations of Business Ethics* series, gave me the opportunity to write this book, and I couldn't be more grateful and appreciative.

As this book is about business ethics and ethical decision making, I want to thank Professor Emeritus Wesley Cragg, my former PhD supervisor, who helped provide me with the tools to enter the academic world of business ethics and who completely exemplifies in my mind the character trait of "integrity."

I want to thank all of my students over the years. By bringing their personal ethical dilemmas into the classroom for discussion, we (and particularly myself) have all gained a much greater understanding of the challenges we face in trying to find ethically optimal solutions in the real world.

Finally, I need to thank my parents, Albert and Eileen Schwartz, who have always been my greatest role models (including ethical role models) throughout my entire life.

I would like to thank the *Journal of Business Ethics*, *Business Horizons*, and Broadview Press for permission to draw on the following previously published articles or book chapters:

Schwartz, M.S. 2016. Ethical decision making: an integrated approach. *Journal of Business Ethics*, 139: 755–776 (adapted for Chapter 2).

Schwartz, M.S. 2011. *Corporate Social Responsibility: An Ethical Approach.* Peterborough, Ontario: Broadview Press, pp. 29–49 (adapted for Chapter 4).
Hoffman, W.M. and Schwartz, M.S. 2015. The morality of external whistleblowing: a commentary on Richard T. De George. *Journal of Business Ethics*, 127: 771–781 (adapted for Chapter 5).
Schwartz, M.S. 2013. Developing and sustaining an ethical corporate culture: the core elements. *Business Horizons*, 56: 39–50 (adapted for Chapter 6).

Introduction to Ethical Decision Making

As we live our lives, whether as a parent or child, spouse or partner, relative or friend, or employee or manager, we presumably try to be the best that we can be in what we are doing. We want to live up to all expectations; those of others and of ourselves. Our basic goals include making a decent living, enjoying our work careers, making our loved ones proud, and taking care of the well-being of our families in relative security and material comfort. But at the very least, we wish to stay out of trouble, not get fired, avoid being sued, not harm others, and certainly not end up in jail. Basically, we hope to fulfill our responsibilities both at work and at home, while living a good life with no major regrets.

We have many motivations to achieve these goals, including feelings of loyalty, love, responsibility, self-worth, and self-satisfaction. But along the way and on a daily basis, as we attempt to fulfill our life objectives, we inevitably face *ethical dilemmas* that need to be resolved. Sometimes we simply don't realize we are facing ethical dilemmas, and make decisions we realize only in hindsight should have been handled differently. In other cases we might realize there are potential ethical implications to our actions but we decide to ignore them, either consciously or subconsciously. Often, this is because we choose to do what will help us achieve what we *want*, rather than what we know we *ought* to do. Either way, there are going to be potential implications as a result of our actions or inaction, both for ourselves and for others, throughout our lives.

Just like everyone else, I have faced and continue to face ethical dilemmas. I still vividly remember being in junior high school and sitting in my mathematics class. Just after class ended I opened one of the textbooks that had been left on the desk. I discovered that a 20 dollar bill had been left inside the textbook. Thoughts immediately crossed my mind. Should I keep it? What would I buy with it? What about the other student who had forgotten about his or her money? Why did the other student leave a 20 dollar bill in a textbook in the

Business Ethics: An Ethical Decision-Making Approach, First Edition. Mark S. Schwartz.
© 2017 John Wiley & Sons, Inc. Published 2017 by John Wiley & Sons, Inc.

first place? Twenty dollars was a lot of money for a teenager at that time. In the end, right after class, I decided to take the money to the Principal's office. Why did I do this? Why didn't I just keep the money? No one would ever have known if I had kept it. To this day I'm still not sure why I returned it.

Later on as a first year law student, without too much disposable cash around, I discovered there was a scholarship I could apply for. I knew of another student who could also use the money, and I was also aware that she had received better grades than I had. If I told her about the scholarship, she would probably apply reducing my chances of receiving the scholarship. Should I tell the other student about the scholarship opportunity? In the end, I told her. Fortunately, we both received the scholarship. But how would I have felt if only she had received it? Or what if I hadn't told her and only I had received it? Would I have felt guilty? Would I have looked back and felt I made the right decision?

After graduating from law school, I started working for a big downtown law firm. Despite generally enjoying the practice of law, I also noticed a number of things that caused me concern. I was invited into the office of an associate lawyer who said he would teach me what I needed to know to become a partner. He showed me how I could "bump up" the time sheets for each client by adding a few minutes to each activity's entry. He said that at the end of the day, he knew he had spent "x" number of hours per day at work, and that he was simply adding in the extra time that he didn't quite document properly during the day. When I expressed a bit of surprise at this technique, he said that corporate clients wouldn't notice or care in any event. I wondered, is everyone doing this, and are the senior partners aware that this practice was taking place? Later, while I was meeting with a senior lawyer in his office, a client called. I heard the lawyer explain to the client that while he could not advise him to destroy a particular document that the client had just found, if the document continued to exist, it would have to be produced to the opposing side and the client would definitely lose his case. The lawyer then hung up. I assume that document was never seen again.

Later, I began to notice that many of the other junior lawyers at the firm were taking advantage of the "free dinner after 7:00 p.m." policy, which was intended to encourage employees to work well past 7:00 p.m. After discovering that my colleagues had no concerns, I also began to wait until exactly 7:00 p.m. to go pick up my meal from a restaurant and eat it at home. This was of course justified in my mind, since everyone seemed to believe they were working hard and deserved the "free" dinners. In any event, I did technically stay until 7:00 p.m., and if this was an issue, the firm could always modify its policy. I wondered how many other ethical issues I would face if I remained in the practice of law.

After deciding to leave the practice of law for academia, I was at a job interview for my first full-time academic position at a business school. The position included teaching both the subjects of business law and business ethics. I felt fortunate to have been invited to the campus, and I wanted to do well during the interviews. With a wife and two young children, getting my first academic appointment was certainly a priority. While meeting with one of the senior professors, I was asked a question that I never expected. She asked: "If you could only offer one course to business students, which one would it be, business law, or business ethics?" I knew that the interviewer was a professor who taught and published in the field of business law, and would therefore presumably prefer to hear "business law" as my response. I immediately asked myself, should I give her the answer which I believed she wanted to hear, and likely improve my chances of being hired?

Without thinking too much, I gave the response I sincerely believed, "business ethics." I indicated my reason, that if students understand their proper ethical obligations, then as future managers most of their legal obligations would necessarily be accounted for. I also suggested that managers that focus only on their legal obligations might neglect their ethical obligations potentially leading to serious negative consequences for others. In the end, I did not receive an offer for the position, and I'll never know if my answer made any difference in making their decision. But I thought how ironic it was that I considered giving an insincere answer during an interview for a position teaching business ethics.

I don't tell these stories to suggest that I am necessarily an ethical or at times unethical person or a good or bad role model. In fact, there's no question that just because someone teaches business ethics or moral philosophy (or is a religious leader, president of a country, politician, prosecutor, judge, police officer, or chief executive officer) means they are necessarily the most "ethical" person.[1] But when I reflect on my life, the most salient decisions made in the past that define who I really am all seem to hinge on those incidents that involved ethical implications. But it's not just the more important decisions in our lives that stand out. In fact, every single day, we face ethical dilemmas or issues that require resolution. Sometimes we recognize these dilemmas as having ethical implications, such as impacting others, and sometimes we don't. Sometimes we only realize the ethical implications days or weeks after we have acted a certain way. And even when we do recognize that we are facing ethical dilemmas, there are many different reasons why we decide how to act a particular way on any given day.

Unethical Activity in Society

So how much unethical or immoral activity is taking place in society in general?[2] It seems that dishonesty, cheating, and breaking promises starts early, and continues throughout life for many. In terms of dishonesty, some researchers have found that on average we lie two to three times for every

10 minutes that we speak, that by age three we know how to fib, and by age six we already know how to lie.[3] One of the more famous lies includes former US President Bill Clinton, who first publicly stated: "I did not have sexual relations with that woman, Ms Lewinski…these allegations are false, and I need to go back to work for the American people."[4] Later, Clinton publically admitted: "While my answers were legally accurate, I did not volunteer information. Indeed, I did have a relationship with Ms Lewinsky that was not appropriate. In fact, it was wrong. It constituted a critical lapse in judgment, and a personal failure on my part for which I am solely and completely responsible…I misled people, including even my wife."[5]

Cycling athlete Lance Armstrong, at one point named one of *Time* magazine's "Most Influential People,"[6] vehemently denied for years taking performance enhancing drugs leading to winning the Tour de France only to later confess that he had been lying the entire time.[7] Armstrong finally publicly admitted during an interview with Oprah Winfrey the following: "In all seven of your Tour de France victories, did you ever take banned substances or blood dope?" "Yes." "For 13 years you didn't just deny it, you brazenly and defiantly denied everything you just admitted just now. So why now admit it?" "That is the best question…I don't know that I have a great answer. I will start my answer by saying that this is too late…this story was so perfect for so long…You overcome the [cancer] disease, you win the Tour de France seven times. You have a happy marriage, you have children. I mean, it's just this mythic perfect story, and it wasn't true."

Brian Williams, a prominent and highly regarded US television news anchor who received several Emmy awards, claimed he had been on a helicopter that was shot down in Iraq when it was later discovered this was not in fact true.[8] Williams later publicly stated: "I made a mistake in recalling the events of 12 years ago. I want to apologize. I said I was travelling in an aircraft that was hit by RPG fire, I was instead in a following aircraft…."[9] From these examples we see that even revered athletes, highly respected journalists, and even US Presidents are capable of publicly lying under certain circumstances, and are able to continue living with the lie for years.

In terms of cheating, one study found that over half of US high school students admitted to cheating on a test the previous year.[10] Business students in graduate university programs may be the worst offenders, with 56% admitting to cheating.[11] Close to half of the professors who catch their students cheating do not report them.[12] The rates of reported infidelity in the United States are approximately 19% for women and 23% for men.[13] Online dating services like Ashley Madison that facilitates extramarital affairs and whose slogan is "Life is short, have an affair," now has according to its website over 45 million members in dozens of countries.[14] In Britain, one study found that there were over 180,000 attempted fraudulent applications for motor insurance in one year, involving motorists who were lying about or knowingly failing to disclose important information.[15] Approximately 17% of Americans cheat on their taxes, either by under-reporting income, not filing taxes, or underpaying taxes.[16] Virtually everyone has at one point faced the dilemma whether to engage in illegally downloading music, television shows, movies, or computer software, or to purchase what we know to be counterfeit fashion products.[17]

Unethical Activity in the Workplace

And what about unethical activity in the *workplace*? Is this of big concern? Unfortunately, the answer is yes. Every day, employees and managers face ethical issues, moral temptations, and organizational pressures, potentially leading to misconduct. Consider the following research on the extent of unethical and illegal activity taking place in the workplace. One national survey found that over 40% of US workers observed misconduct during the previous year, representing tens of millions of Americans.[18] The most significant types of misconduct observed include:[19]

- abusive behavior or behavior that creates a hostile work environment (18%);
- lying to employees (17%);
- a conflict of interest – employee's interests placed over the company's interests (12%);
- violating company policies related to Internet use (12%);
- discriminating against employees (12%);
- violations of health or safety regulations (10%);
- lying to customers, vendors, or the public (10%);
- retaliation against someone who has reported misconduct (10%);
- falsifying time reports or hours worked (10%);
- stealing or theft (9%).

In terms of theft, one study found that two-thirds of employees steal from their workplaces. The most common items stolen by employees include sticky notes, tape, scissors, toilet paper, copier paper, USB memory sticks, notepads, pens, staplers, and highlighters.[20] Another survey revealed the "most ridiculous excuses" actually used by employees in order to skip work including: "My plastic surgery needed some "tweaking" to get it just right"; "I was sitting in the bathroom and my feet and legs fell asleep. When I stood up, I fell and broke my ankle"; "I woke up in a good mood and didn't want to ruin it"; "I got stuck in the blood pressure machine at the grocery store and couldn't get out"; "I caught my uniform on fire by putting it in the microwave to dry"; and "I accidentally got on a plane."[21]

Anyone who has worked at a business organization could likely corroborate observing lying, cheating, broken promises, and other types of misconduct contrary to corporate policies or basic morality taking place at some point. Over the years I have read thousands of personal ethical dilemmas faced by MBA and undergraduate business students in their capacities as employees or managers. In many of these cases students have either witnessed unethical activity or were asked to participate in the misconduct. How can we explain the extent of the wrongdoing taking place? Why don't these employees realize that what they are doing is wrong? And if they understand it is wrong to lie, violate company policies, discriminate, retaliate, falsify, or steal, how do they rationalize or justify their actions to themselves? How will unethical activity ever be reduced if we do not understand why it occurs in the first place?

Major Corporate Ethical Scandals

Each of the examples described has consequences, but since they may not seem overly significant in terms of causing serious harm, we might choose to avoid worrying about such wrongful activity too much. Unfortunately, however, there are also examples of much more serious unethical conduct in the business world with much more significant impacts. Most are now familiar with the more highly publicized corporate scandals that have taken place over the years, resulting from the unethical decision making of a number of individuals including the most senior leaders of business firms. Several significant financial scandals have occurred all over the world including in the United States (e.g., Enron, WorldCom, Tyco International), in Japan (e.g., Toshiba[22]), in the UK and continental Europe (e.g., Barings Bank, Parmalat, Société Générale, Barclays Bank), and in Canada (e.g., Bre-X, Nortel Networks, and Hollinger International).[23] The US subprime mortgage debacle that triggered the 2008 financial crisis and recession only heightened the recognition among the public of the risks of widespread unethical activity within the financial community.[24]

Beyond the financial world, other corporate misconduct has caused significant harm to consumers. For example, significant consumer product scandals that have led to thousands of consumer deaths which could have been avoided include the Bridgestone/Firestone tire blowouts and Ford Explorer rollovers in 2001,[25] Merck's eventual recall of its pain killer Vioxx in 2004,[26] and melamine-contaminated Chinese infant formula leading to hundreds of thousands of sick babies and six deaths in 2008.[27] General Motors finally recalled its vehicles with faulty ignition switches in 2014 after more than 100 deaths.[28] In 2016, Japanese auto supplier Takata recalled tens of millions of air bag inflators that would explode during accidents. The Takata recall represents the largest auto safety recall in US history.[29]

The natural environment continues to be impacted by business decisions, including BP's 2010 massive oil spill in the Gulf of Mexico[30] and the Japanese 2011 Fukushima nuclear reactor leak due to inadequate planning for the effects of a large-scale earthquake and tsunami.[31] Volkswagen was hit in 2015 with a massive scandal involving cheating on their vehicles' emissions tests in order to sidestep pollution standards affecting millions of their vehicles.[32] In 2015, the collapse of a tailings dam owned by mining companies BHP and Vale led to Brazil's worst environmental disaster, killing 19 people and unleashing 60 million cubic meters of mud and mine waste into the river valley below.[33]

In terms of international business, bribery and corruption scandals continue to arise for companies including Siemens in Europe in 2008[34] and Petrobas in Brazil in 2015.[35] Multinational companies appear to disregard their ethical obligations in terms of the safety of the factories of their suppliers in developing countries sometimes leading to building collapses or deadly fires.[36] Annual surveys by the organization Transparency International continue to demonstrate the high levels of perceived corruption taking place within the public sector of many countries around the world.[37] In 2016, the "Panama Papers," consisting of millions of documents, were released revealing billions in assets hidden by government and business leaders through secret shell companies.[38] It seems unfortunately that a single day doesn't go by when we can't read at least one story in the news about misconduct taking place in the business world.

Given the extent of illegal and unethical business activity that continues to transpire and the resultant costs to societal stakeholders including shareholders, employees, consumers, and the natural environment,[39] the importance of *ethical decision making* by individual employees and managers in business organizations is no longer in doubt. Unethical activity continues despite the best efforts of business organizations to implement comprehensive ethics programs, including codes of ethics, compliance and ethics training, and reporting hotlines in the United States,[40] and in the UK and continental Europe.[41] Graduates of business schools continue to engage in misconduct despite the extent to which business schools around the world teach the subject of business ethics.[42] The significant negative yet potentially preventable costs to society resulting from the unethical actions of individual firm agents suggests that ethical decision making might be considered one of the most important processes to understand better, not only for business students and academics, but for the corporate community and society at large.[43]

An "Ethical Decision-Making Approach" to Business Ethics

There are a variety of ways to approach the topic of business ethics. *Business ethics* as an academic field can generally be understood as addressing business practices and behavior in terms of moral right and wrong.[44] The key consideration typically revolves around a normative assessment of the impacts of business activity on various *stakeholders*, meaning those individuals or groups who can affect or are affected by the firm's actions.[45] If the core goal of business ethics had to be reduced to just three words, I would suggest those words would be to *avoid unnecessary harm*.[46] While many still joke that "business ethics is an oxymoron" or as a subject must be the "shortest course in the world" with the "thinnest textbook," I would contend that ethics is absolutely necessary for business. For example, without a minimum degree of trust that the other side will follow through on its promises, business activity could not take place, irrespective of any legal contract.

So how is this book different from other business ethics books? Most traditional business ethics textbooks cover a range of topics, such as moral theory, corporate social responsibility (or the purpose of business),[47] as well as the firm's ethical obligations to its primary stakeholders including customers, employees, shareholders, government, suppliers, and the natural environment.[48] Other business ethics textbooks are anthologies, which consist of a series of key readings by different authors on a variety of business ethics-related topics such as affirmative action, discrimination, sexual harassment, worker health and safety, consumer protection, marketing, whistleblowing, or international business.[49] Rather than discussing a range of business ethics issues, this book takes a different approach and focuses on one particular component of the business ethics field, that of *ethical decision making*.

The reason for taking this particular and more focused approach is as follows. While all of the various business ethics topics are important, in the end each of these issues boils down to one important process, that of ethical decision making by individuals operating within business organizations, and in this respect represents the fundamental component or the underlying foundation for the entire business ethics field. At the core of business activity, ethical or unethical decisions are made by business firm agents that ultimately have important positive or negative impacts for the decision maker, for others, or for society at large. In fact, the ethical decision-making process may be one of the most relevant decision-making processes for every human being living on this planet, and is what potentially distinguishes us from the rest of the animal kingdom. It is for these reasons that I wanted to write this book, both for myself and for others, to begin to understand the range of discussion and research that has taken place on the very important subject of ethical decision making. Ethical decision making may in fact represent one of the most powerful lenses by which virtually all human activity and behavior, whether personal in nature or business-related, can be viewed, judged, and hopefully improved.

About This Book

So what is this book all about, and how does it address the ethical situations that we might face and the current misconduct taking place? When it comes to the subject of ethical decision making in the workplace, I believe that for teachers, students, and especially employees and managers, it is important to reflect on three basic interrelated questions. The first question is *descriptive* in nature: how do people decide whether to engage in ethical or unethical behavior? By understanding the ethical decision-making process, we can become aware of the factors that either assist or impede us from becoming aware that we are facing ethical dilemmas and as a result end up acting inappropriately. The second question is *normative* in nature: irrespective of how ethical decision making descriptively takes place, what standards, principles, or tests *should* we use to determine and ultimately engage in ethical behavior? Understanding the normative decision-making process becomes particularly important when we face and need to resolve more difficult and challenging ethical dilemmas.[50] In addition to knowing why people make ethical or unethical decisions as well as how we should decide what is right and wrong, we also need to move beyond the descriptive and normative questions and ask a more *practical* or instrumental question: What can the senior leadership of business firms do to help ensure that other firm agents act ethically and avoid problems?

This book, entitled *Business Ethics: An Ethical Decision-Making Approach*, will attempt to answer these questions by explaining the ethical decision-making process in terms of how it takes place (descriptive), how appropriate behavior should be determined (normative), and how ethical behavior can be encouraged and supported (practical). The overall goal is to provide readers with a basic roadmap to understand the key challenges we all face in being aware of ethical issues taking place around us all the time, determining the right course of action, and then actually following through with appropriate behavior.

Any book about ethical decision making would necessarily be built on a series of core assumptions. For this book, the following is assumed, with each assumption being open to challenge:

- Individual human nature is such that all behavior is assumed to be driven by two fundamental motives or objectives:[51] (i) self-interest (pleasure/desires/utility/self-preservation, referred to as the "*want* self"); and/or (ii) morality (abiding by one's moral commitments, referred to as the "*should* self"[52]). While these two objectives often merge together, they can also conflict with each other. It is when they are in potential conflict that most ethical issues arise for individuals operating within a business organization.

- In the more specific organizational context, all decision making by the firm or individual agents relates to either the economic (i.e., business or individual self-interest), legal, and/or ethical domains. Moral awareness only arises when we realize the ethical implications of the dilemmas we face, as opposed to merely the business or legal implications.
- The vast majority of firm agents, including executives, managers, and employees, are "good apples" and would prefer to act ethically (the "should self") under the right circumstances and with appropriate organizational support (i.e., "good barrels").
- A minority of firm agents will, however, act unethically (the "bad apples") with the "want self" taking priority when the opportunity exists regardless of the efforts of firms to prevent such unethical activity.
- The academic research community is still at the preliminary stages of properly understanding the ethical decision-making process, despite the fact that nearly 500 empirical studies with over 1,000 findings have already been conducted by ethical decision-making researchers since the late 1970s.[53] This does not negate, however, the need to understand the current state of the research, and only enhances the importance of conducting further research.

A Few Key Definitions

But before we proceed further, a few key definitions are required. An *ethical issue* is defined as a situation in which an individual must reflect upon competing moral standards and/or stakeholder claims in determining what is the morally appropriate decision or action. One might try to distinguish ethical issues or situations involving "ethical dilemmas" from those whereby an individual is facing a "moral temptation" circumstance. *Ethical dilemmas* are defined as those more challenging situations involving "right versus right" or "wrong versus wrong" alternatives, such as deciding which employee to lay-off or whether to anonymously report the misconduct of a manager. With every alternative, there are individuals who might benefit and those who might suffer, have their rights infringed, or be treated unfairly. The goal when faced with an ethical dilemma is to select the "most right" or "least wrong" among the various possible alternatives.

Moral temptations, however, involve "right versus wrong" alternatives linked more directly to our self-interest, such as deciding whether to steal supplies from the office supply cabinet or lie and call into work sick.[54] For moral temptation issues, we generally know we shouldn't act a certain way but might nonetheless rationalize or convince ourselves that the action is acceptable under the circumstances. *Moral judgment* is defined as the determination of the most ethically appropriate or least ethically objectionable course of action among potential alternatives. *Ethical behavior* is not defined merely as conforming to the legal or moral norms of the larger community,[55] but is behavior that can be supported by one or more moral standards.[56] These moral standards will be discussed in more detail in Chapter 4.

The Organization of the Book

To cover the broad topic of ethical decision making in organizations, the book is divided into three parts with seven chapters. As indicated above, the book consists of three interrelated parts: the *descriptive*, or how ethical decision making takes place (Part 1); the *normative*, or how ethical decision making should take place (Part 2); and the *practical*, or how ethical decision making can be improved in an organizational setting (Part 3).

Part 1 of the book provides an overview of the *descriptive theory* underlying ethical decision making. Chapter 1 addresses the question of what determines ethical behavior. Both individual and situational constructs and factors are discussed that can influence or moderate behavior including an individual's moral character along with the situational nature of the issue, the organizational factors, and the personal context. In Chapter 2 a new ethical decision-making framework is proposed which binds together the rationalist (or reason-based) approach with the non-rationalist (or intuition/emotion-based) approach, called "Integrated Ethical Decision Making." The proposed model is described beginning with initial awareness of an ethical issue leading to judgment, forming an intention to act, and finally to actual behavior. Chapter 3 describes the dominant impediments or barriers to ethical decision making including improper framing, cognitive biases, psychological tendencies, moral rationalizations, and self-interest.

Part 2 of the book provides a *normative framework* for ethical decision making. Chapter 4 provides a basis for how ethical decision making should take place which is called "Multifaceted Ethical Decision Making." The framework includes the application of several moral standards, followed by consideration of several ethical decision-making tests referred to as the "Public-Parent-Pillow (3P) Filter." Chapter 5 provides a set of conditions under which it is morally permissible or morally obligatory to report misconduct taking place in a firm, considered to be one of the most significant ethical issues an employee can face during their career.

Part 3 of the book moves into a *practical application* of the descriptive and normative theory described in Parts 1 and 2. Chapter 6 sets out the three pillars that the senior leadership of business firms should make sure exist in order to develop and sustain an ethical corporate culture which can diminish the likelihood of unethical behavior. The pillars include infusing ethical values throughout the organization, developing comprehensive ethics programs, and ensuring ethical leadership. Chapter 7 provides an opportunity for readers to engage in a practical exercise in deciding how they would act. A set of common ethical dilemmas faced by employees in the workplace is presented with commentary on their decisions based on the theories and principles set out earlier in the book. Finally, the conclusion of the book provides a series of key takeaways with respect to improving the quality of the ethical decision-making process.

A few final qualifications are in order. First, I will often refer to previous academic research that has been conducted. But I will also suggest my own approaches to ethical decision making as well. Second, to reduce somewhat the "academic bulkiness" of the chapters, I will use extensive endnotes and several appendices for providing additional theoretical background or commentary to many of the points which may be of interest for those who would like to see additional academic discussion on the topics. While the book is highly theoretical in nature, it does not provide the specific criteria for measuring many of the theoretical constructs which can be found elsewhere in the academic literature.[57] Third, due to its heavy reliance on theory, this book is primarily intended for academics or as a supplemental text for students taking a course in business or professional ethics. The book might also be of some assistance to those business practitioners, including employees, managers, executives, CEOs, board members, and consultants, who are looking to better understand ethical decision making in the workplace but from a more academic perspective. Chapter 1 of the book will now introduce the topic of ethical decision making by reviewing the key *individual* and *situational* constructs or factors that might influence the decision to engage in misconduct.

Notes

1. One study for example found that there was no difference between ethics professors and other professors in terms of their self-reported ethical behavior. See: Schwitzgebel and Rust (2014).
2. Although "ethics" can be distinguished from "moral" (e.g., ethics is the study of morality, while morals are the practice of ethics), throughout the book, the terms "ethics" and "ethical" will be used interchangeably with the terms "morality" and "moral" for ease of reference. See: Jones (1991, p. 367) who uses a similar approach.
3. See: Ulrich Boser, "We're All Lying Liars: Why People Tell Lies, and Why White Lies Can Be OK," *US News and World Report*, May 18, 2009, http://health.usnews.com/health-news/family-health/brain-and-behavior/articles/2009

/05/18/were-all-lying-liars-why-people-tell-lies-and-why-white-lies-can-be-ok (accessed 18 September 2016).

4. See: "Clinton: I Did Not Have Sexual Relations With That Woman," *YouTube* video, August 30, 2006, https://www.youtube.com/watch?v=KiIP_KDQmXs (accessed 18 September 2016).

5. See: "Bill Clinton Admits To Having Inappropriate Relationship with Monica Lewinsky," *YouTube* video, November 18, 2010, https://www.youtube.com/watch?v=UEmjwR0Rs20 (accessed 18 September 2016). Clinton also indicated the reasons for his lie: "I was motivated by many factors, first by a motivation to protect myself, from the embarrassment of my own conduct."

6. See: Elizabeth Edwards, "The 2008 Time 100: Lance Armstrong," *Time*, May 12, 2008, http://content.time.com/time/specials/2007/article/0,28804,1733748_1733756_1735280,00.html (accessed 18 September 2016).

7. See: Telegraph Sport, "Lance Armstrong's Interview with Oprah Winfrey: The Transcript," *The Telegraph*, January 18, 2013, http://www.telegraph.co.uk/sport/othersports/cycling/lancearmstrong/9810801/Lance-Armstrongs-interview-with-Oprah-Winfrey-the-transcript.html (accessed 18 September 2016).

8. See: Emily Steel and Ravi Somaiya, "Brian Williams Suspended From NBC for 6 Months Without Pay," *The New York Times*, February 10, 2015, http://www.nytimes.com/2015/02/11/business/media/brian-williams-suspended-by-nbc-news-for-six-months.html (accessed 18 September 2016).

9. See: Emily Steel and Ravi Somaiya, "Brian Williams Suspended From NBC for 6 Months Without Pay."

10. See: Thomas Ehrlich and Ernestine Fu, "Cheating in Schools and Colleges: What To Do About It," *Forbes*, August 22, 2013, http://www.forbes.com/sites/ehrlichfu/2013/08/22/cheating-in-schools-and-colleges/ (accessed 18 September 2016).

11. See: McCabe *et al.* (2006).

12. Forty-four percent of professors did not report students who they had caught cheating. See: *Maclean's*, "The Great University Cheating Scandal," February 9, 2007, http://www.macleans.ca/general/the-great-university-cheating-scandal/ (accessed 18 September 2016).

13. See: Kim Carollo, "Equal Opportunity Cheating: Women and Men Cheat at Same Rate," *ABC News*, June 21, 2011, http://abcnews.go.com/Health/women-cheating-men-study/story?id=13885519#.UENkZ1QcAi4 (accessed 18 September 2016).

14. See: Ashley Madison website, http://www.ashleymadison.com (accessed 18 September 2016). The Ashley Madison website was hacked leading to the release of the members' identities. See: Alex Hern, "Infidelity Site Ashley Madison Hacked as Attackers Demand Total Shutdown," *The Guardian*, July 20, 2015, http://www.theguardian.com/technology/2015/jul/20/ashley-madison-hacked-cheating-site-total-shutdown (accessed 18 September 2016).

15. See: Rupert Jones, "Fraudulent Insurance Claims Running at 500 a Day," *The Guardian*, September 17, 2014, http://www.theguardian.com/money/2014/sep/17/fraudulent-insurance-claims-500-per-day (accessed 18 September 2016).

16. See: Allison Linn, "Cheat on Taxes? Never! (Really)," *CNBC*, March 3, 2014, http://www.cnbc.com/id/101456854 (accessed 18 September 2016).
17. See: Hilton *et al.* (2004); Koklic *et al.* (2016). Fifty-seven percent of those surveyed admitted to using illegally downloaded software. See: William Jackson, "Surprise: 57 Percent Admit to Using Pirated Software," *GCN*, May 15, 2012, http://gcn.com/articles/2012/05/15/cybereye-57-percent-use-pirated-software.aspx (accessed 18 September 2016).
18. See: Ethics Resource Center (2014). Although the Ethics Resource Center is now part of the Ethics & Compliance Initiative (ECI) as of June 2015, the Ethics Resource Center will be referred to as the original author of the various studies referred to throughout the book. See: Ethics & Compliance Initiative website, https://www.ethics.org/home (accessed 18 September 2016).
19. Other types of misconduct observed include (Ethics Resource Center, 2014, pp. 41–42): violating employee wage, overtime, or benefit rules (9%); delivery of substandard goods or services (9%); abusing substances, such as drugs or alcohol, at work (9%); breaching employee privacy (8%); improper hiring practices (7%); sexual harassment (7%); breaching customer or consumer privacy (5%); violation of environmental regulations (4%); misuse of company's confidential information (4%); violating contract terms with customers or suppliers (4%); falsifying invoices, books, and/or records (4%); accepting inappropriate gifts or kickbacks from suppliers or vendors (4%); offering anything of value (e.g., cash, gifts, entertainment) to influence a potential/existing customer (4%); falsifying expense reports (4%); falsifying and/or manipulating financial reporting information (3%); improper use of competitor's proprietary information (3%); offering anything of value (e.g., cash, gifts, entertainment) to influence a public official (3%); and making improper political contributions to officials or organizations (3%).

    In Canada, similar to the United States, 42% of employees have observed some type of misconduct. The major types of workplace misconduct observed include: misuse of company property (28%) (e.g., misuse of confidential information, customer or employee privacy breach); harm to people (25%) (e.g., abusive behavior, lying to employees, discrimination, health or safety violations, sexual harassment, etc.); privacy violations (17%) (e.g., misuse of confidential information, customer or employee privacy breach); fraud (17%) (e.g., stealing, falsifying time sheets/expense reports, employee benefits violations); conflicts of interest (13%) (e.g., insider trading); environmental violations (12%) (e.g., dumping of hazardous waste, violating environmental standards); misrepresenting company results (11%) (e.g., misrepresenting financial records); and bribery and corruption (9%) (e.g., illegal political contributions, offering/accepting kickbacks or bribes) (9%) (see: Ipsos Reid, "Four in Ten (42%) Employed Canadians Have Observed Some Form of Workplace Misconduct: One in Five (17%) Cite Witnessing Privacy Violations," July 3, 2013, http://www.ipsos-na.com/news-polls/pressrelease.aspx?id=6187 (accessed 18 September 2016).
20. See: KMLE, "Top Office Supplies That Are Stolen & The Average Value of Contents in a Woman's Purse," May 16, 2012, http://kmle1079.cbslocal.com/2012/05/16/top-office-supplies-that-are-stolen/ (accessed 18 September 2016).

21. See: Susan Adams, "The Most Ridiculous Excuses for Skipping Work," *Forbes*, October 23, 2014, http://www.forbes.com/sites/susanadams/2014/10/23/the-most-ridiculous-excuses-for-skipping-work/ (accessed 18 September 2016).

22. See: BBC News, "Toshiba Chief Executive Resigns Over Scandal," July 21, 2015, http://www.bbc.com/news/business-33605638 (accessed 18 September 2016).

23. The list of scandals is quite extensive. Here is an additional list of some of the more significant financial scandals, with the year the scandal broke: Drexel Burnham Lambert (1987) – insider trading, stock parking (defunct); BCCI (1991) – money laundering (defunct); Salomon Brothers (1991) – treasury-bond auction scandal; Barings Bank (1995) – fraudulent trading of Nikkei-index contracts (defunct); Prudential Securities (1995) – fraud in selling limited partnerships; Bankers Trust (1995) – misrepresentations in derivatives trading; Daiwa Bank (1995) – concealed trading losses; Merrill Lynch and Orange County (1996) – leveraged interest-rate losses; Bre-X (1997) – massive fraud over extent of gold find (defunct); Enron (2001) – aggressive accounting (bankrupt); WorldCom (2002) – aggressive accounting (bankrupt); Parmalat (2004) – fraudulent accounting; Nortel Networks (2005) – aggressive accounting/bonuses; Hollinger International (2007) – executive self-dealing; Société Générale (2008) – trading scandal; Madoff Investment Securities (2009) – Ponzi scheme fraud (defunct); Barclays Bank (2012) – Libor rate scandal, Wells Fargo (2016) – fake bank accounts.

24. See: Vikas Bajaj and Louise Story, "Mortgage Crisis Spreads Past Subprime Loans," *The New York Times*, February 12, 2008, http://www.nytimes.com/2008/02/12/business/12credit.html (accessed 18 September 2016).

25. See: Mark Hosenball, "Ford Versus Firestone," *Newsweek*, September 18, 2000, http://europe.newsweek.com/ford-vs-firestone-159587?rm=eu (accessed 18 September 2016).

26. See: Duff Wilson, "Merck Agrees to Pay $950 Million Over Vioxx," *The New York Times*, November 22, 2011, http://www.nytimes.com/2011/11/23/business/merck-agrees-to-pay-950-million-in-vioxx-case.html (accessed 18 September 2016).

27. See: Yanzhong Huang, "The 2008 Milk Scandal Revisited," *Forbes*, July 14, 2014, http://www.forbes.com/sites/yanzhonghuang/2014/07/16/the-2008-milk-scandal-revisited/#669baca64428 (accessed 18 September 2016).

28. See: Margaret Cronin Fisk, "GM Ignition Nightmare Won't Go Away, for Victims or Company," *Bloomberg*, January 8, 2016, http://www.bloomberg.com/news/articles/2016-01-08/gm-ignition-nightmare-won-t-go-away-for-victims-or-company (accessed 18 September 2016).

29. See: Nathan Bomey, "Takata Air Bag Recall Now Largest in U.S. History," *USA Today*, May 4, 2016, http://www.usatoday.com/story/money/cars/2016/05/04/takata-airbag-recall-nhtsa/83926312/ (accessed 18 September 2016).

30. See: *The Guardian* website, "BP Oil Spill," http://www.theguardian.com/environment/bp-oil-spill (accessed 18 September 2016).

31. See: The Guardian website, "Fukushima," http://www.theguardian.com/environment/fukushima (accessed 18 September 2016).

32. See: Karl Russell, Guilbert Gates, Josh Keller, and Derek Watkins, "How Volkswagen is Grappling with its Diesel Deception," *The New York Times*, March

24, 2016, http://www.nytimes.com/interactive/2015/business/international/vw-diesel-emissions-scandal-explained.html (accessed 18 September 2016).

33. See: Stephen Eisenhammer, "Brazil's Prosecutors Hit Vale, BHP With $44 Billion Civil Lawsuit For Dam Collapse," *Reuters*, May 4, 2016, http://www.reuters.com/article/us-brazil-damburst-prosecutors-idUSKCN0XU2AH (accessed 18 September 2016).

34. See: Huffington Post website, "Siemens Bribery Scandal," http://www.huffingtonpost.com/news/siemens-bribery-scandal/(accessed 18 September 2016).

35. See: Mac Margolis, "Brazil's Petrobras Scandal Shakes Up the System," *Independent*, December 23, 2015, http://www.independent.co.uk/news/business/analysis-and-features/brazils-petrobras-scandal-shakes-up-the-system-a6759756.html (accessed 18 September 2016).

36. See: Irene Pietropaoli, "Philippines Factory Fire: 72 Workers Need Not Have Died," *The Guardian*, June 8, 2015, http://www.theguardian.com/global-development-professionals-network/2015/jun/08/philippines-factory-fire-72-workers-unions-human-rights (accessed 18 September 2016).

37. See: Transparency International website, "Corruption Perceptions Index," http://www.transparency.org/research/cpi/overview (accessed 18 September 2016).

38. See: The Guardian, "Panama Papers," http://www.theguardian.com/news/series/panama-papers (accessed 18 September 2016).

39. See: Ethics Resource Center (2014); US Sentencing Commission, *US Federal Sentencing Guidelines for Organizations*, http://www.ussc.gov/guidelines-manual/2014/2014-chapter-8 (accessed 18 September 2016); Association of Certified Fraud Examiners, *Report to the Nations on Occupational Fraud and Abuse: 2014 Global Fraud Study*, http://www.acfe.com/rttn/docs/2014-report-to-nations.pdf (accessed 18 September 2016).

40. See: Ethics Resource Center (2014, p. 48).

41. See: Webley (2011).

42. See: D. Rossouw and C. Stuckelberger (eds), *Global Survey of Business Ethics in Teaching, Training, and Research*, 2012, http://www.globethics.net/documents/4289936/13403236/GlobalSeries_5_GlobalSurveyBusinessEthics_text.pdf/d13e186c-198a-4e77-ac7a-9aa5584e7a8c (accessed 18 September 2016).

43. Treviño (1986, p. 601).

44. See: Velasquez (2012, p. 15). Business ethics as an academic field has a major overlap with other business and society fields including corporate social responsibility, stakeholder management, sustainability, and corporate citizenship. See: Schwartz and Carroll (2008).

45. See: Freeman (1984).

46. Of course, there will always be some degree of harm to others due to the actions of business organizations. The goal then is to diminish the extent of what can be considered to be *unnecessary* harm.

47. For a full discussion of the subject of corporate social responsibility, see: Schwartz (2011).

48. For example, see: Crane and Matten (2010); De George (2010); or Velasquez (2012).

49. For example, see: Beauchamp *et al.* (2009); Hoffman *et al.* (2014). Other business ethics books will focus more on particular subject areas, such as ethics in finance (Boatright, 2014) or ethics in accounting (Duska *et al.*, 2011).

50. Tenbrunsel and Smith-Crowe (2008, p. 549) clarify the difference between descriptive and normative: "[This] is the distinction between descriptive (or behavioral) approaches to ethics versus normative approaches: the goal of the former is to study what people do, and the goal of the latter is to construct argument regarding what people *should* do."

51. See: Etzioni (1988) for a full discussion of the theoretical and empirical basis for this assumption.

52. Bazerman and Tenbrunsel (2011, p. 66) define the "want self" as "…the side of you that's emotional, affective, impulsive, and hot-headed…the want self reflects our actual behavior, which is typically characterized by self-interest and a relative disregard for ethical considerations." In contrast, the "should self" is defined as being "…rational, cognitive, thoughtful, and cool-headed. The "should self" encompasses our ethical intentions and the belief that we should behave according to our ethical values and principles." Others have referred to the basic conflict of morality as a choice between our self-interest and the duty to be "other-regarding" (see: Maitland, 2002, p. 4). The constant daily conflict that takes place between our *want* and *should* selves also relates to Freud's *super-ego* (our moral conscience) versus our *id* (our basic instinctual drives) (see: Freud and Strachey, 1960).

53. Based on the meta-studies conducted so far including: Ford and Richardson (1994); Loe *et al.* (2000); O'Fallon and Butterfield (2005); Craft (2013); and Lehnert *et al.* (2015). The empirical research on the individual and situational factors of ethical decision making is discussed further in Chapter 1 and Appendix A.

54. See: Kidder (1995).

55. One definition of ethical behavior that has been proposed and used by other researchers is as follows: "…an ethical decision is defined as a decision that is both legal and morally acceptable to the larger community. Conversely, an unethical decision is either illegal or morally unacceptable to the larger community" (Jones, 1991, p. 367). I consider this too limited a definition of "ethical" to be utilized for the purpose of properly studying the ethical decision-making process. The author of this definition himself admits that his definition of an ethical decision is "imprecise and relativistic" and refers to the difficulties of establishing substantive definitions for ethical behavior (Jones, 1991, p. 367). Others have also suggested that this definition of what is ethical is "too relativistic" and avoids a precise normative position on right versus wrong (Reynolds, 2008; Tenbrunsel and Smith-Crowe, 2008). In addition, community norms can violate what are referred to as "hypernorms," or universal ethical principles (see: Donaldson and Dunfee, 1999).

56. While there is an extensive literature on moral theory, the *moral standards* can be grouped under three general categories: (i) conventions (e.g., including reference to industry or corporate codes of ethics); (ii) consequences (e.g., net impacts on all those affected); or (iii) duty-based values or principles (including

trustworthiness, respect, moral rights, and justice/fairness). See: Schwartz and Carroll (2003); Schwartz (2005).

57.   See: Agle *et al.* (2014) who provide the criteria and measurement tools for many of the variables and theoretical constructs discussed throughout the book.

References

Agle, B.R., Hart, D.W., Thompson, J.A., and Hendricks, H.M. (eds). 2014. *Research Companion to Ethical Behavior in Organizations: Constructs and Measures.* Cheltenham, UK: Edward Elgar.

Bazerman, M.H. and Tenbrunsel, A.E. 2011. *Blind Spots: Why We Fail to Do What's Right and What to Do About It.* Princeton, NJ: Princeton University Press.

Beauchamp, T.L., Bowie, N.E., and Arnold, D.G. (eds). 2009. *Ethical Theory and Business* (8th edn). Upper Saddle River, NJ: Pearson-Prentice Hall.

Boatright, J.R. 2014. *Ethics in Finance* (3rd edn). Oxford: Wiley-Blackwell.

Craft, J.L. 2013. A review of the empirical ethical decision-making literature: 2004–2011. *Journal of Business Ethics*, 177: 221–259.

Crane, A. and Matten, D. 2010. *Business Ethics* (3rd edn). New York: Oxford University Press.

De George, R.T. 2010. *Business Ethics* (7th edn). New York: Prentice Hall.

Donaldson, T. and Dunfee, T.W. 1999. *Ties That Bind: A Social Contracts Approach to Business Ethics.* Boston, MA: Harvard Business School Press.

Duska, R., Duska, B.S., and Ragatz, J.A. 2011. *Accounting Ethics* (2nd edn). Oxford: Wiley-Blackwell.

Ethics Resource Center 2014. *2013 National Business Ethics Survey.* Arlington, VA.

Etzioni, A. 1988. *The Moral Dimension: Toward a New Economics.* New York: The Free Press.

Ford, R.C. and Richardson, W.D. 1994. Ethical decision making: a review of the empirical literature. *Journal of Business Ethics*, 13: 205–221.

Freeman, R.E. 1984. *Strategic Management: A Stakeholder Approach.* Boston, MA: Pitman.

Freud, S. and Strachey, J. 1960. *The Ego and the Id.* New York: W.W. Norton & Company.

Hilton, B. Choi, C.J., and Chen, S. 2004. The ethics of counterfeiting in the fashion industry: quality, credence and profit issues. *Journal of Business Ethics*, 55: 345–354.

Hoffman, W.M., Frederick, R. and Schwartz, M.S. (eds). 2014. *Business Ethics: Readings and Cases in Corporate Morality* (5th edn). Chichester, UK: John Wiley & Sons, Inc.

Jones, T.M. 1991. Ethical decision making by individuals in organizations: an issue-contingent model. *The Academy of Management Review*, 16: 366–395.

Kidder, R.M. 1995. *How Good People Make Tough Choices: Resolving the Dilemmas of Ethical Living.* New York: Simon & Schuster.

Koklic, M.K., Kukar-Kinner, M., and Vida, I. 2016. Three-level mechanism of consumer digital piracy: development and cross-cultural validation. *Journal of Business Ethics*, 134: 15–27.

Lehnert, K., Park, Y., and Singh, N. 2015. Research note and review of the empirical ethical decision-making literature: boundary conditions and extensions. *Journal of Business Ethics*, 129: 195–219.

Loe, T.W., Ferrell, L., and Mansfield, P. 2000. A review of empirical studies assessing ethical decision making in business. *Journal of Business Ethics*, 25: 185–204.

Maitland, I. 2002. The human face of self-interest. *Journal of Business Ethics*, 38: 3–17.

McCabe, D.L., Butterfield, K.D., and Treviño, L.K. 2006. Academic dishonesty in graduate business programs: prevalence, causes, and proposed action. *Academy of Management Learning & Education*, 5: 294–305.

O'Fallon, M.J. and Butterfield, K.D. 2005. A review of the empirical ethical decision-making literature: 1996–2003. *Journal of Business Ethics*, 59: 375–413.

Reynolds, S.J. 2008. Moral attentiveness: who pays attention to the moral aspects of life? *Journal of Applied Psychology*, 93: 1027–1041.

Schwartz, M.S. 2005. Universal moral values for corporate codes of ethics. *Journal of Business Ethics*, 59: 27–44.

Schwartz, M.S. 2011. *Corporate Social Responsibility: An Ethical Approach*. Peterborough, Ontario: Broadview Press.

Schwartz, M.S. and Carroll, A.B. 2003. Corporate social responsibility: a three domain approach. *Business Ethics Quarterly*, 13: 503–530.

Schwartz, M.S. and Carroll, A.B. 2008. Integrating and unifying competing and complementary frameworks: the search for a common core in the business and society field. *Business & Society*, 47: 148–186.

Schwitzgebel, E. and Rust, J. 2014. The moral behavior of ethics professors: relationships among self-reported behavior, expressed normative attitude, and directly observed behavior. *Philosophical Psychology*, 27: 293–327.

Tenbrunsel, A.E. and Smith-Crowe, K. 2008. Ethical decision making: where we've been and where we're going. *Academy of Management Annals*, 2: 545–607.

Treviño, L.K. 1986. Ethical decision making in organizations: a person-situation interactionist model. *Academy of Management Review*, 11: 601–617.

Velasquez, M.G. 2012. *Business Ethics Concepts and Cases* (7th edn). Upper Saddle River, NJ: Prentice Hall.

Webley, S. 2011. *Corporate Ethics Policies and Programmes: UK and Continental Europe Survey 2010*, London, UK: Institute of Business Ethics.

Part One

Descriptive Theory

Chapter One

What Determines Ethical Behavior?

Why is it that certain individuals engage in unethical behavior in the business world, whereas others behave ethically? Several individuals through their unethical actions helped to contribute to the downfall of their firms, with the more classic examples including Jeffrey Skilling, Andrew Fastow, Bernie Ebbers, Nick Leeson, and Bernie Madoff. Jeffrey Skilling, the former Enron Chief Executive Officer, and Andrew Fastow, the former Enron Chief Financial Officer, engaged in practices that clearly deceived shareholders, leading to the bankruptcy of a firm that once topped the quality of management category in *Fortune* magazine's survey of most admired companies.[1] Former WorldCom Chief Executive Officer Bernie Ebbers helped bankrupt a firm that had become the second largest long distance US telecommunications company by improperly reporting $3.8 billion in expenses.[2] Ebbers was sentenced to 25 years in jail for securities fraud, conspiracy, and filing false reports.[3] Ebbers, who apparently once stated that a code of ethics for his firm would be a "colossal waste of time",[4] tried to defend himself by claiming he "had no idea what was going on."[5] Nick Leeson, unbeknownst to his superiors and while sitting in the Singapore branch office, bet the entire equity of Barings Bank on the Japanese Nikkei stock index leading to the 233-year-old bank's collapse.[6] Bernie Madoff, the founder of Bernard L. Madoff Investment Securities, stole billions from his clients through a fraudulent Ponzi scheme, which became the largest financial scandal of all time. Madoff was sentenced to 150 years in prison.[7]

Other high-profile individuals also caused significant harm to others or reputational damage to their firms through their unethical activity. Jérôme Kerviel brought his French bank Société Générale to the brink of financial collapse through covert trading leading to billions in losses.[8] Raj Rajaratnam, who once had an estimated net worth of over $1 billion, helped orchestrate one of the

Business Ethics: An Ethical Decision-Making Approach, First Edition. Mark S. Schwartz.
© 2017 John Wiley & Sons, Inc. Published 2017 by John Wiley & Sons, Inc.

largest insider trading scandals in Wall Street history and was sentenced to 11 years in prison.[9] Former UBS and Citigroup trader Tom Hayes was sentenced to 14 years in prison after being found guilty of conspiracy to manipulate the benchmark Libor rate. As the UK-based "ringmaster" of a global network, Hayes would apparently bully, bribe, and reward other traders and brokers for their help in skewing the Libor rate, used to price more than $350 trillion of financial contracts from credit cards to mortgages.[10] Former CEO Martin Shkreli of Turing Pharmaceuticals, after being criticized for raising the price of a single pill of a drug used to treat HIV patients from $13.50 to $750, was later arrested for securities fraud.[11]

But it's not just white collar crime that involves unethical activity. Employees call in sick even when they are healthy, use employee discounts to buy clothes for their friends, steal supplies from the office supply cabinet, and overly embellish their skills and qualifications during job interviews. Managers accept expensive gifts and entertainment from suppliers and abuse business expense accounts. Executives hire relatives or friends for positions even when there are more qualified candidates. In order to win contracts, salespeople promise potential customers that their product specification demands and deadlines will be met, despite knowledge that this will not take place. Why does all of this misconduct take place? Are all of these individuals just "bad apples"? Doesn't each of these corporate agents realize that what they are doing is wrong? And why do people engage in unethical behavior even when they realize it is clearly wrong to do so?

To address these questions, let's start by thinking about our own assumptions as to why unethical activity takes place. For example, when you read in the news about managers or employees who have engaged in misconduct, such as bribery, fraud, or insider trading, what are your initial assumptions? Do you assume that the primary reason for the misconduct is because of the person's weak moral character, in other words, their level of greediness versus possessing stronger moral values? Or do you believe that the situational context is equally important to predicting ethical or unethical behavior? Does the decision maker's perceived personal financial situation, the lack of sanctions, or the opportunity to engage in the misconduct without getting caught mainly drive their actions? And if the situational context is most important, does this mean that different people with varying degrees of moral character will tend to act the same way when faced with the same situational context?

Rather than focusing on only one reason or the other, this chapter assumes that both *individual* and *situational* reasons are equally important when it comes to explaining ethical decision making.[12] To explain this "person–situation" approach, we will first explore the impact of *individual* moral character, followed by the *situational* context including the particular issue, organizational factors, as well as personal constraints that drive behavior. Let's now begin by taking a closer look at the importance of an individual's *moral character* on ethical decision making.

The "Good or Bad Apple" Approach to Ethical Decision Making

While there are a number of possible explanations for unethical behavior, one possible starting point is to accept that there are a number of people, including those individuals mentioned above, who unfortunately based on who they are, tend to act unethically, or are more likely to be influenced by their circumstances to act unethically. Others are more likely to act ethically based on their individual ethical predisposition. In other words, we need to take into account the "bad" or "good" apples, or the bad features of otherwise good apples, as playing an important role in the ethical decision-making process.[13]

So how do we explain what makes someone a "good" versus a "bad" apple? While not always sufficiently emphasized, the reason that best explains why different individuals act differently in terms of their ethical behavior when faced with the same set of circumstances, is the person's *moral character*.[14] The moral character approach to ethical decision making and behavior has been around for thousands of years, and is based on the writings of Greek philosopher Aristotle who believed that what counts most is not our actions, but who we ought to be as a person in terms of the nature of our character and the virtues we possess.[15] Aristotle suggested that through training or repetition, we can acquire virtues and our virtuous activity will then become habitual. In other words, for Aristotle, the moral ideal is a person who naturally does the right thing.[16]

While there are several possible definitions of moral character, for our purposes *moral character* can be broadly defined as follows:

Moral character: *the capability to not only avoid acting inappropriately when facing a moral temptation situation, but to be able to engage in the proper resolution of ethical dilemmas, and to ultimately have the commitment and motivation to naturally engage in ethical behavior.*

Individuals like Jeffrey Skilling, Andrew Fastow, Bernie Ebbers, Nick Leeson, Bernie Madoff, Jérôme Kerviel, Raj Rajaratnam, and Tom Hayes all appear to have possessed weak moral character. On the other hand, those executives, managers, and employees who consistently do the "right thing" despite the possible ramifications to themselves, tend to possess strong moral character.

Let's now try to understand what moral character more specifically consists of in relation to ethical decision making.

There are two interrelated but distinct *dimensions* to our *moral character*: (i) our *capability* to determine morally right from wrong; and (ii) our level of *commitment* to consistently behave ethically according to our determination of the morally right course of action. Each of the two basic dimensions to moral character has three elements as follows:

First dimension of moral character – *capability* (the ability to properly determine morally right from wrong)

(i)   Moral maturity
(ii)   Moral value system
(iii)   Moral competence

Second dimension of moral character – *commitment* (the motivation to consistently do what we know or determine to be morally right)

(i)   Moral identity
(ii)   Moral willpower
(iii)   Moral courage

In other words, our moral character is based not only on our capability to recognize ethical situations and reach appropriate moral judgments, but the extent to which we are committed and motivated to act upon those moral judgments even when faced with adversity or pressures to act otherwise. Figure 1.1 uses the metaphor of an apple tree (with both good and bad apples) and its root system to depict how moral character is developed and sustained, along with the various situational pressures and incentives that can challenge a person's moral character (described further later) similar to the environmental forces and pressures that can affect the growth and quality of the apples growing on a tree (e.g., insects, pesticides, rain, or wind). We will now explore the different dimensions and elements of moral character in more detail.

Moral character – capability

The first dimension of *moral character* is a person's *capability* to determine morally right from wrong based on their (i) level of *moral maturity*, (ii) current *moral value system*, and (iii) level of *moral competence*. Let's now examine each of the first three elements of *moral character*.

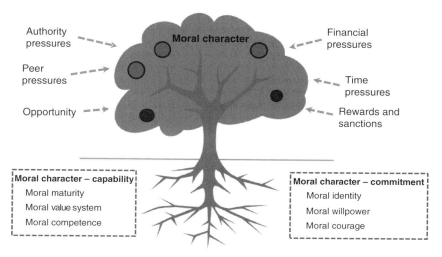

Figure 1.1   The root system of moral character.

Moral maturity

The first element of moral character is our level of *moral maturity*[17] which can be defined as follows:

> Moral maturity: *the stage of moral development by which a person determines morally right from wrong.*[18]

The primary contributor to cognitive moral development theory is moral psychologist Lawrence Kohlberg[19] who suggested that all human beings move through a series of stages of moral development from early childhood through to adulthood based on training or their interactions with others throughout their lives.[20] To come to this conclusion, Kohlberg and his colleagues used a series of ethical dilemmas to establish a person's stage of moral development. Possibly the most famous of the dilemmas Kohlberg used is known as the "Heinz Dilemma." It consists of the following:

> A woman was near death from a special kind of cancer. There was one drug that the doctors thought might save her. It was a form of radium that a druggist in the same town had recently discovered. The drug was expensive to make, but the druggist was charging ten times what the drug cost him to produce. He paid $200 for the radium and charged $2,000 for a small dose of the drug. The sick woman's husband, Heinz, went to everyone he knew to borrow the money, but he could only get together about $1,000 which is half of what it cost. He told the druggist that his wife was dying and asked him to sell it cheaper or let him pay

later. But the druggist said: "No, I discovered the drug and I'm going to make money from it." So Heinz got desperate and broke into the man's store to steal the drug for his wife. Should Heinz have broken into the laboratory to steal the drug for his wife? Why or why not?[21]

Try to decide what you would do if you were Heinz, and why. Would you steal the drug? For Kohlberg, it was not important whether the respondents in his experiments believed that Heinz should or should not steal the drug, but their moral reasoning process and the reasons why they came to their moral judgment. Based on his research findings, Kohlberg proposed three general levels of cognitive moral development each with two stages:[22]

I. The *pre-conventional* level with a focus on *oneself*:
- Stage one (punishment or sanctions): the *punishment and obedience* orientation. The consequences of an action determine its goodness or badness. *Example*: I decide not to engage in insider trading because I might end up in jail.
- Stage two (self-interest): the *instrumental* orientation. Right action is based on satisfying one's own needs and occasionally the needs of others. *Example*: I decide to take the kickback from a supplier because it benefits me.

II. The *conventional* level with a focus on others such as family, group, or nation:
- Stage three (referent others): The *interpersonal concordance or "good boy – nice girl"* orientation. Good behavior is that which pleases or helps others and is approved by them. Intention (he or she "means well") becomes important at this stage. *Example*: I sell the firm's services to clients in an overly aggressive manner in order to conform to my work group's sales expectations.
- Stage four (law): the *law* and *order* orientation. Right behavior consists of doing one's duty, respecting authority, following fixed rules, and maintaining social order. *Example*: I pay custom duties simply because it is legally required even when I could get away with not paying.

III. The *post-conventional* (autonomous) level with a focus on all of *humankind*:
- Stage five (social contract): the *social-contract legalistic* orientation. Right action is based on individual rights and standards which have been agreed upon by society. Society will agree there are times when laws/rules should be changed based on social utility. *Example*: I do not report a colleague for stealing because physical abuse by the police authorities in that country is taking place.

- Stage six (ethical principles): the *universal-ethical-principle* orientation. What is right is based on ethical principles such as justice, human rights, or social welfare. *Example*: I insist the company voluntarily recalls a potentially dangerous product despite the cost in order to avoid harming consumers.

So which stage or stages of moral development do you fall into? Did you reason that Heinz should steal (or not steal) based on the potential of going to jail (stage one) or because it was in Heinz's self-interest to keep his wife alive (stage two)? Was your decision based on expectations of Heinz's friends or relatives or his wife's friends or relatives (stage three) or simply because it was against the law to steal (stage four)? Did you believe it was okay to steal because under the circumstances society would understand and forgive Heinz for breaking the law (stage five)? Or did you believe it was okay for Heinz to steal because you considered human life more valuable than property rights meaning Heinz should steal even for a stranger (stage six)? Of note, Kohlberg believed that most adults end up reaching stages three or four of moral development, with only a small percentage ending up reaching stages five and six.

Kohlberg's theory of moral development, despite facing several criticisms,[23] has been given prominence as part of the *moral judgment* stage of several ethical decision-making models.[24] The presumption of Kohlberg is that a person with a higher level of moral development or moral maturity tends to engage in a higher stage of moral reasoning leading to more ethical behavior. In other words, a person with a high level of moral maturity bases their moral judgments on a set of moral values or principles *before* concerns over possible sanctions, their own self-interest, the views or norms of others, or just the legal system.

Moral value system
The second element of the capability dimension of our *moral character* is our current *moral value system* which can be defined as follows:

Moral value system: *the framework, approaches, or theories that guide our ethical choices and behavior.*[25]

This dimension of moral character overlaps with and provides the content of Kohlberg's fifth and sixth stages of moral development (the autonomy level) for each individual. A person's moral value system forms the basis for their moral character and helps answer the question "Which moral or ethical values or principles, if any, do you generally possess and rely upon to make decisions at a given point in time?"[26] A person with a strong moral value system can be distinguished from those who merely rely on external cues (Kohlberg's first four stages of moral development) for moral guidance (e.g., authority, rewards, norms, law). For example, a person with a strong moral value system would believe that moral values such as honesty, promise-keeping, loyalty, responsibility, respect, caring, and fairness should always be part of their decision-making process and should take priority even if there is a conflict with their self-interest in deciding what is right or wrong.[27]

There are a series of other similar concepts that are related to a person's *moral value system*. For example, *ethical predisposition* refers to the cognitive frameworks that people prefer to use in moral decision making.[28] Similarly, *ethical ideology*[29] refers to an integrated system of values, standards, beliefs, and self-assessments that define a person's orientation toward matters of right and wrong.[30] Others refer to *personal value orientations*[31] or *philosophy/value orientations*[32] that we each possess. These orientations typically distinguish individuals as being either *utilitarian* by basing their decisions on consequences, or *formalists* by basing their decisions on duties, rules, or obligations.[33] All of these related concepts (ethical predispositions, ethical ideologies, or value orientations) converge together in referring to our current *moral value system* that we carry with us on a day-to-day basis and which then makes an impact on the sorts of moral judgments we make.

Moral competence
The third element of moral character is a person's level of *moral competence*, which can be defined as follows:

> Moral competence: *the cognitive capability of a person based on their ethical knowledge and experience to resolve ethical dilemmas using sound critical reasoning skills.*[34]

While a person's *moral value system* might be considered the "fuel" of the moral reasoning process, a person's *moral competence* is the "engine" that allows us to process complex or challenging moral situations.[35] Those who possess strong levels of moral competence tend to be able to judge situations as right or wrong rather than remaining unclear or undecided over what the right action consists of. Those with strong moral competence also tend to possess a higher level of *moral sensitivity* or awareness of ethical situations, possibly due to ethics training they have received or due to reflection and learning from past ethical situations they have encountered.[36] For example, business ethics professors and ethics officers of organizations would presumably possess higher levels of moral competence in terms of their moral reasoning skills and heightened ethical awareness, although this would not necessarily translate into being more ethical in terms of behavior.[37]

The following example might help demonstrate strong *moral competence*. A 19-year-old manager of a Dairy Queen fast food outlet, Joey Prusak, witnessed a blind customer drop $20 on the floor while waiting in line. He saw another female customer pick up the money and immediately put it into her purse. When Prusak confronted the female customer, she said the money was hers. Prusak asked the female customer to leave the store, and then proceeded to give the blind customer $20 from his own pocket. Prusak's response later was as follows: "I was just doing what I thought was right … I did it without even really thinking about it … Ninety-nine out of 100 people would've done the same thing as me." Another customer who had witnessed everything wrote a letter to the store praising Prusak, which was then posted on the internet, and soon went viral.[38]

How should we understand Prusak's actions? It's not clear if other managers would have acted the same way. Why did he do this? One reason may simply be his level of *moral competence*. Based on his level of moral competence, along with his level of *moral maturity* and *core moral value system*, Prusak seems to have had the *capability* to immediately determine the ethically appropriate response to this situation.[39]

Moral character – commitment

Moral character, however, also includes not just our *capability* to reach proper moral judgments, but the willingness or motivation we have to consistently follow through on our moral judgments.[40] This can be referred to as the *commitment* dimension to our moral character, which includes the next three interrelated elements: (iv) *moral identity*; (v) *moral willpower*; and (vi) *moral courage*. Let's take a look at these three additional elements of moral character.

Moral identity
The fourth element of moral character (and the first element of the commitment dimension of moral character) is a person's knowledge about themselves as a moral actor, referred to as a person's *moral identity*[41] which can be defined as follows:

> Moral identity: *a mental representation of a person's moral character that is held both internally as well as projected to others.*[42]

Moral identity involves asking questions like: "What do I stand for?"; "What are my core beliefs?"; "Am I a moral person?"; and "How well do I live up to my core moral values?"[43] People can differ in the degree to which they experience moral identity in terms of how they define themselves. In general, those individuals with a strong *moral identity* possess a reliable *moral compass*, whereby their "true north" consistently defines and directs the person towards ethically appropriate behavior.[44] People with a strong moral identity also tend to have a strong *moral conscience*, and are able to anticipate feelings of *guilt* when they do not intend to act in a manner that supports and maintains their sense of moral identity. When this happens, they are more likely to *self-regulate* themselves in order to remain consistent with their understanding of what it means to be a moral person.[45] In other words, when a person's actions or intended actions are not in alignment with their perceived moral identity, they can experience *mental stress*, creating a desire to rectify the misalignment.

The Hollywood movie *Jerry Maguire* has a classic scene at the beginning that epitomizes the concept of moral identity. When Jerry (played by Tom Cruise), as a sports agent, realizes that what he is doing and how he is treating his clients no longer corresponds with his sense of moral identity, he takes drastic steps. Jerry asks himself "Who had I become? Just another shark in a suit?" We can now also each ask ourselves a similar question: do we believe we have a strong moral identity, and do we try to live up to it on a constant basis?

Moral willpower
Moral willpower is the fifth element of moral character which overlaps with moral identity and can be defined as follows:

> Moral willpower: *the motivation to act in accordance with our current moral value system.*[46]

Having the moral willpower to act on our moral judgments is not always easy. Moral willpower is required in order to sufficiently self-sanction or engage in self-control if we are to overcome and survive *moral temptation* situations with our *moral identities* remaining intact.[47] Anyone who has attempted to go on a diet when they love eating food or stop smoking when they are addicted to cigarettes understands the meaning and importance of willpower. You need not only the goal but the willpower to overcome the physical and mental desire to be able to avoid eating ice cream or smoking cigarettes, especially when they are readily available. When the judge sentenced former trader Tom Hayes for manipulating the Libor rate, he stated: "You succumbed to temptation because you could."[48]

Possessing *moral willpower* means overcoming situations that involve the possibility of personal gain or satisfying our "wants" when there are ethical implications in doing so. Like the muscles in our bodies, our *moral willpower* can be depleted following heavy testing or strengthened over time.[49] When our moral character is weak or has been placed under too much stress, we can more easily reach an *ethical tipping point* or *personal ethical threshold* and *morally compromise* our moral value system leading to unethical behavior.[50] In other words, we have the potential to become more susceptible to various external authority or peer pressures to act unethically. This can happen for example when our managers are putting pressure on us to unfairly take advantage of customers, or when our colleagues are encouraging us to join them in their unethical activity, such as padding expense accounts.

As an example related to moral willpower, I have heard from a number of employees who have faced the moral temptation situation where they can take a look at what they know to be highly useful confidential information.[51] The information could be of great value to themselves in their positions, as well as to their firms. Competitive information, for example, could have been accidentally sent by a competitor to you or accidentally left behind by a client (e.g., a competitor's bid) following a meeting. The expectation is that no one will know or realize that you have looked at the confidential information. What helps explain why one employee succumbs to the moral temptation and will look at the information, while another employee won't? The answer appears to be the *moral willpower* component of a person's moral character.

Moral courage
The sixth and final element of moral character is *moral courage* which can be defined as follows:

> Moral courage: *the ability to act ethically or to resist pressures to act unethically even when we are aware that there is a danger to ourselves in doing so.*[52]

Moral courage involves the question "To what extent am I prepared to stand up for my beliefs?" *Moral courage* determines whether we will act in ways that feel uncomfortable or will potentially harm our own interests when we know it is the right thing to do. Moral courage is often generated only when we feel a sense of *moral responsibility* to take ethical action in a given situation, even when support is not readily available from our peers or organizational leaders. This sense of psychological responsibility or moral "ownership" can be felt over the ethical nature of our own actions, those of our colleagues, or the actions of our organizations.[53]

Moral courage leading to action may be more likely when we believe we have the capability to address a specific ethical issue.[54] In a business organizational context, the strength of our moral character often dictates the extent to which we are prepared to challenge decision making by raising ethical concerns, report ethical misconduct, or report bad news or mistakes to our managers. Moral courage can also involve trying to protect colleagues who are being abused or harassed, or customers or clients who might be harmed, despite the risks placed on us. Whistleblowers like Jeffrey Wigand of Brown & Williamson Tobacco and Sherron Watkins of Enron (discussed further in Chapter 5), who were aware that by reporting misconduct internally within the firm they were putting themselves and their families at great risk, appear to demonstrate strong moral courage. If we have sufficiently strong *moral courage*, we are more committed to keeping our *moral identity* intact, and are prepared to push back and face any adverse consequences as a result.

One example related to moral courage arises from the dilemma faced by the engineers and managers of the company that provided the booster rockets for NASA's space shuttle *Challenger*. Morton Thiokol engineer Roger Boisjoly was aware of the safety dangers of launching the space shuttle in cold temperatures. Boisjoly did initially demonstrate moral courage by trying to convince his managers and NASA to delay the launch, but was apparently told to put on his "manager's hat" instead of his "engineer's hat."[55] It may be that despite a strong set of *moral values*, insufficient *moral courage* prevented Boisjoly as well as others from going outside the chain of command to try to stop the launch of the shuttle which might have prevented the deaths of all seven crew members following an explosion shortly after the shuttle's launch.[56] Examples like this make it clear that a strong moral character includes not only the capability to determine morally right from wrong, but the commitment and moral courage to act as well.

Strong versus weak moral character – examples

As a review, it might be helpful to look at another example of an employee who appears to possess strong moral character. A lifeguard at a Florida beach, Tomas Lopez, received an emergency call. Lopez had to decide whether to leave his lifeguard station to assist a swimmer who was swimming on an unpatrolled neighboring beach. The other beach had signs indicating that swimmers swam at their own risk. Instead of trying to help save the swimmer in such a situation, Lopez was, according to his firm's policy, supposed to call "911" and hope emergency staff arrived in time. Lopez was aware that he could be fired for breaking his company's rules. If you were Lopez, would you violate company policy and leave your station to try to save the swimmer, or just call 911 as you have been instructed to do?

Fortunately, the swimmer was saved in part by Lopez who left his post. But despite Lopez's beach continuing to be patrolled by other lifeguards, his actions led to him being fired by his company, since one of his employment obligations was to never leave his assigned post due to liability concerns. "I have no doubts I did the right thing," Lopez said afterwards. "I believe I did what was right, and that if someone needs help you're going to go help them, regardless if you're a lifeguard or not." In the end, the lifeguard management company realized it had made a mistake firing Lopez and offered him his job back, which Lopez declined.[57] This might be considered a case of strong moral character in terms of both *capability* and *commitment* leading to ethical action by Lopez, regardless of the potential for getting fired.

Not everyone demonstrates strong moral character however. In another case, over 100 student applicants figured out how to hack into a website showing their application status at several top US business schools. After discovering that this was taking place, several schools rejected their applications. The letter written by Harvard's Dean summarized his view that the students by hacking had demonstrated weak moral character. Here is the Dean's letter to the students (emphasis added):[58]

> I would like to have the last word on Harvard Business School's policy regarding applicants who hacked into the ApplyYourself, Inc., Web site containing confidential admissions information. This behavior is unethical at best – a serious breach of trust that cannot be countered by rationalization. Any applicant found to have done so will not be admitted to this School. Our mission is to educate principled leaders who make a difference in the world. To achieve that, *a person must have many skills and qualities, including the highest standards of integrity, sound judgment, and a strong moral compass* – an intuitive sense of what is right and wrong. Those who have hacked into this Web site have failed to pass that test. Kim B. Clark, Dean, Harvard Business School, Boston, Massachusetts

Weak moral character, especially weak *moral competence* and weak *moral willpower*, appears to have played a direct role in the students' lack of moral awareness or inability to self-regulate their actions. In terms of moral awareness, there were a number of students who indicated in online discussions afterwards that "they failed to see the ethical issue presented." There were even some students who thought the hacking students should be praised. One commented online: "Exploiting weaknesses is what good business is all about. Why would they ding you?"[59]

So what leads to a particular person possessing strong moral character in terms of their *capability* and *commitment* to engage in proper moral reasoning, judgment, and behavior? Almost all theoretical ethical decision-making models suggest that there is a set of *individual-based factors* such as demographic variables, psychological or personality variables,[60] personal values,[61] or personal experiences[62] that influence or might relate to the ethical make-up or predisposition of a particular person. To understand this better, Appendix A summarizes much of the key empirical research that examines the key individual *demographic* (e.g., gender, age, nationality, education, work experience, or religiosity) and *personality* or *psychological* factors that might influence a person's *moral character* which then potentially affects ethical decision making. Unfortunately, the research findings are quite mixed, and it can therefore quickly get very confusing to understand exactly which factors or variables might actually play a role and to what extent.[63] It may take some time before we fully understand the real underlying factors leading to strong or weak moral character, but regardless of how moral character develops, it clearly plays a key role in determining whether ethical or unethical behavior takes place.

The Situational Approach to Ethical Decision Making

We have now determined that being a "good" or "bad" apple, or a person with a strong or weak moral character is the critical starting point for predicting ethical behavior. The presumption is that if you put a person with strong moral character in a moral temptation situation alongside an individual with weak moral character, the person with the strong moral character will more likely tend to behave ethically. As a simple example, if someone finds a lost wallet with cash in it, whether they try to return it to the owner or simply keep the money will depend to a large extent on their moral character.[64] So why do good apples sometimes behave unethically?

One important reason is the *situation* they are facing or currently experiencing.[65] In fact, all dominant ethical decision-making models refer to situational or organizational factors that can impact the decision-making process.[66] Building on these past models, the situational context should be comprised of three interrelated components: (i) the *issue*; (ii) the *organizational environment*; and (iii) the *personal context*. I will now discuss each of these three components of the situational context.

Issue

With respect to the first component, rather than focusing on the good or bad "apples" (i.e., individual characteristics) or the good or bad "barrels" (i.e., organizational environment), some have argued that the *issue* itself (e.g., the worm?) should be the focus of ethical decision making.[67] As a factor, the issue variable would consist of three dimensions: (i) issue intensity; (ii) issue importance; and (iii) issue complexity. Let's now consider each of the dimensions of the issue-related variable.

Issue intensity
One approach to ethical decision making suggests that the *moral intensity* of an issue can impact each stage of the ethical decision-making process.[68] Issue intensity is defined as follows:

> Issue intensity: *the degree to which consequences, social norms, proximity, or deontological/fairness considerations affect the moral imperative in a situation.*

According to this view, the moral intensity of an ethical issue incorporates six components:

(1)   Magnitude of consequences (total harm/benefit caused);
(2)   Social consensus (degree of agreement that option is good or evil);
(3)   Probability of effect (likelihood action will cause expected benefit/harm);
(4)   Temporal immediacy (the length of time between the present and the consequences of the moral act);
(5)   Proximity of closeness (the feeling of nearness that the moral agent has for the victims or beneficiaries); and
(6)   Concentration of effect (the inverse function of the number of people affected by an act of given magnitude).[69]

For example, if a manager must decide whether to sell a defective unsafe product to a consumer, this would relate to several issue intensity criteria: *magnitude of consequences* (total harm caused by the unsafe product), *probability of effect* (chances of the consumer being harmed), and *concentration of effect* (large number of people harmed). If the product is expected to cause harm immediately, this would relate to the criterion of *temporal immediacy*. If the manager would be selling the unsafe product to immediate family members or friends, this would relate to the criterion of *proximity of closeness*. The criterion of *social consensus* would apply in terms of the broader community disapproving of the sale of such a product. Based on the criteria being met, *moral intensity* would be strong. The basic idea is that if I face a dilemma where someone could be seriously injured, especially a family member, or if a large number of people would be seriously injured in the near future, or if many people disapprove of a particular action, I would tend to be more aware that I face an issue with moral implications.[70]

In addition to consequences (either positive or negative), social norms, and the proximity or "closeness" the agent has to those affected, the characteristics of moral intensity should also include additional duty-based and fairness dimensions. In other words, the moral intensity of an issue would increase if an individual is facing a situation which might require violating or respecting rules (e.g., codes), laws, or the rights of others, or relate to fairness. This broader definition of moral intensity is in accordance with researchers who have recognized that moral intensity should include a broader range of ethical characteristics.[71] A higher level of moral intensity would then presumably increase the likelihood of moral awareness, as demonstrated in a number of research studies.[72]

Issue importance
Issue importance is another factor that can impact ethical decision making. Issue importance is defined as follows:

Issue importance: *the perceived personal importance or relevance of an ethical issue to an individual.*[73]

The reason for this approach is that any objective determination of issue intensity would be irrelevant unless the decision maker himself or herself perceived the issue as being of importance.[74] It seems to make sense that issues that the decision maker, for whatever reason, believes are important to him or her, would more likely impact the ethical decision-making process. The reasons for *issue importance* may be based on the person's *moral character* including his or her upbringing or past experiences. I might for example see an issue involving discrimination or harassment of others as much more important than someone else due to my past personal experience of being discriminated against or harassed. Issue importance might also be shaped by the firm's corporate policies or reward/sanction systems and the issues the firm focuses on. If issue importance to the decision maker is not considered, the ethical implications of the issue might be ignored altogether leading to a lack of moral awareness.[75]

Issue complexity
Another dimension of an issue that appears to have received little attention but potentially has important implications is the extent to which an issue is perceived to be complex. *Issue complexity* is defined as follows:

Issue complexity: *the degree to which issues are perceived to be hard to understand or difficult to resolve.*

Issue complexity can involve the perceived degree of conflict among competing moral standards or multiple stakeholder claims. More complex issues would require a higher degree of cognitive skill and effort to resolve, and require greater "cognitive expenditure",[76] which could affect our motivation to even attempt to resolve the dilemma or the process by which moral judgment is reached. It may be that a very complex issue lessens the chance that we will be morally aware of the issue,[77] or requires a more reflective reasoning process and a higher level of *moral competence* to resolve, as opposed to less complex issues whereby intuition or gut instinct may be sufficient.[78] For example, deciding whether to downsize and who to let go would represent a more complex ethical issue due to the impact on multiple stakeholders, such as the owners, the employees, and the employees' families. The decision would become even more complex if friendships might be jeopardized.

Issue complexity might also include other components such as the degree to which there are complicated facts involved or multiple factual assumptions that need to be made due to a lack of relevant information available. Such information may be necessary in order to understand properly the ramifications of a particular issue and its potential future harm to oneself or others.[79] As a result, regardless of its intensity or importance, the mere perceived complexity of the issue or dilemma could possibly cause us to ignore facing and addressing the issue altogether, leading to a type of "moral paralysis." For example, deciding whether to blow the whistle on firm misconduct can be a highly complex and difficult decision with ramifications to multiple parties, which might then prevent coming to any judgment on the ethically appropriate action to take.[80] Due to its potential impact, perceived *issue complexity* is also included in addition to *issue intensity* and *issue importance* as part of the issue-related situational construct.

Organizational environment

The second component of the situational context is the organizational environment or the "barrels" (or "baskets") in which employees are situated. One potentially useful way to denote organizational factors is to collectively refer to them as representing the *ethical corporate culture* of the organization.[81] *Ethical corporate culture*, as the overarching concept for all organizational environmental variables, is defined as follows:

> Ethical corporate culture: *the organizational formal and informal elements that contribute to an organization's ethical effectiveness.*[82]

Other ways of collectively referring to the various organizational elements is to refer to them as the firm's *ethical infrastructure*[83] or *ethical context.*[84] The ethical corporate culture would include several *formal* and *informal* systems such as communication, surveillance, and sanctioning systems. The key component of a *communication system* is the firm's *code of conduct* or *ethics*. A code of ethics can be defined as *a written, distinct, and formal document which consists of moral standards used to guide employee or corporate behavior.*[85] The majority of studies support the notion that codes of ethics are positively related to ethical decision making.[86] Other elements of a communication system would include firm mission statements, performance standards, and compliance or ethics training programs.

Surveillance systems are also important, such as performance appraisals and reporting hotlines. The most important element, however, may be sanctioning systems. A *sanctioning system* would include rewards and punishments such as evaluations, promotions, salary, and bonuses. Research has consistently found that rewards and sanctions impact ethical decision making.[87] Both the formal and informal systems form part of the *organizational climate* that supports the firm's ethical infrastructure.[88] A substantial body of empirical research has examined the potential impact the various components of an ethical corporate culture can have on ethical decision making by individuals within organizations.[89] The underlying assumption is that firms with a strong ethical culture and climate generally lead to more employees becoming aware of ethical issues and the importance of behaving in what would be considered by the company to be an ethical manner.[90] The various ways an ethical culture of a firm can be developed and sustained will be discussed in much more detail in Chapter 6.

There are other factors that should also be included as part of the organizational environment. This was made evident in the case of Enron. Enron had all the formal elements of a comprehensive ethics program, including a detailed 64-page code of ethics, ethics training, and a set of core ethical values. Yet other organizational factors clearly pushed executives and employees to act in an unethical manner. In fact, these other factors may ultimately represent the most significant factors that can influence good people to do some very bad things. For example, the impact of *significant* or *referent others/peers* can lead to one imitating or learning from the behavior of others. There is no question that we tend to imitate the behavior of others, even when it is contrary to our own views.[91] The impact of *authority pressures* such as managers or executives would also be included as part of the ethical corporate culture.[92] I have seen many cases of employees who receive ethically questionable orders from their managers and comply rather than risk the repercussions of disobeying an order. Authority pressures are often expressed in the form of setting unreasonable sales objectives or overly aggressive financial targets that can only be attained by subordinates crossing an ethical line.

The *opportunity* or the occurrence of circumstances that permit ethical/ unethical behavior would also be included as a component of an organization's ethical culture.[93] If there is no perceived opportunity to engage in the desired improper behavior, then this alone could prevent unethical behavior from taking place.[94] Other organizational factors have been examined such as the type of industry and the organization's size, but neither seems overall to have much of an impact on ethical decision making.[95] There are a number of other miscellaneous organizational variables that have received insufficient research treatment to date to support any generalized conclusions on whether they impact ethical decision making, but future research may lead to new discoveries.[96]

Personal context

Our *personal context* is the final component of the situational context. I believe this situational component needs to be emphasized much more as a major factor that impacts ethical decision making and behavior, and can influence a lot of seemingly "good" people to do some very "bad" things. Personal context is defined as follows:

> Personal context: *the individual's current situation which can lead to "ethical vulnerability" due to "personal need for gain" or time/financial constraints.*

The key variable of an individual's personal context is what I refer to as our perceived *need for personal gain*. I define "need for personal gain" as the current perceived desire to either improve or sustain our financial situation, status, career, or compensation. The need for personal gain is primarily based on the perceived financial situation of an individual. A strong need for personal gain can result from living beyond one's means, high debt, financial losses, or unexpected financial needs.[97]

The *need for personal gain* needs to be distinguished with a person's *moral character*. Some people are inherently unselfish or selfless, while some people are inherently greedy, meaning they have an insatiable desire for wealth, power, or ego that can never be satisfied, often leading to unethical or illegal behavior. The need for personal gain is a temporary state of affairs, whereas our moral character generally remains stable for a longer period of time. Quite often unethical behavior can be explained simply because of individuals who despite having a strong moral character believe they are in a dire financial situation with dependents to take care of. The variable of *perceived need for gain*, which would be based primarily on our self-interest, does not yet appear to have been proposed in the ethical decision-making literature, but is a critical component in fraud prevention literature. "Financial pressures," in addition to perceived opportunity and rationalization make up the "fraud triangle" that helps explain why most people commit fraud.[98]

Another way of expressing one's "need for personal gain" at any given point in time is what might be referred to as a person's current state of *ethical vulnerability*.[99] Ethical vulnerability means that if we are in a weak financial position, facing significant perceived financial pressures or obligations, with few or non-existent career or job alternatives available, we would presumably be in a much weaker position to resist unethical requests and put our job, promotion, or bonus at risk or be less willing to accept the "personal costs" of taking moral action.[100] In terms of employees that have faced ethical dilemmas at work, it seems that what often impacts their decision on how to act and whether to push back on unethical requests is whether they expect to remain in the job or industry, or require a reference for a future position. It also seems to depend to a large extent on their current family situation, such as being married with young children or with rent or mortgage obligations.[101] When you need your job and have dependents and financial responsibilities, you tend to have much less leeway to take risks on losing your job, even when you know acting a certain way is against your sense of moral identity.

Here's an example of a real dilemma faced by an employee (we'll refer to him as "Adam"), that highlights *ethical vulnerability*. Adam unfortunately lost his job, and during a tough time in the economy had been looking for a new job for over one year. Adam was married, and he and his wife had just had a new baby. Adam's financial situation was becoming extremely difficult, pressures on his marriage were intensifying, and he knew he had to find a job soon. Eventually, an opportunity arose and Adam received an offer to work for a very successful online gambling company. Finally, Adam's financial stress could be alleviated.

There was only one problem, however, but it was a big one. Adam's uncle had become addicted to online poker gambling. It didn't take too long for his uncle to gamble away his life savings and lose the entire equity in his home, leading to a divorce. The devastation of losing everything, including his family, was too much to bear. His uncle unfortunately and tragically committed suicide. Which online gambling site did the uncle use? Coincidentally, his uncle had been gambling on the website of the very same online gambling company from where Adam had finally received an offer, after searching for an entire year. Should Adam work for the online gambling company, which could be seen as contributing to the death of his uncle? What do you think Adam decided to do? When I read Adam's dilemma, I was fairly certain he would have turned it down. But then I realized the potential impact of *ethical vulnerability*. Adam took the job. He was able to convince himself that despite working for this firm, he would do everything he could within the company to make it a more responsible gambling site. It's not clear if Adam was able to do this, but at least he had stabilized his family's financial situation.

Other constraints such as *time pressure* or *limited financial resources* to do what we know to be right can also be considered part of the personal situational context.[102] The impact of *time pressure* on decision making was demonstrated in the famous "Good Samaritan" experiment, whereby seminary students about to give a talk on being a good Samaritan tended not to assist someone in distress when they were in a "high-hurry" condition.[103] Time pressures in an organizational context often arise when authority figures instruct their subordinates to complete a certain project within an unreasonable time frame which creates an incentive to cut ethical corners. In other cases, you might know what the right action to take is, such as properly compensating someone for the injuries you have caused, but do not have the *financial resources* or means to fully implement your moral judgment.

One or more of the situational factors can come into direct conflict with our *moral character* and whether we are able to withstand the pressures we face. These factors or pressures are depicted in Figure 1.1 and represent the "wind" that can cause the apples to fall from the tree or the "insects" that can make apples go rotten.[104] Figure 1.2 depicts each of the components of the situational context construct.

To provide greater clarity, Table 1.1 provides a summary of the definitions of the various constructs influencing ethical decision making.

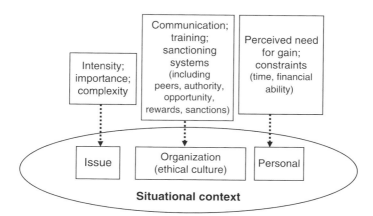

Figure 1.2 Situational context for ethical decision making. *Source:* Schwartz, M.S. 2016. Reproduced with the permission of Springer.

Table 1.1   Individual and situational moderating factors of ethical decision making. *Source*: Schwartz, M.S. 2016. Reproduced with the permission of Springer.

Construct	Definition
Individual	
(1) Individual moral character	The ability to avoid moral temptations, engage in the proper resolution of ethical dilemmas, and be motivated to engage in ethical behavior.
(a) Moral character – capability	An individual's ability to determine right from wrong based on their level of *moral maturity*, current *moral value system*, and level of *moral competence*.[105]
(b) Moral character – commitment	The capability to act consistently according to a person's moral character.[106] It is comprised of *moral identity*, *moral willpower*, and *moral courage*.
Situational	
(1) Ethical issue	A situation requiring a freely made choice to be made among alternatives that can positively or negatively impact others.[107]
(a) Issue intensity	The degree to which consequences, social norms, proximity, or deontological/fairness considerations affect the moral imperative in a situation.[108]
(b) Issue importance	The perceived personal relevance of an ethical issue by an individual.[109]
(c) Issue complexity	The perceived degree of difficulty in understanding an issue. Based on perceived conflict among moral standards or stakeholder claims or required factual information or assumptions needed to be made.
(2) Organization's ethical culture	The organizational formal and informal elements that contribute to an organization's ethical effectiveness. This includes formal and informal communication, surveillance, and sanctioning systems.[110]
(3) Personal context	The individual's current situation which can lead to "ethical vulnerability" due to "personal need for gain" or time/financial constraints.[111]

Chapter Summary

We have now reviewed the factors that might influence or moderate the ethical decision-making process. There are two essential sets of constructs or factors that influence decision making: *individual* and *situational*. The first individual-based set of factors relates to the general concept of *moral character*, that is, what sort of ethical individual are you to begin with? Are you generally someone who has strong ethical values, and tends to stick with them even when you are pressured not to do so? Or are you mainly a person who focuses on your self-interest, to the neglect of others? We initially defined moral character as including your *level of moral maturity*, current *moral value system*, and level of *moral competence*. A strong moral character means you have the *capability* to figure out what is the right thing to do. But moral character also includes your *commitment* to behave ethically. If you have a high level of commitment based on a strong *moral identity*, *moral willpower*, and *moral courage*, you are more likely to form an intention to act and behave according to your moral judgment, no matter what the consequences to yourself.

We also discussed *situational* factors affecting ethical decision making which can challenge a person's moral character. The first situational factor involved the *issue* itself. Was this an issue that had strong *moral intensity*? That you perceived as being *important* to you? That wasn't so *complex* that you could actually work through and formulate a resolution? What sort of *organizational factors* were present or lacking? How strong was the ethical culture of the organization? Was there a code that was well communicated and supported by training? Were there rewards and sanctions for behavior, and what sort of opportunity was there to engage in unethical behavior without getting caught? Finally, what was the *personal context*? Were you facing difficult personal financial circumstances, with dependents to take care of, or under time pressure to act?

Understanding how ethical decision making works and the various factors that affect the process including our individual *moral character*, the *issue*, the *organizational environment*, and our *personal situation* are all important. But possibly more important is trying to understand *how* we arrive at ethical decisions. In Chapter 2, we review a comprehensive ethical decision-making theoretical framework, called "Integrated Ethical Decision Making," which helps to explain the ethical decision-making *process*, from initial awareness of an ethical issue, to moral judgment, to forming an intention to act, to actual behavior.

Notes

1. See: CNN, "Enron Fast Facts," April 26, 2015, http://edition.cnn.com/2013/07/02/us/enron-fast-facts/(accessed 29 August 2016).
2. See: Luisa Beltran, "WorldCom Files Largest Bankruptcy Ever," *CNN Money*, July 22, 2002, http://money.cnn.com/2002/07/19/news/worldcom_bankruptcy/ (accessed 29 August 2016).
3. See: Dionne Searcey, Shawn Young, and Kara Scannell, "Ebbers is Sentenced to 25 Years for $11 Billion WorldCom Fraud," *The Wall Street Journal*, July 14, 2005, http://www.wsj.com/articles/SB112126001526184427 (accessed 29 August 2016).

4. See: Schwartz *et al.* (2005, p. 94).

5. See: *Time* website, "Top 10 Crooked CEOs: Bernie Ebbers," http://content. time.com/time/specials/packages/article/0,28804,1903155_1903156_1903277, 00.html (accessed 29 August 2016).

6. See: Harry Wallop, "Twenty Years On, Is Nick Leeson Really Sorry for Breaking the Bank?" *The Telegraph*, February 25, 2015, http://www.telegraph.co.uk/ finance/newsbysector/banksandfinance/11425522/Twenty-years-on-is-Nick-Leeson-really-sorry-for-breaking-the-bank.html (accessed 29 August 2016).

7. See: Diana B. Henriques, "Madoff Is Sentenced to 150 Years for Ponzi Scheme," *The New York Times*, June 29, 2009, http://www.nytimes.com/2009/06/30/ business/30madoff.html (accessed 29 August 2016).

8. See: Fiona Walsh and David Gow, "Société Générale Uncovers £3.7Bn Fraud By Rogue Trader," *The Guardian*, January 24, 2008, http://www.theguardian.com/ business/2008/jan/24/creditcrunch.banking (accessed 29 August 2016).

9. See: Aaron Smith and Hussein Saddique, "Galleon Manager Rajaratnam Sentenced," *CNN Money*, October 14, 2011, http://money.cnn.com/2011/10/13/ news/companies/insider_trading_raj_rajaratnam/ (accessed 29 August 2016).

10. See: Gavin Finch and Liam Vaughan, "Former Libor 'Ringmaster' Hayes Gets 14 years for Libor Rigging," *Bloomberg*, August 3, 2015, http://www.bloomberg. com/news/articles/2015-08-03/former-libor-ringmaster-hayes-guilty-of-manip ulating-rates (accessed 29 August 2016).

11. See: Julie Creswell, Stephanie Clifford, and Andrew Pollack, "Drug C.E.O. Martin Shkreli Arrested on Fraud Charges," *The New York Times*, December 17, 2015, http://www.nytimes.com/2015/12/18/business/shkreli-fraud-charges. html (accessed 29 August 2016).

12. This position is similar to those who propose a "person–situation interactionist" model of ethical decision making. See: Treviño (1986). This model is described further in Appendix B.

13. See: Watson *et al.* (2009, p. 12).

14. Somewhat surprisingly, the factor of moral character is lacking in most ethical decision-making models. One researcher for example indicates that the models that are presently available are not sufficient because they do not find that an individual's moral character is integral when it comes to identifying and recognizing ethical dilemmas (Pimental *et al.*, 2010, p. 360). Others concur and suggest that the most powerful factor that determines whether our conduct matches our moral judgment is the "centrality of morality to self," in other words our moral character (Damon and Hart, 1992, p. 455). For these reasons, it should be clear that moral character should be incorporated into any ethical decision-making model, as will be discussed later in Chapter 2.

15. The "virtuous" person for Aristotle chooses the reasonable path or the "mean" between the extremes of various emotions or actions (i.e., vices of "deficiency" or vices of "excess"). See: Velasquez (2012, p. 129). Some of Aristotle's virtues include: courage, generosity, pride, good tempered, truthfulness, wittiness, friendliness, and modesty. See: Aristotle (1968).

16. See: Hartman (1998, p. 548). According to Aristotle, good character is not only doing the right thing, but also having the right desires and emotions: "If you do

the right thing reluctantly, you are not really a person of good character, and virtuous actions may or may not be in your best interests" (see: Hartman, 2008, p. 319).

17. The concept of "moral maturation capacities" is introduced by Hannah *et al.* (2011).
18. Kohlberg (1973); Treviño (1986).
19. Kohlberg (1973).
20. Other ethical dilemmas presented in the experiments included the following: "A boy must decide between obeying his father and keeping money he has rightfully gained and that his father unjustly requests; A girl must decide whether to tell on a sister who used her savings to go to a rock concert instead of clothes for school and lied to her mother about it; A doctor must decide whether to kill a dying patient who is asking for an end to her suffering; A marine captain must decide between ordering a man to go on a fatal mission, enabling him to lead the rest of his men to safety, and sacrificing himself, leaving his men to their own devices." See: Colby and Kohlberg (1987); Monin *et al.* (2007, p. 101).
21. For a more recent societal view on dealing with those who steal food in order to feed their families, see: Jennifer Smith, "Police Going Easy on Mothers Who Steal Food 'Simply to Live," *Mail Online*, December 30, 2013, http://www.dailymail.co.uk/news/article-2531059/Police-going-easy-mothers-steal-food-simply-live.html (accessed 29 August 2016).
22. See: Kohlberg (1973, p. 632). In later years, Kohlberg indicated that his model only focused on moral reasoning as opposed to the entire ethical decision-making process, and later clarified that it really only focused on justice/fairness issues (see: Rest *et al.*, 1999).
23. Kohlberg's model is not without criticism, especially from Gilligan (1982) who viewed women as going through different stages of moral development. Gilligan also suggested that stage three (referent others, relationships, caring, responsibility for others) and stage four (law) should be reversed for women.
24. For example, see: Rest (1986); Treviño (1986); Hunt and Vitell (1986); Ferrell *et al.* (1989).
25. See: Jackson *et al.* (2013, p. 236).
26. According to Hartman (2008, p. 317): "To have a [moral] character of significant strength is to have values that consistently guide one's actions."
27. Later in Chapter 4 we will discuss further the core ethical values a person with moral character should possess.
28. Brady and Wheeler (1996); Reynolds (2006, p. 234).
29. A person's "ethical ideology" is made up of their "moral personality" and "moral identity." See: McFerran *et al.* (2010, p. 35). Schlenker (2008, p. 1079) suggests that there is a continuum between a "principled ideology" (a person believes moral principles exist and should guide conduct "… regardless of personal consequences or self-serving rationalizations") and "expedient ideology" (a person believes moral principles have flexibility and that deviations for personal gain are justifiable).
30. Schlenker (2008).
31. Weber (1993); Bartlett (2003).

32. See: O'Fallon and Butterfield (2005).

33. Utilitarianism is discussed further in Chapter 4. Others distinguish between different types of *personal moral philosophies*. Highly *relativistic* individuals believe that moral actions depend on the nature of the situation and the individuals involved (Kohlberg's stage three), rather than acting in ways that are consistent with moral principles (Kohlberg's stages five and six). Highly *idealistic* individuals believe that harming others is always avoidable, rather than believing that harming others is sometimes necessary. See: Forsyth (1992, p. 462).

34. See: Morales-Sánchez and Cabello-Medina (2013, p. 717) who argue that "moral competencies," as moral virtues, can facilitate ethical decision-making. Carroll (1987), based on Powers and Vogel (1980), refers to "moral competence" as representing a major element or capacity that is "essential in making moral judgments" (1987, p. 13) and forms "an integral part of managerial competence" (1987, p. 14).

35. See: Hannah *et al.* (2011, pp. 668–670) who refer to additional related functions such as "moral complexity" and "meta-cognitive ability."

36. See: Reynolds (2008); Hannah *et al.* (2011, p. 669).

37. See: Schwitzgebel and Rust (2014).

38. See: Christina Ng, "Warren Buffett Invites Good Deed Dairy Queen Teen to Shareholders Meeting," *ABC News*, September 20, 2013, http://abcnews.go.com/US/warren-buffett-invites-good-deed-dairy-queen-teen/story?id=20320838 (accessed 29 August 2016).

39. See: James Daniel, "Dairy Queen Manager Who Stuck Up For Blind Customer Now Enjoying Fame as He Gets a Congratulatory Call from Warren Buffet and He May Be on Queen Latifah," *Mail Online*, September 20, 2013, http://www.dailymail.co.uk/news/article-2426695/Joey-Prusak-Dairy-Queen-manager-stuck-blind-customer-enjoying-fame.html (accessed 29 August 2016).

40. See: Jackson *et al.* (2013). The concept that comes closest to capturing this consistency is *integrity capacity* (see: Petrick and Quinn, 2000). Integrity capacity can be defined as a person's capability for repeated alignment of their awareness, deliberation, and conduct with their core moral value system (Petrick and Quinn, 2000, p. 4). Another similar concept is that of *ego strength*, which has been defined as a person's strength of conviction or self-regulating skills (Treviño, 1986, p. 609).

41. See: Hannah *et al.* (2011, pp. 669–670). "Moral identity" has been suggested by several theorists as playing an important self-regulatory role in linking moral attitudes to one's behavior. See: Schlenker (2008, p. 1081). See also: Lapsley and Narvaez (2004) for a review of the concept of moral identity.

42. See: McFerrran *et al.* (2010, p. 37).

43. Hannah *et al.* (2011, p. 671).

44. See: Thompson (2010, p. 20).

45. See: Mayer *et al.* (2012, p. 152).

46. Hannah *et al.* (2011).

47. Hannah *et al.* (2011, p. 664) refer to *moral willpower* as "moral conation" which they define as having the "impetus to act."

48. See: BBC News, "Trader Jailed for 14 Years Over Libor Rate-Rigging," August 3, 2015, http://www.bbc.com/news/business-33763628 (accessed 29 August 2016).
49. See: Muraven *et al.* (1999).
50. See: Comer and Vega (2008) for a description of the "Personal Ethical Threshold" construct.
51. Examples such as these are often provided by my MBA students.
52. See: Hannah *et al.* (2011).
53. See: Hannah *et al.* (2011, p. 674).
54. Hannah *et al.* (2011, p. 675) refer to this belief as "moral efficacy."
55. See: Storer Rowley and Michael Tackett, "Shuttle Rocket Maker Cleaning House," *Chicago Tribune*, June 4, 1986, http://articles.chicagotribune.com/1986-06-04/news/8602090327_1_calvin-wiggins-roger-boisjoly-space-booster-program (accessed 29 August 2016). See also: Howard Berkes, "Remembering Roger Boisjoly: He Tried to Stop Shuttle Challenger Launch," *NPR*, http://www.npr.org/sections/thetwo-way/2012/02/06/146490064/remembering-roger-boisjoly-he-tried-to-stop-shuttle-challenger-launch (accessed 29 August 2016).
56. See: Treviño and Nelson (2011, p. 279).
57. See: John Zarrella and Lateef Munglin, "Florida Lifeguard Says He's Been Offered His Job Back," *CNN*, July 6, 2012, http://edition.cnn.com/2012/07/05/us/florida-lifeguard-fired/ (accessed 29 August 2016).
58. See: Linda Rosencrance, "Harvard Rejects Business-School Applicants Who Hacked Site," *Computerworld*, March 8, 2005, http://www.computerworld.com/article/2568748/cybercrime-hacking/harvard-rejects-business-school-applicants-who-hacked-site.html (accessed 29 August 2016).
59. See: Shaw and Barry (2016, p. 84).
60. Treviño (1986).
61. Ferrell and Gresham (1985).
62. Hunt and Vitell (1986).
63. For example, one study found that 119 different variables, many of which might overlap, have been included in one or more of 11 different ethical decision-making theoretical models demonstrating a lack of consistency (see: Torres, 2001).
64. See: Kieran Corcoran, "Would You Pass the Wallet Test? World's Most Honest Cities Revealed After Researchers Dropped Purse Containing £30 To See If It Would Be Returned," *Mail Online*, September 24, 2013, http://www.dailymail.co.uk/news/article-2430530/Helsinki-worlds-honest-city-Lisbon-lost-wallet-test.html (accessed 29 August 2016). The study suggests that there are some cities with residents who are more honest than others.
65. For example, Nohria *et al.* (2015, p. 1, emphasis added) state: "Contrary evidence has been accumulating, indicating the malleability of character and the critical, sometimes decisive role that *situation* – not character – plays in ethical decision making…."
66. Ferrell and Gresham (1985); Hunt and Vitell (1986); Treviño (1986); Bommer *et al.* (1987); Jones (1991).
67. Jones (1991); Weber (1996); Bartlett (2003); Kish-Gephart et al. (2010). See Appendix B for a description of Jones' issue-contingency model.

68. Jones (1991).
69. Jones' (1991) model appears to draw from philosopher Jeremy Bentham's utilitarianism. Bentham's criteria for measuring pleasure or pain (his principle of utility) is divided into the categories of intensity, duration, certainty, proximity, productiveness, purity, and extent. Jones' first component, "magnitude of consequences," is similar to Bentham's overall calculation of net benefit. "Probability of effect" is similar to Bentham's criteria of "certainty or uncertainty." "Concentration of effect" is similar to its "extent"; that is, "… the number of persons to whom it extends; or (in other words) who are affected by it…." See: Bentham (1970).
70. One initial concern with Jones' moral intensity construct is that the dimensions of moral intensity can simply be incorporated into the moral judgment stage of ethical decision making that will be discussed further in Chapter 2. For example, Herndon states (1996, p. 504): "While Jones (1991) adds the concept of moral intensity which is the degree of "badness" of an act; it can be placed in the consequences and behavioral evaluation portions of the synthesis integrated model."
71. As indicated by some researchers, "… other ethical perspectives should also be considered … such as fairness or law breaking where harm was not involved" as part of the moral intensity construct (Butterfield *et al.*, 2000, p. 1010).
72. See: May and Pauli (2002). O'Fallon and Butterfield (2005, p. 398) state: "Although moral intensity is a relatively new construct in the business ethics literature, there seems to be strong support for its influence on the ethical decision-making process. Magnitude of consequences and social consensus represent the most consistent findings." Lehnert *et al.* (2015, p. 205) indicate that there is a "strong consensus on the positive relationship between moral intensity and ethical decision making."
73. Robin *et al.* (1996, p. 17).
74. A number of researchers have shifted the focus on the moral intensity of an issue to the subjective *perceived* importance placed on a particular issue by a particular individual. See: Haines *et al.* (2008); Valentine and Hollingworth (2012); Yu (2015). Singhapakdi *et al.* (1999) and Dedeke (2015) both refer to the related concept of "perceived moral intensity." Robin *et al.* (1996, p. 18) suggest that "perceived issue importance" could be a component of a broader and more complex concept called "moral involvement."
75. Researchers are beginning to pick up on the concern over Jones' (1991) reliance on the objectivity of the existence of issue intensity, rather than the subjective perception of the individual decision maker. For example, Yu (2015, p. 574) suggests that moral intensity "… should include compositions of subjective perception rather than being merely a fact of objective existence," in other words, "… the existence of an ethical issue is appropriately defined according to individuals and the environment because it must be subjectively conscious by an individual … Furthermore, because the identity, position, thinking, resources, and situation of each individual differ, these factors also influence individuals' subjective recognition of [moral intensity]."
76. See: Street *et al.* (2001).

77. Rest (1984, p. 35) recognized issue complexity as a situational factor that can influence the awareness stage of ethical decision making (i.e., "sheer number of elements in the situation …" and the "… complexity in tracing out cause-effect chains").

78. Warren and Smith-Crowe (2008, p. 90) refer to issue complexity in relation to the type of moral judgment (reason versus intuition) that might take place: "… the intuitionists are not seeking judgments from individuals on issues that are new, complex, or have many options."

79. In a similar vein, relevant knowledge on the issue has been suggested as being linked with "… one's ability to engage in effortful cognitive activity" (see: Street *et al.*, 2001, p. 263).

80. De George (2010).

81. Tenbrunsel *et al.* (2003); Treviño *et al.* (2006).

82. Tenbrunsel *et al.* (2003). This is the same definition used by Tenbrunsel *et al.* (2003, p. 286) for *ethical infrastructure* which for our purposes is considered equivalent to *ethical corporate culture*.

83. Tenbrunsel *et al.* (2003, p. 286).

84. See: Valentine *et al.* (2014). The *ethical context* is considered by Valentine *et al.* (2014) to include both the "ethical culture" (Treviño *et al.*, 1998) and the "ethical climate" (Victor and Cullen, 1998) of the organization.

85. See: Schwartz (2001, p. 248).

86. O'Fallon and Butterfield (2005, p. 397). Kaptein and Schwartz (2008, p. 115) state: "… a thorough review of existing literature reveals at least 79 empirical studies that examine the effectiveness of business codes. The results of these studies … are clearly mixed: 35% of the studies have found that codes are effective, 16% have found that the relationship is weak, 33% have found that there is no significant relationship, and 14% have presented mixed results. Only one study has found that business codes could be counterproductive."

87. O'Fallon and Butterfield (2005, p. 398) state: "The impact of rewards and sanctions is clear – rewarding unethical behavior tends to increase the frequency of such behavior, while effective sanctioning systems tend to decrease such behavior."

88. Tenbrunsel *et al.* (2003, p. 286).

89. See: O'Fallon and Butterfield (2005); Craft (2013).

90. See: Ethics Resource Center (2014). O'Fallon and Butterfield (2005, p. 397) find that: "There is increasing support for the notion that ethical climates and cultures exist within organizations. The research generally supports the notion that ethical climates and cultures have a positive influence on ethical decision making." Mudrack and Mason (2013, p. 585) find, however, that: "There is little evidence that ethical judgments relate systematically to respondent-determined ethical climate."

91. The extent to which one is potentially impacted by others can be based on the notion of *field dependence*, which has been defined as a person's dependence on external social referents to guide their behavior, such as work colleagues. See: Treviño (1986, p. 610).

92. For example, see: Hunt and Vitell (1986); Treviño (1986); Bommer *et al.* (1987).
93. Ferrell *et al.* (1989, p. 61).
94. In terms of rewards and sanctions, O'Fallon and Butterfield (2005, p. 398) find that: "The impact of rewards and sanctions is clear – rewarding unethical behavior tends to increase the frequency of such behavior, while effective sanctioning systems tend to decrease such behavior."
95. In terms of the type of industry: "Due to the fact that different industries were examined in various studies, no overall conclusions regarding the effect of industry can be drawn" (O'Fallon and Butterfield, 2005, p. 397). In terms of organizational size: "The research in this area generally suggests that organizational size has a detrimental effect on ethical decision making. However, given the mixed results, future research appears warranted" (O'Fallon and Butterfield, 2005, p. 397).
96. These other factors include: business competitiveness, subjective norms, stress, and mindfulness of one's environment. Work roles might also influence ethical decision making, as one might be inclined to adopt their functional or hierarchical role in deciding how to behave (see: Crane and Matten, 2010, p. 172; Treviño and Nelson, 2011, pp. 272–276). Future ethical decision-making empirical research may examine these factors further and find that they influence ethical decision making.
97. Albrecht (2003).
98. See: Albrecht (2003, p. 30).
99. The notion of "vulnerability" has apparently received little attention in the business ethics literature (see: Brown, 2013), although Comer and Vega (2008) do refer to one's "personal ethical threshold" which incorporates the notion of vulnerability.
100. Treviño (1986).
101. These conclusions are based on the many MBA student ethical dilemmas I have read as part of a class assignment.
102. Treviño (1986).
103. This is discussed by Prentice (2014, pp. 338–339).
104. As additional empirical support, a number of interview-based studies of managers and employees have confirmed that *situational* factors related to the organization context and our personal situation are perceived to be the most important determiners of our actions and behavior. Executives ranked several factors thought to influence unethical behavior in the following order: (i) the behavior of superiors; (ii) the ethical practices of one's industry or profession; (iii) the behavior of one's peers in the organization; (iv) formal organizational policy (or lack thereof); and (v) personal financial need (Baumhart, 1961). Other studies have found similar results. For example, Brenner and Molander (1977) and Posner and Schmidt (1987) repeated Baumhart's study with the addition of "society's moral climate" as a possible factor. Although there were different rankings of the factors across the three studies, they all found that *behavior of superiors* was considered the number one influence on unethical behavior, with *behavior of one's peers* being ranked high in two of the three studies.

105. Kohlberg (1973); Jackson *et al.* (2013).
106. Petrick and Quinn (2000).
107. Jones (1991).
108. Butterfield *et al.* (2000).
109. Robin *et al.* (1996).
110. Tenbrunsel *et al.* (2003).
111. Albrecht (2003).

References

Albrecht, W.S. 2003. *Fraud Examination*. Mason, OH: Thomson.

Aristotle. 1968. *The Nichomachean Ethics*. H. Rackham Trans., Cambridge, MA: Harvard University Press.

Bartlett, D. 2003. Management and business ethics: a critique and integration of ethical decision-making models. *British Journal of Management*, 14: 223–235.

Baumhart, R.C. 1961. How ethical are businessmen? *Harvard Business Review*, 39: 6–9.

Bentham, J. 1970. *An Introduction of the Principles of Morals and Legislation*. London: Athlone Press.

Bommer, M.C., Gratto., J., Gravender, J., and Tuttle, M. 1987. A behavioral model of ethical and unethical decision making. *Journal of Business Ethics*, 6: 265–280.

Brady, F.N. and Wheeler, G.E. 1996. An empirical study of ethical predispositions. *Journal of Business Ethics*, 15: 927–940.

Brenner, S.N. and Molander, E.W. 1977. Is the ethics of business changing? *Harvard Business Review*, 55: 57–71.

Brown, E. 2013. Vulnerability and the basis of business ethics: from fiduciary duties to professionalism. *Journal of Business Ethics*, 113: 489–504.

Butterfield, K.D., Treviño, L.K., and Weaver, G.R. 2000. Moral awareness in business organizations: influences of issue-related and social context factors. *Human Relations*, 53: 981–1018.

Carroll, A.B. 1987. In search of the moral manager. *Business Horizons*, 30: 7–15.

Colby, A. and Kohlberg, L. 1987. *The Measurement of Moral Judgment*. New York: Cambridge University Press.

Comer, D.R. and Vega, G. 2008. Using the PET assessment instrument to help students identify factors that could impede moral behavior. *Journal of Business Ethics*, 77: 129–145.

Craft, J.L. 2013. A review of the empirical ethical decision-making literature: 2004–2011. *Journal of Business Ethics*, 177: 221–259.

Crane, A. and Matten, D. 2010. *Business Ethics* (3rd edn). New York: Oxford University Press.

Damon, W. and Hart, D. 1992. Self-understanding and its role in social and moral development. In *Developmental Psychology: An Advanced Textbook* (3rd edn) (M. Bornstein and M.E. Lamb, eds). Hillsdale, NJ: Erlbaum, pp. 421–464.

De George, R.T. 2010. *Business Ethics* (7th edn). New York: Prentice Hall.

Dedeke, A. 2015. A cognitive-intuitionist model of moral judgment. *Journal of Business Ethics*, 126: 437–457.

Ethics Resource Center 2014. *2013 National Business Ethics Survey*. Arlington, VA.

Ferrell, O.C. and Gresham, L. 1985. A contingency framework for understanding ethical decision making in marketing. *Journal of Marketing*, 49: 87–96.

Ferrell, O.C., Gresham, L.G., and Fraedrich, J. 1989. A synthesis of ethical decision models for marketing. *Journal of Macromarketing*, 9: 55–64.

Forsyth, D.R. 1992. Judging the morality of business practices: the influence of personal moral philosophies. *Journal of Business Ethics*, 11: 461–470.

Gilligan, C. 1982. *In a Different Voice: Psychological Theory and Women's Development*. Cambridge, MA: Harvard University Press.

Haines, R., Street, M.D., and Haines, D. 2008. The influence of perceived importance of an ethical issue on moral judgment, moral obligation, and moral intent. *Journal of Business Ethics*, 81: 387–399.

Hannah, S.T., Avolio, B.J., and May, D.R. 2011. Moral maturation and moral conation: a capacity approach to explaining moral thought and action. *Academy of Management Review*, 36: 663–685.

Hartman, E.M. 1998. The role of character in business ethics. *Business Ethics Quarterly*, 8: 547–559.

Hartman, E.M. 2008. Socratic questions and Aristotelian answers: a virtue-based approach to business ethics. *Journal of Business Ethics*, 78: 313–328.

Herndon, N.C. Jr 1996. A new context for ethics education objectives in a college of business: ethical decision-making models. *Journal of Business Ethics*, 15: 501–510.

Hunt, S.D. and Vitell, S. 1986. A general theory of marketing ethics. *Journal of Macromarketing*, 6: 5–16.

Jackson, R.W., Wood, C.M., and Zboja, J.J. 2013. The dissolution of ethical decision-making in organizations: a comprehensive review and model. *Journal of Business Ethics*, 116: 233–250.

Jones, T.M. 1991. Ethical decision making by individuals in organizations: an issue-contingent model. *The Academy of Management Review*, 16: 366–395.

Kaptein, M. and Schwartz, M.S. 2008. The effectiveness of business codes: a critical examination of existing studies and the development of an integrated research model. *Journal of Business Ethics*, 77: 111–127.

Kish-Gephart, J.J., Harrison, D.A., and Treviño, L.K. 2010. Bad apples, bad cases, and bad barrels: meta-analytic evidence about sources of unethical decisions at work. *Journal of Applied Psychology*, 95: 1–31.

Kohlberg, L. 1973. The claim to moral adequacy of a highest stage of moral judgment. *The Journal of Philosophy*, 70: 630–646.

Lapsley, D.K. and Narvaez, D. 2004. *Moral Development, Self, and Identity*. Mahwah, New Jersey: Lawrence Erlbaum Associates.

Lehnert, K., Park. Y., and Singh, N. 2015. Research note and review of the empirical ethical decision-making literature: boundary conditions and extensions. *Journal of Business Ethics*, 129: 195–219.

May, D.R. and Pauli, K.P. 2002. The role of moral intensity in ethical decision making. *Business & Society*, 41: 84–117.

Mayer, D.M., Aquino, K., Greenbaum, R.L., and Kuenzi, M. 2012. Who displays ethical leadership and why does it matter? An examination of antecedents and consequences of ethical leadership. *Academy of Management Journal*, 55: 151–171.

McFerran, B., Aquino, K., and Duffy, M. 2010. How personality and moral identity relate to individuals' ethical ideology. *Business Ethics Quarterly*, 20: 35–56.

Monin, B., Pizarro, D.A., and Beer, J.S. 2007. Deciding versus reacting: conceptions of moral judgment and the reason-affect debate. *Review of General Psychology*, 11: 99–111.

Morales-Sánchez, R. and Cabello-Medina, C. 2013. The role of four universal moral competencies in ethical decision-making. *Journal of Business Ethics*, 116: 717–734.

Mudrack, P.E. and Mason, E.S. 2013. Ethical judgments: what do we know, where do we go? *Journal of Business Ethics*, 115: 575–597.

Muraven M., Baumeister, R.F., and Tice, D.M. 1999. Longitudinal improvement of self-regulation through practice: building self-control strength through repeated exercise. *Journal of Social Psychology*, 139: 446–457.

Nohria, N., Sucher, S.J., Badaracco, J., and Gurtler, B. 2015. *Note on Human Behavior: Situation Versus Character*. Harvard Business Publishing, No. 9-316-078: 1–9.

O'Fallon, M.J. and Butterfield, K.D. 2005. A review of the empirical ethical decision-making literature: 1996–2003. *Journal of Business Ethics*, 59: 375–413.

Petrick, J.A. and Quinn, J.F. 2000. The integrity capacity construct and moral progress in business. *Journal of Business Ethics*, 23: 3–18.

Pimental, J.R.C., Kuntz, J.R., and Elenkov, D.S. 2010. Ethical decision-making: an integrative model for business practice. *European Business Review*, 22: 359–376.

Posner, B.Z. and Schmidt, W.H. 1987. Ethics in American companies: a managerial perspective. *Journal of Business Ethics*, 6: 383–391.

Powers, C. and Vogel, D. 1980. *Ethics in the Education of Business Managers*. Hastings-on-Hudson, NY: Hastings Center.

Prentice, R.A. 2014. Teaching behavioral ethics. *Journal of Legal Studies Education*, 31: 325–365.

Rest, J.R. 1984. The major components of morality. In *Morality, Moral Behavior, and Moral Development* (W.M. Kurtines and J.L. Gewirtz, eds). New York: John Wiley and Sons, Inc., pp. 24–38.

Rest, J.R. 1986. *Moral Development: Advances in Research and Theory*. New York: Praeger.

Rest, J., Narvaez, D., Bebeau, M.J., and Shoma, S.J. 1999. *Postconventional Thinking: A New-Kohlbergian Approach*. Mahwah, New Jersey: Lawrence Erlbaum Associates.

Reynolds, S.J. 2006. Moral awareness and ethical predispositions: investigating the role of individual differences in the recognition of moral issues. *Journal of Applied Psychology*, 91: 233–243.

Reynolds, S.J. 2008. Moral attentiveness: who pays attention to the moral aspects of life? *Journal of Applied Psychology*, 93: 1027–1041.

Robin, D.P., Reidenbach, R.E., and Forrest, P.J. 1996. The perceived importance of an ethical issue as an influence on the ethical decision-making of ad managers. *Journal of Business Research*, 35: 17–28.

Schlenker, B.R. 2008. Integrity and character: implications of principled and expedient ethical ideologies. *Journal of Social and Clinical Psychology*, 27: 1078–1125.

Schwartz, M.S. 2001. The nature of the relationship between corporate codes of ethics and behaviour. *Journal of Business Ethics*, 32: 247–262.

Schwartz, M.S. 2016. Ethical decision-making theory: an integrated approach. *Journal of Business Ethics*, 139: 755–776.

Schwartz, M.S., Dunfee, T., and Kline, M. 2005. Tone at the top: an ethics code for directors? *Journal of Business Ethics*, 58: 79–100.

Schwitzgebel, E. and Rust, J. 2014. The moral behavior of ethics professors: relationships among self-reported behavior, expressed normative attitude, and directly observed behavior. *Philosophical Psychology*, 27: 293–327.

Shaw, W.H. and Barry, V. 2016. *Moral Issues in Business* (13th edn). Boston, MA: Cengage Learning.

Singhapakdi, A., Vitell, S.J., and Franke, G.R. 1999. Antecedents, consequences, and mediating effects of perceived moral intensity and personal moral philosophies. *Journal of the Academy of Marketing Science*, 27: 1131–1140.

Street, M.D., Douglas, S.C., Geiger, S.W., and Martinko, M.J. 2001. The impact of cognitive expenditure on the ethical decision-making process: the cognitive elaboration model. *Organizational Behavior and Human Decision Processes*, 86: 256–277.

Tenbrunsel, A.E., Smith-Crowe, K., and Umphress, E. 2003. Building houses on rocks: the role of the ethical infrastructure in organizations. *Social Justice Research*, 16: 285–307.

Thompson, L.J. 2010. The global moral compass for business leaders. *Journal of Business Ethics*, 93: 15–32.

Torres, M.B. 2001. Character and Decision Making. Unpublished Dissertation, University of Navarra.

Treviño, L.K. 1986. Ethical decision making in organizations: a person-situation interactionist model. *Academy of Management Review*, 11: 601–617.

Treviño, L.K. and Nelson, K.A. 2011. *Managing Business Ethics: Straight Talk About How to Do It Right* (5th edn). Hoboken, NJ: John Wiley & Sons, Inc.

Treviño, L.K., Butterfield, K.D., and McCabe, D.L. 1998. The ethical context in organizations: influences on employee attitudes and behaviors. *Business Ethics Quarterly*, 8: 447–476.

Treviño, L.K., Weaver, G.R., and Reynolds, S.J. 2006. Behavioral ethics in organizations. *Journal of Management*, 32: 951–990.

Valentine, S. and Hollingworth, D. 2012. Moral intensity, issue importance, and ethical reasoning in operations situations. *Journal of Business Ethics*, 108: 509–523.

Valentine, S., Nam, S.H., Hollingworth, D., and Hall, C. 2014. Ethical context and ethical decision making: examination of an alternative statistical approach for identifying variable relationships. *Journal of Business Ethics*, 124: 509–526.

Velasquez, M.G. 2012. *Business Ethics Concepts and Cases* (7th edn). Upper Saddle River, NJ: Prentice Hall.

Victor, B. and Cullen, J. B. 1988. The organizational bases of ethical work climates. *Administrative Science Quarterly*, 33: 101–125.

Warren, D.E. and Smith-Crowe, K. 2008. Deciding what's right: the role of external sanctions and embarrassment in shaping moral judgments in the workplace. *Research in Organizational Behavior*, 28: 81–105.

Watson, G.W., Berkley, R.A., and Papamarcos, S.D. 2009. Ambiguous allure: the value-pragmatics model of ethical decision making. *Business and Society Review*, 114: 1–29.

Weber, J. 1993. Exploring the relationship between personal values and moral reasoning. *Human Relations*, 46: 435–463.

Weber, J. 1996. Influences upon managerial moral decision-making: nature of the harm and magnitude of consequences. *Human Relations*, 49: 1–22.

Yu, Y.M. 2015. Comparative analysis of Jones' and Kelley's ethical decision-making models. *Journal of Business Ethics*, 130: 573–583.

Chapter Two

The Ethical Decision-Making Process

In Chapter 1, we looked at the "good or bad apple" approach as well as the situational perspective to help explain ethical and unethical decision making. But this is only one part of the ethical decision-making picture. We also need to understand the ethical decision-making *process* as well. Yes, different people act differently under the same circumstances based on their individual *moral character*, and yes, the same person will act differently when the *situational context* changes in terms of the nature of the issue, the ethical corporate culture, and the personal situation and pressures that are being faced. But we also need to understand the decision-making *process* we go through when we make ethical decisions, and at what stage of the process each of the individual and situational factors we have already discussed might influence or moderate decision making. Building on and borrowing from a series of academic disciplines and theories including moral philosophy, moral psychology, social psychology, social economics, organizational behavior, criminology, behavioral science, cognitive neuroscience, and business ethics, a number of descriptive ethical decision-making *theoretical* models have fortunately been proposed to help explain the decision-making process of individuals leading to ethical or unethical behavior or actions.

Unfortunately, however, to date there does not appear to be a fully comprehensive ethical decision-making model. For example, following a comprehensive review of ethical decision-making research, some researchers suggest the following: "If the field of descriptive ethics is to move forward to strengthen our understanding of the ethical decision-making process, it is imperative that future studies focus more attention on theory development."[1] Similarly, according to others there remains a deficiency in ethical decision-making theory: "Unlike in the past, researchers no longer need to justify their rationale for studying ethics; instead, their attention needs to focus on developing a more

Business Ethics: An Ethical Decision-Making Approach, First Edition. Mark S. Schwartz.
© 2017 John Wiley & Sons, Inc. Published 2017 by John Wiley & Sons, Inc.

comprehensive theoretical platform upon which empirical work in behavioral ethics can continue."[2] In other words, the current disagreement among scholars over which theoretical ethical decision-making model (if any) is the most appropriate, especially when engaging in empirical research, needs to be addressed. In fact, some continue to refer to the ethical decision-making process as a "black box."[3]

After looking at the various approaches and ethical decision-making models, my own version of a descriptive ethical decision-making model is outlined in this chapter that attempts to consolidate the various models that have already been proposed while incorporating other important aspects of the ethical decision-making process that have at times been neglected.[4] The goal is to not only build upon previous ethical decision-making models, but also to address the key divergence between what has been referred to as the rationalist (reason) and non-rationalist (intuition and emotion) approaches to ethical decision making. For those who are interested in reviewing the dominant ethical decision-making descriptive models that have been suggested, please refer to Appendix B, which summarizes the key aspects of each of the models. Since the proposed framework attempts to integrate much of the ethical decision-making literature, the reformulated ethical decision-making model is called *Integrated Ethical Decision Making* (or Integrated-EDM). The proposed model, which is shown in its entirety in Figure 2.1, will now be described.

Try not to be too intimidated by all of the different aspects of Figure 2.1. By the end of the chapter the model should make more sense. At its most basic level, there are two major components to the Integrated-EDM model: (i) the ethical decision-making *process*; and (ii) the *factors* (or variables) that influence the ethical decision-making process. The ethical decision-making *process* is composed of four basic stages: (i) awareness; (ii) judgment; (iii) intention; and (iv) action/behavior, and in this respect continues to reflect the basic process framework proposed by most previous ethical decision-making models.[5] One important additional set of processes takes place when *impediments* potentially interfere with the moral judgment stage. Given their importance, the impediments to ethical decision making which include cognitive biases, psychological tendencies, moral rationalizations, and self-interest will each be discussed further in Chapter 3.

The precursor to the ethical decision-making process includes basic environmental *norms*, while the subsequent stages of the process include potential learning *feedback loops*. The ethical decision-making *factors* that were discussed in Chapter 1 that influence the process fall into two basic categories: (i) *individual*; and (ii) *situational*.[6] The Integrated-EDM model assumes that ethical behavior is contingent on which particular *individual* is facing the ethical dilemma (e.g., different individuals may act differently when faced with the same dilemma depending on their *moral character*), and (ii) the *situational*

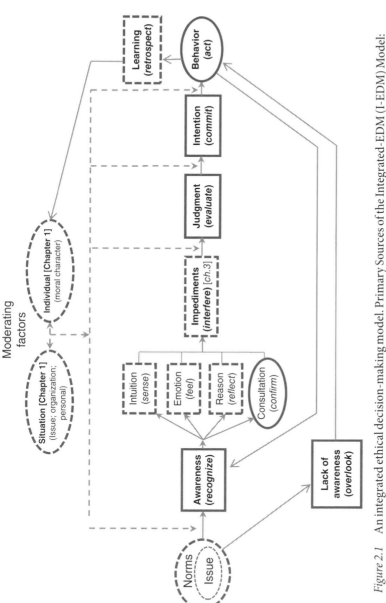

Figure 2.1 An integrated ethical decision-making model. Primary Sources of the Integrated-EDM (I-EDM) Model: Rest (1984) (Four-Component model); Jones (1991) (Issue-Contingency model); Treviño (1986) (Person-Situation Interactionist model); Tenbrunsel and Smith-Crowe (2008) (Lack of Moral Awareness); Haidt (2001) (Social Intuitionist model). Legend: Solid Box – Mental State; Dotted Box – Mental Process; Solid Circle – Active Conduct; Dotted Circle – Factor/Variable. *Source*: Schwartz, M.S. 2016. Reproduced with the permission of Springer.

context within which an individual faces a dilemma (e.g., the same individual can behave differently depending on the particular situation one is facing or environment one is situated within).

In order to gain a better understanding of *how* the Integrated-EDM model works, a common ethical situation faced by many employees and managers in the workplace will be considered. Imagine that you work for a business firm, and *a current supplier has sent you a very expensive bottle of wine* during the holiday season. Your firm does not have a policy specifically addressing receiving gifts. Assuming this is the situation you are facing, let's now see how the Integrated-EDM model would apply in terms of your decision-making process.

Environmental Norms

In terms of the *process* of the Integrated-EDM model, the initial starting point is the *norms* that are prevalent in the external environment that tend to determine whether an ethical issue or dilemma potentially exists. Environmental norms are defined as follows:

> Environmental norms: *those prevailing standards or expectations of behavior held by members of a particular group or community.*

Several ethical decision-making models propose that there is an "environmental" context within which the existence of an ethical issue or dilemma can arise.[7] Norms can simultaneously exist at several different levels, including at the societal/cultural/national level, at the industry, organizational, or professional level,[8] or at the work group level within the organization. The sources of these norms might include deeply embedded sociological, political, economic, legal, or religious considerations or views.[9]

For the Integrated-EDM model, a potential ethical issue or dilemma arises when there is a situation whereby different norms apply, each of which cannot be followed at the same time. This basic starting point of the ethical decision-making process has also been referred to as the *eliciting situation*.[10] For example, there may be norms around gift giving, such as societal norms (bribery is considered unacceptable), industry-level norms (everyone gives and receives gifts in business), organizational norms (the firm frowns upon conflicts of interest), professional norms (which restrict gifts), and work group norms (everyone considers gift receiving acceptable). If your personal view conflicts with any of these norms, or if any of these norms conflict with each other, you face a potential ethical issue that you may or may not be aware of.

The next four stages of the Integrated-EDM model are based on the "Four-Component" model of ethical decision making, which include awareness, judgment, intention, and action.[11] We will now work through each of these four stages of ethical decision making in more detail.

Moral Awareness Stage

Assuming that a situation with a potential ethical issue or dilemma exists due to conflicting norms, the next question is whether we become aware of the existence of the issue or dilemma. Moral awareness is defined as follows:

> Moral awareness: *the point in time when an individual realizes that they are faced with a situation requiring a decision or action that could affect the interests, welfare, or expectations of oneself or others in a manner that may conflict with one or more moral standards.*[12]

Moral awareness that a particular situation raises ethical issues can take place simply due to an individual's moral character and inherent ability to recognize ethical issues,[13] or as a result of a firm's ethical corporate culture (i.e., including codes, training, meetings, or other disseminated ethical policy communications).[14] If you become aware that an ethical issue or dilemma exists, then you have by definition identified at least two different possible courses of action, and you will then potentially engage in an ethical decision-making process consisting of the moral judgment and intention stages.[15] In the case of receiving an expensive gift, the awareness stage involves whether or not I realize that there are ethical implications to receiving a gift from a current supplier, or if I merely see this as an economic (self-interest) issue.

To understand this phenomenon better, the following will now explain how the *lack of moral awareness* process takes place, considered to be an equally important component of the Integrated-EDM model.

Lack of moral awareness

Most ethical decision-making theoretical models presume that only through moral awareness of the potential ethical nature of a dilemma can you ultimately engage in ethical behavior.[16] In other words, moral awareness is viewed as being binary – you either recognize the ethical issue or you fail to do so.[17] As a result, most researchers have tended to focus on whether moral awareness is present or absent as a precondition for activating the other stages of decision making.[18] What appears to be lacking in current ethical decision-making models, however, is the depiction of our *lack* of moral awareness, which is defined as follows:

> Lack of moral awareness: *the state of not realizing that a situation we are experiencing raises ethical implications.*

There are now several overlapping theories that have been proposed in ethical decision-making literature to help explain the processes or reasons by which we might lack moral awareness, also referred to as unintentional "amoral awareness"[19] or unintentional "amoral management."[20] For example, we can lack moral awareness due to *ethical fading*. Ethical fading is defined as the process by which the "moral colors" of an ethical decision fade into "bleached hues" that are void of moral implications.[21] In order for ethical fading to take place, we engage in self-deception through the use of euphemistic language (e.g., "aggressive" accounting practices as opposed to being "deceptive"; "borrowing" company funds with the possible "intention" to return them rather than stealing) and other techniques to "shield ourselves" from our own unethical behavior. Another similar concept used to explain our lack of moral awareness is *ethical blindness*, which means that the decision maker is temporarily unable to see the ethical dimension of a decision at stake.[22] Ethical blindness includes three aspects: (i) people deviate from their own values and principles; (ii) this deviation is temporary in nature; and (iii) the process is unconscious in nature.[23] The classic example of *ethical blindness* comes from Dennis Gioia, the recall coordinator of the defective and deadly 1970s Ford Pinto vehicle that would potentially explode upon being rear-ended. Gioia asked himself after failing to take any action regarding the defect: "Why didn't I see the gravity of the problem and its ethical overtones?"[24]

Another theory related to a lack of moral awareness is the use of *non-moral decision frames*, which occurs when one focuses on the *economic* or *legal* implications of issues rather than on the *ethical* considerations.[25] The process of framing in a non-moral manner leading to a lack of moral awareness can result due to insufficient or biased information gathering, or socially constructing the facts in a particular manner.[26] *Moral myopia* can also take place which is similarly defined as a distortion of moral vision that prevents issues of a moral nature from coming into focus.[27] These initial theories or processes appear to each relate more directly to our work environment leading to a lack of moral awareness. In other words, if we are situated in a work environment which tends to ignore ethical considerations in its decision making or consistently prioritizes the bottom line over ethical concerns, as well as uses non-moral language in its operations, then we would likely be less inclined to be morally aware when facing a dilemma.[28]

The bottom line emphasis at Enron contributed to each of these processes taking place including ethical fading, ethical blindness, non-moral decision frames, and moral myopia. This all led to a lack of moral awareness contributing to misconduct at all levels of the organization. Former Enron CEO Jeff Skilling would reportedly say: "... all that matters is money ... Profits at all costs ...." The use of a "rank and yank" system whereby a percentage of the weakest performing Enron employees would automatically be fired each year also appeared to contribute to the lack of moral awareness among Enron employees.[29] Several of my former students worked for Enron, and although they realized impropriety was taking place, they were able to ignore the misconduct and did not raise any concerns. What was their number one reason for doing nothing? Because they were extremely well paid, and certainly didn't want to "rock" the boat.

Moral awareness, however, could be attributable to the particular individual's inherent nature, and thus directly related to the individual's *moral character* described in Chapter 1. For example, moral awareness can result from *moral attentiveness*, which has been defined as the extent to which a person chronically perceives and considers morality and moral elements in his or her experiences.[30] Similar to the notion of moral attentiveness, others have linked moral awareness to the concept of *mindfulness*, which is described as the awareness of an individual both internally (awareness of their own thoughts) and externally (awareness of what is happening in their environment).[31] It may be that a lack of mindfulness exacerbates our self-serving thoughts, self-deception, and unconscious biases leading to unethical behavior.[32]

Applying the process of *moral imagination* might also potentially lead to moral awareness, while failing to engage in moral imagination might lead to a lack of moral awareness.[33] Moral imagination takes place when a person reframes their situation outside of its current context in order to discern all of the possible alternatives along with the potential impacts of each course of action on others.[34] When we are only able to see one option rather than create imaginative options, we may be unaware that we are even facing an ethical dilemma with potentially more ethical alternatives being available.

For example, when faced with the dilemma whether to accept an expensive bottle of wine from a current supplier, you might initially think that your only option is to accept the gift, because otherwise you will offend the supplier, which might seriously affect the relationship. But if you realize through your sense of *moral imagination* that there are other options, such as accepting the gift in a particular way, you might become morally aware of the situation leading to a different outcome. You might imagine for instance that it could be possible for the gift to become the property of the company (and maybe hold a

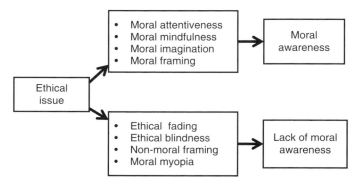

Figure 2.2   Processes affecting moral awareness. *Source*: Schwartz, M.S. 2016. Reproduced with the permission of Springer.

raffle for the gift among the employees), which would diminish the likelihood of a conflict of interest or at least perceived conflict of interest for you individually. You might also imagine that you can still accept the gift as long as the arrangement is reciprocal, whereby you agree to pay for the next meal together with the supplier. The issue would shift from being an *economic* self-interested decision to a *moral* decision, and a moral judgment process could then take place. In terms of the individual factors, a person with a strong *moral character* and in particular strong *moral competence* would also have a high level of moral attentiveness, moral mindfulness, and moral imagination, and would therefore likely be aware that receiving a gift from even a current supplier raises ethical considerations. Figure 2.2 summarizes the theories or processes discussed previously that help explain and contribute to moral awareness or a lack of moral awareness.

By not including the phenomenon of *lack of moral awareness* in ethical decision-making models, an important stream of ethical decision-making research is being ignored. Even if we are not aware that an ethical dilemma exists when we are asked to accept an expensive gift of a bottle of wine, we can still engage in what might be considered "unintentional" ethical or unethical behavior.[35] Due to the importance of understanding why there might be a lack of moral awareness and the processes leading to it, which would presumably increase the potential for unethical behavior, the lack of moral awareness path is depicted in the Integrated-EDM model.

Moral Judgment Stage

The moral judgment stage represents the crux of the Integrated-EDM model, and might be referred to as the actual ethical decision-making process that takes place. *Moral judgment* is defined for the purposes of the model as follows:

> Moral judgment: *the determination of the most ethically appropriate course of action among the alternatives.*

This is the point in the Integrated-EDM model where several different processes either affect moral judgment directly, or potentially interact with each other leading to a particular moral judgment. These mental processes include: (i) *intuition*; (ii) *emotion*; and (iii) *reasoning*. While some would distinguish between the rationalist (reason) and non-rationalist (intuition; emotion) approaches to ethical decision making, the Integrated-EDM model considers each of these interrelated mental processes to be of equal relevance.[36] Each of these three processes will now be described.

Intuition

The Integrated-EDM model presumes that for most ethical situations, including those that are non-complex ethical dilemmas or involve moral temptations with clearly right versus wrong alternatives, an *intuitive* mental process takes place at least initially after being evoked by the situation, and in this respect intuition plays a significant role in the ethical decision-making process.[37] Intuition is defined as follows:

> Intuition: *an automatic and non-deliberative cognitive process leading to an initial judgment that may or may not be acted upon.*

The intuitive process is reflexive in nature, effortless, immediate, and involves a one-step mental process. The position of intuitionists is that people have a "built-in moral sense" that creates pleasurable feelings of approval toward benevolent acts and corresponding feelings of disapproval toward evil acts.[38] The judgment might be considered to be self-evident, with the truth essentially being engrained or innate in each of us as human beings. The process is inaccessible and not controllable, and only the results enter our awareness. Our intuitions may be based on "prototypes" of right and wrong that have been stored over our lifetimes in our hidden memory based on our experiences.[39] When we come to a judgment based on intuition, we can be *morally dumbfounded*, in that we can't provide the reasons for our judgments of approval or disapproval. For example, several situations may provide an automatic gut "sense" of rightness and wrongness, such as paying a bribe or overcharging a customer.

To understand the nature of intuitions better, consider the following experiment. The participants were provided with a series of what were called "harmless-offensive" stories in which an actor does something likely to be considered offensive, yet there are neither harmful consequences nor intention.[40] For example, one story was designed to trigger the emotion of disgust: "A family's dog was killed by a car in front of their house. They had heard that dog meat was delicious, so they cut up the dog's body and cooked it and ate it for dinner."[41] Other stories include a woman who cuts up an American flag and uses it to clean up her bathroom, a son who breaks his promise to his dying mother to visit her grave every week, a brother and sister who make love to each other,[42] and a man who has sexual intercourse with a dead chicken and then eats it.[43] The respondents upon reading the stories know the actions are wrong, but they are also *morally dumbfounded* in that they are not able to provide reasons for their judgments of disapproval.[44]

Just like these stories, we sometimes in the workplace automatically and without any real reflection just know what is right or wrong through our intuitions or "gut sense." When we are asked to cover up mistakes that cause harm to our clients, we automatically and intuitively sense this is wrong. When we see our firm pollute the natural environment, we know this is wrong without reflecting on it. When employees are denied breaks or are required to work on a religious holiday, we intuitively sense this is wrong. As part of the non-rationalist approach to ethical decision making, some argue that intuition should be considered central or "sovereign" to the ethical moral judgment stage of ethical decision making:[45] for these theorists, if moral reasoning takes place at all, it happens after the intuitive judgment has already been reached. In this sense, reasoning is retroactive in nature, in that it is used primarily to rationalize previous judgments and not to arrive at those judgments.[46] One way to express the intuitive process is by saying: "I don't know, I can't explain it; I just know it's wrong."[47]

In the case of receiving an expensive bottle of wine as a gift from a supplier, our inner intuitive sense or gut instinct may simply raise an ethical red flag that there is something possibly wrong in accepting the gift, even if we are not certain exactly why.

Emotions

The second mental process that impacts the moral judgment stage of ethical decision making is *emotion*. While for many years the main focus of most ethical decision-making research was on the *moral reasoning* process, emotion (along with intuition) continues to receive more attention in the literature.[48]

Emotion tends to be defined broadly but for our purposes is defined as follows:

> Emotion: *a person's positive or negative "feeling state" that arises from the appraisal of an arousing situation.*[49]

Emotions can vary in intensity from mild to intense. The sorts of emotions that have been suggested to impact ethical decision making include: anger, anxiety, compassion, disgust, distress, dominance, embarrassment, empathy, fear, grief, guilt, hope, humiliation, love, meaninglessness, mercy, pride, regret, remorse, responsibility, sadness, shame, and sympathy.[50] Several of these emotions have been considered to be *moral emotions*, in the sense that they more directly relate to ethical decision making. *Moral emotions* can be categorized into: (i) *prosocial* emotions which promote morally good behavior such as empathy, sympathy, concern, or compassion; (ii) *self-blame* emotions such as guilt, shame, and embarrassment; or (iii) *other-blame* emotions, such as contempt, anger, and disgust.[51] In many cases, emotion might be the first response when faced with an ethical situation or dilemma.[52]

In order to understand better how emotion can impact our moral judgments, consider the following example, known as the "runaway trolley" dilemma:

> A runaway trolley is headed for five people who will be killed if it proceeds on the present course. The only way to save them is to hit a switch that will turn the trolley onto an alternate set of tracks where it will kill one person instead of five. Should you turn the trolley to save five people at the expense of one?[53]

Did you hit the switch and turn the trolley onto a different track? Most people say "yes" and approve of turning the trolley to a different track. One explanation provided is that since the dilemma is "impersonal" in nature, no emotional response is triggered. Individuals can then fully engage in a moral reasoning process not impeded by emotion by simply reflecting on the consequences of the two alternatives. When this reasoning process takes place, most people determine that it is morally acceptable to kill one person in order to save the lives of five other people. The second version of the dilemma, however, is as follows:

> A trolley threatens to kill five people. You are standing next to a large stranger on a footbridge spanning the tracks, in-between the oncoming trolley and the hapless five. This time, the only way to save them is to push this stranger off the bridge and onto the tracks below. He will die if you do this, but his body will stop the trolley from reaching the others. Should you save the five others by pushing this stranger to his death?[54]

Would you push the stranger off the bridge to save the lives of five other people? Most people now disapprove of the action of saving five people by pushing a stranger to his death. Although there is no consequential difference between the first and second versions of the dilemma, we respond differently due to the harm or violence resulting from the more personal act of actually physically and directly pushing someone to their death. When we think about this more personal involvement, a negative emotional response of disgust is triggered in most people, leading to a judgment of moral disapproval of the act regardless of the fact that additional lives will now be lost.[55]

Just as our emotions affect how we feel about pushing someone to save the lives of others, our emotions can impact how we behave in the workplace and therefore they are considered an important part of the Integrated-EDM model. Several researchers have attempted to explain the relationship between emotion and ethical decision making. Some directly link emotion to intuition with little emphasis placed on reason.[56] Others suggest that emotion can facilitate the reasoning process by acting as a regulator of our conduct.[57] Various emotions such as empathy, guilt, or anger may also impact other stages of the ethical decision-making process in addition to moral judgment, such as the intention stage by creating a motivation to act.[58] Now that we understand the different ways in which emotion can influence the ethical decision-making process, let's look at the various types of moral emotions and how they might influence behavior in the workplace.

Pro-social emotions such as empathy can lead to intuitive judgments or "affect-laden intuitions," often referred to as "gut feelings" about the rightness or wrongness of certain actions.[59] As a manager I might feel empathy towards an employee who is facing serious health and financial issues, which might impact how I handle a situation where the employee in dire straits has engaged in misconduct or needs to be fired. When senior executives of business firms see actual pictures of the injuries their products have caused to their consumers rather than simply reading reports, or when they actually meet the families of the victims, the emotion of empathy might trigger taking responsibility to ensure similar injuries won't happen again to someone else. While pro-social or positive emotions such as empathy are generally associated with ethical behavior, it may also be the case that positive emotions can arise following unethical behavior such as cheating, which can then reinforce and contribute to additional future unethical behavior.[60]

Self-blame emotions such as embarrassment and guilt can also be a powerful motivator of ethical behavior in the workplace. For these emotions, we might not act a certain way because we would expect to be embarrassed if our actions were discovered or because we would simply feel guilty. When I ask my students whether they would inform a friend about a job position during a difficult job market when the friend would be more likely to get the job offer, the majority of students indicate they would tell their friend. For some of these students, the feelings of guilt they would experience if they did not inform their friend and then got the job plays a role in their decision making. Unfortunately, however, we are not always able to foresee the shame and embarrassment we later experience from acting unethically.

Consider these examples. According to Nick Leeson, who went to jail for over four years for fraud and illegal trading after financially crippling his employer Barings Bank, his overwhelming emotion looking back on his fraud was one of embarrassment, rather than shame or remorse. Leeson states: "You go through them all. But the lasting one for me is embarrassment. Because it's the complete opposite of what I wanted. I'd want to be remembered for my successes rather than my failures, but nothing that I do is probably ever going to change that."[61] Bernie Madoff only later realized his fraudulent actions under his Ponzi scheme were problematic in terms of the shame he ultimately caused to his family. After receiving his 150 year sentence, Madoff said: "I've left a legacy of shame to my family and my grandchildren that is something that I will live with for the rest of my life."[62]

In addition to *pro-social* and *self-blame* emotions, we might also experience *other-blame emotions* such as anger or disgust. When we experience other-blame emotions, we tend to act in a less rational manner, and can end up acting unethically as a result. If a manager is observed unnecessarily disparaging an employee, a feeling of anger or disgust might arise among the employee's co-workers. These feelings might then cause the employee's co-workers to act improperly by no longer returning the "evil" manager's emails or no longer fully informing the manager about relevant matters. Feelings of anger towards other employees or the firm itself might even lead to unethical acts of revenge or sabotage. If I have just been fired for what I believe are unjust reasons, I might be tempted due to anger to speak badly about the company to others, take some clients with me, or fail to properly train my successor. If I feel the emotions of envy or resentment towards work colleagues who are paid more than me for the same performance, then I might tend to believe that I am entitled to pad my expense account.[63]

In other cases, our *other-blame emotions* might simply trigger our initial moral awareness. For example, I may feel anger and disgust when I discover that a colleague is watching pornography while at work, or that my firm is selling defective and dangerous goods to unknowing consumers, or that my manager has stolen confidential information from our competitors. This initial moral awareness may then lead to a moral judgment driven by the emotions of anger and disgust that such behavior is unacceptable and needs to be addressed.

Finally, some individuals can be considered to be *psychopathic*. Psychopaths are able to engage repeatedly in criminal and unethical behavior without any feeling of remorse, sympathy, or empathy for those who have been victimized. For these psychopathic employees or managers, emotions would not play a role in their decision making, and while they may be capable of rational thinking and knowing the rules of social behavior, they do not care about the consequences of their actions.[64] While only representing approximately 1% of the population, corporate psychopaths with their lack of emotion can potentially cause great damage within firms and have even been blamed for contributing to the global financial crisis.[65]

Returning to our initial example, it's not clear whether we would have any sort of emotional response to being given an expensive bottle of wine from a current supplier, other than feelings of pleasure and gratitude. But these feelings would not be moral emotions per se, and would therefore not likely play a role in our ethical decision-making process other than relating to our self-interest. If, however, we anticipate experiencing feelings of guilt or embarrassment at the thought of having our actions discovered by others, then we might decide it would be best not to accept the gift.

Reason

The Integrated-EDM model considers the *moral reasoning* process to be just as important as intuition and emotion[66] and not limited to merely after-the-fact rationalization as some theorists suggest.[67] Moral reasoning is defined as follows:

> Moral reasoning: *the conscious and deliberate application of moral standards to a situation in order to reach a moral judgment.*

The moral reasoning process is considered to have several features. It is effortful, non-automatic, slow, inferential, methodological, and involves the application of moral standards to a situation. There are multiple steps in the process, and the person engaged in moral reasoning is potentially aware of and in control of the thought process. For example, in deciding whether to dismiss a colleague who is also considered a close friend, a more deliberative moral reasoning process may take place, leading to a particular moral judgment.

In the case of receiving an expensive bottle of wine from a current supplier, several moral standards would potentially be considered. Initially, self-interest would likely push us to accept the gift, which would necessarily come into conflict with other moral standards. If we are morally aware, we might ask or reflect upon additional issues such as: "By accepting the wine, am I creating a conflict of interest so that I would no longer be acting in a trustworthy and loyal manner towards my firm?" "Would accepting the gift be unfair to the other potential suppliers?" "Are the net benefits of accepting the gift positive for everyone involved?"

If there is a conflict among the moral standards (e.g., consequences versus duties) or competing stakeholder claims, then this conflict would need to be worked out leading to an overall moral judgment on the ethical acceptability of receiving the gift. More complex ethical dilemmas would presumably lead to a more challenging moral reasoning process, the proper resolution of which may require stronger *moral competence.*

Integration

As can be seen in Figure 2.1, the Integrated-EDM model suggests that all three mental processes (intuition, emotion, and reason), are each involved in the moral judgment process. This is in line with a growing number of researchers who are indicating the importance of including what has been referred to as the *dual process* of both reason and emotion/intuition in any ethical decision-making model.[68] Despite this development, very few studies provide a clear visual depiction of the influence of reason, intuition, and emotion on ethical decision making.[69]

While the actual degree of influence of reason, intuition, and emotion and the sequencing or nature of the interaction remain open for debate and further research,[70] virtually everyone now agrees that both approaches play a role in ethical decision making.[71] The relationships between emotion and intuition upon each other, as well as on moral judgment and intention, should therefore be indicated in any comprehensive ethical decision-making model. As indicated by a proponent of the intuitionist approach:

> The debate between rationalism and intuitionism is an old one, but the divide between the two approaches may not be unbridgeable. Both sides agree that people have emotions and intuitions, engage in reasoning, and are influenced by each other. The challenge, then, is to specify how these processes fit together. Rationalist models do this by focusing on reasoning and then discussing the other processes in terms of their effects on reasoning. Emotions matter because they can be inputs to reasoning … The social intuitionist model proposes a very different arrangement, one that fully integrates reasoning, emotion, intuition, and social influence.[72]

Yet despite the claim of "fully" integrating reason, emotion, and intuition, intuitionists clearly make reason play a secondary role to intuition in a potential two-stage process, highlighting its lack of importance to ethical decision making.[73] As opposed to other ethical decision-making models, the Integrated-EDM model equally incorporates intuition, emotion, and reason along with their potential interrelationships as part of a neuro-cognitive-affective process as depicted in Figure 2.1.

To relate this to popular culture, each of the two approaches to ethical decision making would be aligned with a different character in the popular science fiction television and movie series *Star Trek*. First Officer Mister Spock with his use of *reason* and logic to guide decision making would be considered a rationalist, while Doctor Leonard "Bones" McCoy with his reliance on *emotion* would be considered a sentimentalist or non-rationalist. Captain James T. Kirk with his gut instincts or *intuitions* would also be considered a non-rationalist. One might note that together Spock, McCoy, and Kirk make a (hypothetical) formidable decision-making team, and it may be that depending on the issue, a proper combination of intuition, emotion, and reason can ultimately lead to the most appropriate ethical decisions in the workplace supported by a sufficient motivation to act.[74] Reflecting a common divide in philosophy, one other way of perceiving the different approaches to decision making is that rationality can be associated with the "head", while intuition or emotion can be associated with the "heart."[75]

Table 2.1 provides a summary of some of the key features that have been suggested to distinguish between the non-rationalist approach (i.e., intuition/emotion) and the rationalist approach (i.e., reason) to ethical decision making.[76]

Moral consultation

One additional potential process that can impact our judgment, intention, or behavior is that of *moral consultation*. Moral consultation is defined as follows:

> Moral consultation: *the active process of reviewing ethics-related documentation (e.g., codes of ethics) or discussing to any extent our situation with others in order to receive guidance or feedback in relation to the ethical dilemma we are facing.*

While it is clear that not all individuals will engage with others in helping to determine the appropriate course of action when facing an ethical dilemma, any degree of discussion with colleagues, managers, family members, friends, or an ethics officer, or the review of ethics documentation, would constitute moral consultation.

Moral consultation as a procedural step of ethical decision making, while not incorporated into the dominant ethical decision-making models, is referred to by some ethical decision-making theorists.[77] For example, in the intuitionist model individuals are referred to as being influenced or persuaded through their social interactions with others and that most moral change

Table 2.1 Non-rationalist vs rationalist approaches to ethical decision making.
Source: Haidt, J. 2001. Reproduced with the permission of the American
Psychological Association.

Non-Rationalist Approach/System (Intuition/Emotion)	Rationalist Approach/System (Reason)
System 1	System 2
System X (reflexive)	System C (higher order conscious)
"Hot" system (emotions)	"Cold" system (reason)
Effortless	Effortful
Automatic, Rapidity, Fast, Immediate	Non-automatic, Slow
Non-inferential	Inferential
Moral sense, Gut reactions, Moral sentiments/emotions	Application of moral rules to a situation
Mental habits, Flashes of insight, Seems/seemings	Methodical
One step mental process	Multiple step mental process, Sequential
Self-evident truths, Engrained or innate moral judgments	Rules govern cognitive process
Evaluative instincts (not behavioral)	Potentially aware of and in control of the process
Emotionally-valenced intuition, Feels/feelings	Emotions influence but do not cause moral judgments
Process is unintentional and not controllable	Process is intentional and controllable
Process is inaccessible; only results enter awareness	Process is consciously accessible and viewable
Does not demand attentional resources	Demands attentional resources, which are limited
Common to all mammals	Unique to humans over age 2
Context dependent	Context independent

happens as a result of social interaction.[78] Moral consultation should be considered particularly important in an organizational setting given that firms
often encourage and provide opportunities to their employees to discuss and
seek ethical guidance from others or from ethics documentation.[79] While
moral consultation is generally expected to improve ethical decision making, the opposite might also occur. We may discover through discussion that
"unethical" behavior is considered acceptable to others potentially increasing
the likelihood of acting in an unethical manner.

In the case of our example of receiving the gift of the expensive bottle of
wine, moral consultation can take place when we discuss the matter with our
work colleagues, managers, or friends, and then listen to their opinion. We
could also simply refer to the industry or firm's code of ethics or other policies.

For example, the firm's code of ethics may indicate that employees should not place themselves in a conflict of interest situation which would imply the gift should not be accepted. Even though we might consult others or a code of ethics, however, this does not guarantee that the guidance received will necessarily be followed.

Intention Stage

Our moral judgment (*evaluation*) whether based on emotion (*feel*), intuition (*sense*), moral reasoning (*reflect*), and/or moral consultation (*confirm*), may then lead to moral intention (*commitment*), which is defined as follows:

> Moral intention: *the commitment or motivation to act according to our moral judgment.*[80]

Once a *moral intention* to act is formed, the likelihood increases that ethical behavior (*action*) will follow (see Figure 2.1). Whether we reach a proper moral judgment and moral intention to act is often determined by the extent to which various *impediments* or barriers interfere with our rational thought process. These impediments will be discussed further in Chapter 3, which can also be observed in Figure 2.1. Once moral intention is reached, we have essentially prioritized ethical values over other concerns such as our self-interest.

We want, however, to be very careful to distinguish between *intention* and *behavior*. The following well-known riddle might help illustrate the difference: if there are three birds sitting on a wire, and two birds *decide* to fly away, how many birds are left on the wire? We might want to answer that only one bird is left sitting on the wire, but the actual correct response is that all three birds are left sitting on the wire. The two birds did not actually leave yet, although they did "decide" or intend to leave. There are many people who have good intentions to act a certain way, but are unable to follow through with the intended behavior due to weak *moral character* in terms of having a weak *moral identity*, a low level of *moral willpower*, or insufficient *moral courage*. We may intend to let the supplier know they should not have sent us the bottle of expensive wine and return it to them, but we simply never get around to it and bring the bottle of wine home to enjoy instead.

Moral Behavior Stage

Each of the above processes (i.e., emotion, intuition, reason, and consultation) can impact moral judgment either directly or following interaction with each other, leading to forming an intention to act, and then potentially to behavior. *Ethical behavior* is defined as follows:

> Ethical behavior: *action that is supported by one or more moral standards.*

The behavior can either relate to "proscriptive" acts such as avoiding harming others or "prescriptive" actions which involve doing good for others.[81] While we often think of behavior as being either ethical or unethical, we also need to realize that behavior can be of different *degrees* of "rightness" or "wrongness" or "goodness" or "badness." In other words, rather than behavior either being only good or bad or right or wrong, instead there is a spectrum or continuum of what has been referred to as "ethicality."[82] In other words, some actions can be judged as being extremely unethical, while others might be seen as highly ethical.[83] Most actions or behavior fall somewhere in between these extremes.[84]

Here are the various categories of ethicality with examples from least ethical to most ethical: "ethically reprehensible" or "evil" such as knowingly selling a defective and dangerous consumer product; "ethically unacceptable" such as engaging in insider trading or padding expense accounts; "ethically questionable" such as receiving a gift from a current supplier; "ethically tolerable" such as occasionally surfing on the internet for personal matters while at work; "ethically permissible" such as bluffing during negotiations; "ethically acceptable" such as infrequently leaving work a bit early to take care of one's children; "ethically commendable" or desirable such as disclosing a minor mistake to a client that would not have been discovered; or "ethically praiseworthy" or even heroic, such as blowing the whistle on misconduct despite the risk of personal repercussions.[85]

Accepting an expensive bottle of wine from a current supplier would likely be considered at the very least ethically "questionable." If there is a company policy against employees placing themselves in a conflict of interest situation or the employee is a decision maker regarding the supplier, then accepting the wine would more clearly be ethically unacceptable. The fact that no one is directly harmed means that the act is not ethically reprehensible in nature.[86] Figure 2.3 depicts what might be considered an "ethicality continuum."

Feedback loops

Potential feedback loops represent the final procedural step in the Integrated-EDM model. Behavior may be followed by perceived positive or negative *consequences* to others or to ourselves through rewards or punishments/sanctions

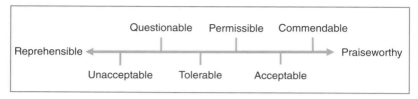

Figure 2.3   Ethicality continuum.

for the decision made or actions taken. When the consequences are observed by the decision maker, *learning* involving internal retrospection over our actions can take place. Learning is defined as follows:

> Learning: *the process of understanding and internalizing the impacts of our decisions.*

Learning may affect our individual moral character and thereby the decision-making process the next time an ethical dilemma arises. We have all stayed awake at night reflecting on our decisions and experiences of the previous day.[87] The learning might be either positive or negative, for example we might determine that acting in an unethical manner was worth the risks taken, or that acting ethically was not worth the personal costs suffered. In either case, such realizations might impact future decision making. When learning does not take place, this can be referred to as *moral amnesia*, or the habitual inability to remember or learn from one's own and others' past mistakes and the failure to transfer that knowledge when new ethical challenges arise.[88] Similar feedback loops including consequences and learning are included in several (but not all) ethical decision-making models. For example, one model refers to "evaluation of behavior",[89] while another model refers to "actual consequences" which is the "major learning construct in the model" which feeds back to our "personal experiences."[90] Another model refers to the feedback loop as our "ethical decision history."[91]

One additional feedback loop of the Integrated-EDM model (see Figure 2.1) flows from behavior to awareness, in that only after we act (e.g., telling a white lie, fudging an account) we may realize that there were ethical implications that ought to have been considered (i.e., if there was originally a lack of awareness) or that the matter ought to have been considered differently. The original issue or dilemma may then potentially be judged again based on any of the processes (i.e., emotion, intuition, reason, and/or consultation) leading to a different judgment and new behavior (e.g., admission of fault, apology, steps to fix the mistake, etc.).

In terms of receiving a gift of a bottle of expensive wine from a supplier, we might learn from the experience of accepting the wine that it was a mistake, in that the supplier now has an expectation of having the supply relationship continue. At the very least, we may realize after the fact that we have created a perceived conflict of interest by our colleagues if they discover that we have received an expensive bottle of wine and then believe we might be influenced in our future decision making regarding this supplier. Based on this *learning*, we might rethink the entire decision-making process, or our moral character might adjust so that in the future we are better able to self-sanction ourselves from receiving expensive gifts from suppliers.

Basic propositions

In general, according to the Integrated-EDM model, ethical behavior is assumed to be more likely to take place when there is strong individual moral character, strong issue characteristics (high level of moral intensity and importance with a lack of complexity), strong ethical corporate culture (including weak perceived opportunity with strong sanctions for unethical behavior), along with weak personal constraints (weak perceived need for personal gain, sufficient time and financial resources). Unethical behavior tends to take place when there is weak individual moral character (weak capability and weak commitment leading to a high degree of ethical vulnerability to situational pressures), weak issue characteristics (weak issue intensity and importance along with a high level of issue complexity), weak ethical corporate culture (including strong perceived opportunities, weak sanctions, along with strong authority pressures and peer influence to engage in unethical behavior), and strong personal constraints (strong perceived need for personal gain and time pressures).[92]

Going back to our case of gift giving or receiving, the employee who refuses the expensive bottle of wine from a supplier likely has strong moral character along with a weak personal "need for gain" at the time (or simply doesn't like wine). The firm more likely has a strong ethical corporate culture with clear guidelines on gift giving and receiving that has been well communicated to employees through proper training or communication of the policy, with strong sanctions for acting improperly. Figure 2.4 summarizes the basic propositions of the Integrated-EDM model. The arrows between the various individual factors (moral character) and situational factors (ethical corporate culture, issue characteristics, and personal constraints) suggests that there is a continuum of strength ("weak" to "strong") for each set of factors.

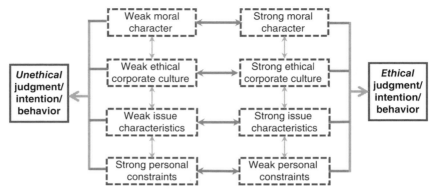

Figure 2.4   Factors leading to ethical/unethical behavior.

In Table 2.2 the definitions of the various process stages and their relationships with other Integrated-EDM model constructs and stages are summarized.

Chapter Summary

This chapter outlines an Integrated Ethical Decision-Making model by building on previous theoretical models, and attempts to illustrate the anatomy or basic structure of ethical decision making. It does so by merging together the key processes, factors, and theories, including *intuition*, *emotion*, and moral *reasoning* along with the key *individual* and *situational* variables. The proposed integrated model might be considered to take a *person–situation interactionist* approach[108] reflected in Chapter 1 along with an *intuition/sentimentalist–rationalist* approach[109] to moral judgment as described in this chapter. As research suggests: "Most all of us may commit unethical behaviors, given the right circumstances."[110] The possibility of *lacking moral awareness* is taken into account, as are key precursors (i.e., moral norms) and subsequent processes (i.e., learning) to ethical decision making.

Obviously, the proposed ethical decision-making model remains subject to further criticism, leading to the need to be further modified as new ethical decision-making research is generated.[111] However, despite its limitations, what has been proposed in this chapter hopefully represents a more robust and comprehensive model that captures the ethical decision-making process undertaken by most people in most situations.[112] Now that we have reviewed the ethical decision-making process in terms of the stages we tend to go through, we turn in Chapter 3 to a discussion of the *impediments* or barriers that hinder or prevent proper ethical decision making.

Table 2.2 Integrated ethical decision-making process stages and constructs. *Source:* Schwartz, M.S. 2016. Reproduced with the permission of Springer.

Process Stages	Definition and Relationship with Other Integrated-EDM Concepts and Stages
Moral awareness	The point in time when an individual realizes that they are facing a situation requiring a decision or action that could the affect the interests, welfare, or expectations of oneself or others in a manner that may conflict with one or more moral standards.[93]
Lack of moral awareness	The state of not realizing that a dilemma has moral implications. Leads to unintentional ethical or unethical behavior.[94]
Moral judgment	Determination of the ethically appropriate course of action among alternatives. Activates the moral intention stage.[95]
Intuition	A cognitive process involving an automatic and reflexive reaction leading to an initial moral judgment. Can lead to moral judgment directly.[96] Can also impact *emotion*[97] or *moral reasoning* when there are unclear or conflicting intuitions.[98]
Emotion	A feeling state. Can impact judgment directly.[99] Can also impact the moral *reasoning* process[100] or trigger *intuitions*.[101]
Reason	The conscious and deliberate application of moral standards to a situation in order to reach a moral judgment. Can impact moral judgment directly.[102] Reason ("cool system") can also control *emotions* ("hot system").[103] Reason through "private reflection" can lead to a new *intuition*.[104]
Moral consultation	Discussing to any extent an ethical dilemma with others or the review of ethical documentation (e.g., codes). Takes place after initial awareness, but could also take place after behavior.
Moral intention	The commitment or motivation to act according to our moral values. Affects moral behavior and can lead to moral consultation.[105]
Ethical behavior	Action that is supported by one or more moral standards. Can be intentional (moral awareness) or unintentional (lack of moral awareness). Typically follows moral judgment and/or moral intention.[106]
Learning	The process of understanding and internalizing the impacts of our decisions. Can impact our moral character for future decisions.[107]

Notes

1. O'Fallon and Butterfield (2005, p. 399).
2. Tenbrunsel and Smith-Crowe (2008, p. 593).
3. See: Liedka (1989, p. 805); Tenbrunsel and Smith-Crowe (2008, p. 584). The challenges and complexity of ethical decision making have led some researchers to suggest a "punch bowl" or "garbage can" approach, which assumes that researchers will never know exactly what takes place leading to ethical judgments in that only what goes into or out of the process is capable of being analyzed (see: Schminke, 1998, p. 207).
4. The model presented in this chapter attempts to illustrate *how* ethical decision making takes place, and is therefore essentially descriptive in nature. Of course, no decision-making model can be completely descriptive, as the model likely reflects my own norms and values to some extent. Later on, Chapter 4 provides a *normative* ethical decision-making model (or "how to" make ethical decisions), by incorporating several key moral standards and ethical decision-making tests into the moral judgment stage of the ethical decision-making process.
5. The essential process framework is Rest's (1986) "Four-Component" model of ethical decision making which is described in more detail in Appendix B.
6. Treviño (1986).
7. Ferrell and Gresham (1985); Hunt and Vitell (1986); Treviño (1986); Randall (1989); Jones (1991); Brass *et al.* (1998).
8. The firm's informal ethical culture should be considered distinct from organizational-level norms although there would clearly be a relationship between them.
9. For example, the market system within which business operates (e.g., capitalistic versus a command economy) certainly has an important influence on environmental norms. Social media can also significantly impact environmental norms. The way in which environmental norms are established, despite the importance of this process is, however, beyond the scope of this book.
10. Haidt (2001).
11. See: Rest (1986). Rest's model was heavily influenced by Kohlberg (1973).
12. Butterfield *et al.* (2000).
13. Hannah *et al.* (2011).
14. Tenbrunsel *et al.* (2003); Tenbrunsel and Smith-Crowe (2008).
15. There is, however, a risk of moral awareness being confounded with moral judgment, especially when the definition of moral awareness includes consideration of one or more ethical standards (see: Reynolds, 2006a, p. 233).
16. Rest (1986).
17. Jones (1991, p. 383).
18. Sonenshein (2007, p. 1026).
19. Tenbrunsel and Smith-Crowe (2008).
20. Carroll (1987) refers to "amoral managers", who can either act intentionally or unintentionally. Unintentional amoral managers "… do not think about business activity in ethical terms. These managers are simply casual about, careless about, or inattentive to the fact that their decisions and actions may have

negative or deleterious effects on others. These managers lack ethical perception and moral awareness; that is, they blithely go through their organizational lives not thinking that what they are doing has an ethical dimension to it. They may be well intentioned but are either too insensitive or egocentric to consider the impacts on others of their behavior" (Carrroll, 1987, p. 11).

21. Tenbrunsel and Messick (2004, p. 224).
22. Palazzo *et al.* (2012, p. 324).
23. Palazzo *et al.* (2012, p. 325).
24. Gioia (1992, p. 383).
25. Tenbrunsel and Smith-Crowe (2008); Dedeke (2015).
26. Sonenshein (2007). Given its importance to unethical decision making, the process of *non-moral framing* will be discussed in more detail in Chapter 3.
27. Drumwright and Murphy (2004, p. 7).
28. This can also take place due to *moral muting*, which involves managers who "… avoid moral expressions in their communications …" (Bird and Waters, 1989, p. 75). In other words, managers tend to frame morally defined objectives in terms of "organizational interests" and "economic good sense" (Bird and Waters, 1989, p. 73).
29. See: Sims and Brinkmann (2003).
30. Reynolds (2008, p. 1027).
31. Ruedy and Schweitzer (2010, p. 73).
32. For example, *mindful* individuals may feel less compelled to explain away, ignore, or rationalize ideas that might be potentially threatening to self-interest, such as a potential bias or a conflict of interest. See: Ruedy and Schweitzer (2010, p. 76).
33. Werhane (1998).
34. See: Werhane (1998; 1999). Werhane (1999, p. 5) defines moral imagination as follows: "Moral imagination entails the ability to understand [a particular] context or set of activities from a number of different perspectives, the actualizing of new possibilities that are not context-dependent, and the instigation of the process of evaluating those possibilities from a moral point of view." Moral imagination as a process of reframing or disengaging from one's context or situation can also assist in avoiding the roles, mental models, moral boundaries, or biases that impede ethical decision making which are discussed next in Chapter 3.
35. Tenbrunsel and Smith-Crowe (2008); Jackson *et al.* (2013).
36. Haidt (2001) is the key proponent of the non-rationalist approach to ethical decision making, while Rest (1986) is the primary proponent of the rationalist approach.
37. Haidt (2001); Reynolds (2006b); Dedeke (2015).
38. Haidt (2001, p. 816).
39. See: Reynolds (2006b).
40. See: Haidt *et al.* (1993, p. 617).
41. See: Haidt *et al.* (1993, p. 617).
42. Haidt (2001, p. 814) presents the following situation, which is designed to avoid any ethical issues: "Julie and Mark are brother and sister. They are travelling together in France on summer vacation from college. One night they are staying alone in a cabin near the beach. They decide that it would be interesting and

fun if they tried making love. At the very least it would be a new experience for each of them. Julie was already taking birth control pills, but Mark uses a condom too, just to be safe. They both enjoy making love, but they decide not to do it again. They keep that night as a special secret, which makes them feel even closer to each other. What do you think about that? Was it OK for them to make love?" Most respondents find the activity to be "wrong", but are unable to present reasons for this.

43. See: Haidt *et al.* (1993, p. 617).
44. See: Haidt (2001).
45. Haidt (2001).
46. Saltzstein and Kasachkoff (2004, p. 276).
47. Haidt (2001, p. 814).
48. Haidt (2001); Greene *et al.* (2001); Sonenshein (2007).
49. See: Gaudine and Thorne (2001, p. 176). There appears to be some disagreement over the relationship and differences between emotions, moods, and affective personality traits.
50. See: Haidt (2001, pp. 824–825); Agnihotri *et al.* (2012). For a review of the research on guilt, shame, empathy, and moods in relation to morality, see: Eisenberg (2000). Damasio (1994) has also provided support linking emotion and its biological underpinnings to decision making. See: Agnihotri *et al.* (2012, p. 246) for a summary of the ethical decision-making theoretical and empirical studies on emotion.
51. See: Prinz and Nichols (2010).
52. Haidt *et al.* (1993).
53. See: Foot (1978, pp. 19–32); Thomson (1985).
54. See: Thomson (1985).
55. Greene (2007).
56. Haidt (2001). Most appear to agree that intuitions are typically based upon or triggered by emotions. One view suggests that "The difference between intuitions and emotions … seems to be that intuitions are behavioral guides or evaluations that directly follow from an emotional experience" (Monin *et al.*, 2007, p. 101). Others refer to intuitive judgments as "… affectively charged, given that such judgments often involve emotions" and are "… detached from rationality" (Dane and Pratt, 2007, pp. 38–39). Another view is that: "The operations of [intuition] are typically fast, automatic, effortless, associative, implicit (not available to introspection), and often emotionally charged" (Kahneman, 2003, p. 698).
57. See: Damasio (1994); Elfenbein (2007, p. 348). One way to explain the relationship between emotion and reason is by describing emotions as the "hot system" ("go"), which can undermine efforts to self-control one's behavior. In contrast, the "cool system" ("know") which is cognitive, contemplative, and emotionally neutral can potentially control the "hot system" through what is referred to as "moral willpower" (Metcalfe and Mischel, 1999).
58. See: Rest (1986); Eisenberg (2000); Gaudine and Thorne (2001); Huebner *et al.* (2009).
59. Toffler (1986).

60. See: Ruedy *et al.* (2013).
61. See: Esther Addley, "Nick Leeson on Banking: Extremely Competitive … and Improperly Policed", *The Guardian*, February 23, 2015, http://www.theguardian.com/business/2015/feb/23/nick-leeson-banking-industry-extremely-competitive-improperly-policed (accessed 29 August 2016).
62. See: Sinclair Stewart, "Madoff Jailed 150 Years for 'Massive' Fraud", *The Globe and Mail*, June 29, 2009, http://www.theglobeandmail.com/report-on-business/madoff-jailed-150-years-for-massive-fraud/article4296656/(accessed 29 August 2016).
63. This is part of the moral rationalization process that will be discussed further in Chapter 3.
64. See: Haidt (2001, p. 824). For a full account regarding psychopaths, see: Babiak and Hare (2006) who suggest that psychopaths are the result of both nature (genetic) and nurture (environment).
65. See: Boddy (2011).
66. Saltzstein and Kasachkoff (2004).
67. Haidt (2001).
68. See: Marquardt and Hoeger (2009); Elm and Radin (2012). For example, Woiceshyn (2011, p. 313, emphasis added) states: "Following the developments in cognitive neuroscience and neuroethics (Salvador and Folger, 2009) and paralleling the general decision-making literature (Dane and Pratt, 2007), most researchers have since come to hold a so-called *dual processing* model of ethical decision making." One ethical decision-making study was identified that shows the links between reason, intuition, *and* emotion, referred to as a "cognitive-intuitionist" model of moral decision making (Dedeke, 2015). In the model, intuitions are referred to as reflexive "automatic cognitions", which may or may not interact with "automatic emotions". This interaction is considered part of the "pre-processing" process which often takes place and is then "… subject to review and update by the moral reflection/reasoning process" (Dedeke, 2015, p. 446). Emotion can also "sabotage" the moral reflection stage for some people and thus an "emotional control variable" is proposed "… that enables an individual to … modify … their feelings stages" (Dedeke, 2015, p. 448). The "cognitive-intuitionist" integrative model recognizes and captures the importance of moving future ethical decision-making theory in a more integrative manner, in other words, one that incorporates reason, intuition, and emotion into the ethical decision-making process.
69. One model includes reason (or reasoning) as well as intuition in the schematic social intuitionist model, although as indicated above, reason serves primarily a post hoc rationalization function and emotion (or affect) appears to be comingled with intuition (Haidt, 2001). Another approach proposes a two-system model which also includes both intuition (the reflexive X-system) and reason (the higher order conscious reasoning C-system) but appears to have left out the impact of emotion (Reynolds, 2006b). Another researcher also attempts to integrate reason and intuition but does not explicitly include emotion (Woiceshyn, 2011). Others focus more on emotion and ignore intuition by visually depicting the influence of emotion on the four ethical decision-making stages (Gaudine

and Thorne, 2001). Other fields, such as social psychology, have attempted to merge intuition and reason together schematically (Strack and Deutsch, 2004).

70. See: Dane and Pratt (2007).
71. Some have argued that the debate over reason versus intuition/emotion is actually based on whether one is experiencing a moral dilemma requiring a reasoning process, versus an affective or emotion-laden process based on reacting to a shocking situation such as considering the prospect of eating one's own dog (Monin *et al.*, 2007, p. 99).
72. Haidt (2001, p. 828).
73. See: Saltzstein and Kasachkoff (2004).
74. See: Shaw (2004).
75. See: Dane and Pratt (2007, p. 39).
76. Table 2.1 is partly based on Haidt (2001, p. 818) and Wright (2005) who discuss the contrasts between the two approaches/systems. See also: Kahneman (2011), who distinguishes between "System 1" thinking (fast/intuitive/emotional) and "System 2" thinking (slow/deliberative/logical).
77. See: Sonenshein (2007); Hamilton and Knouse (2011). Even Aristotle held that in making ethically good decisions "we should respectively consider the opinions of people widely regarded as wise." See: Hartman (2008, p. 318).
78. Haidt (2007, p. 999).
79. Weaver and Treviño (1999); Stevens (2008).
80. Ethical intention is sometimes linked with ethical behavior as being part of the "same phenomenon" (Reynolds, 2006b, p. 741) or they can be combined together as representing one's "ethical choice" (Kish-Gephart *et al.*, 2010, p. 2). It may be, therefore, that "intention" should be eliminated from Rest's (1986) four stage model, but might continue to act as a proxy for measuring judgment or behavior in ethical decision-making empirical research (see: Mencl and May, 2009, p. 205). For the purposes of the Integrated-EDM model, intention remains theoretically distinct from behavior.
81. See: Janoff-Bulman *et al.* (2009).
82. Tenbrunsel and Smith-Crowe (2008, pp. 553–554) refer to "the *ethicality* of a decision" in terms of the decision outcome being either ethical or unethical. Their proposed typology distinguishes between the *process* of decision making ("moral" or intended decision making versus "amoral" or unintended decision making) and *decision outcome* (ethical or unethical). Their typology can be used to evaluate decisions that are "intended unethical" as being worse than "unintended" or amoral decisions that have an unethical outcome.
83. See: Henderson (1984) for his version of a spectrum of ethicality in relation to minimum, maximum, and innovative legal and ethical compliance. Green (1994) also provides a type of spectrum of ethicality in terms of norms of acceptability, while Kaler (2000, p. 163) distinguishes between self-interest and morality as follows: egoism, quasi-egoism, quasi-moral, ordinarily moral, extraordinarily moral, and ultra-moral. One could also rate activity on its ethicality based on a simple scale of 1–10 from very unethical to very ethical (see: Prentice, 2014, p. 335).

84. Of course, the classification of a particular act in terms of where it then falls on the ethicality spectrum becomes much more complicated when the act involves ethical tradeoffs (e.g., duties versus consequences such as lying, cheating, stealing, or bribing in order to save a life or avoid physical injury) or different impacts on multiple stakeholders (e.g., harming someone to benefit others).

85. Kant (a philosopher whose duty-based ethics are discussed further in Chapter 4) makes a distinction between "perfect duties", which must be performed all the time without exception such as telling the truth or keeping our promises, and "imperfect duties", which can be fulfilled in different ways or at different times, such as the duty to help others. The failure to fulfill these two types of duties might also be situated on different ends of the ethicality spectrum. In addition to "forbidden", "permissible", and "required", actions, "supererogatory" actions are those acts that "go beyond the call of duty" (e.g., actions that are morally heroic such as putting one's life at risk by saving a stranger who falls onto the subway tracks) which would be located on the extreme right hand side of the ethicality spectrum.

86. Of course, other potential suppliers or the owners of the firm would be indirectly harmed if the best supplier is not being utilized as a result of the gift being received.

87. According to Reynolds (2006b, p. 742, emphasis added): "… anyone who has lain awake at night contemplating the experiences of the previous day knows that *retrospection* is a key component of the ethical experience …."

88. See: Patricia H. Werhane and Brian Moriarty, "Moral Imagination and Management Decision Making", Business Roundtable Institute for Corporate Ethics, 2009, p. 3, http://www.corporate-ethics.org/pdf/moral_imagination.pdf (accessed 29 August 2016).

89. Ferrell and Gresham (1985).

90. Hunt and Vitell (1986, p. 10).

91. Stead *et al.* (1990).

92. One way to combine several of the key factors discussed in this chapter is through the concept of "Personal Ethical Threshold" (or PET), which represents how ethically vulnerable an individual is to the situational factors in his or her organization. PET accounts for the interaction between an individual's moral character and various situational factors (e.g., organizational pressures, issue moral intensity, and personal financial pressures or opportunities for gain) leading to unethical behavior. See: Comer and Vega (2008).

93. Butterfield *et al.* (2000).

94. Tenbrunsel and Smith-Crowe (2008).

95. Rest (1996).

96. Haidt (2001).

97. Dedeke (2015).

98. Haidt (2001).

99. Greene *et al.* (2001).

100. Damasio (1994); Greene *et al.* (2001); Huebner *et al.* (2009).

101. Haidt (2001).

102. Kohlberg (1973).
103. Metcalfe and Mischel (1999).
104. Haidt (2001).
105. Rest (1986).
106. Rest (1986).
107. Reynolds (2006b).
108. Treviño (1986).
109. Haidt (2001).
110. De Cremer *et al.* (2010, p. 2).
111. The proposed Integrated-EDM model contains a number of important *limitations*. In terms of scope, the Integrated-EDM model is focused on individual decision making and behavior, rather than organizational decision making, and is designed to apply mainly to the business context. One could argue that the model is overly *rationalist* in nature by continuing to rely on the four-component model (Rest, 1986) as the dominant framework to explain the ethical decision-making process. The manner and extent to which the variables and processes are depicted by the Integrated-EDM model as portrayed in Figure 2.1 can be criticized as being too all encompassing and thus lacking sufficient focus. It might on the other hand be criticized as failing to take into account other key variables or processes involved in ethical decision making that have been suggested in the literature. For example, the role of interpersonal processes (rather than intrapersonal processes) may not be sufficiently accounted for in the Integrated-EDM model despite recognizing the influence of peers/referent others, authority pressures, and the moral consultation process (see: Moore and Gino, 2013). Finally, each element of the Integrated-EDM model, including the individual and situational context variables as well as the relationship between and overlap among the variables and each of the process stages of ethical decision making, requires further detailed exploration and explication which hopefully further research will address.
112. Given the extent of theoretical and empirical research that has now taken place, ethical decision making in organizations might be considered to be moving towards developing into a "stand-alone" academic field. Whether this eventually takes place is primarily dependent on the strength of the theoretical ethical decision-making models being developed and tested by empirical ethical decision-making researchers. See: Tenbrunsel and Smith-Crowe (2008, p. 545).

References

Agnihotri, R., Rapp, J., Kothandaraman, P., and Singh, R.K. 2012. An emotion-based model of salesperson ethical behaviors. *Journal of Business Ethics*, 109: 243–257.

Babiak, P. and Hare, R.D. 2006. *Snakes in Suits: When Psychopaths Go to Work*. New York: HarperCollins.

Bird, F.B. and Waters, G.A. 1989. The moral muteness of managers. *California Management Review*, 32: 73–78.

Boddy, C.R. 2011. The corporate psychopaths theory of the global financial crisis. *Journal of Business Ethics*, 102: 255–259.

Brass, D.J., Butterfield, K.D., and Skaggs, B.C. 1998. Relationships and unethical behavior: a social network perspective. *Academy of Management Review*, 23: 14–31.

Butterfield, K.D., Treviño, L.K. and Weaver, G.R. 2000. Moral awareness in business organizations: influences of issue-related and social context factors. *Human Relations*, 53(7): 981–1018.

Carroll, A.B. 1987. In search of the moral manager. *Business Horizons*, 30(2): 7–15.

Comer, D.R. and Vega, G. 2008. Using the PET assessment instrument to help students identify factors that could impede moral behavior. *Journal of Business Ethics*, 77: 129–145.

Damasio, A. 1994. *Descartes' Error: Emotion, Reason, and the Human Brain*. New York: Putnam.

Dane, E. and Pratt, M.G. 2007. Exploring intuition and its role in managerial decision making. *Academy of Management Review*, 32(1): 33–54.

De Cremer, D., Mayer, D.M., and Schminke, M. 2010. Guest Editors' introduction on understanding ethical behavior and decision making: a behavioral ethics approach. *Business Ethics Quarterly*, 20: 1–6.

Dedeke, A. 2015. A cognitive-intuitionist model of moral judgment. *Journal of Business Ethics*, 126: 437–457.

Drumwright, M.E. and Murphy, P.E. 2004. How advertising practitioners view ethics: moral muteness, moral myopia, and moral imagination. *Journal of Advertising*, 33: 7–24.

Eisenberg, N. 2000. Emotion, regulation, and moral development. *Annual Review of Psychology*, 51: 665–697.

Elfenbein, H.A. 2007. Emotion in organizations. *The Academy of Management Annals*, 1: 315–386.

Elm, D.R. and Radin, T.J. 2012. Ethical decision making: special or no different? *Journal of Business Ethics*, 107: 313–329.

Ferrell, O.C. and Gresham, L. 1985. A contingency framework for understanding ethical decision making in marketing. *Journal of Marketing*, 49: 87–96.

Foot, P. 1978. *Virtues and Vices and Other Essays in Moral Philosophy*. Los Angeles, CA: University of California Press.

Gaudine, A. and Thorne, L. 2001. Emotion and ethical decision-making in organizations. *Journal of Business Ethics*, 31: 175–187.

Gioia, D. 1992. Pinto fires and personal ethics: a script analysis of missed opportunities. *Journal of Business Ethics*, 11: 379–389.

Green, R.M. 1994. *The Ethical Manager: A New Method for Business Ethics*. New York: Macmillan Publishing Company.

Greene, J. 2007. Why are VMPFC patients more utilitarian? A dual process theory of moral judgment explains. *Trends in Cognitive Sciences*, 11: 322–323.

Greene, J.D., Sommerville, R.B., Nystrom, L.E., Darley, J.M., and Cohen, J. 2001. An fMRI investigation of emotional engagement in moral judgement. *Science*, 293: 2105–2108.

Haidt, J. 2001. The emotional dog and its rational tail: a social intuitionist approach to moral judgment. *Psychological Review*, 4: 814–834.

Haidt, J. 2007. The new synthesis in moral psychology. *Science*, 316: 998–1002.

Haidt, J., Koller, S., and Dias, M. 1993. Affect, culture, and morality, or is it wrong to eat your dog? *Journal of Personality and Social Psychology*, 65: 613–628.

Hamilton, J.B. III and Knouse, S.B. 2011. The experience-focused model of ethical action. In *Emerging Perspectives on Organizational Justice and Ethics* (S.W. Gilliland, D.D. Steiner, and D.P. Skarlicki, eds). Charlotte, NC: Information Age Publishing, pp. 223–257.

Hannah, S.T., Avolio, B.J., and May, D.R. 2011. Moral maturation and moral conation: a capacity approach to explaining moral thought and action. *Academy of Management Review*, 36: 663–685.

Hartman, E.M. 2008. Socratic questions and Aristotelian answers: a virtue-based approach to business ethics. *Journal of Business Ethics*, 78: 313–328.

Henderson, V.E. 1984. The spectrum of ethicality. *Journal of Business Ethics*, 3: 163–171.

Huebner, B., Dwyer, S., and Hauser, M. 2009. The role of emotion in moral psychology. *Trends in Cognitive Sciences*, 13: 1–6.

Hunt, S.D. and Vitell, S. 1986. A general theory of marketing ethics. *Journal of Macromarketing*, 6: 5–16.

Jackson, R.W., Wood, C.M., and Zboja, J.J. 2013. The dissolution of ethical decision-making in organizations: a comprehensive review and model. *Journal of Business Ethics*, 116: 233–250.

Janoff-Bulman, R., Sheikh, S., and Hepp, S. 2009. Proscriptive versus prescriptive morality: two faces of moral regulation. *Journal of Personality and Social Psychology*, 96: 521–537.

Jones, T.M. 1991. Ethical decision making by individuals in organizations: an issue-contingent model. *The Academy of Management Review*, 16: 366–395.

Kahneman, D. 2003. A perspective on judgment and choice. *American Psychologist*, 58: 697–720.

Kahneman, D. 2011. *Think Fast and Slow*. New York: Farrar, Straus and Giroux.

Kaler, J. 2000. Reasons to be ethical: self-interest and ethical business. *Journal of Business Ethics*, 27: 161–173.

Kish-Gephart, J.J., Detert, J., Treviño, L.K., Baker, V., and Martin, S. 2014. Situational moral disengagement: can the effects of self-interest be mitigated? *Journal of Business Ethics*, 125: 267–285.

Kohlberg, L. 1973. The claim to moral adequacy of a highest stage of moral judgment. *The Journal of Philosophy*, 70: 630–646.

Liedka, J.M. 1989. Value congruence: the interplay of individual and organizational value systems. *Journal of Business Ethics*, 8: 805–815.

Marquardt, N. and Hoeger, R. 2009. The effect of implicit moral attitudes on managerial decision-making: an implicit social cognition approach. *Journal of Business Ethics*, 85: 157–171.

Mencl, J. and May, D.R. 2009. The effects of proximity and empathy on ethical decision-making: an exploratory investigation. *Journal of Business Ethics*, 85: 201–226.

Metcalfe, J. and Mischel, W. 1999. A hot/cool system analysis of delay of gratification: dynamics of willpower. *Psychological Review*, 106: 3–19.

Monin, B., Pizarro, D.A., and Beer, J.S. 2007. Deciding versus reacting: conceptions of moral judgment and the reason-affect debate. *Review of General Psychology*, 11: 99–111.

Moore, G. and Gino, F. 2013. Ethically adrift: how others pull our moral compass from true north, and how we can fix it. *Research in Organizational Behavior*, 33: 53–77.

O'Fallon, M.J. and Butterfield, K.D. 2005. A review of the empirical ethical decision-making literature: 1996–2003. *Journal of Business Ethics*, 59: 375–413.

Palazzo, G., Krings, F., and Hoffrage, U. 2012. Ethical blindness. *Journal of Business Ethics*, 109: 323–338.

Prentice, R.A. 2014. Teaching behavioral ethics. *Journal of Legal Studies Education*, 31: 325–365.

Prinz, J. and Nichols, S. 2010. Moral emotions. In *The Moral Psychology Handbook* (J. M. Doris and The Moral Psychology Research Group, eds). Oxford Scholarship Online. www.oxfordsholarship.com.

Randall, D.M. 1989. Taking stock: can the theory of reasoned action explain unethical conduct? *Journal of Business Ethics*, 8: 873–882.

Rest, J.R. 1986. *Moral Development: Advances in Research and Theory*. New York: Praeger.

Reynolds, S.J. 2006a. Moral awareness and ethical predispositions: investigating the role of individual differences in the recognition of moral issues. *Journal of Applied Psychology*, 91: 233–243.

Reynolds, S.J. 2006b. A neurocognitive model of the ethical decision-making process: implications for study and practice. *Journal of Applied Psychology*, 91: 737–748.

Reynolds, S.J. 2008. Moral attentiveness: who pays attention to the moral aspects of life? *Journal of Applied Psychology*, 93: 1027–1041.

Ruedy, N.E. and Schweitzer, M.E. 2011. In the moment: the effect of mindfulness on ethical decision making. *Journal of Business Ethics*, 95: 73–87.

Ruedy, N.E., Moore, C., Gino, F., and Schweitzer, M.E. 2013. The cheater's high: the unexpected affective benefits of unethical behavior. *Journal of Personality and Social Psychology*, 105: 531–548.

Saltzstein, H.D. and Kasachkoff, T. 2004. Haidt's Moral Intuitionist Theory: a psychological and philosophical critique. *Review of General Psychology*, 8: 273–282.

Salvador, R. and Folger, R.G. 2009. Business ethics and the brain. *Business Ethics Quarterly*, 19: 1–31.

Schminke, M. 1998. The magic punchbowl: a nonrational model of ethical management. In *Managerial Ethics: Moral Management of People and Processes* (M. Schminke, ed.). Mahwah, New Jersey: Lawrence Erlbaum Associates, pp. 197–214.

Schwartz, M.S. 2016. Ethical decision-making theory: an integrated approach. *Journal of Business Ethics*, 139: 755–776.

Shaw, B. 2004. Hollywood ethics: developing ethics … Hollywood style. *Journal of Business Ethics*, 49: 167–177.

Sims, R.R. and Brinkmann, J. 2003. Enron ethics (or culture matters more than codes). *Journal of Business Ethics*, 45: 243–256.

Sonenshein, S. 2007. The role of construction, intuition, and justification in responding to ethical issues at work: the Sensemaking-Intuition Model. *Academy of Management Review*, 32: 1022–1040.

Stead, W.E., Worrell, D.L., and Stead, J.G. 1990. An integrative model for understanding and managing ethical behavior in business organizations. *Journal of Business Ethics*, 9: 233–242.

Stevens, B. 2008. Corporate ethical codes: effective instruments for influencing behavior. *Journal of Business Ethics*, 78: 601–609.

Strack, F. and Deutsch, R. (2004). Reflective and impulsive determinants of social behavior. *Personality and Social Psychological Review*, 8: 220–247.

Tenbrunsel, A.E. and Messick, D.M. 2004. Ethical fading: the role of self-deception in unethical behavior. *Social Justice Research*, 17: 223–236.

Tenbrunsel, A.E. and Smith-Crowe, K. 2008. Ethical decision making: where we've been and where we're going. *Academy of Management Annals*, 2: 545–607.

Tenbrunsel, A.E., Smith-Crowe, K., and Umphress, E. 2003. Building houses on rocks: the role of the ethical infrastructure in organizations. *Social Justice Research*, 16: 285–307.

Thomson, J.J. 1985. The trolley problem. *Yale Law Journal*, 94: 1395–1415.

Toffler, B.L. 1986. *Tough Choices: Managers Talk Ethics*. New York: John Wiley & Sons, Inc.

Treviño, L.K. 1986. Ethical decision making in organizations: a person-situation interactionist model. *Academy of Management Review*, 11: 601–617.

Weaver, G.R. and Treviño, L.K. 1999. Compliance and values oriented ethics programs: influences on employees' attitudes and behavior. *Business Ethics Quarterly*, 9: 315–336.

Werhane, P.H. 1998. Moral imagination and the search for ethical decision-making in management. *Business Ethics Quarterly*, Ruffin Series (1): 75–98.

Werhane, P.H. 1999. *Moral Imagination and Management Decision-Making*. New York: Oxford University Press.

Woiceshyn, J. 2011. A model for ethical decision making in business: reasoning, intuition, and rational moral principles. *Journal of Business Ethics*, 104: 311–323.

Wright, J.C. 2005. The role of reasoning and intuition in moral judgment: a review. PhD Comprehensive Exam, University of Wyoming.

Chapter Three

Impediments to Proper Ethical Decision Making

In Chapter 1, we considered the basic reasons to help explain why particular people may act ethically or unethically in certain situations, and in Chapter 2 the typical process we go through when we decide whether or not to act ethically. But now we need to ask a series of additional questions: Why do we intentionally or subconsciously ignore or choose to block out the ethical implications of the situations we are facing? Why do our moral judgments not always translate into ethical behavior? How are we able to justify our unethical activity to ourselves and others?

Consider a typical day. You wake up and on the way to work go into a coffee shop to pick up your regular bagel and coffee, and enter the line-up of customers. Someone cuts the line, not directly in front of you, but in front of the person in front of you. Do you say anything? At work, you spend your time on the internet planning your next vacation. You realize you probably should get back to work, but you'd rather take care of this now rather than at home. Do you stop surfing and wait until you get home? Your manager then comes back from lunch and appears intoxicated. You have suspected for a while that he might be developing a drinking problem. You know he is about to meet an important client. Do you say or do anything? On your way home from work, you go into the grocery store to pick up some items. You know you have well over 10 items, but you are in a hurry to get home and think about going into the express lane for "10 items or less." Do you do this? While leaving the parking lot, you are still in hurry mode and unfortunately drive your car too close to another parked car. You hit the car and leave a small dent, but after checking you notice the other car already has a bunch of scratches. Do you do anything, like leave a note on the other car's windshield with your name and phone number, or drive away?

Business Ethics: An Ethical Decision-Making Approach, First Edition. Mark S. Schwartz.
© 2017 John Wiley & Sons, Inc. Published 2017 by John Wiley & Sons, Inc.

In reflecting on each of these dilemmas, try to assess what you think you would do and why. If you are having trouble, imagine as one set of possibilities you decide to do the following:

- politely tell the person you were ahead of them in line and hope the person would react by getting behind you;
- continue planning your vacation on the internet at work, since you know you are a good employee and will finish your assigned workload on time;
- don't say anything to your intoxicated boss or anyone else since you are worried he might not react favorably and instead you leave the matter for the client or others to deal with;
- use the express lane at the supermarket because everyone else does this, and finally;
- don't leave a note on the car you hit because the dent is so small and the car is already scratched they might not even notice or care.

If these were your responses, how did you come to these conclusions? Presumably you went through a mental process in deciding what to do. As we covered in Chapter 2, you might have immediately *intuitively* sensed what the right thing to do was, you might have reflected somewhat through a moral *reasoning* process before deciding based on certain moral standards or principles, or you might have been influenced by possible *emotions* of guilt in acting or not acting a certain way. Maybe you *morally consulted* on each issue with a friend or colleague. Each of these steps allows us to move from moral awareness to moral judgment as part of the ethical decision-making process we discussed in Chapter 2. *But when we know or should know that a particular action is ethically wrong, why do we engage in the act nonetheless?*

This chapter will attempt to address this important and fundamental question. In doing so, we will discover that there are several key interrelated categories of *impediments* or barriers that help explain why we are able to engage in unethical decision making, even when we do know or should know better. These barriers include: (i) *improper framing*; (ii) *cognitive biases* and *psychological tendencies*; (iii) *moral rationalizations*; and (iv) *self-interest*.

In Figure 3.1, the major impediments to ethical decision making are depicted. This represents a further clarification of the "impediments" and "lack of awareness" boxes in Figure 2.1 from Chapter 2. Improper *framing* through *ignoring* ethical concerns can lead to a lack of moral awareness, *biases/tendencies* can lead to a person *downplaying* ethical concerns, *rationalizations* can lead to *justifying* initial intuitions in a flawed manner, and *self-interest* can cause a *non-prioritization* of ethical concerns. Each of these impediments can minimize or neutralize the impact of *emotions* (such as anticipatory guilt),

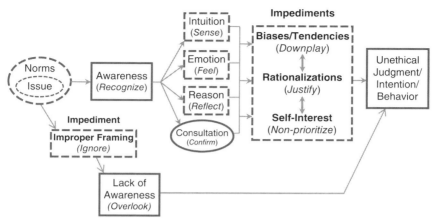

Figure 3.1   Impediments to ethical decision making. *Source*: Schwartz, M.S. 2016. Reproduced with the permission of Springer.

intuitions, the moral *reasoning* process, or the moral *consultation* process, which can then lead to unethical judgments, intentions, and/or behavior. Let's now review each of these impediments to proper ethical decision making.

Improper Framing

So what is the starting point for what prevents us from acting ethically? The first impediment to ethical decision making is *improper framing*. Improper framing takes place when we *ignore the ethical implications of the situation, and instead only recognize the economic and/or legal implications of the situation*. Unless we frame the dilemma we are facing as *ethical* in nature, we can remain in a state of *lacking moral awareness*, which can increase our chances of engaging in unethical behavior.[1] As we saw in Chapter 2, in many situations and for a variety of reasons such as *ethical fading*, *ethical blindness*, or *moral myopia*, we remain unaware that we are facing an ethical dilemma. In other cases we simply assume particular roles as employees and managers which can lead to ethical concerns being ignored in our framing of situations.[2] If we end up engaging in what can be considered ethical or unethical behavior, it's not because we intended to do so. If, however, we are *morally attentive, morally mindful,* or *morally imaginative*, we increase the chances that we will realize we are facing an ethical dilemma with several different alternatives, and then potentially engage in a proper moral reasoning process.

In reflecting on the nature of the situation we are facing before determining the possible courses of action, we tend to ask ourselves a series of possible questions that help frame the situation we are facing. The three frames include: (i) economic; (ii) legal; and (iii) ethical.[3] Let's now examine each of these possible frames.

Economic frame

When applying the *economic* frame, we are focused on whether the situation relates to our self-interest or the interests of our company. In terms of our self-interest, any decision or consideration that would either in the short or long term sustain or improve our net convenience, pleasure, happiness, compensation, job security, wealth, status, power, or prestige would be considered as falling under the economic frame. For the firm, it would include decisions that are intended to sustain or improve our firm's bottom line. The economic frame tends to dominate decision making in the business world, since without economic considerations being taken into account, firms would no longer be in business and employees including ourselves would no longer have jobs. A person applying an economic frame might ask the following questions when faced with particular situations:

- Should I report a co-worker's mistake to make myself look better in my upcoming salary review?
- Should I stay at work late when my boss will appreciate this or go home from work early?
- Should I claim a sick day so I can go away with my spouse for our anniversary?

Legal frame

For the *legal* frame, a person is most concerned with either themselves or their employers abiding by laws, and not getting sued. The legal domain would potentially capture many situations in the business world including those related to: bribery, anti-competition, fraud, intellectual property, privacy, sexual harassment, or discrimination. A person looking at a situation using a legal frame might ask these questions:

- Should I ask my subordinate out on a date, or will this be considered sexual harassment?
- Should I break a contract with a supplier when it is no longer in our interests to continue the relationship, when I might be sued as a result?
- Should I tell a potential client that my competitor provides lousy service, when I might be sued for defamation?

Ethical frame

When applying an ethical frame, we ask whether the situation relates to any abstract principles of right and wrong.[4] As opposed to the economic frame, where you think about what you *want* to do based on what's best for you or your firm, or the legal frame, where you think about what you *must* do to comply with the law or avoid lawsuits, the ethical frame is thinking about an issue in terms of what you *should* do based on moral standards. For example, while using an ethical frame we wouldn't look at breaking a contract with a supplier merely from the perspective of the financial loss or gain, or potentially being legally sued for breach of contract. Instead, we would frame the issue in terms of our ethical obligation to try to keep our promises and act with loyalty towards our current suppliers. Here are some questions a person would ask when they are applying an *ethical* frame:

- Should I ask an employee to work on their non-legally recognized religious holiday, when this might be considered exploiting them or an infringement of their moral rights?
- Should I pretend to be a student in order to receive information from our competitor, when this might be considered deceptive?
- Should I anonymously post a rave review about my product or service to increase sales, when this might be considered unfair to my competitors?

Figure 3.2 depicts the three *frames* of decision making: *economic, legal,* and *ethical*.[5] For most decisions or situations we face in the business world, there are degrees of overlap among the various frames. Due to the overlap, there are actually seven different types of framing, including situations that are purely economic, purely legal, purely ethical, economic/ethical, economic/legal, legal/ethical, and economic/legal/ethical. If the ethical frame is not being applied, you would end up in a state of lacking moral awareness.

Let's now look at an example to see the range of ways you can frame a dilemma. Assume you are considering dropping a client. You have discovered that the client is not paying their taxes, is cheating their customers, and permits discrimination to take place when hiring employees. The client has also been a lucrative one for your firm, and is the same client which you succeeded in convincing to use your firm's services. How would you frame this dilemma? The way you frame the dilemma can have a direct impact on its resolution. You might only consider the *economic* implications to yourself (your compensation or promotion) or your firm (its bottom line). You might consider the *legal* obligations of dropping the client while in the middle of the engagement. Would the client potentially take legal action against you? You might

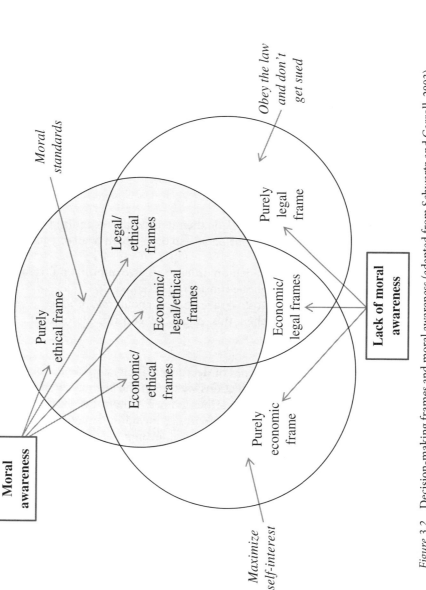

Figure 3.2 Decision-making frames and moral awareness (adapted from Schwartz and Carroll, 2003).

also consider the *ethical* implications of working with an unethical client. Is it morally right to provide services to a client who is acting unethically, and causing harm to others? Isn't it wrong to provide indirect support of unethical practices, and doesn't this make you partially morally responsible as well? The way you frame the dilemma can impact the decision you make. If you apply each of the economic, legal, and ethical frames, you would end up in the center of Figure 3.2.

Take former Chief Financial Officer Andrew Fastow of Enron for instance. Fastow, who went to jail for six years for securities fraud, explained his lack of awareness this way: "In the real world, it's very rare to see a black-and-white decision. No one's going to come up to you and say, 'Would you like to sell tainted baby formula, or pollute the river at night? Join this Ponzi scheme; it's a great deal'. It's more likely that you're going to be confronted with that gray area, where you're not even sure you have an ethical decision to make." Fastow indicated that at the time it was not clear to him that he was doing anything wrong. He justified his unethical deals to himself by "… pointing to the approval granted to his decisions by attorneys and board members, the bonuses he received when he made them, and by believing that if he did not make one of these deals, someone else would."[6] Fastow's *frames* for judging the acceptability of what he was doing were *legal* in nature due to receiving the approval of lawyers and Enron's board of directors and *economic* in terms of the bonuses he could earn, but lacked any *ethical* framing, unfortunately leading to unethical decision making.

In the case of Bernie Madoff, his only framing for his actions appears to have been *economic* in nature. Madoff was able to set aside any potential legal or ethical ramifications of his fraudulent Ponzi scheme leading to the loss of billions of dollars for investors. Since Madoff completely disregarded the law and any ethical implications of his actions, his only real framing of what he was doing was economic in nature based on whether his Ponzi scheme fraud would continue to make money for himself and his family. When Madoff admitted his guilt in the courtroom, he stated: "I knew what I was doing was wrong, indeed criminal. When I began the Ponzi scheme, I believed it would end shortly and I would be able to extricate myself and my clients."[7]

For many others, legality is simply equated with ethicality. How often do we hear in the workplace, "If it's legal, it's ethical"? Another example demonstrating a lack of *ethical framing* leading to a lack of moral awareness takes place in the movie *Margin Call*. The movie is loosely based on what took place at investment bank Lehman Brothers prior to the 2008 financial crisis. In a critical scene, a board meeting takes place to decide whether the firm should dump its toxic (worthless) assets on its clients in order to avoid bankruptcy. The CEO (John) appears focused on the *economic* and *legal* frames after checking that what they are planning to do is considered legal by the company lawyer. Here is the boardroom exchange with Sam, one of John's senior managers:[8]

Sam: The real question is: who are we selling this to?
John: The same people we've been selling it to for the last two years, and who-ever else would buy it.
Sam: But John, if you do this, you will kill the market for years. It's over.
        [John nods grimly]
Sam: And you're selling something that you 'know' has no value.
John: We are selling to willing buyers at the current fair market price.
        [Sam lowers his gaze]
John: So that we may survive.
Sam: You would never sell anything to any of those people ever again.
John: I understand.
Sam: Do you?
John: Do 'you'?
John: [pounding on the desk] This is it! I'm telling you, this is it!

Many people, including the CEO John, unfortunately assume that business decisions or dilemmas are only economic and legal in nature. However, many if not most decisions taking place in the business world have ethical implications as well, and a primary reason for unethical decision making may be that decision makers do not frame their decisions as having an ethical component. After a devastating fire destroyed his textile firm's factory, Malden Mills CEO Aaron Feuerstein had to decide whether to take $300 million in insurance money and retire or use cheaper labor overseas. Instead of retiring or relocating, Feuerstein decided he would remain in Lawrence, Massachusetts and continue to pay tens of millions of dollars in salary and benefits to his employees during the period the factory was being rebuilt, despite no legal obligation to do so. Feuerstein said: "It was a good business decision but that isn't why I did it. I did it because it was the right thing to do."[9] Feuerstein did not frame the situation as merely being economic or legal in nature, but was able to frame it as an *ethical* issue by taking into account the potential impacts of his decision on his employees and his obligations of loyalty towards them and the community.

As we'll now see, however, even if you are able to frame the dilemma as having ethical implications, a series of other biases, tendencies, and rationalizations, along with the impact of self-interest, can still prevent you from engaging in rational decision making or in following through and doing what you have determined is the right thing to do.

Cognitive Biases and Psychological Tendencies

While we would like to hope that we all engage in rational ethical decision making, there is now a substantial literature based on empirical research that suggests otherwise. For example, those who adopt a rationalist approach to ethical decision making that involves a reflection of moral standards are now beginning to recognize its limitations, including constraints or barriers such as "bounded rationality" or more specifically "bounded ethicality."[10] *Bounded ethicality* is defined as making decisions counter to values or principles without being aware of it.[11] In other words, people are generally ethical, but with limits. It can be difficult to be ethical, even when we want to be, due to biases, psychological tendencies, and organizational pressures.[12] Let's now consider the various types of significant biases and psychological tendencies that can impede moral reasoning.[13]

The first psychological tendency, *obedience to authority*, takes place when people believe or rationalize that they are not responsible for their misdeeds if their actions are based on the orders of an authority figure like their manager or CEO. It's now clear that even normally good people are capable, when working under an authority figure, of engaging in completely unethical acts. This was demonstrated in the famous Stanley Milgram electric shock experiments conducted during the 1960s whereby two thirds of participants (the "teachers") were willing to administer the most dangerous level of shock voltage to an innocent participant (the "learners"). The reason for the potentially lethal action was simply based on an "experimenter" taking responsibility for any consequences of the action.[14] Similarly, many of my students as employees have been directed by their managers or senior executives to act unethically in terms of covering up mistakes, and in many cases the students obey.

As one example, a former student of mine worked for an investment firm that was raising funds for a new client. The client firm had developed a new heart medical device, and had received several doctors' reports on its safety and efficacy. While four of the doctors provided positive reports, one doctor highlighted the safety risks of the new device in his report. The student discovered that her firm's client had buried the negative report, with their lawyers' approval. The student indicated her discomfort to her manager at the investment bank, given the potential risk to future patients. The manager's response was "This is not our responsibility. It's the client's responsibility and their lawyers. Our job is to make sure we raise sufficient funds for our client to be successful." The student was not prepared to take the matter further, but did decide to quit the firm. Several years later, the student read in the newspaper that there was a negligence lawsuit against the client for producing a faulty medical device leading to several deaths.

We can also be affected in our decision making by what others are doing or what others believe is acceptable. This is referred to as *conformity bias*. In terms of *conformity bias*, the famous Asch conformity experiments regarding peer influence provide empirical support for this psychological tendency.[15] In these experiments, a line of a particular length was first shown to a group of participants. Then three other lines of different lengths were shown, with only one of

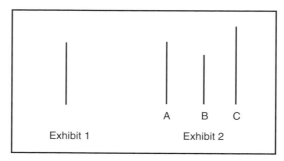

Figure 3.3   The Asch Conformity Experiment (adapted from Asch, 1955).

the three lines being the same length as the length of the original line shown (see Figure 3.3). The participants were then asked which of the three lines was the same length as the original line they were shown. All of the other participants other than the real subject of the experiment were confederates and would indicate one of the three lines that was clearly not the same length. More than one third of the time, the real subject who would answer last would conform to the response of the confederates and also give the incorrect answer.[16]

This tendency of imitating others can also lead an employee to perceive unethical actions such as insider trading, conflicts of interest, or personal internet surfing on company time, as being completely legitimized and therefore acceptable. I have heard several times from students indicating that while they were on business abroad, they would be asked to go with clients to special clubs that cater to gentlemen, with plenty of alcohol and exotic dancing. Despite their unease, the students felt compelled to be part of their team, and would tend to conform to what was considered the acceptable norm and go to the clubs.

One of the best examples of another psychological tendency is *incrementalism*, which means that what starts out as a minor ethical infraction eventually slides into more significant misconduct. Unethical activity can often proceed as a slippery slope in small steps. We have all experienced or witnessed how easily small lies can become much bigger lies very quickly, or small mistakes become much bigger issues once we try to cover them up hoping the problem will go away. This can also occur due to repeated exposure causing "psychic numbing" or "routinization" of unethical behavior. This is best represented by the actions of Nick Leeson of Barings Bank. What started as a small trade using client money to cover up the mistake of a subordinate, escalated into Leeson betting his entire bank on the Japanese Nikkei stock index. Unfortunately, the Japanese Kobe earthquake of 1995 led to the collapse of the Nikkei index, causing Barings Bank to collapse and be sold to ING Bank for one pound.[17] Incrementalism is well reflected in one of the final lines in the John Grisham movie *Rainmaker*: "Every lawyer, at least once in every case, feels himself crossing a line that he doesn't really mean to cross ... it just happens ... And if you cross it enough times it disappears forever. And then you're nothing but another lawyer joke. Just another shark in the dirty water."[18]

With respect to another psychological tendency, known as *moral equilibrium*, people tend to keep a running scorecard on their ethical self-image. When they perceive they have a deficit they try to make up for it ("moral compensation") and if they believe they have a surplus might give themselves permission to deviate ("moral license").[19] A television interview on the news program *60 Minutes* with former ImClone CEO Sam Waksal seems to demonstrate his view that he had done so much good with his drug company, there might have been a degree of moral license for him to benefit through engaging in illegal insider trading.[20] Waksal stated: "The day I was arrested was a horrible day in my life ... It is very difficult for someone who thinks about himself as someone who does good things for society to be led away, in handcuffs, and thought about as a common criminal."[21]

Moral equilibrium also tends to come out during the sentencing proceedings of white collar criminals. The lawyer for Raj Rajaratnam argued, during his sentencing for insider trading, that his charitable work should entitle him to a more lenient sentence. His lawyer stated to the court: "Raj Rajaratnam has attempted to make the world a better place. If there is a ledger in one's life, he should have some credit to draw upon in that ledger now that things have gone bad."[22] It may be that Mr Rajaratnam also felt his good works should have permitted him some leeway to engage in his insider trading activities. Lance Armstrong also appears to believe that the positive impact he had on the sport of cycling and the tremendous good his Livestrong cancer foundation was doing for society by raising $500 million for cancer research may have made it easier for him to live with himself while taking performance-enhancing drugs.[23]

There may also be other cognitive biases or tendencies that affect how information is processed and help explain the often unethical decisions that managers and executives make. Several of these biases relate to how we take into account the perceived possible *consequences* or *outcomes* of our actions. One such bias is *loss aversion*, which means that people dislike losses more than enjoying similar sized gains. This can lead to taking riskier and even less ethical decisions to avoid a loss rather than making a decision to secure an equivalent gain.[24] Martha Stewart appears to have demonstrated loss aversion in her actions. Although worth hundreds of millions of dollars at the time, Martha Stewart sold off her ImClone stock the day before news was released that a new ImClone drug had not received governmental approval. Although Stewart was able to avoid losing approximately $200,000 on the value of her stock portfolio, in the end, she was convicted and went to jail for obstructing justice and lying to investigators about the timing of her share sale.[25]

Other biases related to our perception of consequences exist as well. For example, we tend to consider only the *tangible versus the abstract*, which means that certain factors, if removed in time and space, like an unsafe product that might harm customers whom you will never encounter in the future, can be disregarded.[26] It may be much easier for scammers to engage in online fraudulent schemes promising millions of dollars to their victims due to an inheritance or lottery winnings when the scammers have no actual physical contact with their victims. *Sunk costs* and the *escalation of commitment* mean that good money can often be thrown after bad money, because most people take into account sunk costs when making decisions. This could relate to the inability to scrap a product with safety defects or discharge an unethical client, due to the sunk costs that have occurred. There are also *time delay traps*, which means that we often have the inability to appreciate long-term consequences. For example, dumping environmental waste may not be of great concern, since the health implications are so long term in nature. We can also engage in *over-optimism*, which means believing in an irrational manner that there will be positive outcomes. In this case, executives might engage in deceptive financial disclosure irrationally believing that the firm's prospects would eventually be positive. Other biases that permit or facilitate ignoring possible outcomes or consequences include ignoring low-probability events, limiting the search for stakeholders, and ignoring the possibility that the public will "find out."[27]

Other biases or tendencies simply lead to irrational decision making. Sometimes we engage in the *false consensus effect*, or the tendency to believe that others think the same way we do. This can take place when employees believe until the very end that their bosses are not crooks. We can also engage in *overconfidence*, where we tend to believe that we are more ethical than others. This allows us to accept our own decisions without serious reflection. We might engage in insider trading or bribery based on a view that we still remain at least as ethical as others. In other cases, we simply allow ourselves to be affected by a *self-serving bias*. When this happens, we might gather, process, and even remember information in unfair and biased ways when it serves our self-interest to do so. Bernie Madoff clearly operated his massive Ponzi scheme defrauding investors of billions and processed information under a self-serving bias.[28]

In other cases we gather and process information in a biased manner that simply supports the position we have already taken, known as *confirmation bias*.[29] As discussed earlier, the managers of Morton Thiokol, the company that manufactured the NASA Space Shuttle Challenger's rocket boosters, decided to ignore the safety concerns raised by engineer Roger Boisjoly. Instead, the managers continued to recommend launching the shuttle leading to the tragic deaths of seven crew members in 1986, a decision that appears to have taken place due to a confirmation bias.[30] The presence of *transparency* can also affect ethical decision making, in other words people tend to act more ethically when they believe they are being observed. For example, experiments with pictures of eyes on the wall or well-lit rooms increased levels of honesty.[31]

Together, these tendencies make it possible for good people to act in unethical ways that they could never have initially predicted.[32] These tendencies might also increase the chances that someone with a strong *moral character* might nonetheless act inappropriately. The importance of these other tendencies or processes on the moral reasoning process cannot be ignored or understated: "What is less often studied is the fact that many of these heuristics, biases, and related psychological tendencies can render even well-intentioned people susceptible to committing unethical and even illegal acts. With a few exceptions ... this body of thought has received insufficient attention in academic ethics literature."[33] The bulk of the research in this area has been referred to as "behavioral ethics," a relatively new academic field,[34] which has been defined as understanding how people actually behave when confronted with ethical dilemmas,[35] and helps to explain why so many people seem to be unaware of the ethical implications of the dilemmas they face. The root causes of the US 2008 financial crisis might even be explained by these irrational processes, including the notion of *paying for peril*, meaning rewarding short term but suffering long term, as well as the *normalization of questionable behavior*.[36] Both of these psychological processes allowed banks to lend to homeowners well beyond what would have normally been considered rational and reasonable, and for investment banks to then repackage this debt as new securitized financial instruments despite the risks to clients.

As an example of the potential impact of psychological tendencies, consider the following dilemma actually faced by an employee, Susan. Susan's boss asked her to write an application essay for his five-year-old daughter's entrance into grade one of a prestigious private elementary school. Susan strongly believed that in general, only university applicants themselves (or in this case the child applicant's parents) should write their own admission essays in terms of basic honesty, and that any cheating in this respect defeats the purpose of the educational system. Susan also realized, however, that her boss would determine whether she would be promoted. Her boss was terrible in written communication, with English being his second language. If you had been in Susan's shoes, would you have written the reference letter on behalf of your boss even though you believe it would normally be wrong to do so?

Several biases and psychological tendencies can kick in and affect your moral judgment. For example, you might assume many people are likely to do this (*conformity bias*). You do know the child a little bit so it's not really completely dishonest, while in any event the letter probably won't be the major factor related to the admission decision (*over-optimism*). You also believe it's difficult to identify anyone including other children that will actually get hurt by this (*the abstract and the intangible*). In the end, the desire to ensure your position at work (*self-serving bias*) due to the instructions of your boss (*obedience to authority*) may take precedence, and you might decide to write the letter (as did Susan) feeling that overall you can live with yourself for taking this action.

Finally, the process of *moral disengagement* provides another important psychological tendency that works in tandem with many of the biases and tendencies indicated above often leading to a lack of moral awareness.[37] Moral disengagement involves a process or tendency by which we convince ourselves in a particular context that ethical standards do not apply. Moral standards regulate behavior only when self-regulatory mechanisms or "moral self-sanctions" (i.e., our *moral conscience*) are activated. There are a series of psychological processes or tendencies that can be used to prevent this activation. They include the following:

(i)   restructuring inhumane conduct to become neutral or praiseworthy conduct by moral *justification, sanitizing language,* and *advantageous comparison*;
(ii) denial of being personally responsible by diffusing or displacing *responsibility*;
(iii) disregarding or minimizing the *negative impacts* of one's actions;
(iv) *blaming* and *dehumanizing* of the victims.[38]

Let's try to apply an example to understand moral disengagement. I am instructed to fire an employee by my manager. I am aware, however, that this employee is a single mother supporting her three children. I also strongly suspect that my manager wants the employee fired because of personal reasons, rather than performance-related reasons. Although I realize I am facing an ethical dilemma, I ultimately decide to obey my manager's instructions. To maintain my moral identity and not feel guilty over my actions, I engage in the process of *moral disengagement*. Instead of using the term "firing," I decide to refer to what I am doing to myself and others as "rightsizing" (*sanitizing language*). Since the employee is being provided with two weeks' notice and other firms will fire their employees with no notice given, I believe that the firing is morally acceptable when compared with how other firms tend to behave (*advantageous comparison*).

Of course, I am not personally responsible for firing the employee, since I was asked to do so by my manager (*denial of responsibility*). Since I am not completely aware of the employee's exact personal financial situation, I am able to disregard any negative effects of firing the employee (*minimize negative impacts*). And probably this employee wasn't sufficiently pulling her weight in any event and therefore really did deserve to be fired (*blame and dehumanize victim*). Based on the process of *moral disengagement*, I am able to disengage from the moral implications of firing the employee. I am able to frame the dilemma as merely an *economic* decision, and proceed to fire the employee believing this is in my own best interests as well as the firm's best interests (*self-serving bias*). The Hollywood movie *Up in the Air* clearly depicts how a professional corporate downsizer (played by George Clooney) can morally disengage from feeling any emotion or concern during the act of firing employees.

While we may want to think of moral reasoning as a dominant force in the moral judgment process, we now see that not only can other processes such as *emotion* interfere with moral reasoning, but that the moral reasoning process can be impeded by various *biases* or *psychological tendencies*. These key psychological or cognitive factors or tendencies can affect not only regular judgments and beliefs, but ethical decisions and actions as well, unfortunately leading good "apples" to act unethically. Table 3.1 summarizes the various biases and psychological tendencies that can impede ethical decision making.[39]

Moral Rationalizations

Moral rationalization, which has a clear overlap with the biases and psychological tendencies described above, has over time become recognized as a more important psychological process with respect to ethical decision making. Moral rationalization has been defined as *the cognitive process that is used by individuals to convince themselves that their behavior does not violate their moral standards*.[45] Rationalizations permit a person to maintain their *moral identity* intact as well as avoid experiencing the emotions of guilt, or anticipatory shame or embarrassment. It can be used to justify both small unethical acts as well as serious atrocities.[46] There's a well-known lawyer joke that helps demonstrate moral rationalization:

> A dying man gives each of his best friends – a lawyer, an accountant, and a clergyman – an envelope containing $25,000 in cash to be placed in his coffin after he dies, since he believes he may need money for the afterlife. A week later the man dies and the friends each place an envelope in the coffin. Several months later, the three friends get together. The clergyman confesses that he only put $10,000 in the envelope and sent the rest of the money to a charity for the homeless. The accountant confesses that his envelope had only $8,000 because he had worked on his friend's estate and believed he was owed the money for his services. The lawyer is outraged, and says "I am the only one who kept my promise to our dying friend. I want you both to know that the envelope I placed in the coffin contained my own personal check for the entire $25,000."[47]

Table 3.1 Biases and psychological tendencies that impede ethical decision making.

Bias/Tendency	Definition	Example
Obedience to authority	People rationalize they are not responsible for their misdeeds if done based on the orders of an authority figure.	Deceiving a consumer or fudging the budget based on a directive from a manager or supervisor.
Conformity bias (or "social proof")	People suspend their ethical judgment and defer to the perceived group norm (i.e., "group think").	Padding expense accounts due to everyone else also doing it.
Incrementalism	Unethical activity can often proceed as a slippery slope in small steps.	Nick Leeson at Barings Bank. When an initial trading mistake threatened his self-perception of being a success, Leeson then took greater and greater risks leading to the bank's collapse.[40]
Moral equilibrium	People tend to keep a running scorecard on their ethical self-image giving themselves permission to deviate.	Sam Waksal indicating that because his firm ImClone Systems did so much good for society, insider trading was not so problematic.[41]
Loss aversion	People dislike losses more than they enjoy similar sized gains.	Martha Stewart selling her ImClone shares to avoid a loss and then covering up the sale.[42]
Sunk costs and escalation of commitment	Most people take into account sunk costs in making decisions, such as throwing good money after bad.	Inability to scrap a product with safety defects or discharge an unethical client given sunk costs.
Time-delay traps	Inability to appreciate long-term negative consequences.	Dumping environmental waste with long-term health implications.
Over-optimism	Believing in an irrational manner that there will be positive outcomes.	Executives engaging in deceptive financial disclosure irrationally believing that the firm's prospects will eventually be positive.

False consensus effect	The tendency to believe that others think the same way we do.	Employees believing until the end that their bosses are not crooks.
Overconfidence	People tend to believe they are more ethical than others. They therefore accept their own decisions without serious ethical reflection.	Engaging in insider trading based on a view that one remains at least as ethical as others.
Self-serving bias	Gathering, processing, and even remembering information in unfair and biased ways that benefits oneself.	Bernie Madoff operating his massive Ponzi scheme, defrauding investors of billions, under a self-serving bias. [43]
Confirmation bias	Gathering, processing, and even remembering information in unfair and biased ways that support the position one has already taken.	Ignoring information related to ethical risks because the decision to launch the product has already been taken, such as the decision to launch the Space Shuttle Challenger.
The tangible versus the abstract	Individuals are impacted more by vivid, tangible, contemporaneous factors rather than factors that are removed in time and space. [44]	One might be more likely to make a decision that causes harm to customers (unsafe products), employees (when fired), or shareholders (fraud) as the harm is both intangible and abstract.
Moral disengagement	Shutting off conscience and self-sanctioning mechanisms by convincing ourselves in a particular context that ethical standards do not apply.	There is no reason to feel guilty or concerned when employees are let go even under questionable circumstances.

There is a definite element of truth in the joke. All three friends knew that keeping any part of the money was morally wrong. But each was able to convince themselves that it was okay to do so, either for the greater good (the clergyman), or because they deserved it (the accountant). The lawyer was able, however, to convince himself that he had actually kept his promise to his friend in its entirety and had therefore not done anything wrong. How can this rationalization process be explained?

One way of thinking about rationalization is based on the theory of *belief harmonization* which means revising and arranging our needs, beliefs, and personal preferences into a cohesive cognitive network that mitigates against *cognitive dissonance*.[48] Cognitive dissonance is *the mental stress we experience when we try to hold two contradictory beliefs or values at the same time*. Moral rationalization might be seen as a type of faulty or flawed moral reasoning, where moral standards are used to explain or justify a decision or action to reduce cognitive dissonance. Here is one way to explain the rationalization process:[49]

> ... a person may distort the feelings of obligation by denying the need to act, denying personal responsibility, or reappraising the situation so as to make alternative actions more appropriate. In other words, as subjects recognize the implications of [their moral judgment and intention] and the personal costs of moral action become clear, they may defensively reappraise and alter their interpretation of the situation [i.e., the awareness stage] so that they can feel honorable, but at less cost to themselves.

Other theories have been proposed to help explain the moral rationalization process. Moral rationalization may be based on the notion of *moral appropriation*, which is defined as *the desire for moral approval from others or oneself*.[50] The moral rationalization process has also been tied to what has been referred to as *fudge factor* theory, which helps explain how many are prepared to cheat a little bit through "flexible" moral reasoning while still maintaining their sense of moral identity.[51] Similarly, *moral balance* theory permits us to engage in moral deviations as long as our moral identity remains "satisfactory."[52]

Moral rationalization can take place through the process of moral disengagement discussed above[53] or any other series of rationalization or "neutralization" techniques.[54] Moral rationalization, like moral reasoning, is a cognitive process, which as a form of "self-deceptive" rationality overlaps to a large extent with the moral reasoning process. For example, Sam Waksal, former CEO of ImClone, who went to jail for insider trading, states: "Did I know that I had committed an illegal act? Yeah, I knew. I tried to rationalize beyond rationality that I hadn't ... It was sort of playing with linguistics. But I knew."[55] Due to its importance in the ethical decision-making process, the following will attempt to describe the different types or techniques of moral rationalization that have been suggested. Each category will be briefly described with a few examples provided.[56]

Denial of responsibility

This technique of neutralization involves a claim by the offender that he or she was not responsible for the consequences of their actions.[57] This can be due to the actions or its consequences being unintentional, that the offender was provoked or otherwise "unable to think clearly while performing it," that there was no choice, that the act was done out of necessity, or was an accident.[58] In an organizational context, this typically takes place by blaming our firm, superiors, or subordinates for our actions. In addition to *obedience to authority* described above, where we can shift blame for our actions on our supervisors, this rationalization can also relate to blaming or assigning responsibility for unethical conduct on our clients or customers.

For example, consider the following interview conducted with former Swiss-based UBS banker Bradley Birkenfeld. The banker "conveniently" neglected to tell US officials about his assistance in helping a US client hide $200 million in revenues by introducing him to a consultant who specialized in creating shell companies that concealed the ownership of the UBS accounts. Birkenfeld's response suggests that he was not responsible for any tax evasion: "I don't sign people's tax returns, so what they do with their taxes is not my business. I'm a banker …" "So you would steer them to somebody who would help them hide their money? You would recommend them to these service providers?" [the interviewer] asked. "That's correct," Birkenfeld said. "You must have known deep down that it was illegal," [the interviewer] remarked … "That's correct," Birkenfeld said.[59] Birkenfeld appears to believe that only his client was responsible for his tax evasion, rather than himself.

Denial of the injury

This form of rationalization takes place when the offender tries to minimize or *deny that any harm* has taken place.[60] In other words, the intentions were good and no one was really harmed in the end.[61] This relates to the "faceless" character of the victims of crime or unethical actions, often due to the diffusion of the harm over a large number of persons. In the corporate world, anti-trust actions, or illegally copying software might take place since no one can identify the competitors or shareholders (e.g., of Microsoft) who would be affected. Executives of firms who attempt to evade taxes through various techniques can more easily justify the actions since it is difficult to identify the regular "taxpayer" or citizen who is harmed as a result. This rationalization relates to the *tangible versus the abstract* psychological tendency described previously.

Denial of the victim

For this rationalization, the offender acknowledges the harm or injury caused, but claims that the victim is unworthy of concern because, in some way, the victim *deserved* it.[62] The offender might even try to claim that the unethical activity can be characterized as a form of righteous justice or as a means to ensure that the crimes or unethical activity of others be punished. For example, rather than "stealing" from the company, an employee takes firm property for personal use as a means to punish the employer for treating other employees improperly or unfairly.[63] In other cases, if the firm is involved in illegal or unethical activity, an employee may view their own theft as merely seizing "ill-gotten gains." This rationalization has been referred to as convincing ourselves that targets deserve their fate due to "past unfairness or corruption on their part."[64]

The other version of denying the victim is to "depersonalize" the victim into a "faceless statistic" or even "subhuman status." This process relates to the *tangible versus the abstract* and *moral disengagement* psychological tendencies described above. Depersonalization may have taken place during the Ford Pinto case, when the decision not to recall the defective vehicles shifted from being about human life to financial considerations, or for Wall Street traders who view clients as "suckers asking to be conned."[65] Following his 150 year imprisonment for his massive multi-billion dollar Ponzi scheme fraud, Bernie Madoff indicated that he believed his victims deserved their losses. Madoff stated: "People just kept throwing money at me ... Some guy wanted to invest, and if I said no, the guy said, 'What, I'm not good enough?'" In terms of his victims deserving what happened, Madoff stated: "F— my victims ... I carried them for 20 years, and now I'm doing 150 years."[66] This rationalization relates to fairness: "The actors counter any blame for their actions by arguing that the violated party deserved whatever happened."[67]

Condemnation of the condemners

For this rationalization, the offender believes that they really did nothing seriously wrong and are being singled out unfairly by those who are charging them with acting improperly, especially when no one else is being punished for doing the same offence.[68] A review of former Imclone CEO Sam Waksal's statements during his interview on the television show *60 Minutes* suggests that Waksal, who went to jail for insider trading, felt he was unfairly targeted by the US government due to the simplicity of his case, along with his profile and association with popular personality Martha Stewart. Waksal stated: "… I know that I would have, at another point in time, gone to court … And I doubt that the US attorney, absent other situations, would have ever taken that case to court. This was done because the US attorney was trying to make an example out of me."[69] A similar example of this rationalization appears to be the case for cyclist Lance Armstrong, who felt that he was singled out and ultimately stripped of his record seven Tour de France titles simply because he fought back so aggressively against those who accused him of doping.[70]

Appeal to higher authorities

Rather than being based on pure self-interest, here the offender claims that their actions were motivated by a higher moral obligation such as loyalty to others including family, managers, the firm and its owners, co-workers, customers, or society in general.[71] In other words, "The actors argue that their violation of norms is due to their attempt to realize a higher-order value."[72] The actions of former Enron CEO Jeffrey Skilling seemed to be justified for himself on the basis that his actions were always supposedly with the best interests of Enron in mind. Skilling stated: "We are the good guys. We are on the side of angels."[73] The children's movie *Monster's Inc.* has a similar scene where the CEO declares that he would be willing to "kidnap children" in order to save the company and avoid an energy crisis for the community. Like *Monster's Inc.*, Enron was also an energy company, helping to provide electricity to its customers. The actions of the senior executives of Chiquita Brands International may have demonstrated this rationalization when they were willing to fund a terrorist organization in Columbia contrary to US law in order to keep their employees safe there.[74]

Everyone else is doing it

This rationalization is based on the notion that since everyone else or the majority of everyone else is engaged in similar unethical activity, then I should be able to do so as well. Whenever there is a widespread violation of a law, rule, or policy, especially when no one is being punished despite awareness of the violations taking place, suggests that we should also be able to engage in the improper activity. If everyone is padding their expense accounts, then why shouldn't I be entitled to do so as well? It also becomes easier to justify unethical activity when you can find someone else who appears even worse.[75] Former champion cyclist Lance Armstrong indicated that if he had to do the Tour de France cycling race over again, he would still dope since "… everyone else in cycling was doping too." Armstrong stated: "I knew what my competitors were doing. We [his US Postal Service team] were doing less."[76] Armstrong, who himself was a cancer survivor, was clearly able to rationalize his actions as not taking advantage of anyone else. Armstrong indicated during his interview with talk show host Oprah Winfrey that he had never felt like he was cheating due to the pervasiveness of banned drugs in professional cycling: "I ... looked up the definition of cheat and the definition of cheat is to gain an advantage on a rival or foe that they don't have. I didn't view it that way. I viewed it as a level playing field."[77] This rationalization technique is related to *conformity bias* discussed above whereby other people's actions affect how we end up behaving.

Claim to entitlement

For this rationalization technique, the offender convinces himself or herself that for some reason they are entitled to engage in the unethical action. This rationalization might be referred to as the "metaphor of the ledger," in that we rationalize that we are entitled to indulge in deviant behaviors because of our accrued credits (time and effort) in our jobs.[78] These actual or anticipated "good work" credits are then used to offset unethical acts. For example, you might believe it is acceptable to use the internet for personal reasons at work since you work overtime without any additional pay. Individuals might also rely on the past glory of their firm to justify current unethical behavior, such as what appears to have taken place at Arthur Andersen when clients were billed excessively.[79] This rationalization is similar to the *moral equilibrium bias* described above whereby the accumulations of "credits" for ethical actions might lead to rationalizing unethical behavior.

Prohibition should not apply

In some cases, we believe that we can act in whatever manner we wish because we do not see the prohibition itself as justified or legitimate.[80] We may perceive the law, a rule, or the provisions of a code of ethics as being vague, complex, complicated, inconsistent, rarely enforced, or merely politically motivated and therefore we can rationalize that there is nothing wrong or unethical when we contravene it. In others cases, we might rationalize that a certain prohibition only applies to *other* people and not to ourselves, especially when we are well connected, wealthy, and powerful.[81] Former ImClone CEO Sam Waksal appears to have believed that he might have deserved special treatment permitting him to engage in insider trading. Waksal states: "And who cared? ... what difference does it make that I do a couple of things that aren't exactly kosher? ... I think, in that way, there may have been an arrogance where I didn't have to deal with details - that these details were *meant for other people*, not for me."[82] Andrew Fastow, the former CFO of Enron, believed that the firm's conflict of interest provisions in its code of ethics should not apply towards his own self-enriching activities.[83] Martha Stewart, despite being trained as a stock broker as well as being a board member of the New York Stock Exchange, may also have applied this rationalization to justify her actions involving obstruction of justice of an investigation into possible insider trading.[84] Table 3.2 summarizes the different possible rationalizations along with some example statements.

In terms of the timing of rationalization in the ethical decision-making process, rationalizations can be invoked prospectively before the act to forestall guilt and resistance or retrospectively after the act to ease misgivings about our behavior. Once invoked, the rationalizations not only facilitate future wrong-doing but dull awareness that the act is in fact wrong.[92] If our moral judgment based on moral reasoning is contrary to our self-perceived moral identity, typically due to a preference or desire to act towards fulfilling our self-interest, then we may engage in a biased or distorted process of moral rationalization. By doing so, we are able to avoid experiencing the emotions of guilt, shame, or embarrassment. Some refer to this state as being one of *moral hypocrisy* or the appearance of being moral to themselves or others while avoiding the cost of actually being moral.[93] While moral rationalization is a cognitive (albeit possibly subconscious) process, it may also affect, be affected by, or work in conjunction with (i.e., overlap) the moral reasoning process,[94] intuition,[95] or emotion.[96] With few exceptions, moral rationalization is often unfortunately ignored or simply assumed to exist by most ethical decision-making models.[97]

Self-Interest

Throughout the entire ethical decision-making process, *self-interest*, which is often ignored in ethical decision-making research[98] despite its acknowledged importance in influencing behavior,[99] should be considered to play an important role as an impediment to ethical behavior.[100] As part of the Integrated-EDM model, the importance attached to self-interest would directly relate to our *moral character* in terms of our level of moral maturity with respect to moral development (e.g., Kohlberg's pre-conventional level, stages one and two). Self-interest would also relate indirectly as part of some individual's moral personality (e.g., "Machiavellianism" meaning a person who acts in an opportunistic, deceptive, and manipulative manner in order to benefit themselves). It would also relate to the personal context of the *perceived need for personal gain* variable or a person's *ethical vulnerability* (e.g., current financial situation and pressures), as well as the organization's *ethical culture* in terms of perceived opportunity for gain, rewards, and sanctions for engaging in misconduct. Self-interest overlaps with the *self-serving bias* described previously,

Table 3.2 Summary of rationalizations (adapted from Anand *et al.*, 2005; Heath 2008).

Rationalization	Explanation	Example Statements
Denial of responsibility	You can live with yourself because you are not responsible.	"Don't blame me." "What could I do? My arm was being twisted." "It is none of my business."[85]
Denial of the injury	You believe the act is acceptable because there is no real injury.	"No one was really harmed." "It could have been worse."[86]
Denial of the victim	You believe the act is acceptable because there is no real victim.	"They deserved it." "They chose to participate."[87]
Condemnation of the condemners	You believe you should not be blamed because you are being unfairly attacked.	"You have no right to criticize me."[88]
Appeal to higher authorities	You believe the act is acceptable because your motivation was selfless.	"It was in the company's best interests." "I did it for my family."[89] "I answered to a more important cause." [90]
Everyone else is doing it	You believe the act is acceptable because others are doing the same thing.	"If others are doing it, why can't I?" "Others are worse than I am."[91]
Claim to entitlement	You believe because of your accrued good credits you are able to offset any unethical acts.	"I deserve this." "We earned the right."
Prohibition should not apply	You believe the act is acceptable because the prohibition is no longer relevant or should not apply to you.	"The law is ridiculous or out of date and should not be enforced." "This rule (or law) is meant for other people, not for me."

as well as often playing a direct role influencing the *moral rationalization* process of justifying unethical decision making. For example, when employees and managers lie on their resumes about their educational backgrounds or work experience, or on other occasions obtain fake academic diplomas, it seems clear that getting the job and serving their own self-interest outweighs any ethical considerations of basic honesty, truthfulness, and transparency.[101]

The impact of self-interest has been demonstrated in interview-based studies that have looked for the specific factors that are most likely to cause people to compromise an organization's ethical standards, such as the company's code of ethics. The most common pressures in the workplace that are perceived to influence unethical behavior include: (i) the pressure to meet unrealistic business objectives/deadlines (70%); (2) the desire to further our careers (39%); and (3) the desire to protect our livelihoods (34%).[102] According to another study of employees, the following are the greatest sources of pressure to compromise standards (in rank order): (i) keeping your job; (ii) meeting personal financial obligations; (iii) financial stability and success of your company; and (iv) advancing your career.[103] In other words, self-interest in the form of "personal survival" such as keeping our jobs and being able to pay our bills is considered the top source of pressure to compromise standards, and thus represents a major impediment to ethical behavior. Self-interest would also play a role during ethical decision making including the moral judgment and reasoning process, when acting in our self-interest would potentially conflict with other moral standards. The prioritization of self-interest over morality can also affect whether we move from judgment to intention to act,[104] or from intention to actual behavior based on the strength of our *moral character*.[105] Unfortunately, one of the main reasons for not doing what we intend to do, or know is the right thing to do, is because our "want" self (self-interest) dominates our actual behavior with a disregard for other ethical considerations, leaving our "should" self behind (or disengaged) in the process.[106]

Chapter Summary

In this chapter, we reviewed the major impediments to ethical behavior. The first relates directly to moral awareness, in that we sometimes *improperly frame* the issues we face in terms of their economic or legal considerations, rather than their ethical implications. When we do so, we often remain unaware that we are facing an ethical dilemma, and if we end up acting ethically, it is not because we intended to do so for moral reasons. The second impediment includes the *cognitive biases* and *psychological tendencies* that we each possess. Each of these biases and tendencies can impact our rational thought processes leading to unethical decisions. These might include *obedience to authority* such as commands from our manager to do something we know is unethical, *conformity bias* to what is considered acceptable behavior taking place around us, or *incrementalism* where we start with small violations which then become much bigger violations. *Moral rationalizations* can distort the moral reasoning process so that we can still feel okay about our moral identities despite acting unethically. Finally, *self-interest* can sometimes lead us to act in a way that harms others, and is often the source of improper framing, biases, or moral rationalizations.

Going back to the very beginning of the chapter, we can now better understand how *improper framing, biases and tendencies, rationalizations,* and *self-interest* can all work together leading us to justify spending time surfing on the internet at work, not saying anything about our intoxicated boss, using the express lane despite having more than 10 items, and not doing anything when we damage another car when the other car owner is not there. For example, our decision how to act for each of these situations may be dependent on our self-interest alone in terms of not suffering any personal repercussions by acting a certain way that is of self-benefit, combined with the fact that we do not perceive that anyone else really gets hurt by our actions.

Now that we have reviewed the ethical decision-making process in terms of how we decide what is right or wrong, we move on in Chapter 4 to considerations of how we *should* or *ought* to behave, in other words, the *normative framework* of ethical decision making.

Notes

1. See: Hosmer (2008); Tenbrunsel and Smith-Crowe (2008); Dedeke (2013).
2. See: Crane and Matten (2010, p. 172) for a discussion on "work roles" affecting ethical decision making. This is sometimes referred to as "role-morality."
3. The importance of a three-prong approach to ethical decision making has been referred to as follows: "In ethical decision making ... we tend to ... focus on ethical expectations and, especially, those forces that primarily come into tension with ethics – economics (the quest for profits) and law. Thus, in most decision-making situations, ethics, economics, and law become the central expectations that must be considered and balanced against each other in the quest to make wise decisions" (Karakowsky *et al.*, 2005, p. 174). Others agree that a three-prong approach including consideration of the economic outcome, legal requirements, and ethical duties, is appropriate. See: Hosmer (2008, p. 64).
4. The moral standards will be discussed further in Chapter 4.
5. This Venn diagram is also used to represent the three overlapping domains (economic, legal, and ethical) of corporate social responsibility. See: Schwartz and Carroll (2003).
6. See: Selah Maya Zighelboim, "Former Enron CFO Andrew Fastow Reflects on Business Ethics," *McCombs Today*, February 18, 2015, http://www.today.

mccombs.utexas.edu/2015/02/former-enron-cfo-andrew-fastow-ethics (accessed 29 August 2016).

7. See: Diana B. Henriques and Jack Healy, "Madoff Goes to Jail After Guilty Pleas," *The New York Times*, March 12, 2009, http://www.nytimes.com/2009/03/13/ business/13madoff.html?_r=0 (accessed 29 August 2016).

8. See: IMDb website, "Margin Call: Quotes," http://www.imdb.com/title/ tt1615147/quotes (accessed 8 May 2016).

9. See: Rebecca Leung, "The Mensch of Malden Mills," *60 Minutes*, July 3, 2003, http://www.cbsnews.com/news/the-mensch-of-malden-mills/ (accessed 29 August 2016).

10. Chugh *et al.* (2005); Palazzo *et al.* (2012, p. 324).

11. Chugh *et al.* (2005); Palazzo *et al.* (2012, p. 324).

12. Prentice (2014).

13. The following discussion is based primarily on Prentice (2004; 2014); Gentile (2010); and Harris *et al.* (2015). In a similar vein, Ariely (2012) has conducted a series of experiments in an attempt to understand why people are dishonest. The following factors or forces were found to contribute to dishonesty: ability to rationalize, conflicts of interest, creativity, one immoral act, being depleted, others benefitting from our dishonesty, watching others behave dishonestly, and culture that gives examples of dishonesty. The following forces were found to decrease dishonesty: pledge, signatures, moral reminders, and supervision. Two forces were surprisingly found to have no impact on dishonesty: amount of money to be gained, and the probability of being caught. See: Ariely (2012, p. 245).

14. See: Prentice (2014). Note, the innocent participants (the "learners") were actors and did not actually receive any electrical shocks.

15. See: Prentice (2014).

16. Asch (1955). When there was no pressure to conform, the error rate was less than 1%.

17. Leeson (1996).

18. See: IMDb website, "The Rainmaker: Quotes," http://www.imdb.com/title/ tt0119978/quotes (accessed 8 May, 2016).

19. This is similar to the "metaphor of the ledger" moral rationalization proposed by Anand *et al.* (2005).

20. See: Rebecca Leung, "Sam Waksal, I Was Arrogant," CBS *60 Minutes*, October 2, 2003, http://www.cbsnews.com/news/sam-waksal-i-was-arrogant-02-10-2003/ (accessed 29 August 2016).

21. See: Rebecca Leung, "Sam Waksal: I Was Arrogant."

22. See: Susan Pulliam and Chad Bray, "Trader Draws Record Sentence," *The Wall Street Journal*, October 14, 2011, http://www.wsj.com/articles/ SB10001424052970203914304576627191081876286 (accessed 29 August 2016).

23. Armstrong indicated that he did not regret the impact his career had had on the sport or on his cancer foundation, Livestrong: "I know what happened to the sport, I saw its growth," he said. "I know what happened to Trek Bicycles [his bike supplier] – $100-million in sales to $1-billion in sales. And I know what happened to my foundation, from raising no money to raising $500-million,

serving three million people. Do we want to take it away? I don't think anybody says 'yes.'" See: Tom Cary, "Lance Armstrong Says He Would Still Dope If He Could Start All Over Again," *The Telegraph*, January 26, 2015, http://www. telegraph.co.uk/sport/othersports/cycling/lancearmstrong/11370341/Lance-Armstrong-says-he-would-still-dope-if-he-could-start-all-over-again.html (accessed 29 August 2016).

24. Prentice (2014, p. 346).

25. See: Constance L. Hays, "Prosecuting Martha Stewart: The Overview," *The New York Times*, June 5, 2003, http://www.nytimes.com/2003/06/05/business/prosec uting-martha-stewart-overview-martha-stewart-indicted-us-obstruction.html (accessed 29 August 2016).

26. Prentice (2014, pp. 348–349).

27. Messick and Bazerman (1996, p. 10). See also: Prentice (2014) for a review of the various barriers to rational decision making.

28. See: Steve Fishman, "Bernie Madoff, Free at Last," *New York Times Magazine*, June 6, 2010, http://nymag.com/news/crimelaw/66468/ (accessed 29 August 2016).

29. This also relates to the concept of "motivated reasoning" (using a variety of cognitive mechanisms to arrive at a conclusion that was initially desired) or "moral seduction" (being unaware of the gradual accumulation of pressures to modify our conclusions). See: Prentice (2014).

30. See: Douglas Martin, "Roger Boisjoly, 73, Dies; Warned of Shuttle Danger," *The New York Times*, February 3, 2012, http://www.nytimes.com/2012/02/04/us/ roger-boisjoly-73-dies-warned-of-shuttle-danger.html (accessed 29 August 2016).

31. Prentice (2014). See also: Treviño *et al.* (2006, pp. 958–959) for a discussion of cognitive biases.

32. Prentice (2014, p. 333) explains how good people do bad things while at the same time thinking of themselves as good ethical people: "Their accomplice is their brain, which manipulates frames of reference, compartmentalizes thoughts and actions, conjures up rationalizations, manufactures memories, and otherwise shades perceived reality in self-serving ways."

33. See: Prentice (2004, p. 56). Some of the exceptions include: Etzioni (1988); Messick and Bazerman (1996); Tenbrunsel and Messick (2004).

34. Prentice (2014, p. 326), provides a useful summary of the key references on behavioral ethics.

35. Bazerman and Tenbrunsel (2011, p. 4). See also: Bazerman and Gino (2012, p. 90) for several other proposed definitions of behavioral ethics.

36. See: Donaldson (2012).

37. It's not clear at what stage of ethical decision making moral disengagement takes place. Lehnert *et al.* (2015, p. 213) state: "More research is needed to better understand whether moral disengagement occurs at the moral awareness stage, the moral judgment stage, or even perhaps as part of post hoc rationalization of unethical behavior."

38. Bandura (1999, p. 193).
39. Table 3.1 is based on the biases and tendencies suggested by Prentice (2004; 2014) and Gentile (2010).
40. Leeson (1996).
41. See: Rebecca Leung, "Sam Waksal: I Was Arrogant."
42. See: Constance L. Hays, "Prosecuting Martha Stewart: The Overview."
43. See: Steve Fishman, "Bernie Madoff, Free at Last."
44. Prentice (2014, pp. 348–349).
45. Tsang (2002, p. 26).
46. Tsang (2002, p. 25).
47. Adapted from Jokes website, "The Lawyer Keeps His Promise," http://jokes.cc. com/funny-lawyer/coxno8/the-lawyer-keeps-his-promise (accessed 29 August 2016).
48. Jackson *et al.* (2013, p. 238).
49. Rest (1986, p. 18).
50. Jones and Ryan (1997, p. 664).
51. Ariely (2012, p. 53).
52. Nisan (1991).
53. Bandura (1999).
54. Sykes and Matza (1957); Anand *et al.* (2005); Heath (2008).
55. See: Rebecca Leung, "Sam Waksal: I Was Arrogant."
56. Much of what follows is based on Anand *et al.* (2005) and Heath (2008).
57. See: Heath (2008).
58. Heath (2008, p. 603).
59. See: CBS News, "Banking: A Crack in the Swiss Vault," *CBS 60 Minutes*, December 30, 2009, http://www.cbsnews.com/news/banking-a-crack-in-the-swiss-vault/ (accessed 29 August 2016).
60. Heath (2008, p. 603).
61. Anand *et al.* (2005, p. 11).
62. Heath (2008, p. 603).
63. Heath (2008, p. 607).
64. Anand *et al.* (2005, p. 12).
65. Anand *et al.* (2005, p. 13).
66. See: Steve Fishman, "Bernie Madoff, Free at Last."
67. Anand *et al.* (2005, p. 11).
68. Heath (2008).
69. See: Rebecca Leung, "Sam Waksal: I Was Arrogant."
70. See: ESPN, "Lance Armstrong: Singled Out," December 12, 2013, http://espn. go.com/sports/endurance/story/_/id/10124453/lance-armstrong-singled-nice (accessed 29 August 2016).
71. Heath (2008).
72. Anand *et al.* (2005, p. 11).
73. See: Michael Chandler, "Blackout Program," *PBS Frontline*, June 5, 2001, http:// www.pbs.org/wgbh/pages/frontline/shows/blackout/etc/script.html (accessed 29 August 2016).

74. See: Laurie P. Cohen, "Chiquita Under the Gun," *Wall Street Journal*, August 2, 2007, http://online.wsj.com/news/articles/SB118601669056785578 (accessed 29 August 2016).

75. Anand *et al.* (2005, p. 13) refer to this rationalization as *social weighting* by engaging in "selective social comparison" with others who appear even worse in their actions.

76. See: ESPN, "Lance Armstrong: Singled Out."

77. See: Telegraph Sport, "Lance Armstrong's Interview with Oprah Winfrey: The Transcript," *The Telegraph*, January 18, 2013, http://www.telegraph.co.uk/sport/othersports/cycling/lancearmstrong/9810801/Lance-Armstrongs-interview-with-Oprah-Winfrey-the-transcript.html (accessed 29 August 2016).

78. Anand *et al.* (2005, p. 11).

79. Toffler and Reingold (2003).

80. Anand *et al.* (2005, p. 13).

81. Heath (2008, p. 609) refers to this category of rationalization as part of his discussion of the "entitlement" rationalization.

82. See: Rebecca Leung, "Sam Waksal: I Was Arrogant."

83. Fastow did, however, receive approval from Enron's board of directors for his partnerships which contravened Enron's code of ethics. See: Reed Abelson, "Enron's Collapse: The Directors," *The New York Times*, January 19, 2002, http://www.nytimes.com/2002/01/19/business/enron-s-collapse-directors-one-enron-inquiry-suggests-board-played-important.html (accessed 29 August 2016).

84. See: Landon, Thomas, Jr, "Martha Stewart Settles Civil Insider-Trading Case," *The New York Times*, August 7, 2006, http://www.nytimes.com/2006/08/07/business/07cnd-martha.html?_r=0 (accessed 29 August 2016).

85. Anand *et al.* (2005, p. 11).

86. Anand *et al.* (2005, p. 11).

87. Anand *et al.* (2005, p. 11).

88. Anand *et al.* (2005, p. 11).

89. Heath (2008, p. 608).

90. Anand *et al.* (2005, p. 11).

91. Anand *et al.* (2005, p. 11).

92. Anand *et al.* (2005, p. 11).

93. Batson *et al.* (1999, p. 525).

94. Tsang (2002).

95. Haidt (2001).

96. Bandura (1999).

97. Three notable exceptions include Reynolds (2006), who makes rationalization explicit in his model as a retrospective (e.g., post hoc analysis) process operating as part of the higher order conscious reasoning system, while the decision-making model proposed by Tsang (2002) positions moral rationalization (along with situational factors) as being central to the ethical decision-making process. Dedeke (2015) also indicates that rationalization of one's reflexive (intuitive or emotion-based) judgment can be part of the "moral reflection" stage of ethical decision making where moral reasoning also takes place.

98. See: Watson *et al.* (2009); Woiceshyn (2011, p. 315).
99. See: Miller (1999, p. 1053); Kish-Gephart *et al.* (2014, p. 267).
100. Hunt and Vitell (1986, p. 10) indirectly refer to self-interest. For example, a person can modify their judgment leading to a different alternative due to certain "preferred consequences" to themselves as a result of choosing the "less ethical" alternative. Treviño (1986) indirectly refers to self-interest by including the "personal costs" of moral behavior (as a component of the situational moderator of "immediate job context").
101. See: Jon Mitchell, "10 Executives Who Lied On Their Resumes – And 2 Who Got Away With It," *Readwrite*, May 3, 2012, http://readwrite.com/2012/05/03/10-executives-who-lied-on-their-resumes-and-2-who-got-away-with-it (accessed 29 August 2016). In Pakistan, a massive fake diploma scandal has apparently taken place. See: Saba Imtiaz and Declan Walsh, "Axact Chief Executive Arrested in Pakistan Over Fake Diplomas Scandal," *The New York Times*, May 27, 2015, http://www.nytimes.com/2015/05/28/world/asia/axact-chief-executive-arrested-in-pakistan-over-fake-diplomas-scandal.html (accessed 29 August 2016).
102. See: American Management Association, *The Ethical Enterprise: A Global Study of Business Ethics*, 2006, http://www.amanet.org/images/HREthicsSurvey06.pdf (accessed 8 May 2016). The rest of the factors influencing unethical behavior include: working in an environment with cynicism or diminished morale (31%); improper training/ignorance that the act was unethical (28%); lack of consequences if caught (24%); need to follow boss's orders (23%); peer pressure/desire to be a team player (15%); desire to steal from or harm the organization (9%); wanting to help the organization survive (9%); desire to save jobs (8%); and a sense of loyalty (7%). A review of the reasons provided above suggests three main categories of justification: acting according to perceived self-interest; acting in the firm's self-interest; and/or situational factors related to the organization's culture or climate.
103. Ethics Resource Center (2012).
104. Rest (1986).
105. Whether we shift from intention to behavior would be based on our "integrity capacity" according to Petrick and Quinn (2000).
106. See: Bazerman and Tenbrunsel (2011, p. 66).

References

Anand, V., Ashforth, B.E., and Joshi, M. 2005. Business as usual: the acceptance and perpetuation of corruption in organizations. *Academy of Management Executive*, 19: 9–23.

Ariely, D. 2012. *The (Honest) Truth About Dishonesty*. New York: HarperCollins.

Asch, S. 1955. Opinions and social pressure. *Scientific American*, 193: 31–35.

Bandura, A. 1999. Moral disengagement in the perpetration of inhumanities. *Personality and Social Psychology Review*, 3: 193–209.

Batson, C.D, Thompson, E.R., Seuferling, G., Whitney, H., and Strongman, J.A. 1999. Moral hypocrisy: appearing moral to oneself without being so. *Journal of Personality and Social Psychology*, 3: 525–537.

Bazerman, M.H. and Gino, F. 2012. Behavioral ethics: toward a deeper understanding of moral judgment and dishonesty. *Annual Review of Law and Social Science*, 8: 85–104.

Bazerman, M.H. and Tenbrunsel, A.E. 2011. *Blind Spots: Why We Fail to Do What's Right and What to Do About It*. Princeton, New Jersey: Princeton University Press.

Chugh, D., Banaji, M.R., and Bazerman, M.H. 2005. Bounded ethicality as a psychological barrier to recognizing conflicts of interest. In *Conflicts of Interest: Challenges and Solutions in Business, Law, Medicine, and Public Policy*, (D.A. Moore, D.M. Cain, G. Loewenstein, and M. Bazerman, eds). New York: Cambridge University Press, pp. 74–95.

Crane, A. and Matten, D. 2010. *Business Ethics* (3rd edn). New York: Oxford University Press.

Dedeke, A. 2015. A cognitive-intuitionist model of moral judgment. *Journal of Business Ethics*, 126: 437–457.

Donaldson, T. 2012. Three ethical roots of the economic crisis. *Journal of Business Ethics*, 106: 5–8.

Ethics Resource Center 2012. *2011 National Business Ethics Survey*. Arlington, VA.

Etzioni, A. 1988. *The Moral Dimension: Toward a New Economics*. New York: The Free Press.

Gentile, M.C. 2010. *Giving Voice to Values: How to Speak Your Mind When You Know What's Right*. New Haven, CT: Yale University Press.

Haidt, J. 2001. The emotional dog and its rational tail: a social intuitionist approach to moral judgment. *Psychological Review*, 4: 814–834.

Harris, J.D., Slover, S.L., Hernandez, M., and Guarana, C. 2015. Ethics Beneath the Surface. Technical Note (UV7092), Darden Business Publishing.

Heath, J. 2008. Business ethics and moral motivation: a criminological perspective. *Journal of Business Ethics*, 83: 595–614.

Hosmer, L.T. 2008. *The Ethics of Management* (6th edn). New York: McGraw-Hill.

Hunt, S.D. and Vitell, S. 1986. A general theory of marketing ethics. *Journal of Macromarketing*, 6: 5–16.

Jackson, R.W., Wood, C.M., and Zboja, J.J. 2013. The dissolution of ethical decision-making in organizations: a comprehensive review and model. *Journal of Business Ethics*, 116: 233–250.

Jones, T.M. and Ryan, L.V. 1997. The link between ethical judgment and action in organizations: a moral approbation approach. *Organization Science*, 8: 663–680.

Karakowsky, L., Carroll, A.B., and Buchholtz, A.K. 2005. *Business and Society: Ethics and Stakeholder Management*. Toronto, Ontario: Thomson Nelson.

Kish-Gephart, J.J., Detert, J., Treviño, L.K., Baker, V., and Martin, S. 2014. Situational moral disengagement: can the effects of self-interest be mitigated? *Journal of Business Ethics*, 125: 267–285.

Leeson, N. 1996. *Rogue Trader*. London: Little, Brown Book Group.

Lehnert, K., Park. Y., and Singh, N. 2015. Research note and review of the empirical ethical decision-making literature: boundary conditions and extensions. *Journal of Business Ethics*, 129: 195–219.

Messick, D.M. and Bazerman, M.H. 1996. Ethical leadership and the psychology of decision making. *Sloan Management Review*, 37: 9–22.

Miller, D.T. 1999. The norm of self interest. *American Psychologist*, 54: 1053–1060.

Nisan, M. 1991. The moral balance model: theory and research extending our understanding of moral choice and deviation. In *Handbook of Moral Behavior and Development* (vol. 3), (W. Kurtines and J. Gewirtz, eds). Hillsdale, NJ: Erlbaum, pp. 213–249.

Palazzo, G., Krings, F., and Hoffrage, U. 2012. Ethical blindness. *Journal of Business Ethics*, 109: 323–338.

Petrick, J.A. and Quinn, J.F. 2000. The integrity capacity construct and moral progress in business. *Journal of Business Ethics*, 23: 3–18.

Prentice, R.A. 2004. Teaching ethics, heuristics, and biases. *Journal of Business Ethics Education*, 1: 55–72.

Prentice, R.A. 2014. Teaching behavioral ethics. *Journal of Legal Studies Education*, 31: 325–365.

Rest, J.R. 1986. *Moral Development: Advances in Research and Theory*. New York: Praeger.

Reynolds, S.J. 2006. A neurocognitive model of the ethical decision-making process: implications for study and practice. *Journal of Applied Psychology*, 91: 737–748.

Schwartz, M.S. 2016. Ethical decision-making theory: an integrated approach. *Journal of Business Ethics*, 139: 755–776.

Schwartz, M.S. and Carroll, A.B. 2003. Corporate social responsibility: a three domain approach. *Business Ethics Quarterly*, 13: 503–530.

Tenbrunsel, A.E. and Messick, D.M. 2004. Ethical fading: the role of self-deception in unethical behavior. *Social Justice Research*, 17: 223–236.

Tenbrunsel, A.E. and Smith-Crowe, K. 2008. Ethical decision making: where we've been and where we're going. *Academy of Management Annals*, 2: 545–607.

Toffler, B.L. and Reingold, J. 2003. *Final Accounting: Ambition, Greed, and the Fall of Arthur Andersen*. New York: Broadway Books.

Treviño, L.K. 1986. Ethical decision making in organizations: a person-situation interactionist model. *Academy of Management Review*, 11: 601–617.

Treviño, L.K., Weaver, G.R., and Reynolds, S.J. 2006. Behavioral ethics in organizations. *Journal of Management*, 32: 951–990.

Tsang, J.A. 2002. Moral rationalization and the integration of situational factors and psychological processes in immoral behavior. *Review of General Psychology*, 6: 25–50.

Watson, G.W., Berkley, R.A., and Papamarcos, S.D. 2009. Ambiguous allure: the value-pragmatics model of ethical decision making. *Business and Society Review*, 114(1): 1–29.

Woiceshyn, J. 2011. A model for ethical decision making in business: reasoning, intuition, and rational moral principles. *Journal of Business Ethics*, 104: 311–323.

Part Two

Normative Framework

Chapter Four

Distinguishing Right from Wrong

In the previous three chapters, we looked at *descriptive* ethical decision making through an *Integrated Ethical Decision-Making* model. Chapter 1 identified the *individual* and *situational* considerations underlying ethical decision making. Chapter 2 described the ethical decision-making *process* from initial awareness to behavior. We then considered the *impediments* to ethical decision making in Chapter 3. All of this relates to a *descriptive* explanation of how people make or do not make ethical decisions. It describes a state of affairs of how we tend to determine and engage in ethical or unethical behavior.

While it is important to understand the *descriptive* question of *how* we decide to behave, in Part 2 we begin in this chapter to shift to the more *normative* question: regardless of how we decide what's ethically right and wrong, how *should* we decide or determine what is right versus wrong?[1] In other words, what exactly should take place during the *moral judgment* stage to ensure that we determine the proper or best ethical decision to make, hopefully then leading to ethical behavior?[2]

Imagine the following scenario. You have begun working as a new supervisor on a construction site. The relatively low-skilled labor positions are filled by a group of workers who have recently immigrated to your country. Several weeks after your promotion to supervisor, one of the managers takes you aside and explains that a previous manager, who is no longer with the company, had hired some employees who had provided false documentation when they were hired. This means that a few of the current workers are not legally permitted to work in the country. It is illegal to hire undocumented employees and this could lead to legal trouble for the firm. On the other hand, you are aware that these workers are merely trying to earn enough to feed their families with no legitimate job opportunities elsewhere. What do you do?[3]

Business Ethics: An Ethical Decision-Making Approach, First Edition. Mark S. Schwartz.
© 2017 John Wiley & Sons, Inc. Published 2017 by John Wiley & Sons, Inc.

This might be considered to represent a true ethical dilemma, in that whatever you decide will have negative outcomes. On what basis will you decide what to do? Emotions of empathy towards the workers and their families, initial intuitions over what's right or wrong, and moral rationalizations such as everyone is hiring illegal workers, might each impact your judgment. But at the end of the day, you still have the responsibility to determine through a moral reasoning process the appropriate course of action based on a set of moral standards. Your considerations might include respecting the law, the consequences to workers (and their families) of being fired, as well as the best interests of the firm. In the end, the employee who actually faced this dilemma decided not to disclose to anyone that the workers were illegal. The employee was prepared to personally face any possible consequences, but did make it clear to his manager that he would not directly participate in the future hiring of any more illegal workers. Was this the ethical decision to make, which essentially condoned breaking the law? What is the normative process by which we can distinguish right from wrong?

To achieve this objective, a second framework is proposed, called *Multifaceted Ethical Decision Making (Multifaceted-EDM)*. The multifaceted framework attempts to incorporate the dominant moral standards and key ethical decision-making tests into the moral judgment stage of the ethical decision-making process, while trying to account for the emotions, biases, psychological tendencies, rationalizations, and impact of self-interest that prevents us from making moral decisions and ultimately acting ethically. The Multifaceted-EDM framework runs in tandem with the *moral awareness* and *moral judgment* process stages of the Integrated-EDM model described in Chapter 2. The Multifaceted-EDM framework is depicted in Figure 4.1.

Similar to the Integrated-EDM descriptive model, the Multifaceted-EDM normative framework consists of several stages. These stages include: (i) moral reasoning through an application of each of the moral standards to the various alternatives; and (ii) an ethics "filter." Only through working through this reasoning process can we be most assured that the decision enjoys a solid ethical justification that has hopefully not been tainted by emotions, biases, tendencies, rationalizations, or self-interest. The two basic stages of the Multifaceted-EDM framework will now be described.

Stage 1: Application of Moral Standards

Let's assume you are already aware that you are facing a dilemma that you realize has ethical implications, in other words, you have already engaged in proper *moral framing*. What sort of additional moral reflection of each of the alternatives should take place leading to a morally appropriate or justified decision?

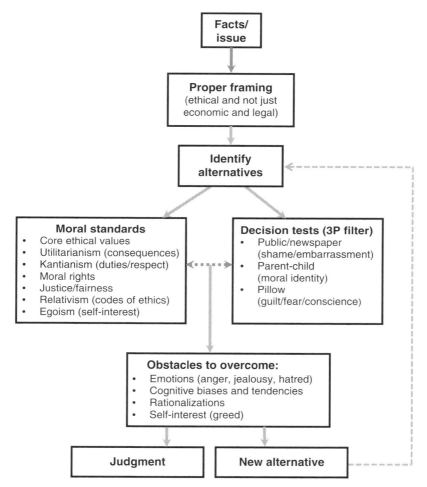

Figure 4.1   The Multifaceted Ethical Decision-Making model.

Which moral standards (ethical values, principles, or theories) can be used or should be used in the moral reasoning process? This question is one of the fundamental issues in moral philosophy.

To understand the moral reasoning process, we need a basic understanding of the key *moral standards* that can help us determine what is morally right versus wrong, or at least what is most right versus least morally wrong.[4] Several moral standards provide a set of analytical tools to help us determine the best course of action among the alternatives.[5] The moral standards can be distinguished into two general categories: (i) those moral standards that tend to support ethical behavior; and (ii) those moral standards that tend to be improperly used to support or rationalize unethical behavior. The moral standards can be categorized as follows:

(i)   Moral standards that tend to *support ethical behavior*:
   * universal core ethical values;
   * utilitarianism (consequences);
   * Kantianism (duties);
   * moral rights;
   * justice/fairness.
(ii)   Moral standards that tend to *support unethical behavior*:
   * relativism (group norms);
   * egoism (greed).

Let's turn now to a discussion of the key moral standards that can be used to guide us in resolving ethical dilemmas.

Moral standards that generally support ethical behavior[6]

Universal core ethical values

The first moral standard is really a collection of core ethical values: trustworthiness, responsibility, caring, and citizenship. These four values are universal, as they exist among different nationalities, religions, and corporate codes of ethics.[7] This moral standard may be thought of as common morality, because everyone seems to understand and accept the basic ethical values it includes.[8] This moral standard also comes closest to Greek philosopher Aristotle's virtue ethics approach,[9] although here the core ethical values not only represent traits of an individual's moral character, but are intended to provide actual guidance on determining right versus wrong.[10]

The initial core ethical value is *trustworthiness*. There are, however, a number of other sub-values that must be exhibited before an individual would be considered trustworthy. The first component of trustworthiness is *honesty*: individuals must tell the truth and avoid deceiving others. Will you rewrite a report to make the numbers look better for a client if your manager asks you to? Honesty can also be indirect, for example, if a conference call has formally ended but you remain connected and can hear people in the meeting room complaining about others at the firm, do you say something, hang up, or keep listening?

The second component of trustworthiness is *integrity*, which comes from the Latin adjective "integer" meaning "wholeness" or "being complete." Integrity is achieved by acting consistently according to your stated values or principles. In other words, you stick to your principles even when there are pressures to do otherwise. When firms have a mission, credo, or code of ethics, do they act accordingly and thus with integrity? One should note that based on this definition, a person or an organization could act with integrity but still be unethical; for example, the Mafia, the Nazis, and terrorist organizations all act with integrity (i.e., they consistently act according to their stated ethical principles and beliefs).[11]

A third component of trustworthiness is *promise-keeping*, which doesn't just mean keeping your promises, but also means not making promises you may not be able to keep. For example, when it comes to confidentiality in business, when someone, including a good friend, says to you: "I want to tell you something confidentially. Can you keep it a secret?" the response really should be "It depends." What if the information could lead to the direct harm of others if not disclosed? (e.g., imminent layoffs). Fourth, *loyalty* is also part of trustworthiness: in other words, acting in the best interests of your firm, profession, managers, work colleagues, customers, suppliers, or your family. The main difficulty with loyalty is that when there is a conflict, for example when choosing between loyalty towards your firm versus your family, which should take precedence?

Finally, *transparency* is also important. In order for an individual or a firm to be considered transparent, sufficient relevant information must be disclosed on a timely basis for interested stakeholders (employees, customers, government regulators) to judge properly the decisions and actions of the individual or firm. As one example, transparency (along with honesty) means being fully open regarding your qualifications and capabilities to your future employer or client.

The second core value is *responsibility*, or what is often referred to as accountability. This is a question not just of individuals doing what they are supposed to do, but also of being accountable for their actions. Responsibility is about acknowledging when one has made a mistake. Often as individuals, however, we unfortunately tend not to admit fault, even when we clearly realize that we are at fault. This value often comes into play when we make a mistake with respect to preparing a report for a client. Will the mistake be disclosed to both our manager and our client, even though there is little chance of the mistake being detected? For business firms, this lack of accountability can often be due to pressures exerted from the firm's legal department to act defensively, in other words, once the firm admits fault, the lawsuits commence. While this may be true, there may also be cases where individuals or firms ultimately benefit by immediately admitting fault and by sincerely apologizing to those who were harmed. For many plaintiffs of lawsuits (e.g., the injured consumer), all they may want to hear from executives or the store's manager is that they admit they were wrong, and that they are sorry for the harm caused. The last thing they want to hear is that someone else such as a competitor, the government, the supplier, or even the consumer himself or herself is at fault.[12]

One example demonstrating a lack of moral responsibility took place when McDonalds' executives blamed 79-year-old customer Stella Liebeck for her third degree burns. Liebeck had spilled coffee on herself after trying to open the lid of her 185 °F hot cup of coffee while in a parked car, causing third degree burns. Despite reports of 700 burns over the years including third degree burns, McDonalds still refused to lower the temperature of their coffee.[13] In another case, Ford's CEO blamed their tire supplier Bridgestone/Firestone for the defective tires causing tire blowouts, leading to hundreds of deaths, rather than assuming responsibility for the rollovers of the Ford Explorer vehicle itself.[14] Responsibility also means that once you admit fault, you will take reasonable steps to correct what led to the mistake, so that it will hopefully not happen again in the future.

The third core value is *caring*. This ethical value involves taking necessary precautions to prevent unnecessary harm in order to be considered a caring person.[15] The reason for indicating "unnecessary" harm is that in the production of goods or the delivery of services, there will always be some degree of harm. For example, the production of cars means that some people will unfortunately be killed in car accidents, but on this basis alone we would not prohibit the production of cars. Firms and their executives can be expected to take reasonable steps, however, to prevent harm from occurring, and certainly can disclose to others through warnings of potential risks and dangers. But caring goes beyond avoiding unnecessary harm. It also means doing good when it requires relatively little cost to oneself. Such actions tend to fall into the prosocial or self-sacrificing category, and tend to be judged by others as being morally praiseworthy, rather than morally obligatory. The last component of caring is being sensitive to others' feelings, for example being sensitive to the manner in which layoffs take place or by trying not to offend others through potentially offensive advertising, jokes, or comments.[16]

The fourth core value is *citizenship*. As individual citizens, we have certain obligations, including obeying both the letter and the spirit of the law, assisting the community, and protecting the natural environment. This core value can also be used to justify many philanthropic acts, such as community involvement or charitable contributions to community or environmental organizations.

Criticisms   Unlike the other moral standards to follow, it is difficult to raise any significant criticisms against the core ethical values. Nonetheless, an application of each universal value can lead to other ethical concerns. For example, in terms of trustworthiness, there may be times when you might be considered to be too honest, leading to insensitivity towards others, or even a breach of your obligation of confidentiality. You might also be too loyal toward your manager or your firm, even when that person or your firm is engaged in illegal or unethical behavior, leading to complicit acceptance of the wrongdoing.

Being fully responsible and accepting complete fault might also help others to avoid blame and to take the corrective steps they should be taking. This can lead at the firm level to crippling class-action lawsuits. In terms of caring, it is often difficult to determine what constitutes "unnecessary harm" which must be avoided as opposed to reasonable and unavoidable harm. Abiding by the law as part of good citizenship can also sometimes be ethically problematic, especially when the law itself might be considered unethical (e.g., South Africa's Apartheid laws). In other cases, ethical values can simply come into conflict, and there is often no clear way to resolve such conflicts.

Utilitarianism
This moral standard focuses on the consequences of a given action and in this respect is a teleological or consequentialist theory. It is often expressed as a classic phrase attributed to nineteenth-century philosopher Jeremy Bentham: "The greatest good for the greatest number of people." His other important statement is that "The greatest happiness of the greatest number is the foundation of morals and legislation."[17] Unlike egoism (described later), which focuses only on the consequences of an action upon a particular individual or firm, utilitarianism focuses on the impact of a decision on all those affected. The typical process for applying utilitarianism is to first identify all the alternatives, determine the costs and benefits for each stakeholder (e.g., shareholders, employees and their families, customers, suppliers, competitors, community, etc.) under each alternative, and then select the alternative that produces (or tends to augment) the greatest net good (i.e., also referred to as utility, happiness, benefit, pleasure, or absence of pain).

For example, should the engineers and executives of self-driving cars such as Google design their cars to swerve off the road and into a tree or pole potentially injuring the driver or other passengers in order to avoid hitting children who suddenly run onto the street?[18] If your answer is yes, then you appear to be deciding on the basis of utilitarianism, that is, the greatest net good for all those affected. One has to be careful, however, as there are several traps that can be fallen into when applying utilitarianism. First, if the sum total of the benefits is greater than the sum total of the costs for a given action, is it ethical? The answer is no. The action is ethical only when the net benefits are greater than *all other* possible alternatives. Second, if the net benefits are greatest for the person performing the action versus all other possible alternatives, is it ethical? Again, the answer is no. The action is ethical only if the net benefits are greatest for *all people* affected by the action, and not just the decision maker.[19]

Criticisms   One major criticism of utilitarianism has to do with the difficulties of measuring utility. For example, how does one put a value on life or health? Such determinations are often subject to individual, subjective assessments. In addition, it is very difficult to predict the future reliably, and it is not always so clear whether something is a benefit or a cost. While these remain important criticisms, utilitarians might respond by suggesting that despite the difficulties, society does place economic value on things like life (e.g., life insurance policies, wrongful death lawsuits, etc.). In addition, we can still attempt to make reasonable predictions about the future. Others, known as "preference utilitarians" have their own response to any concerns raised over the measurement of utility. They would suggest that what is determined as "good" or as a "benefit" should simply be based on whatever action leads to the greatest satisfaction of the preferences and desires of all those involved which can be unique for each individual.[20]

The second major criticism of utilitarianism is that it is either "unable" to address or possibly "ignores" other moral standards, such as moral rights or justice (described later). This is even more problematic if the individual or the firm could keep secret the violation of rights or justice. One could justify a totalitarian regime or a sheriff arresting an innocent man to prevent a racial riot on the basis of utilitarianism. Pharmaceutical firms would be justified testing new drugs on thousands of uninformed African patients or homeless alcoholics in order to develop drugs that could save millions of other lives.[21] But in doing so, the standards of moral rights (particularly for those individuals in the minority), or justice, would be violated. One response of some utilitarians is to apply "rule" utilitarianism, whereby the net benefit of adopting a general rule is considered, as opposed to the net benefit of a particular act (i.e., "act" utilitarianism).

Kantianism

The next moral standard is based on one particular philosopher, and it is significant enough to deserve its own representation as a distinct moral standard. Known as "Kantianism" it is based on the work of eighteenth-century German philosopher Immanuel Kant. For Kant, the moral worth of an action is based on the reasons or motive for acting (i.e., one's "good will"). The motive to act should be based on your moral duty, as opposed to inclination or self-interest. As a duty-based approach to right and wrong behavior, this moral standard is often referred to as being deontological in nature.[22] The question then becomes, how do you determine your moral duty? Kant developed a particular principle to determine moral duty, which he called the "categorical imperative." While there have been numerous explanations of Kant's categorical imperative, I would suggest the following three different formulations: (i) universalizability; (ii) reversibility; and (iii) respect.

Universalizability   Kant's first formulation is that we should act only according to that maxim (i.e., rule) which can be universalized. He states, "Act only according to that maxim whereby you can at the same time will that it should become a universal law without contradiction."[23] The basic idea is that if the rule applied universally is self-defeating, then the act is immoral. Upon first reading, however, it's not very clear what Kant means by this, or how it could ever be applied. In fact, this formulation of the categorical imperative may be one of the more difficult moral principles not only to understand, but also to apply to dilemmas.

The following will provide a more simplistic example in an attempt to demonstrate how universalizability might apply. Consider the following: should you drive on the shoulder of a busy highway? An egoist approach would focus on the perceived self-interest calculation of saving travel time versus potentially receiving a fine. Utilitarianism would determine the net benefits to all those affected, taking into account your own needs (e.g., not to miss an important meeting) versus the possible harm caused to others as a result. To answer this question according to universalizability, however, you should not consider the consequences of the action. Instead, you first need to determine the intended purpose of the shoulder of the highway, in other words, that the shoulder exists for emergency vehicles (e.g., police, fire, ambulance) or for car breakdowns. If everyone were to drive on the shoulder, would the purpose of the shoulder become self-defeating, in other words, no longer be able to be fulfilled? The answer is yes; therefore, according to Kant's universalizability principle, you should not drive on the shoulder. In other words, you cannot "will" driving on the shoulder of a highway into a universal law.

As another example, wealthy mothers from Manhattan, New York were apparently hiring handicapped people so their children could jump the lengthy lines at Disney World's rides. If the mothers had applied universalizability and asked themselves whether the purpose of the physically handicapped ride policy would become self-defeating if everyone hired handicapped people to jump the lines, they would have recognized that they should not be engaging in this practice.[24] Given the widespread abuse, Disney was forced to modify its policy.[25] This type of ethical analysis would also apply to those thinking about using the "10 items or less" express lane in the supermarket when they clearly have more than ten items, or bribing a government official in order to win business.

Other possible examples where Kant's universalizability can be applied include the following:

- Should I cheat on a test? (ask: if every student cheated on tests, would the purpose of tests, presumably to test a student's knowledge relative to other students, become self-defeating?).
- Should I break my promise? (ask: if all promises were broken, would the purpose of making promises become self-defeating?).

- Should I fudge the budget or "massage" the forecasts? (ask: if all budgets or forecasts were fudged, would the purpose of keeping a budget become self-defeating?).
- Can I violate the company code of ethics? (ask: if all codes of ethics were violated, would the purpose of the code provisions become self-defeating?).

If the answer is yes to any of these questions (i.e., the act cannot be universalized), then according to Kant's universalizability, one cannot engage in the action.

In the movie *Quiz Show*, based on true events taking place in the 1950s, a contestant (Charles Van Doren played by Ralph Fiennes) is probed during an interview by studio executives to see whether he would agree to be asked during the live broadcast the same questions he has previously been asked. The contestant poses: "I wonder what Kant would say?" One of the studio executives responds: "I don't think he would have problem with it." Of course, the executive's response is not correct, as Kant would argue that you cannot universalize cheating on a game show, since the purpose is to have two contestants compete against each other. One should try to be careful whenever applying universalizability, however, since it can be quite easy to slip into considering the consequences of the action instead of the motive for the action (e.g., and end up applying egoism or utilitarianism).

Reversibility   The second formulation of the categorical imperative has been referred to as being directly related to universalizability. As part of universalizing the reasons for our decision, we must also consider whether we would be willing to have others act toward us the same way based on similar reasons. In other words, the basic question we each need to ask is "How would I feel if I were in the other person's shoes?" (e.g., discriminate, withhold information, break a promise, etc.). "How would I feel if someone else did the same thing to me?" "Would I still act the same way?" Some suggest that the "golden rule" ("do unto others as you would have them do unto you") is the basis for this formulation of Kant's categorical imperative (although Kant clearly indicates that they are not one and the same).[26] The difficulty of applying reversibility, however, is that it is not always clear into whose shoes you ought to put yourself into when it comes to ethical dilemmas. Generally, the answer should be the party most directly affected. For example, when considering whether you should cheat your customer, you should put yourself into the customer's shoes, as opposed to the shoes of other employees or shareholders who may benefit from the action and are only indirectly affected.

Respect   This third formulation of the categorical imperative is based on Kant's position that we should treat people as "ends" in themselves (i.e., having intrinsic worth as free rational human beings) rather than merely as a "means" to an end. In other words, we should not treat others only as a means to advance our own or the firm's self-interest (e.g., profits) or be able to exploit, manipulate, or take advantage of others, even for the greater good. Kant states, "Act in such a way that you treat humanity, whether in your own person or in the person of any other, always at the same time as an end and never merely as a means to an end."[27] In business, this typically refers to the prohibition against taking advantage of customers or exploiting our employees, even if this improves the firm's bottom line or even the overall good of society. In the movie *Boiler Room*, based on true events taking place at a Long Island brokerage firm, the manager instructs his trainees as follows: "And there is no such thing as a no-sale call. A sale is made on every call you make. Either you sell the client some stock or he sells you a reason he can't. Either way a sale is made; the only question is: who is gonna close? You or him? Now be relentless, that's it, I'm done."[28] Of course, such treatment of clients is a clear example of disrespect to the clients and using them as merely a means to an end.

Criticisms   Several criticisms have been raised against Kant and the application of his categorical imperative. First, there can be difficulties in trying to determine whether or not someone is being used merely as a means to an end. Second, a racist might come to a different conclusion regarding the universalizability of discrimination from a non-racist. Third, Kant is inflexible when it comes to certain actions such as lying, stealing, or breaking promises: they can never be justified even in saving a life, according to Kant.[29] In addition, it can be argued that the categorical imperative is ultimately consequentialist. In other words, in determining whether or not the maxim can be applied universally, we must ultimately make reference to consequential considerations.[30]

Moral rights

Similar to Kantianism, this moral standard is also deontological (duty-based) in nature. Moral rights, unlike legal rights which are determined by social institutions, exist by the mere fact that we are human beings, or arise based on our interactions with other human beings. They essentially represent an individual's entitlement to something. When applied to decision making, an action is considered morally right or wrong only if it respects the rights of individuals affected by the action. While there are many different classifications of moral rights, the primary category that relates to ethical decision making is negative rights. Negative rights can, as expected, be distinguished from positive rights, which create a duty on others such as the government to provide, for example the right to employment, housing, health care, or even education.[31] If one possesses a negative right, this tends to impose a duty on others not to interfere with or infringe on those rights.

There are two important examples of negative rights related to ethical decision making. The first involves the consumer or employee's right to life, health, and safety. The existence of this negative right places a duty on managers to take reasonable steps to eliminate or mitigate against known dangers regarding products or the work environment and to fully disclose to consumers or employees when any dangers or hazards remain. The second important negative right is the shareholder's right to property, which creates a duty on employees, managers, and the board of directors not to "steal" their property (e.g., through fraud, theft, conflicts of interest, or possibly even charitable giving).[32] Quite often, full disclosure (or transparency) of a firm's activities addresses at least to a certain extent the moral rights of its stakeholders (i.e., it better allows stakeholders to insist on their rights not being infringed). The process for applying moral rights is as follows: (i) determine the moral rights each stakeholder (including shareholders) possesses and the duties owed to other stakeholders;[33] (ii) determine the relative significance of these rights and duties; and (iii) choose the alternative that best respects the rights and duties of individual stakeholders.

Criticisms   The major criticism of moral rights as a standard is that it is often difficult to resolve conflicting rights. For example, while we may possess the right to use our property as we wish, others may possess a right to health and therefore not to be polluted. The smoker's right to smoke (e.g., outdoors) might come into conflict with the non-smoker's right to a healthy environment. An employer that monitors its employees in order to better safeguard the assets of the firm (i.e., thereby protecting the property rights of the shareholders) could come into conflict with the privacy rights of employees. Unfortunately, there is no clear and simple method for resolving rights that conflict with each other. However, this does not mean that we cannot still consider the importance or significance of certain rights vis-à-vis others. In addition to the problem of conflicting rights, a strict application of moral rights, similar to the Kantian approach, means that important consequences can often be ignored, with the interests of the minority then taking precedence over the well-being of the majority.

Justice (or fairness)
When it comes to ethical decision making, another major ethical concern is whether our actions can be considered just or fair. When individuals use the term "fairness", however, they often use it in different ways, each with its own meaning and criteria. The different types of justice or fairness include distributive justice, compensatory justice, retributive justice, procedural justice, and societal justice, each of which will now be briefly reviewed.

Distributive justice deals with the equitable or fair distribution of the benefits (e.g., wages) and burdens (e.g., taxation) imposed by an action or policy. In order for a decision to be considered fair, similar individuals should be given similar benefits and suffer similar burdens, or people should be treated the same unless they differ in relevant ways. The difficulty, however, is how to determine whether individuals deserve similar or different treatment. Several different criteria of similarity or difference can be utilized, including the following: (i) contribution/ productivity (i.e., how much output); (ii) effort (i.e., how hard one tries); (iii) merit/seniority (i.e., how long have you been there); (iv) needs and abilities (i.e., how much is able to be produced or how much is required); or (v) equality (i.e., everyone being treated the same regardless of differences). Based on the criteria, we could try to answer the following questions:

- Is it fair that the CEO's child should be given a job position over a more qualified candidate?
- Is it fair to read a competitor's information on a bid that was inadvertently sent to your firm by mistake?
- Is it fair to treat certain clients better because they often take you out for nice dinners?
- Is it fair that someone who has worked at the firm longer than all the others gets to keep his/her job over someone who is more productive?

In each of the above cases, the answer would be "no" if the distributive justice criterion of merit or contribution/productivity is applied.

Compensatory justice is concerned with appropriately compensating people for a past harm or injustice (e.g., restitution). Of course, we should not be morally obligated to compensate others unless our actions were the cause of the injury and the injury was intentional, as opposed to accidental. Quite often this involves actions that have caused injury or harm to others such as employees (e.g., unsafe workplace), customers (e.g., product defects), or communities (e.g., pollution), despite our awareness of the hidden dangers.

Retributive justice is concerned with punishing an individual (e.g., through a fine or imprisonment) or a firm (e.g., through a fine or even requiring dissolution of the firm) that has inflicted harm on others. Unlike compensatory justice, which focuses on providing compensation to the one who has been injured, retributive justice focuses on punishing the agent or firm committing the harm (e.g., sexual harassment or discrimination). Before enacting punishment, however, it should be established that the person or firm was actually responsible for the harm, and that the punishment is consistent with and proportionate to the harm inflicted on others.

Procedural justice relates to fairness in the process of decision making. For example, when suppliers are bidding on a contract, has the decision been made in an impartial, unbiased, and objective manner? Or was it due to a personal relationship with one of the suppliers, or due to being given a nice gift? Has the decision been transparent? Have reasons been given for the decision, such as firing someone? If not, the decision would be considered procedurally unfair.

Societal justice is a more complicated type of justice and often more difficult to apply when determining our ethical responsibilities. Societal justice is based primarily on the writings of philosopher John Rawls, who developed the idea of a "veil of ignorance" in order to establish appropriate principles for society.[34] Rawls asks us to engage in a mental exercise by starting in the "original position" as follows: close your eyes – you are about to be born, you have no idea if you will be born physically handicapped, if you will be mentally challenged, if you will be a man or a woman, intelligent, or what color your skin will be. What principles would you like to establish for your society? One of Rawls's key principles is that inequalities should be arranged so that they are to the greatest benefit of the least advantaged (while remaining under conditions of fair equality of opportunity). Another expression of this principle is that we should adopt the alternative whose worst outcome is superior to the worst outcome of all the other alternatives.

Criticisms   Unfortunately, there's no agreement on which criterion should apply with respect to distributive justice. It's also difficult to assess at what point and to what extent compensatory justice must take place, and whether at some point an individual (or a firm) should no longer be held financially responsible for past injustices. One of the concerns of applying Rawls' societal justice principle is that more advantaged individuals (or firms) could likely end up in a worse position in order to improve (those who would otherwise be) the least advantaged. Disagreement also persists in determining the appropriate punishment according to retributive justice. Finally, there is a real danger that justice or fairness could be inappropriately used as the basis to support several *impediments* to proper moral judgment discussed in Chapter 3, including the moral rationalization of claim to entitlement ("I deserve it"), that there is no real victim (since "they deserved it"), or that I am being unfairly attacked ("attack the attacker").

Moral standards that tend to be used to rationalize unethical behavior

The application of each of the above moral standards to an ethical situation tends to lead to a proper moral reasoning process increasing the likelihood of a proper moral judgment. In this respect there is an overlap between the above moral standards and Kohlberg's fifth (social contract) and sixth (universal ethical principles) stages of moral development discussed in Chapter 1. There are, however, two moral standards, *relativism* and *egoism*, which unfortunately if relied upon solely or even in combination when deciding how to act, tend to lead to unethical decision making and behavior.

Relativism

Relativism can be considered a moral standard, although a potentially dangerous one solely to rely on. This conventionalist approach might in fact be one of the more dominant approaches applied around the world in the workplace to establish right versus wrong. In other words, we ask this question: does the majority of a group of individuals (i.e., a particular reference point) believe that the action in question is morally acceptable? Many refer to this position as "when in Rome, do as the Romans do." Relativism rejects the view that there are universal standards or rules to determine the morality of an act. In order to apply relativism, however, we need to identify the particular reference point being used as a basis for judgment. In terms of analyzing business cases, the following are the typical reference points: the firm itself (which could include the employees, managers, executives, and/or board of directors), industry/competitors, customers, or the community. One can turn to levels of activity, polls or surveys, legislation, or codes of ethics (e.g., organizational, industrial, professional, or international) as evidence of what the majority of a particular reference point believes is morally acceptable. The moral standard of relativism overlaps with stage three of Kohlberg's stages of moral development, which is based on approval of referent others (family, group, or nation) to determine what is right or wrong.

For example, should you open up a store when the law prevents doing so on a particular holiday? Using relativism, you could refer to the majority view of the competitors, and ask whether they will also be opening up, meaning that they presumably believe it is morally acceptable to do so. What does the majority of employees want you to do? The majority of your customers? The majority of the residents in the neighborhood community? Based on relativism, you are justified in opening up the store as long as the majority of one or more reference points, at a particular point in time, believes that it is morally acceptable to do so. For our purposes, however, the views of a single person should not constitute sufficient justification for determining what is ethical (known as "naïve relativism"). There must instead be a group reference point that is referred to (known as "cultural relativism"); otherwise, the moral standard collapses completely by being entirely based on our own individual whims and preferences.

As a moral standard, relativism is quite weak, and relates to both *conformity bias* and the rationalization of "everyone else is doing it" as discussed in Chapter 3. Rather than relying on polls or surveys or the behavior of the majority of a group, reference to formalized and documented ethical norms such as industry, professional, or corporate codes of ethics tends to provide a more solid ethical justification for behavior when based on relativism.

Criticisms   There are many potential deficiencies to using relativism as a moral standard. First, if we merely rely on relativism, our moral judgments can easily change based on time, circumstance or culture. It becomes almost too easy to justify our actions. As long as the majority of the firm, industry, or any other reference point believes that the action is morally acceptable, then the argument ends. Even if the majority position on a particular matter changes from one day to the next, it would still be considered morally legitimate under relativism.

Second, an application of relativism can lead to certain results that might be considered problematic. For example, consequences or individual moral rights can be ignored; if the majority of a particular society accepts genocide or female circumcision as being appropriate, then such practices are ethically justified and must be respected. Activities such as slave labor in the chocolate industry,[35] the padding of expense accounts by an entire group of employees, or bribes to government officials in order to win contracts[36] would also all be considered morally acceptable according to relativism. As a matter of practical application, there may also be difficulties in establishing the relevant community to refer to, owing to both the internal pluralism in most countries as well as economic globalization, which has blurred national borders and their distinct communities. Finally, there may be some philosophers who would reject relativism as a moral standard, yet still argue that community standards remain important to consider when determining what should be considered morally acceptable.[37]

Egoism

Egoism indicates that what is perceived to maximize the long-term best self-interest of the individual (or the business firm) is the morally appropriate action. In this respect egoism as a moral standard overlaps with Kohlberg's first stage (punishment) and second stage (self-interest) of moral development discussed in Chapter 1. For example, any decision that would in the short or long term either increase or avoid the diminishment of our net utility, pleasure, happiness, compensation, job security, wealth, status, power, or prestige, would be considered as falling under egoism. For the purposes of business decisions, egoism would also include the best interests of the firm, typically based on either perceived long-term profits or share value. For the individual, the extent of the "guilt" or embarrassment we might feel upon making a particular decision and then carrying it out, or the extent to which it is inconvenient time-wise to engage in a certain action relative to other actions, should also be taken into account in the calculation of perceived best self-interest.

Egoism (i.e., self-interest) can be seen as the ethical basis of laissez-faire capitalism, and is often referred to in connection with eighteenth-century economist and moral philosopher Adam Smith (but only as "conditional egoism"; in other words, self-interest is acceptable, but only when it leads to the betterment of society). Others typically connected with egoism as a moral standard include economist Milton Friedman in his 1970 *New York Times Magazine* article "The Social Responsibility of Business is to Increase its Profits," and philosopher Ayn Rand in her various novels such as *The Fountainhead* or *Atlas Shrugged*. For many, such as Smith and Friedman, individual egoism is often justified in terms of the moral standard of utilitarianism, in that self-interest moves the marketplace toward optimal efficiency.[38] It may be that egoism has been the most dominant moral standard driving individual and firm behavior in the marketplace since the beginning of commerce.

Criticisms   Many criticize egoism as leading to significant unethical actions by individuals or their firms. Some of the more significant scandals mentioned earlier might include Enron, WorldCom, or Bernie Madoff's massive Ponzi scheme. Many have suggested that the 2008 US financial crisis, primarily involving sub-prime mortgages, was caused by unrestricted egoism or self-interest on the part of mortgage lenders and investment banks.[39] Typically, such criticism of egoism is contingent on regarding it as equivalent to the notion of "greedy" individuals or firms, often leading to highly problematic consequences for others who are taken advantage of. This comparison, however, is not accurate. Instead, greed should be considered as representing only one extreme end of the entire spectrum of egoism.[40] *Greed* can be defined as acting to gain something, typically money, wealth, power, or status, in an insatiable (i.e., never satisfied) and excessive manner. In addition, greed leads people to cut ethical corners, harm others, or even break the law (if they don't think they will get caught) in order to fulfill their insatiable desires.[41]

According to former trader Nick Leeson of Barings Bank, greed is a major factor leading to unethical activity: "Being an ex-banker, everybody keeps away from the word greed, but that's what the industry is about. I don't think you could find a bank that sets themselves a target and, once they get there, is happy with it in terms of their turnover or profit. They always want to exceed that and go further."[42] Some researchers have even begun to study a new variable called "love of money" in relation to the prioritization of self-interest.[43] While some might argue that any self-interested act is unethical, not all self-interested acts should necessarily be considered unethical, unless such acts are based on excessive forms of self-interest such as greed, selfishness, avarice, hedonism, or narcissism, lead to unnecessary harm to others,[44] or are engaged in through unethical means.[45]

Greed should be contrasted with other expressions of egoism, such as self-ishness (i.e., concern excessively or exclusively with oneself, love of oneself, or the inability to share with others), self-interest (i.e., our own perceived inter-est or material well-being), or enlightened self-interest (i.e., initially focusing on the interests of others based on the belief that, by doing so, our own best self-interest will ultimately be served). In other words, we can argue on behalf of egoism while still rejecting the notion of greed as ethically unacceptable. Whether egoism is expressed merely as self-interest or as greed can nonethe-less, however, lead to ethically problematic results, as discussed in Chapter 3. The danger is that a proper moral reasoning process can be compromised through biases or moral rationalizations (e.g., the "self-serving" bias or the rationalization of "claim to entitlement") when decision makers face *moral temptation* situations and their own self-interest is at stake. Another criticism of egoism as a moral standard is that if everyone believed they were obligated to act only in their own self-interest, self-sacrifice or altruism would become morally unacceptable in society. Many, however, would not wish to live in such a society and thus reject egoism as a guiding ethical principle. Table 4.1 sum-marizes the key moral standards, along with possible criticisms and examples of business executive decisions or actions related to each.

Resolving conflicts between the moral standards

One of the major difficulties encountered when trying to come to a moral judgment is that often the various moral standards can come into conflict. The major conflict typically involves egoism, relativism, and the moral property rights of the firm's shareholders versus the other moral standards. Conflicts between utilitarianism and the duty-based moral standards (Kantianism, moral rights, and justice) also tend to arise requiring a resolution. Unfor-tunately, no uncontroversial solution to reconciling conflicts has ever been established. On this basis, the best we can do is attempt to apply the various moral standards in order to identify on what basis a given action may be ethically justified. This essentially means taking a *pluralistic* approach to moral judgment, which is the position I would recommend as well.[57]

Regardless whether or not one adopts a pluralistic approach to morality, at the end of the day, each individual will have to decide which moral standard or standards are the ones that make the most sense to them to apply in deter-mining what is ethically right or wrong in the workplace. At the very least,

Table 4.1 Summary of the moral standards. (*Source:* Schwartz, 2011. Reproduced with the permission of Broadview Press.)

Moral standard	Brief definition	Potential criticisms	Examples
1(a) Core ethical values: trust-worthiness	We act in a trustworthy manner if we are honest, act with integrity (consistent with our stated values/principles), and are transparent, loyal, and keep our promises.	Difficult to resolve conflicting loyalties (e.g., to firm versus to our family).	*Dishonesty:* lack of full disclosure of known potential harmful impacts (e.g., tobacco industry's deception to public regarding health impacts[46]).
1(b) Core ethical values: caring	We act in a caring manner if we avoid unnecessary harm, do good when of relatively little cost to ourselves or the firm, and are sensitive to others' feelings.	Difficult to establish what constitutes "unnecessary" harm.	*Not avoiding harm:* failure to recall vehicle or disclose dangerous fuel tank defect (e.g., Ford Pinto[47]). *Doing good:* provide drugs in Africa for free (e.g., Merck and the river blindness pill[48]).
1(c) Core ethical values: responsibility	We are responsible if we do what we're supposed to do, are accountable for our actions, accept fault, apologize, and don't blame others.	Taking full responsibility can lead to substantial lawsuits.	*Not accepting fault:* blaming supplier for faulty product and failing to take reasonable steps to ensure problem is rectified (e.g., Ford rollovers vs. Firestone tires[49]).
1(d) Core ethical values: citizenship	We are a good corporate citizen if we obey the law, protect the natural environment, and assist the community.	Could lead to abiding by even unethical laws.	*Good corporate citizen:* engaging in recycling, community assistance, or fair trade (e.g., The Body Shop[50]).
2 Utilitarianism	Action ethical if it achieves the greatest net good (or benefit/utility) for all those affected.	Difficulties in measurement (e.g., life or health). May violate individual's moral rights to achieve greater net good.	*Best for society:* using child labor (when children would otherwise be on the streets) in the Third World leading to source of income for families (e.g., Nike in Asia[51]).

(continued)

Table 4.1 (Continued)

Moral standard	Brief definition	Potential criticisms	Examples
3 Kantianism	Action ethical if our motive is based on our moral duty. Duty must be based on categorical imperative (i.e., universalizability; reversibility; respect).	One can never lie for any reason. Consequences are potentially ignored.	*Lack of universalizability:* aggressive accounting which defeats the purpose of financial statements (e.g., Enron[52]).
4 Moral rights	Action must respect the moral rights of individuals affected by the action (e.g., rights to safety or property rights of shareholders).	No method to resolve conflicting moral rights.	*Disregard for moral rights:* providing a repressive government with personal information of customers (privacy rights) leading to their arrest (health and safety rights) (e.g., Yahoo in China[53]).
5 Justice/fairness	Action ethical if outcomes are determined to be fair (e.g., compensatory/retributive/ distributive/procedural/societal).	Not clear which criterion should be used to determine whether the distribution of benefits and burdens is fair.	*Lack of distributive justice:* millions in bonus compensation paid to executives after receiving billions in US government bailouts (e.g., AIG[54]).
6 Relativism	Action ethical if the majority of the reference point (e.g., firm, industry, society) believes the act in question is morally acceptable.	Moral judgment constantly changes depending on the circumstances.	*Justified due to accepted behavior of majority:* bribe your potential customers because if you don't, your competitors will (e.g., Siemens telecom bribery case[55]).
7 Egoism	Act according to our (or our firm's) own perceived long-term best self-interest.	Focus on profit maximization can lead to harming others (i.e., danger of greed). Altruism or self-sacrifice is unacceptable.	*Best for bottom line:* long-term perceived self-interest of firm leading to actions that put worker health and safety or the natural environment at greater risk (e.g., BP oil spill in Gulf of Mexico[56]).

attempting to apply or reflect upon all seven of the moral standards discussed will provide several potentially differing ethical views or perspectives that can lead us to justify better our own decision making, or better critique the decision making of others including the actions of business firms. Coming to a moral judgment through a moral reasoning process based on the moral standards is one critical component of the entire ethical decision-making process potentially leading to ethical behavior.

Stage 2: The Public-Parent-Pillow (3P) Filter

Assuming we realize we are facing a dilemma with ethical implications, and we have engaged in moral reasoning by applying the moral standards to come to a moral judgment, the final stage of the Multifaceted-EDM framework consists of applying a series of simple decision-making tests, which I call the *3P Filter*. The *3P Filter* attempts to incorporate a variety of other decision-making tests that other business ethics commentators have proposed.[58] For those who would like to see other approaches, several additional ethics tests are indicated in Appendix C. While there is an overlap between the 3P Filter and the moral standards, the 3P Filter also attempts to address the potential for emotions, biases, or rationalizations that might enter into the process leading to faulty or misguided moral reasoning. Let's now consider the three filters.

The 3P Filter completes the process by using three core tests to substantiate further the application of the moral standards. These tests include: the *public test*, being a *parent test*, and the *pillow test*. If you are able to make it through the 3P Filter, you will have a greater degree of assurance that your moral reasoning is sound. The *public* (or newspaper) test reflects your concern for the approval of others. To apply the public test, ask yourself, "how would I feel if my decision was reported in the newspaper?"[59] The public or newspaper test is essentially based on the moral standard of relativism, with the reference point being your family, friends, firm, or community, similar to Kohlberg's third stage of moral development described in Chapter 1. One goal of this test is to avoid later feeling embarrassment or shame through public disclosure of wrongdoing. We might consider whether some of the biggest scandals might have been avoided if this question had simply been asked prior to the misconduct taking place. For example, if Andrew Fastow, the former CFO of Enron, had considered the possibility of future news headlines of his actions, or Nick Leeson of Barings Bank, would they still have acted the same way? Of course, many individuals might not care about the views of others or actually enjoy being in the media spotlight, including those who may have psychopathic tendencies and do not suffer from feelings of guilt for their actions even when observed by others.[60]

The *parent* (or child) test can be a very powerful decision-making test, especially if the decision maker has children. When faced with a dilemma, ask yourself, "what would I as a parent tell my child to do?" Once a problem is framed in this way, many people realize that they have higher expectations for their child's behavior than they do for their own. Consequently, they tend to behave more ethically. In real life, we often forget that our children are observing, judging, and emulating our behavior. For example, when the phone rings and you're busy, do you tell your child, "tell them I'm not home", encouraging your child to tell a lie? Dr Jeffrey Wigand, who blew the whistle on his tobacco firm Brown & Williamson for their use of a dangerous chemical additive in their cigarettes, when asked why he did this, said "By this time I had a significant problem looking at myself in the mirror. For my own children, who had the benefit of my affluence and were going to private schools, were asking me, Why, Dad, [are you] killing people with the job [you] do?"[61] In some cases, grandchildren are the main concern, leading to feelings of guilt and embarrassment. A former Prime Minister of Israel, after being convicted of receiving bribes from a businessman in order to receive favorable building approvals, said to the judges: "The real punishment is the shame. What do I say to my grandchild?"[62] This test is related to the concept of *moral identity* mentioned in Chapter 1, or how you maintain your view of yourself as a moral person when faced with challenges.

The *pillow* (or sleep) test is perhaps the most important ethical decision-making test. Ask yourself: "If I engage in a certain course of action, will I be able to sleep peacefully through the night, or will my guilty conscience keep me awake?" You can apply this test either before or after taking action. For example, how many times have we woken up during the middle of the night unable to sleep, only to realize that we are in the midst of an ethical dilemma that requires resolution? This has certainly been the case for me. Applying this test might help you avoid the emotions of guilt you might experience after acting improperly. Of course, we might imagine that there are a number of individuals, especially those who are psychopathic, who lack feeling any guilt, shame, or embarrassment for their actions. Such individuals will be able to sleep quite peacefully at night, despite engaging in activity that others would find morally reprehensible.[63] For example, it seems that Bernie Madoff might not have been persuaded to change his actions based on the pillow test.

As one final step in the process, it may be that only through an application of the moral standards and the 3P Filter (along with the process of moral imagination) that we realize that another potentially better alternative exists. If this takes place, we can then go through the same process by considering the new alternative to see if it can be supported by the moral standards and the 3P Filter.

Putting It All Together: A Normative Framework for Ethical Decision Making

Let's now try to put it all together. In this final section of the chapter, I will summarize the steps of the Multifaceted-EDM framework based on the discussion above.

1. *Becoming aware of an ethical dilemma.* The first step in ethical decision making is realizing that you are facing an ethical dilemma involving more than one alternative course of action. This takes place through proper framing, for example by initially applying all three *frames* discussed in Chapter 3. We need always to recognize whether our decisions involve *ethical* implications as well as any economic and legal concerns. If the ethical concerns conflict with the economic or legal considerations, then this constitutes an ethical dilemma.

2. *Moral reasoning.* When facing an ethical dilemma, a proper moral reflection or reasoning process should take place that includes a reflection of the moral standards discussed above including the core ethical values (i.e., trustworthiness, responsibility, caring, citizenship), utilitarianism, Kantianism, moral rights, and justice/fairness. Relativism might also be applied but only based on moral norms or conventions as reflected in a formal code of ethics rather than being based merely on peer norms. If egoism (self-interest) is applied, we need to be careful not to base our decisions due to greed. Any conflicts among the moral standards must then be resolved, meaning priority might be given to one moral standard or standards over another.

3. *Apply the 3P Filter.* Asking yourself if you would be willing to have your decision publicized, tell your child to act the same way, and still be able to sleep at night, are the final considerations. These tests can assist in mitigating emotions such as anger, jealousy, or hatred, can eliminate possible bias or tendencies, and counter moral rationalizations. For example, you might decide to fire someone because of feelings of jealousy, anger, or resentment rather than on reasonable grounds such as competency. Applying the 3P Filter can capture and thwart this sort of misguided and non-rational decision making.

Chapter Summary

This chapter focused on understanding the basis upon which we should determine what is ethically right or wrong using a framework called *Multifaceted*

Ethical Decision Making. The starting point is first ensuring that we realize or recognize that we constantly face issues not only with economic or legal considerations but with *ethical* implications as well. Once there is initial awareness, the moral standards can be applied including the core ethical values, utilitarianism, Kantianism, moral rights, and justice/fairness. Egoism in terms of self-interest (rather than greed) and relativism in terms of codified moral norms such as codes of ethics can also be taken into account.

Returning to the example of illegal workers raised at the beginning of the chapter, the core ethical value of caring (avoiding unnecessary harm) as well as utilitarianism would clearly support not taking any action against the workers, given the extent and intensity of the harm they (and their families) would suffer. Kantianism might seem to suggest based on reversibility and respect that they should continue to be employed. However, breaking the law, even if we disagree with its purpose, cannot be universalized, and would be contrary to the core ethical value of citizenship which includes obeying the law. Relativism and egoism would support continuing to employ the workers. There is a clear conflict between the moral standards, and a compromise solution such as making sure the practice does not continue and assisting the current workers to take the necessary steps to become legally employed, might represent the best overall moral action.

The next step is to apply the public-parent-pillow (3P) Filter, by asking yourself whether you would be comfortable with your intended action being publicized in a newspaper or in social media, whether you would tell your child to act the same way, and whether you can sleep at night following your decision. These tests can assist in preventing rationalizations from taking place to justify unethical activity, such as egoism (greed) or relativism (everyone else is doing it). For the immigrant workers, it might be difficult to sleep at night knowing you have put their families at risk.

Next in Chapter 5 we shift our focus to possibly one of the most significant ethical issues faced by employees during their careers, that of deciding whether to report the wrongdoing or misconduct of their work colleagues or firms.

Notes

1. Unfortunately, very few behavioral ethics researchers provide a definition of an "ethical decision." One attempt is provided however by Treviño *et al.* (2006, p. 952) along with a few examples: "…behavioral ethics refers to individual behavior that is subject to or judged according to generally accepted moral norms of behavior…some researchers have focused specifically on unethical behaviors, such as lying, cheating, and stealing. Others have focused on ethical behavior defined as those acts that reach some minimal moral standard and are therefore not ethical, such as honesty or obeying the law. Still others have focused on ethical

behavior defined as behaviors that exceed moral minimums such as charitable giving and whistle-blowing. Our definition accounts for all three areas of study."

2. This line of questioning relies on several initial fundamental assumptions: (i) that a morally correct or more appropriate decision can be known or discovered for any given ethical dilemma; (ii) individuals possess the volition or freedom to decide whether to act ethically or unethically; and (iii) individuals have the potential to surpass or overcome the obstacles discussed in Chapter 3 that inhibit doing the right thing. Each of these assumptions, while subject to potential challenge and thus worthy of further discussion and consideration, is beyond the scope of this book.

3. This example is based on an actual MBA student dilemma presented in a business ethics class.

4. As indicated in the Introduction, *ethical behavior* for our purposes is not defined merely as conforming to the legal or moral norms of the larger community, but is behavior that can be supported by one or more moral standards.

5. While there are a multitude of different moral standards to choose from, the following moral standards are considered to be the most dominant in the business ethics literature as reflected in business ethics textbooks and journal articles. See: Schwartz (2011).

6. This section of the chapter up to and including Table 4.1 is adapted from "The Nuts and Bolts of Determining Ethical Responsibility" (Chapter 2) from *Corporate Social Responsibility: An Ethical Approach.* Copyright © 2011 by Mark S. Schwartz. Reprinted with the permission of Broadview Press.

7. See: Schwartz (2005) and Josephson (1996). It has to be recognized, however, that there is a danger when attempting to derive "ought" from "is", also known as the "naturalistic fallacy" as discussed by G.E. Moore in *Principia Ethica* (1968).

8. See: Beauchamp *et al.* (2009, pp. 35–38).

9. For further discussion on Aristotle's virtue ethics approach as opposed to a principles-based approach in relation to business ethics and business education, see: Bragues (2006); Hartman (1998; 2008); Velasquez (2012); Wittmer and O'Brien (2014).

10. Aristotle's virtues, such as courage or wisdom, have been criticized as not providing clear guidance on how to behave ethically (see: Velasquez, 2012, p. 132). Others suggest, however, that universal moral virtues such as prudence (knowledge and practical wisdom), justice (give people exactly what they deserve), fortitude (perseverance), and temperance (moderation or self-control) can influence various stages of the ethical decision-making process (see: Morales-Sánchez and Cabello-Medina, 2013).

11. The core values of various unethical organizations seem at least on paper to be quite ethical in nature. For example, the Mafia's "core values" include loyalty, obedience, and honor while their version of the "Ten Commandments" mandates respect and truthfulness. Organized crime syndicates in Russia apparently have a "Thieves' Code" that includes maintaining confidentiality and keeping promises. Los Angeles street gangs have "honor codes" that are apparently based on the values of respect, reputation, pride, and dignity. See: Jim Nortz, "Do Your Corporate

Values Pass the Mafia Test?" *The Business Journals*, June 23, 2014, http://www.bizjournals.com/bizjournals/how-to/growth-strategies/2014/06/do-your-corporate-values-pass-the-mafia-test.html?page=all (accessed 8 September 2016). The problem is that such entities also act in ways that clearly violate other ethical values or moral standards, such as the right to life, demonstrating that integrity by itself does not equate with ethics.

12. See: Schweitzer *et al.* (2015).
13. See: Retro Report, "Scalded by Coffee, Then News Media," *The New York Times*, October 21, 2013, http://www.nytimes.com/video/us/100000002507537/scalded-by-coffee-then-news-media.html (accessed 8 September 2016).
14. See: Dan Ackman, "Ford, Firestone Face Off," *Forbes*, June 19, 2001, http://www.forbes.com/2001/06/19/0619ff.html (accessed 8 September 2016).
15. This could also be considered a duty of "non-maleficence." See: Ross (1930).
16. Avoiding unnecessary harm and sensitivity towards others might include attempting reasonably to accommodate whenever possible with respect to employees' religious practices including holidays or food requirements.
17. See: Bentham (1970).
18. See: Matt Gurney, "If the Only Way Out of Traffic is a Robo-Car That May Murder Me, Fine," *National Post*, May 30, 2014, http://fullcomment.nationalpost.com/2014/05/30/matt-gurney-if-the-only-way-out-of-traffic-is-a-robo-car-that-may-murder-me-fine/ (accessed 8 September 2016).
19. See: Velasquez (2012, p. 79).
20. For example, economists use this approach when they establish people's preferences based on the choices they make in the marketplace.
21. See: Stephanie Kelly, "Testing Drugs on the Developing World," *The New Yorker*, February 27, 2013, http://www.theatlantic.com/health/archive/2013/02/testing-drugs-on-the-developing-world/273329/ (accessed 8 September 2016).
22. Deontology, which comes from the Greek word "deon" meaning duty or obligation, is a branch of moral philosophy whereby the morality of an action is based on adherence to a set of rules or principles rather than a consideration of the consequences of an action. Kant might be considered to be the primary contributor to deontological or duty-based moral theory.
23. Kant (1964, p. 70).
24. See: Tara Palmert, "Rich Manhattan Moms Hire Handicapped Tour Guides So Kids Can Cut Lines at Disney World," *New York Post*, May 14, 2013, http://nypost.com/2013/05/14/rich-manhattan-moms-hire-handicapped-tour-guides-so-kids-can-cut-lines-at-disney-world/ (accessed 8 September 2016).
25. See: Katia Hetter, "Disney Tightens Up Resort Disability Program," *CNN*, September 25, 2013, http://www.cnn.com/2013/09/23/travel/disney-disability-policy-changes/ (accessed 8 September 2016).
26. It is of note that almost all of the world's religions have a version of the Golden Rule, including Buddhism, Confucianism, Hinduism, Islam, Judaism, and Taoism. See: Hosmer (2008, p. 104).
27. Kant (1964, p. 96).
28. See: IMDb website, "Boiler Room: Quotes," http://www.imdb.com/title/tt0181984/quotes/ (accessed 8 September 2016).

29. This may be one reason why Kant never got married, since according to some the ability to lie and be lied to at least a little bit is necessary in order to be in a relationship. See: Clancy Martin, "Good Lovers Lie," *The New York Times*, February 7, 2015, http://www.nytimes.com/2015/02/08/opinion/sunday/good-lovers-lie.html?_r=1 (accessed 8 September 2016).
30. Whether or not this highly contentious interpretation of Kant is correct, the risk remains for those attempting to apply Kant to slip into a discussion of the consequences of universalizing a particular action.
31. For example, see: Velasquez (2012, p. 96).
32. See: Friedman (1970).
33. For example, using company assets such as the photocopier for personal use without consent can be considered an infringement of the firm owner's moral property rights.
34. Rawls (1971, pp. 136–142).
35. See: Velasquez (2012, pp. 64–65).
36. For example, the $1.4 billion in bribes paid by Siemens Corporation to government officials around the world to convince them to purchase Siemens equipment. See: Velasquez (2012, p. 222).
37. Such philosophers would still argue, however, that some actions, such as slavery, would violate certain universal ethical principles and should be rejected despite being upheld by community norms. See: Donaldson (1996).
38. The view of such economists is that egoists, based on self-interest, move the distribution or allocation of goods toward "Pareto optimality" (i.e., it is impossible to make one person better off without negatively affecting someone else). This happens when egoists are involved in the marketplace under conditions of perfect competition (i.e., no market participant can influence prices in the market).
39. For example, "greedy" mortgage lenders were lending even to those who had no incomes, while investment banks created complex investment vehicles based on such highly speculative mortgages. See: Rithholtz (2009).
40. See: Haynes *et al.* (2015, p. 267) who state that there is a "tipping point" where healthy self-interest turns into the excesses of greed. The famous quotation of corporate raider Gordon Gekko (played by Michael Douglas) in the movie *Wall Street* (1987), that "Greed, for lack of a better word, is good," might have more appropriately been "Enlightened self-interest, for lack of a better expression, is good." The quotation from the movie was apparently taken from an actual statement made by former stock trader and arbitrageur Ivan Boesky during a University of California commencement speech when he said, "Greed is all right, by the way…I want you to know that. I think greed is healthy. You can be greedy and still feel good about yourself." Boesky later went to jail for three years and paid a $100-million fine for insider trading. See: Stewart (1992). Later, in *Wall Street: Money Never Sleeps* (2010), the same character, Gordon Gekko (played again by Michael Douglas), after leaving jail decades later and promoting his new book, *Greed is Good*, makes the following statement during a university guest lecture: "Someone once reminded me I once said "Greed is good." Now it seems greed is legal."
41. See: Haynes *et al.* (2015).

42. See: Esther Addley, "Nick Leeson on Banking: Extremely Competitive…and Improperly Policed," *The Guardian*, February 23, 2015, http://www.theguardian.com/business/2015/feb/23/nick-leeson-banking-industry-extremely-competitive-improperly-policed (accessed 8 September 2016).

43. See: Singhapakdi *et al.* (2013); Tang (2007).

44. See: Maitland (2002).

45. Etzioni (1988).

46. See: Matthew Myers, "Time to Crack Down on Big Tobacco," *CNN*, June 30, 2010, http://www.cnn.com/2010/OPINION/06/29/myers.big.tobacco/index.html (accessed 8 September 2016).

47. See: Hoffman (2001).

48. See: Bollier and Weiss (1991).

49. See: Joann Muller, "Ford versus Firestone: A Corporate Whodunit," *Bloomberg Business Week*, June 11, 2010, http://www.bloomberg.com/news/articles/2001-06-10/ford-vs-dot-firestone-a-corporate-whodunit (accessed 8 September 2016).

50. See: The Body Shop website, https://www.thebodyshop.com/en-gb/commitment (accessed 8 September 2016).

51. Spar and Burns (2002).

52. See: *The New York Times*, "Enron Jury Hears of 'Aggressive' Accounting," February 6, 2006, http://www.nytimes.com/2006/02/06/business/worldbusiness/06iht-enron.html (accessed 8 September 2016).

53. See: Marc Gunther, "Yahoo's China Problem," *Fortune*, February 22, 2006, http://money.cnn.com/2006/02/21/news/international/pluggedin_fortune/ (accessed 8 September 2016).

54. See: Associated Press, "Bonus Furor May Prompt Limits on AIG Bailout," *MSNBC*, March 17, 2009, http://www.msnbc.msn.com/id/29714402/ (accessed 8 September 2016).

55. See: Siri Schubert and Christian Miller, "At Siemens, Bribery Was Just a Line Item," *The New York Times*, December 21, 2008, http://www.nytimes.com/2008/12/21/business/worldbusiness/21siemens.html (accessed 8 September 2016).

56. See: CBC News, "BP Downplayed Oil-Rig Disaster Risk," May 1, 2010, http://www.cbc.ca/world/story/2010/04/30/louisiana-oil-spill.html (accessed 8 September 2016).

57. For statements on how conflicts among moral standards might be addressed, see: White (2003, p. 11); Velasquez (2012, p. 125); Hoffman *et al.* (2014, pp. 5–6). Although subject to criticism, I also adopt a pluralistic approach or perspective to moral judgment similar to others including Crane and Matten who state (2010, p. 128): "…all of the theoretical approaches…throw light from different angles…and thus work in a complementary rather than a mutually excluding fashion."

58. For example, see: Barr *et al.* (2011) for examples of ethical decision-making tests.

59. Given the significant changes taking place in mass electronic communication through social media including Facebook, Twitter, and Instagram, this test might be relabelled as the *social media test*.

60. The public/newspaper test might be considered to be the exact opposite of a thought exercise proposed by Plato in book two of his *Republic*. In the book, there

is a story about the ring of Gyges, which when turned around makes the wearer invisible allowing him to do whatever he wants, including stealing, rape, or killing, with no fear of being captured and punished. Would anyone who found the ring not use it to fulfill all their desires? If you were completely invisible, what sorts of actions would you take? Would you act illegally and unethically to your own advantage? See: Corvino (2006, p. 4).

61. See: "Special Section: The Anti-Tobacco Campaign, Jeffrey Wigand and the Anti-Tobacco Campaign," *The Other Side: Journal of Socialist Thought and Action*, 26(11), November 2013, http://theotherside.org.in/nov_2013/special_section. html (accessed 8 September 2016).

62. See: Yonah J. Bob, "Olmert To Judges: 'The Real Punishment is the Shame. What Do I Say To My Grandchild'," *The Jerusalem Post*, May 5, 2015, http://www.jpost. com/Israel-News/Blair-supports-Olmert-at-sentencing-hearing-commitment-to-peace-should-be-admired-402108 (accessed 8 September 2016).

63. In other words, the "pillow test" assumes that one possesses at least a degree of moral conscience which can be activated after reflecting upon one's behavior or intended actions.

References

Barr, D., Campbell, C., and Dando, N. 2011. *Ethics in Decision-making*. London: Institute of Business Ethics.

Beauchamp, T.L., Bowie, N.E., and Arnold, D.G. (eds). 2009. *Ethical Theory and Business* (8th edn). Upper Saddle River, NJ: Pearson-Prentice Hall.

Bentham, J. 1970. *An Introduction of the Principles of Morals and Legislation*. London: Athlone Press.

Bollier, D. and Weiss, S. 1991. Merck & Co. Inc. (A). The Business Enterprise Trust, Boston, MA: Harvard Business School Publishing.

Bragues, G. 2006. Seek the good life, not money: the Aristotelian approach to business ethics. *Journal of Business Ethics*, 67: 341–357.

Corvino, J. 2006. Reframing 'morality pays': toward a better answer to 'why be moral?' *Journal of Business Ethics*, 67: 1–14.

Crane, A. and Matten, D. 2010. *Business Ethics* (3rd edn). New York: Oxford University Press.

Donaldson, T. 1996. Values in tension: ethics away from home. *Harvard Business Review*, September – October: 5–12.

Etzioni, A. 1988. *The Moral Dimension: Toward a New Economics*. New York: The Free Press.

Friedman, M. 1970. The social responsibility of business is to increase its profits. *New York Times Magazine*, 32–33, 122–126.

Hartman, E.M. 1998. The role of character in business ethics. *Business Ethics Quarterly*, 8: 547–559.

Hartman, E.M. 2008. Socratic questions and Aristotelian answers: a virtue-based approach to business ethics. *Journal of Business Ethics*, 78: 313–328.

Haynes, K.T., Josefy, M., and Hitt, M.A. 2015. Tipping point: managers' self-interest, greed, and altruism. *Journal of Leadership & Organizational Studies*, 22: 265–279.

Hoffman, W.M. 2001. The Ford Pinto. In *Business Ethics: Readings and Cases in Corporate Morality* (4th edn), 2001. (W.M. Hoffman, R.E. Frederick, and M.S. Schwartz, eds), pp. 497–503. New York: McGraw Hill.

Hoffman W.M., Frederick, R. and Schwartz, M.S. (eds). 2014. *Business Ethics: Readings and Cases in Corporate Morality* (5th edn). Chichester, UK: John Wiley & Sons, Ltd.

Hosmer, L.T. 2008. *The Ethics of Management* (6th edn). New York: McGraw-Hill.

Josephson, M. 1996. *Making Ethical Decisions* (4th edn). Marina del Rey, CA: Josephson Institute of Ethics.

Kant, I. 1964. *Groundwork of the Metaphysics of Morals*, trans. H.J. Patron. New York: Harper & Row.

Maitland, I. 2002. The human face of self-interest. *Journal of Business Ethics*, 38: 3–17.

Moore, G.E. 1968. *Principia Ethica* (1903). London: Cambridge University Press.

Morales-Sánchez, R. and Cabello-Medina, C. 2013. The role of four universal moral competencies in ethical decision-making. *Journal of Business Ethics*, 116: 717–734.

Rawls, J. 1971. *A Theory of Justice*. Cambridge, MA: Harvard University Press.

Rithholtz, B. 2009. *Bailout Nation*. Hoboken, NJ: John Wiley & Sons, Inc.

Ross, W.D. 1930. *The Right and the Good*. Oxford: Clarendon.

Schwartz, M.S. 2005. Universal moral values for corporate codes of ethics. *Journal of Business Ethics*, 59: 27–44.

Schwartz, M.S. 2011. *Corporate Social Responsibility: An Ethical Approach*. Peterborough, Ontario: Broadview Press.

Schweitzer, M.E., Brooks, A.W., and Galinsky, A.D. 2015. The organizational apology. *Harvard Business Review*, September: 44–52.

Singhapakdi, A., Vitell, S., Lee, D.J., Nisius, A., and Yu, G. 2013. The influence of love of money and religiosity on ethical decision-making in marketing. *Journal of Business Ethics*, 114: 183–191.

Spar, D. and Burns, J. 2002. *Hitting the Wall: Nike and International Labor Practices*. Harvard Business School Publishing (9-700-047).

Stewart, J.B. 1992. *Den of Thieves*. New York: Simon and Schuster.

Tang, T.L.P. 2007. Income and quality of life: does the love of money make a difference? *Journal of Business Ethics*, 72: 375–393.

Treviño, L.K., Weaver, G.R., and Reynolds, S.J. 2006. Behavioral ethics in organizations. *Journal of Management*, 32: 951–990.

Velasquez, M.G. 2012. *Business Ethics Concepts and Cases* (7th edn). Upper Saddle River, NJ: Prentice Hall.

White, T.L. 2003. *Business Ethics: A Philosophical Reader*. New York: Macmillan.

Wittmer, D. and O'Brien, D. 2014. The virtue of "virtue ethics" in business and business education. *Journal of Business Ethics Education*, 11: 1–18.

Chapter Five

The Decision to Report Misconduct

So far we have covered the *descriptive* theory in Part 1 and essential *normative* frameworks in Chapter 4 that underlie ethical decision making. We will now attempt in this chapter to integrate both frameworks together by focusing on what may be one of the most important and challenging ethical dilemmas we can ever face in the workplace – *the decision whether to report misconduct we observe taking place*. The goal of this chapter is to contribute to a better understanding of not only *how* the decision to report misconduct takes place, but when it can be considered morally permissible or even obligatory to report wrongdoing.

For example, imagine the following scenario.[1] You are responsible for managing the assets of a wealthy client from an overseas country. The investment firm you work for has established a private holding company on behalf of the client in order to transfer cash to dozens of small holding companies in the client's home country. There are more than a dozen transfers, each for about US$2–3 million. The recipient country is currently under United Nations sanction for sheltering terrorist organizations. You become suspicious that the money is funding terrorism, and discuss the matter with your boss. You indicate that the amount of money is significant for the country, and ask whether your firm knows who is receiving the money or what the client is getting in return for the money. Your boss says: "These are questions we do not need to ask. We just need to follow the federal rules for reporting wire transfers, and that's what we do."

You press further, and ask whether there are still obligations on the firm to report if something looks suspicious. Your boss turns red and slams his fist on the desk. He says "No, absolutely not. It's up to the regulators to tell us if there is

Business Ethics: An Ethical Decision-Making Approach, First Edition. Mark S. Schwartz.
© 2017 John Wiley & Sons, Inc. Published 2017 by John Wiley & Sons, Inc.

anything suspicious. All we need to do is our jobs. This client is a very private person and we will lose him as a client if we start prying into his business." The client makes up over half of the personal assets under your direct management, and if the firm lost the client, three other analysts would be out of a job. What do you do?

Do you push your boss harder, notify the appropriate government authorities, or do nothing? What does your decision depend upon? Does it depend on the possible harm your actions might cause to the client or your firm, the quality of the proof you have, or whether there might be retaliation for raising your concerns further? Are you morally obligated to do something? The scenario above, while it might be unique, highlights the difficulties we face as employees when we discover actual or possible misconduct taking place either within or by the organizations we work for. At what point should we take action and report the misconduct to others? This chapter will try to answer this question.

The ethical dilemma whether to report misconduct continues to be a challenging issue for societal members, whether in the public or the private sector. For example, it has been suggested that "whistleblowing is one of the classic issues in business ethics."[2] Despite the challenges and risks, there have been a number of prominent whistleblowers. Famous whistleblowing cases over the years include:

- General Electric manager Chester Walsh, who blew the whistle on GE's submission of fictitious bills to the US government for F-16 fighter jet parts;[3]
- Executive Richard Lundwall, who secretly taped other senior executives during a meeting talking about the racial discrimination practices taking place at Texaco. His evidence helped lead to a $140 million settlement;[4]
- The discovery by Union Bank of Switzerland security guard Christoph Meili that the bank was secretly shredding documents detailing the Jewish assets seized by the Nazis. Meili's evidence helped lead to a $1.4 billion settlement with Holocaust survivors and their families. Unfortunately, Meili received death threats and was ostracized from Switzerland, eventually moving to the United States with his family after being granted political asylum;[5]
- Dr Nancy Olivieri, who blew the whistle on the Canadian drug firm Apotex when she discovered there were potentially life-threatening side effects during clinical trials of a new drug. Following her disclosures of the risks, Dr Olivieri suffered harassment along with threats of a lawsuit from the drug company;[6]
- Hervé Falciani of HSBC, who reported how the Swiss subsidiary of the bank allegedly helped more than 100,000 clients evade billions in taxes;[7]

- John Kopchinski, who reported on his pharmaceutical firm Pfizer for fraudulent marketing practices leading to $2.3 billion in fines, representing one of the largest criminal fines ever imposed in the United States;[8]
- Various whistleblowers, who have emerged in relation to the emissions scandal at Volkswagen involving billions of dollars in potential criminal fines and civil lawsuits against the company;[9]
- A whistleblower disclosed millions of documents known as the "Panama Papers" revealing offshore shell companies used to hide the assets of hundreds of politicians, officials, current and former national leaders, celebrities, and sports stars.[10]

Occasionally whistleblowers are able to benefit financially from reporting misconduct. Under the US *False Claims Act*, whistleblowers can receive up to 30% of any settlement for reporting wrongdoing by their companies against the US government. Since 1986 more than 2,400 lawsuits have been filed, leading to the US government recovering over $2 billion and putting more than $350 million in the pockets of whistleblowers.[11] In 1992, Chester Walsh mentioned above received over $13 million for blowing the whistle on General Electric.[12] In 2009, Robert Ferro reported on aerospace and defense technology company Northrop Grumman for selling faulty electronic equipment to the US government for military satellites leading to a $325 million settlement and a payment of $48 million to Ferro.[13] Employee Bradley Birkenfeld received $104 million in 2012 for blowing the whistle on his firm UBS for assisting their clients in tax evasion, but Birkenfeld also went to jail himself for assisting one particular wealthy client evade taxes.[14]

Several Hollywood movies have portrayed whistleblowing dilemmas based on true events including *Silkwood* (employee Karen Silkwood disclosing safety violations at the Kerr-McGee plutonium fuel fabrication site), *The Insider* (Dr Jeffrey Wigand disclosing the misleading practices of his tobacco company Brown & Williamson); *Erin Brockovich* (paralegal Erin Brockovich discovering from a former Pacific Gas Company employee that the company had dumped dangerous chemicals into the drinking water supply), and *The Informant* (employee Mark Whitacre disclosing the price fixing practices of his agro-business firm Archer Daniels Midland).[15] And of course there's *We Steal Secrets: The Story of WikiLeaks*, which tells the story of Julian Assange who founded WikiLeaks, which continues to publish classified information on its website obtained from anonymous whistleblowers.

For business students, whether to report wrongdoing is consistently raised as possibly one of the most difficult ethical dilemmas to resolve, as it typically involves a direct conflict between our loyalty to our firm and our colleagues (i.e., *trustworthiness*), versus doing the "right thing" by potentially preventing harm to others (i.e., *caring, utilitarianism*). What makes the dilemma of whether or not to blow the whistle even more intense and difficult is the fact that in order to "do the right thing" and prevent possible harm, the whistle-blower must almost always suffer the personal negative consequences (i.e., *egoism*) that follows reporting misconduct. There is no question that for many employees the decision whether and how to blow the whistle on workplace misconduct can have a significant impact on their entire future business careers. This includes the decision whether to quit their jobs or even leave their industries due to the misconduct that is being observed.

In terms of the extent to which whistleblowing takes place in business firms, a national US survey found that while 41% of US employees witnessed illegal or unethical misconduct during the previous year, a significant percentage (37%) did not report it.[16] In a global whistleblowing study of 2,500 middle and senior-level managers, 12% said they had been involved in whistleblowing, while 13% said they knew of a colleague who blew the whistle. When reporting concerns, 52% of respondents said they would go to their manager first, 14% would go to a regulator, 7% to an external organization, and 4% would go to the media.[17] One UK and Continental Europe study found that "speaking up" or whistle-blowing is considered the most significant ethical issue to the organization.[18]

The range of illegal and unethical activity that goes unreported is extensive and includes corruption, bribery, receiving and giving gifts and entertainment, kickbacks, extortion, nepotism, favoritism, money laundering, improper use of insider information, use of intermediaries, conflicts of interest, fraud, aggressive accounting, discrimination, sexual harassment, workplace safety, consumer product safety, and environmental pollution.[19] One study by the Association of Certified Fraud Examiners estimates that the global total fraud cost alone to organizations per year is US$3.7 trillion.[20] According to the study, whistleblowing "tips" were the primary method of detection (42%), followed by management review (16%) and then internal audit (14%).[21] The major source of whistleblowing tips were employees (49%), followed by customers (22%) and then by anonymous sources (15%).[22]

As indicated in the Introduction to the book, we unfortunately don't have to look very far over recent years to see significant examples of crime and unethical activity within or on behalf of business organizations and the serious negative impact such scandals have had on investors, employees, customers, competitors, the natural environment, and society in general. While we might hope that the internal reporting of misconduct would help alleviate the problem, research surveys instead indicate that 21% (up from 12% in 2007) of those reporting misconduct experience some form of retaliation in return.[23] Examples of retaliation include exclusion from work activity, receiving the cold shoulder, verbal abuse by managers and other employees, almost losing one's job, and not receiving promotions or raises.[24] Forty-six percent of employees indicate fear of retaliation as the reason they did not report wrongdoing.[25] Such empirical evidence suggests that it may be unwise for an employee to report any wrongdoing.

Due to its continued importance, frequency of occurrence, and normative complexity as an ethical dilemma, this chapter will examine the issue of whistleblowing, particularly in light of new developments in whistleblowing legislation and corporate compliance and ethics programs. In so doing, an attempt is made to build on and refer to existing whistleblowing literature.[26] For the purposes of this chapter, while there are numerous definitions, reliance will be placed on a relatively broad and general definition of *whistleblowing* as consisting of *an attempt by a member or former member of an organization to disclose wrongdoing in or by the organization.*[27] Whistleblowing can be of two general types. *Internal* whistleblowing involves reporting misconduct to a party within the organization including a manager, senior executive, the CEO, legal counsel, human resources manager, security, internal auditor, ombudsperson, compliance officer, ethics officer, or the board of directors. *External* whistleblowing consists of reporting misconduct to a party outside the firm such as a government regulator, police, media, or a special interest group.

In order to understand ethical decision making in relation to whistleblowing, the chapter first provides a brief overview of the decision-making process that takes place. Next, the key normative arguments and criteria that have been raised by several business ethics commentators are presented.[28] The chapter then applies the proposed criteria to three classic whistleblowing cases to test the criteria's practicality: (i) Dennis Gioia and the Ford Pinto; (ii) Sherron Watkins at Enron; and (iii) Dr Jeffrey Wigand at the tobacco firm Brown & Williamson. The chapter concludes with the implications of the criteria. The primary goal of the chapter is to provide readers with a sense of how whistleblowing on workplace misconduct takes place, as well as when it might be morally permissible or even morally obligatory to blow the whistle.

How Does the Decision to Blow the Whistle Take Place?

Let's review the Integrated-EDM model discussed in Chapters 1 and 2 to see how the decision to blow the whistle might take place. For illustration purposes, we will focus on two significant categories of misconduct often reported in the media; consumer product defects and fraud. For both activities, there are often other managers and employees within the firm who suspect that wrongdoing is taking place and must decide whether to take any action. If you recall from Chapter 2, there are several *process* stages that we typically go through, from the existence of an issue, to initial awareness of the ethical implications of the issue, to judgment and intention, leading to behavior, resulting in possible learning.

Prior to initial awareness that one is facing an ethical issue, there is a set of norms in which an issue arises. In the case of whistleblowing, this means that there are norms that exist that prohibit certain types of activity. The norms may exist at multiple levels, such as society, industry, the organization, the workgroup, or the profession. In the case of selling defective products that are potentially dangerous, or employees or managers fraudulently stealing from their companies or clients, the norms are very clear; these activities are completely morally unacceptable. The assumption is that the majority of employees who observe that their companies are selling a dangerous and defective product to consumers, or when they see other employees or managers stealing from their companies, realize that such activities raise an issue with ethical implications. This would be even more clearly the case for those employees who are *morally mindful* or *morally attentive*. There may, however, be some employees who nonetheless *lack moral awareness*, due to *non-moral framing, ethical fading, ethical blindness, moral myopia*, or a lack of *moral imagination*. These employees would presumably not blow the whistle on the misconduct since there would be no potential moral justification to do so, unless they perceived a legal or economic (self-interested) reason to blow the whistle.

For those employees who are morally aware they face the ethical issue of whether or not to blow the whistle, the *moral judgment* process then becomes engaged. In some cases, employees might feel an *emotion* of disgust for fraudulent activity or empathy for the unknowing consumers who might be physically harmed from the defective product that triggers a judgment that something must be done to stop or prevent the misconduct. Feelings of emotion may or may not trigger *intuitions* that something must be done. Employees might not be able to explain the reasons for their automatic intuition that something must be done about the misconduct, they just know they must act. In some cases, the emotion of guilt of doing nothing especially when this may cause physical or significant financial harm to others may be so powerful that judgment, intention, and action to blow the whistle are all directly triggered.

The *moral reasoning* process, if applied, would then impact decision making. As part of this process, an application of the *moral standards* discussed in Chapter 4 such as caring (avoiding unnecessary harm), Kantianism (reversibility into the consumers' shoes and treating them with respect), moral rights (consumers' rights to life, health and safety in the case of dangerous products, shareholders' moral property rights in the case of fraud), and justice/fairness in the case of fraud (why should the employee, manager, or executive deserve to benefit from the fraud?) could all lead to a moral judgment that the misconduct or intended wrongdoing needs to be reported. While the *parent/child* and *pillow/sleep* tests would tend to support blowing the whistle, the *public/newspaper* test may actually lead someone to reconsider whether they would want to be recognized for their actions which may end up harming the firm's interests. But if the whistleblowing can take place anonymously, the necessity of considering the *public/newspaper* test is essentially avoided.

But even if we reach the moral judgment that we should blow the whistle on misconduct, will we necessarily do so? The impediments discussed in Chapter 3 may prevent us. For example, *biases* and *psychological tendencies* such as "obedience to authority" may come into play if our manager instructs us to keep quiet. The "conformity bias" may also play a role when everyone else seems to be accepting the wrongdoing as the norm. Rationalizations such as "denial of responsibility" when so many others could report the wrongdoing but have chosen not to, or an "appeal to higher authorities" when the misconduct is good for the firm, can also interfere with our moral judgment and lead us to accept the status quo.

The moral standards that might support refraining from blowing the whistle would include relativism (others would not believe I have an obligation to act) or egoism in terms of your self-interest of losing your job or being harassed if you say or do anything about the misconduct. These sorts of moral standards could lead to a moral rationalization process taking place as discussed in Chapter 3, leading to the employee believing that he or she does not have to take responsibility for correcting the situation. *Moral consultation* may take place, either through the employee checking their code of ethics to confirm whether they are obligated to report wrongdoing, or by asking others such as their colleagues, friends, or family members for advice over what they should do. All of these processes may then lead to a decision whether or not to blow the whistle.

Once *moral judgment* takes place, the employee may form an *intention* to act, which might lead to actual whistleblowing. The *moral character* of the employee as discussed in Chapter 1 will primarily determine if whistleblowing takes place. It seems that only an employee who possesses a strong *moral character* with a high level of *moral maturity*, strong current *moral value system*, and a high level of *moral competence*, along with a strong *moral identity* and sufficient *moral courage* to act according to those values, ultimately blows the whistle and risks the difficulties he or she may face as a result. For example, Dr Nancy Olivieri (referred to above) appears to have a strong moral character leading to her decision to report the risks of the new drug. The American Association for the Advancement of Science presented Dr Olivieri its Award for Scientific Freedom and Responsibility. The association noted: "Nancy Olivieri is honored for her indefatigable determination that patient safety and research integrity come before institutional and commercial interests and for her *courage* in defending these principles in the face of severe consequences."[29] Finally, once whistleblowing takes place, there may be consequences that lead to *learning* and an impact on the employee's *moral character* for the future.

Summary of Positions on the Morality of Reporting Misconduct

Now let's turn to the *normative* considerations underlying reporting misconduct through whistleblowing. In the literature on external whistleblowing, there are two extreme positions on moral permissibility or obligation, each of which to date have always been rejected. One extreme position is that employees are never permitted to externally blow the whistle, typically based on the notion of loyalty to the firm and/or due to confidentiality agreements. This position is always rejected because it is morally repugnant to a free and democratic society to completely prohibit whistleblowing or because absolute loyalty towards anyone or any entity should never exist.[30] The other extreme position is that employees are always morally permitted to externally blow the whistle for any reason, typically based on the notion of free speech. This position is also always rejected as free speech has never been considered an absolute moral principle,[31] or due to the unnecessary harm caused to the firm by externally blowing the whistle.

Most proposed sets of criteria for *external* whistleblowing take a position somewhere between these two extremes. For example, one initial starting principle is based on the ethical value of caring or the moral right to life, health, and safety, meaning that companies have a moral obligation not to unnecessarily harm others.[32] While it's the case that employees owe a degree of loyalty to their firms, this obligation is not the highest obligation and can therefore be overridden in order to prevent harm.[33] That being said, based on societal norms and the views of many employees and managers, external whistleblowing can be viewed as an act of "disobedience", which will also tend to cause injury to the firm.[34] This then requires a proper moral justification for external whistleblowing, in that more good will result than harm when an employee externally blows the whistle.[35]

Of course, the motivation underlying whistleblowing can also be considered an issue. Does there need to be a "moral motivation" when you blow the whistle? What if it is done out of revenge? Others have made proper motivation an explicit criterion for morally justified whistleblowing.[36] A proper moral motive for blowing the whistle would involve exposing illegal or unethical actions, and not based on seeking profit or attention. Personally, I am not as concerned with proper motivation for whistleblowing as some commentators, if the end result of the whistleblowing is that unnecessary harm to others is avoided. I would suggest, however, that a proper motive (e.g., not based merely on financial reasons, for revenge, or to try to make it more difficult for oneself to be fired) should still relate to whether the whistleblowing should be considered morally praiseworthy.[37] I will now explain the criteria that render whistleblowing morally permissible or obligatory.

Proposed Criteria for *External* Whistleblowing

Harm criterion

The first criterion for *externally* blowing the whistle might be referred to as the "Harm Principle". With reference to the moral standards from Chapter 4, the harm criterion is based on both *caring* in terms of avoiding unnecessary harm and *utilitarianism* with respect to selecting the alternative that leads to the least overall harm. In other words, without the possibility of serious harm resulting from the misconduct (i.e., the harm threatened by a firm's product or policy), we are morally *prohibited* from blowing the whistle externally. The word "harm" is ambiguous, as we can argue that every product or action of every company has a potential negative impact (i.e., harm) on one or more stakeholders. The qualifier "serious" can be clarified somewhat by suggesting that any matters that threaten death are serious. For example, one commentator suggests that toxic metal drums being dumped into a river by a firm which can later cause cancer should be considered as being serious.[38] Tires sold as premium quality but blowing out at 60–70 mph are also considered serious.[39]

All commentators require serious potential harm (e.g., pollution), or some activity that is currently seriously wronging other parties (e.g., product defect), as a criterion to whistleblowing.[40] Others also require harm, but suggest a broader scope. For example, the criterion can be broadened by using the words "moral wrongdoing" rather than "harm".[41] Similarly, others refer to "non-trivial or unethical actions" that are deemed to violate the dignity of one or more stakeholders.[42]

Empirical research appears to support the practicality of the harm criterion. One study found that employees weigh the severity of the problem when deciding whether or not a problem should be externally reported.[43] The following factors were found to be related to whether employees believed the issue was sufficiently serious to report externally: whether it was a very serious crime (83%); the potential harm to people (78%); the potential harm to the environment (68%); and the potential for the company to get into big trouble (59%).[44]

My position is that "potential harm" should be defined relatively broadly and not limited to "physical" harm alone.[45] The harm criterion should therefore explicitly also include those actions that could result in serious *financial* harm, as well as serious *psychological* harm.[46] I would also include actions that are clearly in serious breach of the law (i.e., would potentially lead to legal disciplinary action such as a significant fine against the firm or legal disciplinary action taken against an individual within the firm[47]). Actions that infringe basic moral rights or involve serious injustice should also be included in the harm criterion.[48] The harm criterion would potentially capture matters such as sexual harassment, violations of privacy, industrial espionage, insider trading,[49] or the falsification of previous serious misconduct,[50] as each involves a serious violation of basic moral rights or constitutes a serious injustice.

It could be argued that requiring the employee to first determine whether the harm can be considered "serious" before blowing the whistle externally is too difficult, onerous, or subjective a criterion. For example, we could ask how an employee could ever make a determination of what might be "serious" harm due to the lack of awareness of all of the potential implications of even minor misconduct, or whether the minor misconduct might actually represent the tip of major wrongdoing or a scandal. Instead, external whistleblowing might be suggested as being morally required for any observed misconduct with any degree of potential harm, leaving the recipient of the whistleblower's information (e.g., government regulators, the media, or special interest groups) with the responsibility to determine whether the reported activity is "serious" enough to render appropriate action to be taken.

I agree that some sort of distinction between minor misconduct and misconduct involving "serious" potential harm must necessarily be determined by the employee before external whistleblowing takes place. For example, an employee should not be considered to be morally required to externally blow the whistle on a co-worker taking scotch tape from the supply room for personal use, or when a purchasing manager is observed receiving a coffee mug from a current supplier as a gift (although observation of such acts might still require internal whistleblowing as discussed below). To assist in the determination of what might be considered "serious" misconduct, we might attempt to link the harm criterion to the *public/newspaper* test used in ethical decision making mentioned in Chapter 4, for instance, do you believe that the misconduct is sufficiently serious that it should be reported as a story in the newspaper?

As a result, the first criterion for external whistleblowing would therefore be as follows:

> *Misconduct has taken place or is expected to take place that violates the law or involves serious physical harm, serious psychological harm, serious financial harm, serious infringement of basic moral rights, or a serious injustice.*

Internal reporting

The next criterion might be labeled the "Internal Reporting Principle." This criterion requires that internal whistleblowing must take place, initially to your supervisor, and then if no action is taken, all the way up the corporate hierarchy to the board of directors if necessary. This criterion is based on *caring* in terms of avoiding unnecessary harm to the firm and its stakeholders such as owners and employees, and *trustworthiness/loyalty* to the firm by giving the firm an initial opportunity to address the wrongdoing. Commentators agree that "reasonably serious attempts" to prevent the wrong through internal whistleblowing have been attempted and have failed,[51] or that except in special circumstances, the whistleblower has exhausted all internal channels before going public.[52] Empirical research supports the proposition that most employees are both willing and able to report matters *internally* first. One national US study found the following (emphasis added)[53]:

> The current stigma assigned to a "whistleblower" as a rogue and disloyal employee is inaccurate. Only one in six reporters (18%) ever chooses to report externally. Of those who do go outside their company at some point, *84% do so only after trying to report internally first*. Furthermore, many of those who are "whistleblowers" in the narrowest sense of the word still try to address the problem within their own company; half of those who choose to report to an outside source initially later report internally as well. Only 2% of employees solely go outside the company and never report the wrongdoing they have observed to their employer.

There are certainly risks and often difficulties faced by those wanting to report matters.[54] Despite the challenges, *internal* whistleblowing should take place whenever possible and be a requirement before *external* whistleblowing takes place. If discussing the misconduct with your supervisor, senior management, or the board of directors (e.g., audit committee) is not possible, then you would fulfill the internal reporting criterion by taking your concerns through the designated reporting channel (e.g., legal counsel, human resources manager, internal auditor, ombudsperson, compliance officer, or ethics officer), if a reporting channel exists. The internal reporting criterion would still be met if the whistleblowing takes place anonymously. The second criterion for *external* whistleblowing would therefore consist of the following:

> *The misconduct must first be reported internally whenever feasible to your direct supervisor and, if no action is taken, all the way up to the board of directors or through the designated reporting channel if one exists (e.g., compliance or ethics officer).*

While I would not go so far as to make it a criterion, I would, however, strongly recommend one additional procedural step whenever possible (and it may not always be possible), that the perpetrator be informed that the misconduct will be reported if it does not cease. Informing the person first has been referred to as a "… preferable course of action, providing one can do so tactfully and with relative personal impunity…."[55] Warning your colleagues of their improper misconduct or of your intention to blow the whistle should always be considered as a first step whenever possible before reporting the misconduct in accordance with principles of *procedural justice*.

This would obviously be easier with respect to the perpetrator being a co-worker or a colleague in a more junior position, rather than your own supervisor or a senior manager. If the primary objective is to reduce harm, then taking the initial step of warning the perpetrator can potentially cause the misconduct to come to an end prior to any additional steps needing to be taken. Rather than being related to the moral permissibility or moral obligation of blowing the whistle, taking the additional step of ensuring that the perpetrator has been warned supports the moral praiseworthiness of ultimately blowing the whistle either internally or externally.

Anti-retaliation policy

Due to the risks of internal whistleblowing, another level of protection to the whistleblower should be added by suggesting that if the firm does not have a written anti-retaliation policy against whistleblowing that is enforced, you are not obligated to blow the whistle. This is based on *distributive justice*; the employee does not deserve to experience any personal harm for blowing the whistle. It should be completely up to the employee to make this determination, and if no formal anti-retaliation policy exists or if there is no evidence to suggest an existing policy will be upheld by the firm's management, then you would not be required to internally report wrongdoing. The existence of an effective firm anti-retaliation policy should still be required, even when anonymous whistleblowing is possible, due to the inherent risks of the employee's identity ultimately being discovered and the demonstrated negative harm caused to the employee as a result. Recent cases demonstrate that without such protection, whistleblowers remain at the mercy of their firm's retribution.[56] The exception would be for *professionals* working within a firm, who would still be bound by their professional ethical obligations to take steps to avoid potential harm by reporting misconduct even when facing personal risk to themselves by doing so. The next criterion for whistleblowing would therefore be as follows:

> *Unless you are a professional working within the firm, an effective written anti-retaliation policy must exist at the firm before you are required to report misconduct.*

Reasonable evidence

The next criterion involves the requirement to have documented evidence (i.e., the "Evidentiary Principle") of the misconduct before you can report it. This criterion is based on *procedural justice*, and is intended to avoid frivolous claims or claims being made based on improper motives. Others agree that the existence of proper evidence should be required before external whistleblowing takes place. For example, commentators suggest that there should be clear, substantiated, and reasonably comprehensive[57] or compelling evidence,[58] while still others require that the whistleblower's beliefs are "justified" and "true."[59] It would be difficult to argue that some sort of evidentiary standard should not exist before you are morally obligated to externally blow the whistle, or morally permitted to blow the whistle at all for that matter.

Some have questioned the limits, however, over the evidentiary requirement and do not believe that whistleblowers are required to have enough evidence to convince others of the wrong in question.[60] While you should not blow the whistle based on mere suspicion, guess, or hunch, and you should take steps to gather as much evidence as you can,[61] the view that "documented" evidence must also exist should be seen as being too strict. Instead of requiring "documented" evidence, the less stringent legal test of "reasonable belief" might be subscribed to.[62] In other words, you should hold a reasonable belief that the misconduct is taking place based on first-hand knowledge.

It should be the case that appropriate responsibility can also be expected of and placed upon the media or government regulators to engage in proper fact-finding and confirmation before any misconduct is reported to the general public. Libel laws and accusations of lack of due process would hopefully ensure some protection against erroneous claims being made by either the media or government based on a whistleblower's report. The requirement of internal whistleblowing will also act as an evidentiary screening mechanism by providing the firm with the opportunity to properly investigate and then verify or dispute the evidentiary basis of the claim being made before it goes public. Therefore requiring documented evidence for external whistleblowing is too stringent.[63] The next criterion would therefore be as follows:

> *Reasonable evidence or belief of misconduct based on first-hand knowledge should exist before misconduct is reported externally.*

Make a difference

Another criterion that should be met before reporting misconduct might be referred to as the "Make a Difference Principle," in other words, you have good reason to believe that externally blowing the whistle will lead to changes in the firm's practices. This criterion would be based on *utilitarianism*, meaning there is a likelihood of net positive consequences to all those affected resulting from the whistleblowing. For example, some might require that: "it is reasonably certain that external whistleblowing will prevent the wrong"[64] or that "whistleblowing has some chance of success."[65] Others, however, disagree by arguing that if applied, this criterion would prevent whistleblowing from ever becoming morally obligated.[66] While empirical research shows that the vast majority of employees (79%) who blow the whistle believe that corrective action will take place,[67] it's not clear what percent erroneously decide not to blow the whistle because they believe changes in practice will not take place.

The assertion for the requirement that employees should have "good reasons" to believe that external whistleblowing will result in changes in practice is too stringent. If internal whistleblowing has already taken place up to the board of directors with no changes being effected, then we might reasonably expect that even the media or government regulators will face a challenge in causing the firm to change its practices as well. It is simply too great a hurdle to require employees to first have "good reasons" to believe that external whistleblowing will likely lead to change, as opposed to merely *hoping* that things will change. It would be ethically offensive that a major corporate scandal involving loss of life resulted from an employee not acting because he or she believed that there was a low likelihood of any changes taking place through reporting the misconduct. In addition, at the very least, the fact that there was a whistleblowing report that was not acted upon could be used later on with respect to punishing those (e.g., firm executives or government regulators) who did not act appropriately after receiving the information, which can hopefully deter similar inaction in the future. For all of these reasons, the "Make a Difference Principle" will not be included as one of the requirements for whistleblowing.

Legal protections

The concern over the potential harm to the whistleblower for reporting misconduct is a valid one. In other words, the chance of being successful must be worth the risk a whistleblower takes and the dangers to which they expose themselves.[68] As a result, laws protecting whistleblowers must also exist.[69] Similar to the requirement of anti-retaliation policies existing for morally obligated whistleblowing, the concern for the well-being of the whistleblower is partially addressed in the next criterion for whistleblowing as follows:

> *Unless you are a professional working within the firm, legal protections against retaliation for employees that blow the whistle externally must exist and be effective (i.e., enforced) in order for external whistleblowing ever to be morally required.*

If an employee decides to blow the whistle externally when *no* legal protection exists (e.g., for private firms), this is the point where such actions should be labelled as not only morally permissible but supererogatory, that is, going above and beyond one's moral duty. These acts are what we often label as morally heroic. This criterion might therefore be looked upon as an exempting condition with respect to the moral obligation to blow the whistle externally. The employee, after doing all he or she can do internally to rectify the misconduct, due to a lack of legal protection against retaliation, should not be morally compelled to place the interests of others who might be harmed by the company's actions before his or her own interests as well as the interests of the employee's family.[70] This action is similar to placing your entire financial, mental, and physical well-being at risk in order to save the lives of others. We should not therefore morally criticize an employee who does not blow the whistle externally when there are insufficient legal protections. Such an employee, however, if required to be involved in the misconduct or in a cover up, would at that point have a moral obligation to *quit* the firm after first finding another position elsewhere to avoid becoming an accomplice in harming or wronging others.

The only exception to this criterion is with respect to professionals (e.g., engineers, lawyers, accountants) working within a firm.[71] Due to their professional codes of ethics, professionals possess additional ethical obligations to prevent harm to society, even when their own personal self-interests are at stake.[72] Professionals are aware of this obligation upon receiving their professional designations, and are therefore aware of the risks of working for a firm that is engaged in misconduct that can harm society. Employees who are not professionals with inherent additional ethical obligations should not be held to the same standard in terms of being morally obligated to blow the whistle externally when no legal protections exist.

This position is in alignment with that proposed by others: "if an employee has compelling evidence of organizational misconduct, he or she has a duty to blow the whistle *unless* that person has reason to believe that his or her own dignity would be seriously harmed by doing so."[73] Due to the empirical research on the high likelihood of negative implications of blowing the whistle,[74] along with the current lack of legal protections,[75] the suggested legal protection criterion provides at least some protection for the whistleblower against otherwise being morally required to risk seriously harming his or her personal well-being.

To summarize, the proposed criteria in order for external whistleblowing to be morally obligatory consist of the following:

1. Misconduct has taken place or is expected to take place that seriously violates the law or involves serious physical harm, serious psychological harm, serious financial harm, serious infringement of basic moral rights, or a serious injustice.
2. Reasonable evidence or belief of misconduct based on first-hand knowledge can be provided.

3. Misconduct must first be reported internally whenever feasible to your direct supervisor and if no action is taken, all the way up to the board of directors or through the designated reporting channel if one exists (e.g., compliance or ethics officer).
4. Unless one is a professional, an effective written anti-retaliation policy must exist at the firm.
5. Unless one is a professional, effective legal protections against retaliation for employees must exist.

Proposed Criteria for *Internal* Whistleblowing

While the discussion up to this point focuses on the moral permissibility or moral obligation of *external* whistleblowing, it should also be pointed out how the proposed criteria would apply to *internal* whistleblowing, which as previously indicated is much more common than external whistleblowing.

Internal whistleblowing should always be considered morally *permissible* as long as the first three criteria are met. In terms of the first criterion with respect to internal reporting, harm need not be considered "serious" in nature by the employee. Any potential ethical misconduct should be included, including any misconduct involving a violation of the firm's code of ethics if one exists. For example, the harm criterion could be broadened substantially in terms of the moral permissibility of internal whistleblowing to include other less serious types of harm to the firm including padding expense accounts, taking kickbacks from suppliers, or accepting large unreported gifts from suppliers.[76] Based on a broader harm criterion, reporting activity internally is morally permitted if the activity is against the law or causes harm to individuals or serious harm to the company.[77] Internal whistleblowing above your supervisor should *always* be considered morally permissible as long as any misconduct or harm (physical or financial) is or is about to take place, if reasonable belief of the misconduct or potential misconduct exists, and if you have already reported the matter to your supervisor when feasible.

If the firm has an effective anti-retaliation policy in place, then you would be *morally obligated* under such circumstances to blow the whistle internally. As a professional, you would be morally obligated to internally blow the whistle if only the first three criteria are met, even when there is no effective anti-retaliation policy in place. In other words, business firms should not require employees in their codes of ethics to blow the whistle internally (the failure of which can lead to dismissal) unless business firms are prepared to take the necessary steps to ensure that their employees will be protected against reprisals for doing so. If an employee decides to blow the whistle internally on wrongdoing without guaranteed protections from the firm against reprisals, they have simply acted in a morally praiseworthy (but non-obligatory) manner.[78]

Table 5.1 Criteria for morally permissible or obligatory whistleblowing.
(*Source*: Hoffman and Schwartz, 2015. Reproduced with the permission of Springer.)

	Criteria for Whistleblowing	
	Internal whistleblowing	External whistleblowing
Morally permissible	1. Misconduct 2. Reasonable belief 3. Internal reporting	1. Serious harm 2. Reasonable belief 3. Internal reporting
Morally obligatory	1. Misconduct 2. Reasonable belief 3. Internal reporting 4. Anti-retaliation policy	1. Serious harm 2. Reasonable belief 3. Internal reporting 4. Anti-retaliation policy 5. Legal protection

Table 5.1 summarizes the criteria in relation to morally permissible/ obligatory and internal/external whistleblowing.

Application of Criteria

In order to preliminarily evaluate the practicality of the proposed criteria, let's apply the criteria to several classic business ethics cases including Dennis Gioia and the Ford Pinto, Sherron Watkins of Enron, and Dr Jeffrey Wigand of Brown & Williamson.

Dennis Gioia and the Ford Pinto[79]

In the 1970s, the Ford Motor Company manufactured its Pinto vehicle, only to discover through later testing that its rear placed fuel tank could explode due to impact from other vehicles even at low speeds.[80] It was expected that numerous deaths and serious burns would result from the fuel tank defect unless the vehicle was recalled. In such a case, we can argue that a Ford employee or manager, such as Dennis Gioia who was Ford's recall coordinator at the time, would only have been morally *permitted* to blow the whistle externally (which would also have been a morally praiseworthy act), but would not have been morally *obligated* to do so.

Gioia became aware that there was clear potential for serious physical *harm* to the users of the vehicle (first criterion), *reasonable belief* that the defect existed (second criterion), while *reporting internally* was irrelevant since even senior management was aware of the defect and had decided to continue to manufacture the vehicle (third criterion). One might assume, however, that

Ford did not possess any *anti-retaliation policy* at the time (fourth criterion), and that *legal protections* against retaliation for whistleblowing were non-existent (fifth criterion). For the latter two reasons, employees would not have been obligated to blow the whistle either internally or externally, although it would have been morally praiseworthy to do so.

Ford engineers, however, including possibly Gioia with his engineering degree, would have been morally *obligated* to blow the whistle internally up to the Board of Directors even if no effective anti-retaliation policy existed (fourth criterion), and externally against Ford despite any lack of effective legal protections (fifth criterion). This duty to report would be based on their additional professional ethical obligations as professional engineers to protect society from harm. Although not obligated to blow the whistle externally, any Ford employee who might be complicit in covering up the defect from the public would be morally obligated to quit Ford once another job was found.[81]

Sherron Watkins and Enron

Enron grew to become one of the world's major energy companies, with over 20,000 employees and revenues of over US$100 billion in 2000. The company went bankrupt, however, in 2001 as the result of an accounting fraud. According to our proposed criteria, Sherron Watkins of Enron, as a professional accountant and former Vice President of Finance at the firm, was morally *obligated* to blow the whistle both internally and externally based on the fraud taking place.[82] In terms of the first criterion, there was a reasonable expectation held by Watkins that if no action was taken immediately, Enron would financially "implode," leaving employees and shareholders in a serious and precarious financial situation. This would be considered to constitute significant financial harm leading to a potential obligation to blow the whistle internally.

In terms of the second criterion, Watkins had more than reasonable evidence. As Watkins reported her concerns directly to Kenneth Lay, who was not only the CEO but was also the Chairman of the Board of Directors, and no action was taken (even after receiving guidance from a law firm), the third criterion of internal reporting was also met (although Watkins might have also taken her concerns to the Board's audit committee). With respect to the fourth criterion, although an effective anti-retaliation policy did not clearly exist at Enron, as a Certified Public Accountant (i.e., professional) working within the firm, this criterion would not act as an exempting condition, and she would have to be prepared to face the personal consequences that would result from whistleblowing.[83] In terms of the fifth criterion, although sufficient legal protections did not exist to protect her at the time, once again as a professional she would still need to report externally regardless of the repercussions.[84] In summary, Watkins was morally obligated to blow the whistle internally and externally as well (which might, however, have taken place anonymously) despite the apparent lack of anti-retaliation protections for whistleblowers.[85]

Dr Jeffrey Wigand and Brown & Williamson

Dr Jeffrey Wigand, former Vice President of Research and Development at the US tobacco firm Brown & Williamson, had much to lose by blowing the whistle on his firm.[86] Dr Wigand was receiving a significant salary, and had a child who required expensive medical care covered through his firm's health benefits. Dr Wigand also at one point signed an expanded confidentiality agreement with his firm. Dr Wigand had become aware, however, that the company was intentionally manipulating its tobacco blend by adding the chemical coumarin, which increased the level of addiction and danger to the users of its already dangerous product. While the additional harm was not clear, we can argue that the product, if even more addictive and dangerous, did represent significant potential harm to the users (first criterion). Dr Wigand had reliable first-hand evidence (second criterion), and had reported his concerns internally to the CEO, which were ignored (third criterion).

On this basis, it was morally permissible and morally praiseworthy for Dr Wigand to externally blow the whistle to the news television program *60 Minutes*, but not morally obligatory due to the lack of an effective anti-retaliation policy (fourth criterion) and the lack of legal protections for blowing the whistle (fifth criterion). In other words, Dr Wigand was not morally required to sacrifice his job, his career, and put his own family's health coverage at risk, even though he had information that might indirectly save additional lives. This would not be true, of course, if Dr Wigand were subject to higher ethical standards by being a member of a profession,[87] which demanded that he protect the public from harm.[88]

Implications

Any proposed set of criteria that renders external whistleblowing obligatory will be subject to criticism, exceptions, and potential modifications due to changes in practical reality. Various commentators have provided the business and academic communities with various sets of normative criteria for external whistleblowing. Everyone rejects the position that external whistleblowing is *always* morally justifiable, and everyone also rejects the position that external whistleblowing is *never* morally justifiable. Due to the high likelihood of negative consequences to the whistleblower, however, such as being fired, blackballed in the industry, denied promotions, or becoming a target for revenge, according to all commentators the decision to report wrongdoing by an employee cannot be taken lightly and precautions should be undertaken.[89]

Should we be obligated to lose our job, be harassed, or blackballed from our industry, in order to save the lives of others or protect them from serious physical or financial harm? Is this not similar to the basic life-saving ethical dilemma of whether we can be morally compelled to put ourselves at risk in order to save someone else? Our answer to this question may determine where on the spectrum we fall in terms of the moral obligation to blow the whistle externally, and the sort of criteria we should reflect upon. The issue becomes more complex when a situation is faced whereby the firm might go bankrupt due to a scandal being disclosed. Should we be required to blow the whistle externally to protect someone from being seriously physically harmed by our company, if the expected result is that thousands might lose their jobs and tens of thousands of shareholders might lose their wealth?

The answer to both of these questions should be "yes", but would typically be "no" as matters currently stand today due to the lack of effective anti-retaliation policies at many firms,[90] and insufficient legal protections in many jurisdictions.[91] Unlike other proposed criteria, I would also impose corresponding ethical obligations on business firms and governments as well. First, firms have an ethical obligation to ensure that there are proper whistleblowing channels for their employees.[92] Such whistleblowing channels should provide for anonymity when desired, confidentiality whenever possible, guaranteed protections against harassment and retaliation, due process taking place during investigations, and there must be a follow-up with the employee who has blown the whistle on the outcome. There must also be a designated individual who receives the complaints (e.g., compliance or ethics officer) who then reports not to the CEO but directly to the board's audit committee consisting of independent (non-executive) directors.

Second, there should be an ethical obligation placed on governments around the world to ensure that proper legal whistleblowing protection is in place and is being properly enforced for employees of all firms, including both public and private firms. While progress on both of these fronts has taken place over the years (e.g., US *False Claims Act*, *Sarbanes Oxley Act*, *Dodd-Frank Act*, UK *Public Interest Disclosure Act*, and Canada's *Criminal Code*[93]), there is certainly room for improvement. It is only when firms establish effective internal whistleblowing channels for their employees with effective anti-retaliation policies (the fourth criterion) and when there is effective government legislation to protect external whistleblowers (the fifth criterion) will we be able to argue that non-professional employees are morally obligated to blow the whistle externally when the proposed criteria as set out above are otherwise met.

If firms were to take reasonable steps to ensure that they possess an ethical corporate culture (discussed next in Chapter 6), then the vast majority of instances of potential internal and external whistleblowing of misconduct may become greatly reduced. Research supports the proposition that "strong ethical cultures" diminish organizational misconduct and thereby the need for employees to blow the whistle internally or externally.[94] While employees based on the criteria proposed previously may on rare occasions have a moral obligation to blow the whistle externally, firms through their boards of directors and senior management possess a contemporaneous ethical obligation to ensure that their employees work within an organization that has a strong ethical corporate culture that reduces the need for whistleblowing while simultaneously protecting those employees who do choose to blow the whistle. Ultimately, employees need to have complete confidence that they can internally report wrongdoing to their managers without the risk of harm or retaliation.

If external whistleblowing is going to take place, certain practical steps should first be undertaken given the repercussions that can be expected. First, you need to confirm that you have your family's support. It will not be an easy process, and you need to know that your loved ones are behind your decision. Second, you should contact a lawyer who can advise you of any potential legal ramifications of externally blowing the whistle. Third, if at all possible, you should first find another job before blowing the whistle, since there is a high likelihood you will lose your job or otherwise face harassment. Fourth, you should report anonymously if this is possible to reduce the likelihood of repercussions taking place. Fifth, you should document everything since the basis of your claim will likely be raised as an issue. Finally, you should find others to come forward with you if possible, since it will be more difficult (although not impossible) to fire several employees rather than only one.

Chapter Summary

This chapter provides a normative framework by which to decide if it is ethically justifiable to report misconduct, both internally within the employee's firm, and externally outside the firm to government regulators or the media. In terms of reporting misconduct externally, this only becomes obligatory under rare circumstances including a situation involving serious potential *harm*, when you have a reasonable *belief* the misconduct is taking place, when *internal reporting* has already been attempted, and when there is an *anti-retaliation* policy as well as *legal protections* against retaliation.

Going back to the beginning of the chapter, the employee would seem to have an obligation to report the activity to a higher level internally within the organization. The potential harm is serious in terms of indirectly funding terrorist activities, and she seemed to have a reasonable belief that there might be a serious problem. If nothing was done internally, she would only have an obligation to report the potential misconduct externally if there was an anti-retaliation policy at her firm, and there were sufficient legal protections for her, which was not likely the case. She could nevertheless externally report the misconduct, which would have been a heroic and praiseworthy act on her part.

Now that the specific ethical dilemma of reporting misconduct through whistleblowing has been considered, Chapter 6 will discuss what managers and firms can do to develop and sustain an *ethical corporate culture*, which will hopefully lessen the extent of misconduct taking place in the first place.

Notes

1. This was an actual dilemma from a former MBA student. As the economy was terrible and the student needed her job, she chose to say nothing. The cash transfers continued and it was never known what they were being used for. The student still wonders what would have happened if the authorities had been notified and whether the funds were actually used for illicit terrorist activities.
2. Hartman and Desjardin (2008, p. 128).
3. See: Richard W. Stevenson, "G.E. Guilty Plea in U.S. Aid to Israel," *The New York Times*, July 23, 1992, http://www.nytimes.com/1992/07/23/business/company-news-ge-guilty-plea-in-us-aid-to-israel.html (accessed 9 September 2016).
4. See: Thomas S. Mulligan and Chris Kraul, "Texaco Settles Race Bias Suit for $176 Million," *Los Angeles Times*, November 16, 1996, http://articles.latimes.com/1996-11-16/news/mn-65290_1_texaco-settles-race-bias-suit (accessed 9 September 2016).
5. See: Louise Jury, "Saved from the Shredder in a Swiss Bank: Are the Victims Still Alive?" *Independent*, December 6, 1997, http://www.independent.co.uk/news/world-saved-from-the-shredder-in-a-swiss-bank-are-the-victims-still-alive-1287404.html (accessed 9 September 2016); Chelsea J. Carter, "Swiss-Bank Whistle-Blower Pays a High Price," *Los Angeles Times*, March 4, 2001, http://articles.latimes.com/2001/mar/04/local/me-33054 (accessed 9 September 2016). Meili eventually returned to Switzerland in 2009 after his wife and his two children moved there following their divorce. See: Swissinfo website, "Christoph Meili Returns – As Hero or Villain?" April 9, 2009, http://www.swissinfo.ch/eng/christoph-meili-returns—as-hero-or-villain-/7330344 (accessed 9 September 2016).
6. See: Gary Schwitzer, "Medical Research Ethics Whistleblower Nancy Olivieri Honored Again," *HealthNewsReview*, May 31, 2012, http://www.healthnewsreview.org/2012/05/medical-research-ethics-whistleblower-nancy-olivieri-honored-again/ (accessed 9 September 2016).

7. See: BBC News, "Profile: HSBC Whistleblower Hervé Falciani," February 9, 2015, http://www.bbc.com/news/world-europe-31296007 (accessed 9 September 2016). See also: Robert Chalmers, "Hervé Falciani: HSBC Switzerland Was a Tax Haven in Itself," *Newsweek*, April 24, 2015, http://www.newsweek.com/2015/05/01/herve-falciani-hsbc-switzerland-was-tax-haven-itself-324768.html (accessed 9 September 2016).

8. See: Rita Rubin, "Pfizer Fined $2.3 Billion for Illegal Marketing in Off-Label Drug Case," *USA Today*, September 3, 2009, http://usatoday30.usatoday.com/money/industries/health/2009-09-02-pfizer-fine_N.htm (accessed 9 September 2016).

9. See: BBC News, "VW Scandal: Company Warned Over Test Cheating Years Ago," September 27, 2015, http://www.bbc.com/news/business-34373637 (accessed 9 September 2016). See also: Jack Ewing, "VW Whistle-Blower's Suit Accuses Carmaker of Deleting Data," *The New York Times*, March 14, 2016, http://www.nytimes.com/2016/03/15/business/energy-environment/vw-diesel-emissions-scandal-whistleblower.html (accessed 9 September 2016).

10. BBC, "Panama Papers: Source Breaks Silence on Mossack Fonseca Leaks," May 6, 2016, http://www.bbc.com/news/world-latin-america-36232142 (accessed 9 September 2016).

11. See: Ghillyer (2012, p. 135).

12. See: Jonathan Peterson, "Whistle-Blower in GE Scandal Gets $13 Million," *Los Angeles Times*, December 5, 1992, http://articles.latimes.com/1992-12-05/business/fi-1438_1_ge-employee (accessed 9 September 2016).

13. See: Christopher Drew, "Military Contractor Agrees to Pay $325 Million to Settle Whistle-Blower Lawsuit," *The New York Times*, April 2, 2009, http://www.nytimes.com/2009/04/03/business/03whistle.html (accessed 9 September 2016).

14. See: CBS News, "IRS Pays Whistleblower Bradley Birkenfeld $104 Million," September 12, 2012, http://www.cbsnews.com/news/irs-pays-whistleblower-bradley-birkenfeld-104m (accessed 9 September 2016).

15. See: Appendix D for a summary of other Hollywood movies addressing business ethics dilemmas.

16. Ethics Resource Center (2014).

17. See: Freshfields Bruckhaus Deringer, "Fair Game or Foul Play: Tackling the Rising Tide of Global Whistleblowing," http://www.freshfields.com/uploadedFiles/SiteWide/News_Room/News_/02268_MBD_MBD_Whistleblower_Interactive%20PDF_AW2.pdf (accessed 9 September 2016).

18. See: Webley (2011, p. 22).

19. U.S. Sentencing Commission, "Organizations Receiving Fines or Restitution." *Sourcebook for Federal Sentencing Statistics*, 2015, http://www.ussc.gov/research-and-publications/annual-reports-sourcebooks/2015/sourcebook-2015 (accessed 9 September 2016). See also: Ethics Resource Center (2014).

20. Association of Certified Fraud Examiners, *Report to the Nations on Occupational Fraud and Abuse: 2014 Global Fraud Study*, http://www.acfe.com/rttn/docs/2014-report-to-nations.pdf (accessed 9 September 2016).

21. Association of Certified Fraud Examiners, *Report to the Nations on Occupational Fraud and Abuse: 2014 Global Fraud Study*, p. 19.

22. Association of Certified Fraud Examiners, *Report to the Nations on Occupational Fraud and Abuse: 2014 Global Fraud Study*, p. 21.
23. Ethics Resource Center (2014, p. 13).
24. Ethics Resource Center (2014, p. 45).
25. Ethics Resource Center (2012, p. 5).
26. This includes: Bowie (1982); Davis (1996); Lindblom (2007); De George (2010); Hoffman and McNulty (2010); and Velasquez (2012).
27. See: Velasquez (2012, p. 428).
28. The focus will be on the arguments as expressed by one of the most important business ethics commentators, Richard De George, in his classic textbook *Business Ethics* (2010, pp. 298–318). Although De George's 7th edition of *Business Ethics* (2010) is referred to, his criteria have not changed significantly from his first edition in 1982.
29. See: Dalhousie University website, "Convocation: Nancy F. Olivieri, May 2012 Honorary Degree Recipient," http://www.dal.ca/academics/convocation/ceremonies/honorary_degree_recipients/hon_degree_2012/nancy_olivieri.html (emphasis added) (accessed 9 September 2016).
30. Lindblom (2007); Duska (2009).
31. The classic example used to counter an unlimited right to free speech is that no one is morally entitled to scream "fire" in a crowded movie theater when there is no fire.
32. See: De George (2010, p. 299). Based on this fundamental notion, De George restricts his initial discussion to external whistleblowing by "employees of profit-making firms" that produce a product or provide a service that "threatens to produce serious bodily harm to the public in general, to employees, or to individual users of the product." See: De George (2010, p. 301).
33. De George (2010, p. 304). Such initial principles lead to De George's three criteria or conditions under which external whistleblowing can be considered to be morally *permissible*:

    1. "The firm, through its product or policy, will do serious and considerable harm to employees or to the public, whether in the person or the user of its product, an innocent bystander, or the general public.
    2. Once employees identify a serious threat to the user of a product or to the general public, they should report it to their immediate superior and make their moral concern known. Unless they do so, the act of whistle-blowing is not clearly justifiable.
    3. If one's immediate superior does nothing effective about the concern or complaint, the employee should exhaust the internal procedures and possibilities within the firm. This usually will involve taking the matter up the managerial ladder and, if necessary – and possible – to the board of directors."

    De George's next two conditions, in addition to the previous three, lead to a moral *obligation* to externally blow the whistle:

    4. "The whistle-blower must have, or have accessible, documented evidence that would convince a reasonable, impartial observer that one's view of the situation is correct, and that the company's product or practice poses a serious and likely danger to the public or user of the product.

5. The employee must have good reasons to believe that by going public the necessary changes will be brought about. The chance of being successful must be worth the risk one takes and the danger to which one is exposed."

34. De George (2010, p. 306).
35. De George (2010, p. 306).
36. Bowie (1982).
37. In terms of financial motives, the issue is, however, potentially more relevant today in light of the US *Dodd-Frank Act* of 2011 which provides for significant monetary payouts to whistleblowers who report directly to the US Securities and Exchange Commission (SEC) even if they don't report internally within their own firms. The primary concern is that providing monetary incentives may motivate and thereby prevent many employees from reporting misconduct internally before going to the SEC. (See: Gilley and Hoffman, 2011 for a debate over this issue.)
38. De George (2010, p. 307).
39. De George (2010, p. 307).
40. Velasquez (2012, p. 430).
41. Davis (1996, p. 10).
42. Hoffman and McNulty (2010, p. 51).
43. Ethics Resource Center (2012, p. 14).
44. Ethics Resource Center (2012, p. 15).
45. For example, De George states (2010, p. 308): "The notion of serious harm might be expanded to include serious financial harm, as well as kinds of harm other than death and serious threats to health and body."
46. For example, see: James (1990).
47. This could include illegal practices such as tax evasion, anti-competitive practices, fraud, environmental pollution, or deceptive advertising.
48. Velasquez (2012).
49. James (1990, p. 294).
50. Davis (1996).
51. Velasquez (2012, p. 430).
52. Bowie (1982).
53. Ethics Resource Center (2012).
54. De George (2010, p. 303).
55. De George (2010, p. 313).
56. See: The National Whistleblowers Center website, http://www.whistleblowers.org (accessed 9 September 2016).
57. Velasquez (2012, p. 430).
58. See: Bowie (1982); Hoffman and McNulty (2010).
59. Davis (1996, p. 10).
60. Davis (1996, pp. 12–13).
61. James (1990, p. 297).
62. See: *U.S. Dodd-Frank Act of 2010*, https://www.sec.gov/about/laws/wallstreet reform-cpa.pdf (accessed 9 September 2016).
63. James (1990); Davis (1996).
64. Velasquez (2012, p. 430).

65. Bowie (1982, p. 143).
66. Davis (1996) refers to what he calls the "paradox of failure", i.e., since the history of whistleblowing demonstrates its general ineffectiveness in causing change, external whistleblowing will paradoxically never be morally obligated if we are required to be reasonably certain whistleblowing will make a difference. As a result, Davis argues that external whistleblowing: "… does not require [belief] that [the] revelation will prevent…the wrong" (Davis, 1996, p. 12).
67. Ethics Resource Center (2012, p. 5).
68. De George (2010, p. 311).
69. Hoffman and McNulty (2010) make it clear that legal protections, despite improvements over the years, remain insufficient or are not enforced leaving external whistleblowers extremely vulnerable to personal harm.
70. See: Vandekerckhove and Tsahuridu (2010).
71. For example, see: James (1990); Velasquez (2012).
72. For example, the National Society of Professional Engineers "Code of Ethics" states as its first "fundamental canon" the following: "Engineers, in the fulfillment of their professional duties, shall: (1) Hold paramount the safety, health, and welfare of the public." See: National Society of Professional Engineers website, "NAPS Code of Ethics," http://www.nspe.org/resources/ethics/code-ethics (accessed 9 September 2016).
73. Hoffman and McNulty (2010, p. 52, emphasis added).
74. Velasquez (2012).
75. Hoffman and McNulty (2010).
76. De George (2010, p. 312).
77. De George (2010, p. 313).
78. According to De George (2010), whether internal whistleblowing is morally required or obligatory can depend on other factors to be considered including the severity of the harm, your position within the firm and vis-à-vis the perpetrator, and the firm's policies including whether the code of ethics requires misconduct to be reported. See: De George (2010, p. 313).
79. See: Gioia (1992; 2011) and Malcolm Gladwell, "The Engineer's Lament," *The New Yorker*, May 4, 2015, http://www.newyorker.com/magazine/2015/05/04/the-engineers-lament (accessed 9 September 2016).
80. See: Hoffman (2001).
81. De George (2010) would come to a similar conclusion but for different reasons. De George does appear to indicate that despite the relatively low risk of harm "… it is not immoral not to make the safest automobile possible…" (De George, 2010, p. 307). The defect's potential seriousness of harm (i.e., death) suggests that his first criterion would be met. As mentioned, one might assume that the matter was already well known internally up to the most senior levels of management. There also appeared to be accessible, documented evidence that would convince an impartial observer that the Ford Pinto posed a serious danger to the users of the vehicle. However, De George's criterion of the likelihood of "making a difference" is not as clear. While De George asks the question: "Did anyone at Ford have an obligation to make known to the public the facts that Ford knew but did not make public?" (De George, 2010, p. 299), he unfortunately does not clearly answer

the question for the reader. But according to De George's criteria, Gioia and Ford's professional engineers might not be morally obligated to blow the whistle externally.

82. See: Swartz and Watkins (2003).

83. De George (2010) addresses the Enron case and appears to hold that Watkins was not morally obligated to blow the whistle externally. The primary reason is that it was not clear according to his criteria whether blowing the whistle would lead to any change ("… it is not clear that the investors and employees who suffered as a result of Enron's demise would have fared any better [by Watkins going public]" (De George, 2010, p. 316)). De George does later state, however, that "[Watkins] would have been morally permitted to go public" (De George, 2010, p. 316), suggesting he is prepared to extend his notion of "harm" to include serious financial harm as well as physical harm.

84. See: Sinzdak (2008).

85. Watkins was later recognized as one of three "Persons of the Year" by *Time* magazine for her internal whistleblowing efforts. See: Richard Lacayo and Amanda Ripley, "The Whistleblowers," *Time Magazine*, December 22, 2001, http://www.wanttoknow.info/021222time.personofyear (accessed 9 September 2016).

86. See: "Jeffrey Wigand on 60 Minutes," JeffreyWigand.com website, February 4, 1996, http://www.jeffreywigand.com/60minutes.php (accessed 9 September 2016).

87. For example, Wigand may have believed that as a research scientist he was a professional similar to lawyers and accountants and should therefore be held to a higher ethical standard when it comes to protecting society from harm.

88. According to De George's criteria, however, Dr Wigand might have assumed that there was little chance that blowing the whistle would lead to any changes of practice by tobacco companies, and thus for this reason alone he would not have been morally obligated to blow the whistle externally. The concern, however, is that even if legal protections exist for whistleblowers, De George's criteria would morally permit individuals (including professionals) to walk away from whistleblowing situations that could lead to the deaths of others simply because they do not have "good reasons" to believe that blowing the whistle externally will necessarily make a difference.

89. De George (2010, p. 303).

90. For example, see: Hassink *et al.* (2007).

91. See: Lewis (2008).

92. For US public firms, ensuring proper reporting channels is now a legal obligation under the *Sarbanes-Oxley Act*. See: U.S. Senate, *Sarbanes-Oxley Act 2002*, http://www.sec.gov/about/laws/soa2002.pdf (accessed 9 September 2016).

93. Canada's *Criminal Code* (Section 425.1) prohibits employers from retaliating or threatening to retaliate against employees who provide information to law enforcement officials. See: Government of Canada: Justice Laws Website, http://laws-lois.justice.gc.ca/eng/acts/C-46/page-89 (accessed 9 September 2016).

94. Ethics Resource Center (2014).

References

Bowie, N.E. 1982. *Business Ethics*. Englewood Cliff, NJ: Prentice Hall.

Davis, M. 1996. Some paradoxes of whistleblowing. *Business & Professional Ethics Journal*, 15: 3–19.

De George, R.T. 2010. *Business Ethics* (7th edn). New York: Prentice Hall.

Duska, R. 2009. Whistle-blowing and employee loyalty. In *Ethical Theory and Business* (8th edn) (T.L. Beauchamp, N.E. Bowie, and D.G. Arnold, eds). Upper Saddle River, NJ: Pearson Education, pp. 155–159.

Ethics Resource Center. 2012. *Inside the Mind of a Whistleblower*. Arlington, VA.

Ethics Resource Center. 2014. *2013 National Business Ethics Survey*. Arlington, VA.

Ghillyer, A. 2012. *Business Ethics Now*. New York: McGraw-Hill.

Gilley, M. and Hoffman, W.M. 2011. Will rewards for whistleblowers encourage ethical behavior? *The CQ Researcher*, 21: 409–432.

Gioia, D. 1992. Pinto fires and personal ethics: a script analysis of missed opportunities. *Journal of Business Ethics*, 11: 379–389.

Gioia, D. 2011. Reflections on the Pinto fires case. In *Managing Business Ethics: Straight Talk About How To Do It Right* (5th edn) (L.K. Treviño and K.A. Nelson, eds). Hoboken, NJ: John Wiley & Sons, Inc., pp. 98–101.

Hartman, L. and Desjardins, J. 2008. *Business Ethics: Decision-Making for Personal Integrity & Social Responsibility*. New York: McGraw Hill.

Hassink, H., de Vries, M., and Bollen, L. 2007. A content analysis of whistleblowing policies of leading European companies. *Journal of Business Ethics*, 75: 25–44.

Hoffman, W.M. 2001. The Ford Pinto. In *Business Ethics: Readings and Cases in Corporate Morality* (4th edn), 2001. (W.M. Hoffman, R.E. Frederick, and M.S. Schwartz, eds). New York: McGraw Hill, pp. 497–503.

Hoffman, W.M. and McNulty, R.E. 2010. A business ethics theory of whistleblowing: responding to the $1 trillion question. In *Whistleblowing: In Defense of Proper Action* (M. Arszulowicz, ed.). New York: Transaction Publishers, pp. 45–59.

Hoffman, W.M. and Schwartz, M.S. 2015. The morality of external whistleblowing: a commentary on Richard T. De George. *Journal of Business Ethics*, 127: 771–781.

James, G.G. 1990. Whistle blowing: its moral justification. In *Business Ethics: Readings and Cases in Corporate Morality* (4th edn), 2001. (W.M. Hoffman, R.E. Frederick, and M.S. Schwartz, eds). New York: McGraw Hill, pp. 291–302.

Lewis, D. 2008. Ten years of public interest disclosure legislation in the UK: are whistleblowers adequately protected? *Journal of Business Ethics*, 82: 497–507.

Lindblom, L. 2007. Dissolving the moral dilemma of whistleblowing. *Journal of Business Ethics*, 76: 413–426.

Sinzdak, G. 2008. An analysis of current whistleblower laws: defending a more flexible approach to reporting requirements. *California Law Review*, 96: 1633–1668.

Swartz, M. and Watkins, S. 2003. *Power Failure: The Inside Story of the Collapse of Enron*. New York: Doubleday.

Vandekerckhove, W. and Tsahuridu, E.E. 2010. Risky rescues and the duty to blow the whistle. *Journal of Business Ethics*, 97: 365–380.

Velasquez, M.G. 2012. *Business Ethics Concepts and Cases* (7th edn). Upper Saddle River, NJ: Prentice Hall.

Webley, S. 2011. *Corporate Ethics Policies and Programmes: UK and Continental Europe Survey 2010*. London, UK: Institute of Business Ethics.

Part Three

Practical Application

Chapter Six

Developing and Sustaining an Ethical Corporate Culture

We have now reflected on the descriptive question of *how* ethical decision making takes place in Chapters 1, 2, and 3. We have also considered the normative question as to how the moral reasoning process *should* take place in Chapter 4, along with the decision whether to report misconduct in Chapter 5. But now we need to shift to more *practical* or *instrumental* questions: what can be done by managers and executives to improve ethical decision making within their organizations? What steps can firms take to reduce the extent of misconduct from taking place in the first place and thereby the need to have it reported?

To answer these questions, this chapter provides a general framework for managers and their firms to help minimize the potential for unethical or illegal activity from occurring, that is, *developing* and *sustaining* an *ethical corporate culture*. An ethical corporate culture is the key component of the *organizational* factors discussed in Chapter 1 which can impact each stage of the ethical decision-making process including awareness, judgment, intention, and behavior. So how can firms through an ethical corporate culture prevent or minimize significant unethical behavior, while at the same time provide proper guidance to managers and employees in how to address day-to-day ethical dilemmas?

To begin to understand the nature and potential impact of ethical corporate culture, consider the following letter written by former investment banker Greg Smith after deciding to no longer work for his firm Goldman Sachs. In the end, Smith decided to quit based on the culture change at the bank that in his opinion no longer prioritized the clients' interests. Smith wrote the following in his letter in 2012 to the *New York Times*:[1]

> Today is my last day at Goldman Sachs. After almost 12 years at the firm – first as a summer intern while at Stanford, then in New York for 10 years, and now in London – I believe I have worked here long enough to understand the

Business Ethics: An Ethical Decision-Making Approach, First Edition. Mark S. Schwartz.
© 2017 John Wiley & Sons, Inc. Published 2017 by John Wiley & Sons, Inc.

trajectory of its culture, its people and its identity. And I can honestly say that the environment now is as toxic and destructive as I have ever seen it. To put the problem in the simplest terms, *the interests of the client continue to be sidelined in the way the firm operates and thinks about making money*. Goldman Sachs is one of the world's largest and most important investment banks and it is too integral to global finance to continue to act this way. The firm has veered so far from the place I joined right out of college that I can no longer in good conscience say that I identify with what it stands for. It might sound surprising to a skeptical public, but culture was always a vital part of Goldman Sachs's success. It revolved around teamwork, integrity, a spirit of humility, and always doing right by our clients. The culture was the secret sauce that made this place great and allowed us to earn our clients' trust for 143 years. It wasn't just about making money; this alone will not sustain a firm for so long. It had something to do with pride and belief in the organization. I am sad to say that I look around today and *see virtually no trace of the culture that made me love working for this firm for many years*. I no longer have the pride, or the belief…

Smith's letter highlights the importance of corporate culture to employees. The perceived shift from a focus on the clients' interests to the bottom line became the new cultural norm at Goldman Sachs, which apparently conflicted with Greg Smith's *moral value system* and his sense of *moral identity* discussed in Chapter 1. But how do we understand exactly what *ethical corporate culture* means, and how it might influence the actions of employees?

Corporate culture can be defined as the shared values, assumptions, and beliefs or "social glue" that holds the organization together.[2] Building on this general definition, an *ethical corporate culture* can be defined as *representing a "slice" or "subset" of the organization's broader culture and is maintained through an interplay and alignment of formal organizational systems [i.e., policies, leadership, authority structures, reward systems, training programs] and informal organizational systems [i.e., peer behavior and ethical norms].*[3] In terms of how an ethical corporate culture can lead to expected ethical behavior, employees can act consistently in accordance with the firm's ethical norms either through a *socialization* process (i.e., employees feel they are expected to behave accordingly) or an *internalization* process (i.e., employees adopt the ethical norms as their own).[4] The goal then is for firms to possess a "strong" ethical corporate culture (rather than a "weak" one) which increases the probability that employees will conform to desired ethical norms.[5]

While a vast array of potential solutions has been presented to address illegal and unethical activity,[6] many have argued that the presence of an *ethical corporate culture* is a necessary (although insufficient) condition if the extent to which illegal or unethical activity is taking place is to be minimized.[7] This position is at least initially supported by empirical evidence. For example, the *National Business Ethics Survey* of thousands of US employees found that in organizations with the strongest "ethical cultures" (versus the "weakest" ethical cultures), far fewer employees feel pressure to compromise standards (7% instead of 33%), rates of observed misconduct are much lower (30% instead of 89%), employees who observe misconduct are more likely to report it (only 6% in strong cultures did *not* report misconduct they observed instead of 48% in weak cultures), and those who report misconduct are less likely to experience retaliation (28% instead of 46%).[8]

One initial issue with respect to the goal of developing an ethical corporate culture is to ask whether its existence will actually make a difference with respect to *all* employees and managers. This position is clearly unrealistic, since illegal and unethical activity will always continue despite the existence of even an "ideal" ethical corporate culture. For example, there are many in the fraud prevention field who accept a "20-60-20" rule,[9] in other words, approximately 20% of a given workforce possess *strong moral character* and will always do the right thing (e.g., act legally or ethically) regardless of the circumstances or work environment. Another 20% possess *weak moral character* and will always engage in illegal or unethical behavior when the opportunity exists, the rewards are sufficient, and there is a perceived low likelihood of getting caught.

The remaining 60% of the workforce, however, while basically honest, may decide to engage in illegal or unethical behavior, depending on the strength of their *moral character* as well as the environment in which they work, based on the organizational factors discussed in Chapter 1 such as authority (managerial) pressure, peer pressure, opportunity, or reward systems,[10] or in the belief that they are acting in the best interests of their firm.[11] Such employees have been referred to as "fence sitters".[12] This position has support from researchers who believe that unfortunately the majority of employees can be socialized into behaving unethically.[13]

Turning this fact into a potential positive, it is this majority group of employees that can also potentially be influenced to do the "right thing" when they work within an ethical corporate culture, and thus these "fence sitters" are the real target for firms intending to develop an ethical corporate culture. In other words, the goal is to identify those measures that can help mitigate or minimize (as opposed to completely eliminate) the extent to which illegal or unethical activity is taking place within or on behalf of business firms. If a majority of employees are in fact influenced by their work environments with respect to their behavior, it becomes extremely important for board members, executives, and managers to understand how best to develop and sustain an ethical corporate culture. While recognizing that there may not be a "one size fits all" solution for all business organizations,[14] we can certainly propose that certain core elements should be in place at a minimum if firms are to have the greatest chance of developing and maintaining an ethical corporate culture.

So the key question becomes: "what are the key elements that are necessary to develop and sustain an ethical corporate culture?" Rather than providing a comprehensive "to do" list for organizations and their senior leaders, I will focus on three key elements or fundamental building blocks that must necessarily exist if crime, corruption, and other illegal or unethical activity within and on behalf of business firms by their agents is to be minimized through building an ethical corporate culture. The three elements are:

1. the existence of a set of *core ethical values* infused throughout the organization in its policies, processes, and practices;
2. the establishment of a *formal ethics program* (e.g., code of ethics, training, hotline, and an ethics officer); and
3. the continuous presence of *ethical leadership* (i.e., "tone at the top") as reflected by the board of directors, senior executives, and managers.

While each of these three elements is distinct, they also overlap, relate to, and potentially reinforce each other. Each of the three key elements necessary to develop and maintain an ethical corporate culture will now be discussed.

First Pillar: Core Ethical Values

Just as the presence of a strong current *moral value system* contributes to an individual's *moral character*, the existence and reinforcement of a set of *core ethical values* is critical to establishing an *ethical corporate culture*. In fact, corporate values have for a long time been referred to as the central dimension of an organization's culture.[15] An ethical corporate culture has in turn been recognized as important to ethical decision making.[16] Despite the recognized importance of core ethical values, however, research suggests that many employees perceive their firms as lacking ethical values. In a survey of 23,000 US employees, only 15% felt that they worked in a high-trust environment, only 13% had highly cooperative working relationships with other groups or departments, and only 10% felt that their organization held people accountable for results.[17]

Of course, several issues remain. For example, which set of core ethical values should a firm utilize? On what basis should the ethical values be selected? Should they be selected because they currently exist within the firm, or because their existence is desired? What happens when the core ethical values conflict with each other, or with the bottom line? Which should take priority?

Although there are a number of potential ethical values to choose from, we need to identify those ethical values which can be considered to be *universal* in nature. In other words, to the greatest extent possible, the selected ethical values should retain their significance despite differences in culture, religion, time, and circumstance. The ethical values should be accepted by a large number of diverse individuals and social groups as being of fundamental importance in guiding or evaluating behavior, actions, or policies.[18] To discover a set of universal ethical values, three separate sources were reviewed.[19] The sources included: (i) companies' codes of ethics; (ii) global codes of ethics; and (iii) the business ethics literature.[20] Based on these sources the following list of core ethical values was generated, each of which was discussed in Chapter 4:

1. *trustworthiness* (including honesty, promise-keeping, integrity, transparency, and loyalty);
2. *responsibility* (accountability, accept fault, don't blame others);
3. *caring* (including the notion of avoiding unnecessary harm);
4. *citizenship* (including notions of obeying laws, assisting the community, and protecting the environment);
5. *respect* (including notions of respect for human rights based on Kantianism); and
6. *fairness* (including procedural, distributive, and societal justice).

While in some cases the listed core ethical values if applied to business practices constrain the firm's self-interest (egoism), in other cases, their consistent application helps to ensure the long-term financial prosperity of the firm. What may be most important, however, is that the company's senior executives always make it very clear that when there is a conflict between the core ethical values (or the code of ethics) and the bottom line, *the ethical values must always take priority to profits.*

In terms of prioritization, Canadian Scotiabank CEO Brian Porter states in his letter introducing the bank's "Guidelines for Business Conduct" that ethics should take priority in decision making: "Doing the right thing, and acting with integrity, is essential to maintaining our good name – even when it is difficult, or seems to conflict with other priorities. Meeting sales goals or profitability targets is important, but absolutely nothing is more important than staying true to our values."[21] Johnson & Johnson is famous for its *Credo*, which prioritizes its responsibilities first to the users of its products and services before taking into account the interests of stockholders.[22] Regardless whether the application of ethical values always leads to profit maximization, it can be argued that all business firms, through their management, should attempt to *infuse* core ethical values and their prioritization over profits throughout their organizations as the basic starting point to establishing an ethical corporate culture. This infusion should take place within the firm's (i) policies, (ii) processes, and (iii) practices. Let's now look at each of these measures.[23]

Policies

First, the core ethical values must be made explicit in the firm's policy documents whenever possible.[24] The most important document in which the ethical values should be present is the firm's code of ethics with the values being stated upfront.[25] The values should also be included in the firm's annual report, public accountability statement, or social report, and should be indicated as clearly as possible on the initial homepage of the firm's website.[26] Johnson & Johnson's Credo for example can be found engraved in limestone in the lobby of the company's headquarters and hangs throughout the company's hallways and corridors.[27] The Credo can also be found after just one click on the company's homepage.[28]

Although being explicit about ethical values might expose a firm to additional critique from academics, the media, special interest groups, customers, or even employees,[29] this should be considered a necessary but insufficient step towards establishing an ethical corporate culture. Even firms such as Enron, despite explicitly displaying their core ethical values (including "integrity", "honesty", and "respect") on its office banners and training videos, failed to live up to them,[30] making it clear that the values must be incorporated into other processes and practices as well.[31]

Processes

The ethical values only become alive, leading to a more ethical corporate culture, when they are infused and observed to be operating throughout the firm's processes.[32] The first process involves hiring. Recruiting the right people and building an ethical reputation that precedes the organization's representatives wherever they go, can help avoid ethical problems.[33] There are various methods that can be used to build ethical values like honesty and integrity into the hiring process, such as testing and interviews. Questions such as "have you ever faced an ethical dilemma before? If so, how did you handle it?" have the potential to reveal an applicant's general level of awareness of ethical issues and perspective on ethical decision making. The answer "me? I don't think I've ever faced an ethical dilemma" suggests a lack of moral awareness and might represent a red flag during the hiring process.[34]

While concerns have been raised over the use and effectiveness of integrity testing,[35] this tool also remains an important measure for employers to screen out "executive psychopaths." Psychopaths, despite their "polish", "charm", and "cool decisiveness" are also "…cunning, manipulative, untrustworthy, unethical, parasitic, and utterly remorseless" which can make them dangerous to their companies due to their inability to feel any empathy, as noted in Chapter 2.[36] Ideally, the first stage of the hiring process should consist of an applicant demonstrating the possession of a set of core ethical values. This should be considered the filter or "gate" which a potential employee must first get through before other performance capabilities of the applicant are even considered.[37] In addition, firms might consider utilizing a group decision-making approach (as opposed to only using one-on-one hiring interviews) when hiring at the more senior levels, as this process might better facilitate raising ethical "red flags" regarding candidates.[38]

The values should also be part of any employee *orientation* process, such as *ethics training*. In this manner the organization's values and guiding principles can be communicated in its orientation programs. By providing ethics train-ing, the organization is communicating that it values ethical behavior and that ethical dimensions should be considered in all decision making.[39] *Performance appraisals* should also incorporate consideration of employees' behavior with respect to the ethical values, and represent an important component of the eth-ical culture. An effective performance management system plays a key role in alignment or misalignment of the ethical culture because employees pay close attention to what is measured, rewarded, and disciplined.[40] While it is some-times more difficult in a performance appraisal to measure behavior that con-forms to the ethical values, it may be easier to identify employees' actions that fail to reflect the values.

Decisions regarding *promotion* should also be based on the ethical values.[41] Employees who are promoted only on the basis of their financial performance when they have not lived up to the ethical values, only reinforces the percep-tion for other employees that the firm does not consider ethical values to be important; this can have a severe potential impact on the firm's ethical cor-porate culture.[42] It is only when employees observe that their colleagues are being rejected for promotion due to not living up to the firm's ethical values that the ethical values are taken seriously. *Disciplinary* or even *dismissal deci-sions* should also be based on whether the values are being lived up to. Possibly most important is that the firm aligns its *reward system*, including compensa-tion, as far as reasonably possible with the firm's ethical values.[43]

Practices

In general, if the firm has a set of core ethical values, it needs to be perceived to live up to them – that is, it must "walk the talk."[44] Without this general per-ception, the ethical values quickly become meaningless. To prevent this from occurring, there are a variety of practices that should explicitly incorporate the firm's values. In general, all decision making and behavior at all levels and functions should be based on the firm's ethical values, whenever possible. This would include not only executives, managers, and employees, but at the board of director's level as well.[45] Surveys of employees and customers should also attempt to include feedback on the performance of the firm and its agents with respect to the ethical values. All meetings, additional training efforts, and speeches (especially by senior executives) should make reference to the core ethical values. All these actions reinforce the core ethical values, helping to sustain an ethical corporate culture.

Another method is to build the ethical values into *stories* about the actions or decisions of employees, managers, or senior executives. Through organizational stories which can sometimes become part of a firm's mythology, greater meaning is given to the organizational culture.[46] This includes *positive stories*, whereby an employee, manager, or even the CEO acted consistently according to the values despite pressures to do otherwise. *Negative stories* are also important, whereby the firm failed to live up to its values but discussion then takes place as to why mistakes were made and how to avoid such mistakes in the future.

As an example, a bank employee was able to think outside of the "policy" box when a customer called asking for information on his 18-year-old daughter's recent debit card transactions.[47] The customer said his daughter was severely depressed and was missing. He was not yet able to call the police, since she had not yet been missing for more than 24 hours. The father was extremely concerned that his daughter might be suicidal. How would you have responded if you had been the bank employee at the call center? The bank's employee, who was just finishing a lengthy shift, considered ending the conversation by simply informing the client that unfortunately there was nothing she could do in terms of releasing the information about the daughter, given the bank's privacy regulations.

But instead of ending the phone call, the employee decided to elevate the request to a manager in the bank's security department. The bank then contacted the police after discovering the daughter had made a recent purchase at a pharmacy. The police fortunately found the daughter alone in a field near the pharmacy after taking an entire bottle of sleeping pills and were able to take her to the hospital in time where she recovered. Due to the bank employee's awareness of being in an ethical situation, she had managed to think outside of a "legalistic" frame and take additional steps that indirectly saved the daughter's life, while still maintaining the bank's privacy policies. The bank employee received an award from the bank, and the story became part of the bank's culture of always focusing whenever possible on the needs of the customer within legal requirements.

In another case, the exact opposite occurred. Southwest Airlines has a number of ethical values for its employees to follow, including: "Follow the Golden Rule"; "Treat others with respect"; "Put others first"; and "Demonstrate proactive customer service".[48] Just before a Southwest Airlines plane was about to take off, a very distressed passenger asked the flight attendant if she could call the police. The passenger's husband had just texted her saying that he was about to commit suicide. The airline's policy was that phone calls are not permitted during takeoff, and that the pilot should only be contacted if the safety of the passengers was directly involved. How would you have responded if you had been the flight attendant?

Instead of realizing the potential implications, the flight attendant "slapped" down the phone and insisted it be put on flight mode. Despite the passenger's pleas, the flight attendant denied her request to make an emergency call to the police during the flight and she never informed the pilot about the situation. The flight attendant was not able to think outside of the "policy" box of her training despite Southwest's core ethical values, and may have feared repercussions to herself of permitting the call or informing the pilot unnecessarily. The passenger called the police immediately upon landing and after arriving at her home discovered that her husband had in fact committed suicide.[49] While this is clearly an unfortunate and tragic outcome and a *negative* story for Southwest Airlines, the company might nonetheless learn from the experience to ensure that situations like this will hopefully never happen again.

Second Pillar: Formal Ethics Program

Most commentators agree that a formal, comprehensive ethics program is necessary to help establish and ensure an ethical corporate culture, particularly for larger organizations. While there are several definitions and types of ethics programs (e.g., compliance or integrity-based),[50] an *ethics program* can generally be defined as *the mechanisms in place at the firm including a code of ethics, ethics training, and a person responsible for the ethics program that help to ensure ethical behavior on the part of corporate agents.* Changing US regulations have now virtually made it a legal requirement for large firms or public firms through their boards of directors to ensure that they have such programs in place.

For example, the US *Federal Sentencing Guidelines for Organizations* (Guidelines), enacted by the US Sentencing Commission in 1991, may be applied when judges sentence organizations for violating US federal law. The Guidelines permit firms to have their fines reduced by federal judges if the firm is able to establish that they possessed an "effective compliance and ethics program" prior to the offence. The Guidelines, revised in 2004 and again in 2010, now state that to have an effective compliance and ethics program an organization "…shall promote *an organizational culture that encourages ethical conduct* and a commitment to compliance with the law" (emphasis added).[51] The Guidelines go on to identify the minimum requirements for a firm to be considered as possessing an "effective" program, including a code of ethics, ethics training, an individual responsible for the ethics program (e.g., an ethics officer), and a reporting system (e.g., a whistleblowing hotline) for improper behavior.[52]

What is not clearly provided are the details regarding each of the elements of the program. For example, although a code of ethics is necessary, what specific content should it include? How lengthy should the code be? Should the code merely be positive and aspirational in tone, or more specific and negative in tone? What about ethics training? Who should conduct it? What format should be used? What should a whistleblowing hotline involve? What protections should be given? Should employees be forced, with threat of discipline, for failure to blow the whistle? Given the lack of agreement over these issues, the following will review the key recommendations that have been provided in terms of: (i) the *development* of an ethics program (e.g., code of ethics); (ii) the *implementation* of the ethics program (e.g., ethics training); and (iii) the *administration* of the ethics program (e.g., ethics hotline/helpline, ethics officer, auditing effectiveness).[53]

Developing an ethics program

A code of ethics
The starting point for an ethics program is to ensure the existence of a distinct and formal document known as a code of ethics or code of conduct. One US survey firm found that 97% of firms of various sizes now have an employee code of conduct.[54] While we saw earlier in Chapter 1 that studies on codes are somewhat mixed as to whether they actually affect employee behavior,[55] one study found that while codes may not necessarily influence ethical behavior directly, they often do so in several indirect ways.[56]

For example, the code can act as: (i) a "sign-post," leading employees to consult other individuals or corporate policies to determine whether certain behavior is appropriate, part of the moral consultation stage discussed in Chapter 2; (ii) a "shield," allowing employees to better challenge and resist unethical requests from suppliers, customers, or even managers; (iii) a "smoke detector," leading employees to try to convince others and warn them of their inappropriate behavior; and (iv) as a "fire alarm," encouraging employees to contact the appropriate authority (e.g., the ethics office) and report violations as discussed in Chapter 5. Overall, codes should be considered a necessary component of any ethics program.

Code content
In terms of code content, as discussed, the code must explicitly indicate the firm's core set of ethical values.[57] With respect to possible code provisions, one study of the codes of 60 US companies found that over two-thirds of the

companies' codes included these topics which might serve as a basic initial template for code content:[58]

- Confidential information
- Conflicts of interest
- Equal employment, discrimination
- Gifts and entertainment
- Sexual harassment
- Anti-trust compliance
- Internet usage
- Use of organizational assets
- Financial reporting accuracy
- Intellectual property

- Employee substance abuse
- Health, environment, and safety
- Political campaign contributions
- Employee expense reporting
- Workplace relationships
- Monitoring employee e-mail
- Monitoring employee activity
- Government contracting
- Purchasing procedures

Nature of code content

When it comes to the nature of code content, many recommendations have been made, with empirical research suggesting a relationship between "high quality" code content and a more ethical and socially responsible corporate culture.[59] For example, codes of ethics must be written in easy-to-understand language,[60] and avoid being legalistic.[61] Codes should include relevant examples,[62] and avoid using too negative a tone (e.g., a series of "thou shalt nots").[63]

In one case, however, a bank manager I interviewed indicated that his company's code of ethics stated that "not all gifts are unacceptable" and whether to accept a gift "depends on the circumstances" and "whether a conflict of interest is created." This led the bank branch manager to conclude after reviewing his bank's code of ethics that it was acceptable for all of his branch employees including himself to each accept a small cash gift of $50 from a very wealthy client. The manager's reasoning was that the gift was given to all employees at Christmas time and therefore no conflict of interest was established from the monetary gift. The bank manager did not realize, however, that the bank also had another more specific policy that indicated that cash gifts were never acceptable. This example may suggest that sometimes codes of ethics should be negative in tone and sufficiently specific for certain types of activity.

Code content must also be relevant,[64] and should include expected behavior and sanctions for non-compliance.[65] While many have suggested that employees should be directly involved in the code creation process[66] in order to enhance the employees' sense of ownership over the code,[67] the major benefit may be that employee involvement increases the chances that the code's content will be relevant and realistic.[68]

Get support from senior management and the board of directors

One of the factors affecting code effectiveness is the necessity of employees knowing that senior management supports their company's code.[69] Ultimately it is an ethical obligation of members of the board of directors to fully support their firm's ethics program.[70] It's important for employees to hear management speak about the code, see their managers lead by example, and discover that managers know and understand the code.[71]

Application and sign-off process
In order for the code to be effective, it should be distributed and apply to everyone within the firm.[72] Some firms go further and recommend that share-holders, recruitment agencies, industry organizations, customers, and suppli-ers should also receive a copy of the code.[73] There is also a general consensus that in order for codes to be effective, they must be accompanied by a sign-off provision whereby employees acknowledge that they have read, understood, and/or complied with the code.[74] One US survey found that over half (57%) of the respondent firms require all employees to acknowledge the code annually.[75]

Others, however, raise concerns that this process might provoke possible cynicism among employees. Some of the concerns with the sign-off procedure include: general hesitation; the request of unions not to sign; lack of benefit; reflects lack of trust; and suggests "pushiness" on the part of their company.[76] Most suggest that requiring employees to sign off on the code is a good idea, primarily because it increases awareness and provides an incentive to read the document. It's also important that managers be perceived to take the sign-off process seriously in order for employees to take it seriously.[77]

Implementing an ethics program

Ethics training
Without sufficient ethics training, codes remain ineffective in influencing behavior.[78] To engage in training, firms are using a variety of methods includ-ing lectures, role-playing, online training, videos, ethical dilemmas, or cases.[79] While some still doubt the value of such training, others suggest that busi-ness ethics training improves ethical behavior.[80] One US survey found that the majority of organizations (69%) offer code training on an annual basis.[81]

The purpose of ethics training for employees is not merely to restate ethi-cal principles or examine the code of ethics, but more importantly to *sensitize* people to the circumstances in which those ethical principles could lie hidden and indistinct.[82] In other words, the main objectives of ethics training are to improve an employee's level of *moral competence* (Chapter 1) and to enhance *moral awareness* among employees, as the first stage of the ethical decision-making process (Chapter 2). Ethics training should be based as much as pos-sible on an examination of cases, preferably taken from real situations, and even more preferably taken from the experiences of those in the workshop. Various types of cases can be used during training including general scenarios reflecting ethical dilemmas faced by managers and employees where the ethical implications are not readily apparent.[83] While training has been perceived positively by most, too much training could be perceived by employees to be a waste of time and money, which may reduce the legitimacy of the code.[84] Essentially, training sessions provide the explanation required in order to raise employees' awareness of the code's usefulness by making the code more "real," or at least to indicate the importance the company attaches to the code.[85]

Ethics training might also include a "Giving Voice to Values" (GVV) component, which as a new educational approach is designed to provide employees with the confidence, skills, and "moral muscle" to "get done" what they already know to be right.[86] GVV is based on the idea that employees need to develop "scripts" or implementation plans, and practice delivery of those scripts. Working through actual dilemmas that have been faced by employees through role playing during ethics training can be crucial for employees to be prepared to act when faced with real ethical situations. Techniques such as enlisting allies, discussing issues one-on-one, working through incremental steps, finding win–win solutions, and appealing to shared purpose and values, can all make it easier to speak and act on one's values.[87] Through GVV ethics training, employees are more likely to transition from moral judgment and intention, to actual behavior as part of the ethical decision-making process discussed in Chapter 2. This might also include having the confidence and *moral courage* to approach managers with ethical concerns before deciding to blow the whistle externally as discussed in Chapter 5.[88]

The decision over who should conduct the training might have an impact on how employees perceive the code.[89] In general, ethics training should be conducted in-house (i.e., by managers or ethics officers) as opposed to being conducted by outside consultants.[90] Managers are generally perceived as understanding better the particular corporate culture, and therefore better equipped to do the training. Greater buy-in from employees may also be achieved when their manager conducts the training. There are several reasons, however, as to why an outside consultant, as opposed to a manager, should conduct training. Some managers may not have the ability to engage in code training or lack the legitimacy to conduct the training due to their own lack of ethics. In addition, discussion by employees during training sessions may not be as "open" if certain managers were to conduct the training.

Reinforcement

Reinforcement through websites, newsletters, department meetings, notices, e-mails, and executive speeches all play an important role in code effectiveness.[91] Without constant reinforcement, codes would tend to have only a minimal impact on employee behavior.[92] Reinforcement allows employees to perceive the seriousness and importance their company places on compliance with the code. Otherwise, the document becomes less of a concern, and more easily disregarded.[93]

Administering an ethics program

Appoint an administrator

In many large business firms, a person is typically appointed to the position of "ethics officer" or "compliance officer," who may oversee an entire staff within the firm's ethics office.[94] One US survey found that the most common job title (56%) for the person with overall responsibility for ethics is "(Chief) Ethics and Compliance Officer."[95] This person must be responsible for the ethics program's operations, and employees must have at least one number to call with day-to-day questions about the code's application. The designation of a person or the creation of an ethics office for larger organizations that employees can contact increases the chances that *moral consultation* will take place, one of the processes in the Integrated-EDM model discussed in Chapter 2.

In addition to appointing an ethics officer,[96] the board of directors must maintain responsibility for the ultimate oversight of the ethics program.[97] It is extremely important that the ethics officer has a direct channel to the board of directors, rather than just to the CEO, given the possibility the CEO or other senior executives may be engaged in misconduct themselves.[98] One survey found that more than half of the US ethics and compliance departments who responded report directly to the board, while approximately 25% report to the CEO.[99] Others recommend that the board of directors itself hires, fires, and sets the compensation of the chief ethics officer, rather than the CEO or other senior executives.[100]

Set up a reporting mechanism and enforcement

Following our discussion in Chapter 5, a mechanism for reporting misconduct must be set up by companies.[101] Protections against harassment and retaliation must be provided and lived up to. The ability to report anonymously and confidentially should also be provided whenever this is possible and practical. Employees should be informed of the result of their reporting whenever practical to do so. Caution, however, should be taken on setting up a reporting system which might evoke images of "Big Brother" and not be consistent with the corporate culture of many companies.[102] For this reason, firms might prefer to call their hotline a "helpline" to encourage employees to gain advice on ethical issues through *moral consultation* prior to mistakes being made.

In addition, consistent enforcement of the code as well as the communication of enforcement is essential to a code's effectiveness.[103] Without consistent and unbiased enforcement, the code may not be taken seriously,[104] with the perception of unfairness directly influencing the level of misconduct of observers.[105] The penalty applied to a code offender should also be fair and proportionate to the violation.[106]

Monitoring/auditing/revision

Finally, the effectiveness of the ethics program should be monitored, audited, and the program should be periodically revised.[107] One US survey found that 83% of respondents indicated that they perform compliance and ethics programs assessment.[108] To audit program effectiveness, firms might use regular and random testing of employees' adherence to the code.[109] In addition, employee surveys should be used to monitor the effectiveness, identify weaknesses, and make improvements to the code of ethics. Codes should also be updated periodically as new issues such as the use of the internet can arise.[110] All of these measures are part of developing a comprehensive and effective ethics program.

Ultimately, the ethics program should be based on the core ethical values discussed previously. However, a firm that possesses core ethical values infused throughout its policies, processes, and practices, even when supported by the establishment of a comprehensive ethics program, may still be insufficient.[111] The presence of *ethical leadership* is also necessary, as we will now see.

Third Pillar: Ethical Leadership

In addition to infusing a set of core ethical values throughout the organization and establishing a formal ethics program, there is a third pillar of an ethical corporate culture, which may ultimately be more important than the other elements: *ethical leadership*. To understand its significance, try to imagine what you would immediately do if faced with the following crisis situations if you were the CEO of the company:[112]

- As CEO of a major chemical producer, you discover that a poisonous gas leak from your pesticide plant in India has led to the deaths of thousands of squatters who were living close by. What do you do? Do you immediately accept responsibility? Do you fly to India and express deep concern? Do you remain in the United States and take a defensive stance? What are your other options?
- As CEO of a large oil company, you hear that one of your oil tankers has struck a reef off the coast of Alaska and a significant amount of oil is leaking. Do you go to Alaska right away? Or do you go on a television show and state that you are running a multi-billion dollar company and have more important issues to deal with?

- As CEO of a major global coffee chain you learn that a newspaper reporter wants to talk to you about the fact that one of your employees in Manhattan charged an ambulance crew $130 for three cases of bottled water that were needed for survivors of the 9/11 tragedy. What do you do? Do you ignore the reporter? Do you speak to the reporter and personally apologize to the ambulance crew? Do you identify and fire the employee?

In each of these cases, CEOs of prestigious high profile companies faced an ethical crisis that could threaten their firms' reputations. In 1984, the CEO of Union Carbide, Warren Anderson, after initially going to Bhopal, India, then claimed that the company's operations met all existing Indian legally mandated safety standards and instructed his firm to deny all liability. Eventually, in 2010 after a $470 million settlement and legal battles lasting more than 25 years, Indian executives of the company were convicted of causing death by negligence.[113] In 1989, Exxon's CEO did not go to Alaska even after hearing about the *Valdez* oil tanker, and was heavily criticized for this decision. Eventually Exxon had to pay billions in fines and settlements.[114] In 2001, the CEO of Starbucks, Howard Schultz ignored a reporter's request for an interview related to charging the ambulance crew for the bottled water on 9/11, leading to a news story and then a call for a consumer boycott of Starbucks. Only then was an apology provided by the CEO Schultz.[115] Now consider the following situations:

- As CEO of a major pharmaceutical firm, you are informed that seven people have died in the Chicago area from cyanide-laced capsules of one of your most popular drugs. How do you respond? Do you announce an investigation and promise to provide assistance to the police to identify the culprit? Do you issue an immediate local recall in the Chicago area only? Or do you immediately order a nation-wide recall at significant expense?
- As CEO of a major tuna canner, you discover that dolphins are getting caught in tuna nets and drowning as a result. The media is showing an interest in the issue. Animal rights activists are beginning a campaign. Do you ignore the complaints? Do you promise an investigation? Or do you commit the funds required to solve the problem and promise immediate action?

Unlike the first set of CEOs, this group responded quite differently when faced with an ethical crisis. In 1982, the CEO of Johnson & Johnson, James Burke, immediately ordered a costly nation-wide recall of Tylenol. Although the short-term costs were substantial and generated criticism from some business commentators, the Tylenol brand became one of the most trusted brands on the market.[116] In 1990, StarKist insisted on the design of fishing nets that did not trap dolphins, announced that the company would no longer purchase tuna captured in nets that trapped dolphins, then added "Dolphin-Safe" to their tuna can labels and in the process gained a significant competitive advantage over other tuna companies.[117]

Each of these examples demonstrates the importance of *ethical leadership*. Beyond infusing ethical values throughout the organization and developing a comprehensive ethics program, an ethical *tone at the top* must also exist in order to develop and sustain an ethical corporate culture.[118] In fact, many suggest that an ethical corporate culture is contingent upon ethical leadership. The moral tone of an organization is best set by top management which then provides ethical cues to the employees who observe what their bosses do.[119] In other words, leaders should provide the key source of ethical guidance for employees.[120] *Ethical leadership* can be defined as *demonstrating normatively appropriate conduct through personal actions and interpersonal relationships, as well as promoting conduct to employees through two-way communication, reinforcement, and ethical decision making.*[121] Ethical leaders are critical to establishing the presence of ethical values within an organization.[122]

The relationship between ethical leadership and ethical behavior has been observed. Perceptions of employees that their managers possess a set of core ethical values and act upon them, has been shown to have a significant impact upon the ethical corporate culture of the firm and the behavior of employees.[123] According to one study based on a survey of over 10,000 US employees, when the employees perceived that their supervisors and executives regularly paid attention to ethics, took ethics seriously, and cared about ethics and values as much as the bottom line, there was significantly less unethical/illegal behavior and greater awareness of ethical/legal issues, while employees were more likely to look for advice within the firm, deliver bad news to management, report ethical violations, and were more committed to the organization.[124] Another study also found employees' perceptions of the ethical culture of top management was more significant than perceptions of the ethical culture of direct supervisors or co-workers in terms of leading to reductions in pressures to compromise standards, less observed misconduct, increased reporting of observed misconduct, and less retaliation against those who reported misconduct.[125]

Despite the recognized importance of ethical leadership within business, there appears to be a perception that such leadership is lacking. For example, in a survey of over 1000 of its readers from around the world, *Harvard Business Review* magazine found that 76% of those surveyed had less trust in US senior management than they had the previous year, and 51% had less trust in senior management at non-US companies.[126] A Gallup survey of over 1000 US adults found that while 80% rated nurses "high" or "very high" for honesty and ethical standards, only 17% perceived business executives as having "very high" or "high" honesty and ethical standards, with 32% receiving a rating of "low" or "very low." The 17% rating for business executives was lower than for lawyers (21%) but at least higher than for car salespeople (8%).[127]

In Britain, over 1000 respondents were asked who they trusted. While doctors were trusted to tell the truth by 89% of the population, business leaders were trusted by only 34% of the public, with bankers being trusted by only 21%.[128] In Canada, only 11% of over 1000 Canadians sampled indicated they found CEOs extremely trustworthy, even less than auto mechanics at 16%.[129] The research suggests that there is significant room for improvement in society's perception of the ethical values of business leaders.

So how exactly do managers and executives exemplify ethical leadership? For larger firms, most employees will not have direct contact with their senior managers, and thus the firm's leaders must develop a reputation for ethical leadership. Various studies have examined how this reputation is developed. Some suggest that there are two dimensions to ethical leadership: a "moral person" dimension and a "moral manager" dimension.[130] The *moral person* dimension (e.g., the manager acts with integrity, honesty, and trustworthiness) is based on being observed to do the right thing, treating people with dignity and respect, showing concern and being open and listening, and by living a personally moral life.[131] The *moral manager* dimension is affected by communicating openly and regularly with employees about ethics and values, visibly role-modeling ethical conduct, and by applying the reward system to hold everyone accountable to the firm's standards.[132] If a leader is perceived as being a strong moral manager but a weak moral person, they would be seen as a hypocrite (i.e., they talk about the importance of ethics but do not act accordingly), thus managers must be perceived as being both strong moral managers and moral persons.[133]

Probably the most significant means of demonstrating ethical leadership, however, is to ensure that all decision making is in accordance with the ethical values as discussed previously. This becomes even more apparent when executives are seen to make such decisions even when there is a financial cost to the firm. In other words, the ethical values must be seen to take *priority* over other interests, or they quickly become irrelevant. In one famous example, at the age of 28, Arthur Andersen, the founder of his accounting firm, refused to yield to the questionable demands of an important railway client during an audit. He lost the client as a result, but when the client later went bankrupt, Arthur Andersen developed a personal reputation as someone who could be trusted to act with integrity.[134] This decision set an ethical tone for the Arthur Andersen firm for many years, leading to Arthur Andersen later acting as a watchdog over the entire US accounting industry. Unfortunately, such ethical behavior did not continue long term at Arthur Andersen, and eventually led to the firm's collapse when its corporate culture, especially in relation to its client

Enron, began to focus more on the generation of consulting revenues rather than the ethical values originally underlying its auditing business.[135]

As another example, former CEO of Alcoa, Paul O'Neill, developed a reputation for caring about the safety of his employees. He managed this by visiting plants and indicating to employees that there would be no set budget for safety matters, and that they should spend money to fix any safety hazard regardless of the cost. He also gave his home phone number for employees to report safety problems, and would personally fly anywhere in the world to visit employees who had been injured.[136] Ethical leadership was also demonstrated in the following example. Following a series of scandals at the Canadian bank CIBC, including a multi-billion dollar settlement related to its dealings with Enron, the new CEO, Gerald McCaughey, decided to voluntarily accept a compensation package that delayed the vesting of his share options extensively, and also included a provision that his compensation could be taken away retroactively if a scandal was later discovered to have taken place during his term as CEO of the bank.[137] Such actions could be seen to demonstrate a commitment to ethical values (i.e., responsibility), leading to a perception of the CEO as an ethical leader.

Unfortunately, however, there are too many examples of companies that failed to establish an ethical "tone at the top", leading to significant scandals which sometimes caused their downfall.[138] For example, US firms and their former CEOs such as WorldCom (Bernie Ebbers), Tyco International (Dennis Kozlowski), and Adelphia (John Rigas), Canadian firms such as Hollinger (Conrad Black) and Livent (Garth Drabinsky), and Italian firm Parmalat (Calisto Tanzi) appear to have been lacking an appropriate tone at the top. These examples represent firms with "unethical leadership" leading to behavior that costs firms billions of dollars a year due to lost productivity, increased absenteeism, increased health care costs, and costs associated with defending lawsuits.[139]

Even Enron, despite possessing a comprehensive compliance or ethics program, collapsed at least in part due to an inappropriate tone at the top led by former CEO Jeffrey Skilling, who as indicated earlier emphasized bottom-line results as opposed to ethical values.[140] Kenneth Lay, also a former CEO and board chairman of Enron, demonstrated a lack of ethical leadership when he requested that Enron's managers use his sister's travel agency for all of their overseas flights.[141] The US government bailout of American International Group (AIG), the collapse of Lehman Brothers, and the sale of Merrill Lynch, appear to demonstrate how the self-interested pursuits of these firms' senior leaders led to severe financial repercussions for their investors, clients, employees, and other stakeholders.[142] These examples seem to support the claim that leadership which lacks ethical conduct can be "dangerous, destructive, and even toxic."[143]

One significant example demonstrating a lack of ethical leadership in terms of the core ethical values of *responsibility* and *caring* was exemplified by BP's CEO Tony Hayward in 2010 following an explosion on one of the oil rigs BP was leasing in the Gulf of Mexico, the *Deepwater Horizon*, resulting in the death of 11 workers, and causing the largest oil spill in US waters. Hayward made statements and engaged in activity following the spill that suggested he was disconnected from the ethical significance of the tragedy. In 2010, in an interview with the *Guardian* newspaper, Hayward stated: "The Gulf of Mexico is a very big ocean. The amount of volume of oil and dispersant we are putting into it is tiny in relation to the total water volume".[144]

After being criticized for downplaying the oil spill, Hayward unfortunately continued to demonstrate insensitivity. Two weeks later, Hayward stated in response to media pressure and public criticism: "I'd like my life back."[145] After apologizing for making that comment,[146] several weeks later Tony Hayward decided to go sailing on his yacht as the oil spill recovery faltered. This took place merely two days after Mr Hayward angered lawmakers on Washington's Capitol Hill with his refusal to provide details during testimony about the offshore oil spill. In his defense, a BP spokesman said it was the "first break" Hayward had had following the *Deepwater Horizon* oil rig explosion.[147]

In contrast, other examples demonstrate the ethical leadership of some firms' boards of directors to discipline their own CEOs when they are perceived to have acted unethically. Harry Stonecipher, a former CEO of Boeing, was asked by the board to resign following the discovery that he was having an intimate consensual relationship with an executive. Stonecipher had been instrumental in both turning the firm around financially and leading a new emphasis on ethical behavior at Boeing through a revised code of ethics. According to Boeing's non-executive chairman: "It's not the fact that [Harry Stonecipher] was having an affair that caused him to be fired, but as we explored the circumstances surrounding the affair, we just thought there were some issues of poor judgment that … impaired his ability to lead going forward."[148]

In another similar case, Hewlett-Packard's CEO Mark Hurd was asked to resign for being in violation of the firm's code of conduct when he hired a former porn star "marketing consultant" without disclosing his close personal relationship with her, along with submitting inaccurate expense claims for meals together. The HP board only discovered the relationship after investigating sexual harassment claims made by the consultant against Hurd. Hurd was asked to resign despite begin credited with financially turning around the firm, with the board's decision leading to an immediate 10% drop in HP's share value.[149]

As one more example, Kenneth Lonchar, the chief financial officer of the firm Veritas, was fired despite his contribution to the firm after it was discovered his claim of having an MBA degree was not true.[150] The actions of these boards of directors despite facing criticism might be contrasted with the board directors of Enron and WorldCom, who continued to support their senior executives' actions despite a series of ethical red flags being raised.[151]

To summarize, an ethical leader is trustworthy, honest, transparent, responsible, caring, respectful, fair, acts with integrity, and puts the interests of the firm's shareholders and other stakeholders before his or her own personal interests. All of this must be demonstrated through the leader's actions, and not just through words (in fact it may only create greater cynicism among employees if the leader talks about the importance of ethical behavior but does not act accordingly). One of the best examples of this was Jeffrey Skilling, former CEO of Enron. In Enron's training video "Vision and Values," Skilling declares to Enron employees: "It's a tough world out there and a very competitive world. There probably are times that there's a desire to cut corners, but we can't have that at Enron."[152] Skilling was sentenced to 24 years in prison (later reduced to 14 years) and fined $45 million for a number of infractions including insider trading and securities fraud.[153]

The failure of senior executives to act accordingly must lead to disciplinary action by their firm's board of directors, regardless of the financial implications, in order to ensure a sense of accountability. Without ethical leadership across the organization, including at the level of the board of directors, there is little chance of establishing and sustaining an ethical corporate culture, with employees taking their ethical (or unethical) cues from their formal leaders.[154] Figure 6.1 summarizes the interaction of all three elements necessary to develop and sustain an ethical corporate culture within a firm.

Figure 6.1   The key elements of an ethical corporate culture. (*Source:* Schwartz, M.S. 2013. Reproduced with the permission of Elsevier.)

Other Considerations to Sustaining an Ethical Corporate Culture

Once an ethical corporate culture is developed, the assumption is that the extent of crime, corruption, and unethical activity within organizations or on behalf of their agents will be minimized. Of course, developing an ethical corporate culture is only the first step, with multiple constant challenges to be overcome. For example, sustaining an ethical corporate culture becomes exceptionally difficult for large multinational organizations which may have tens if not hundreds of thousands of employees around the world, each with their own distinct ethical perspective and culture.[155] In other words, a general or overarching "corporate culture" may not exist or at least be extremely difficult to ever identify in any large multinational organization.

Constant acquisitions or mergers between firms which each possess very distinct ethical corporate cultures make it even more difficult to establish and maintain consistent ethical norms across an entire organization.[156] A single change in top management can also have a significant negative impact on ethical corporate cultures, as demonstrated with respect to CEO Jeffrey Skilling at Enron.[157] In addition, while difficult economic conditions or intense competition that might lead to financial ruin can actually strengthen ethical corporate cultures due to increased scrutiny,[158] such conditions might also intensify the pressure on firms to reject their ethical norms in favor of the bottom line.[159]

Unfortunately, it is often difficult to measure the success of an ethical corporate culture in terms of outcomes, as the ethical scandal that was avoided as a result of an ethical work environment cannot always be identified and quantified. In any event, while significant and sustained efforts by firms must be undertaken to ensure high ethical standards, they must take place along with the decisions and actions of other stakeholders, including: governments (e.g., through regulation, enforcement, incentives, etc.); employees (e.g., deciding where to work); customers (e.g., which companies' products to buy or services to use); suppliers (e.g., which companies to work with); creditors (e.g., where to lend); shareholders (e.g., where to invest, shareholder resolutions, etc.); non-governmental organizations (e.g., through the development of ethical codes and pressure tactics); academics (e.g., through research and teaching); and the media (e.g., through investigative reporting). As a "multi-pronged" approach, all of these stakeholders can collectively create pressure on firms and their agents to engage in legal and ethical behavior.

With respect to the efforts of the firms themselves, we have now seen that there are three fundamental elements that form the basis of an ethical corporate culture: (i) the existence of a set of *core ethical values*; (ii) the establishment of a *formal ethics program*; and (iii) the continuous presence of *ethical leadership* (i.e., "tone at the top"). As a summary, Table 6.1 highlights the key

Table 6.1 Three pillars of an ethical corporate culture: recommendations and examples. (*Source*: Schwartz, M.S. 2013. Reproduced with the permission of Elsevier.)

	Recommendations	Examples
(1)(a) Core ethical values: *policy*	• Establish a set of core ethical values for the firm including: trustworthiness; responsibility; caring; citizenship; fairness; and respect. • Emphasize that when in conflict, the ethical values must take *priority* to the bottom line. • The ethical values should be posted prominently in the firm's code of ethics and on the home page of the firm's website.	• *Good*: Johnson & Johnson's Credo establishes stakeholder priorities by stating that their first responsibility is to the users of their products and services, while their "final responsibility" is to their stockholders. • *Bad*: Toyota's actions leading to the brake pedal recall appeared to equate the value of "safety" with "quality", rather than making safety a priority in and of itself.[160]
(1)(b) Core ethical values: *process*	• An ethical values filter should be applied to decision making including hiring (e.g., testing/interviews), performance appraisals, and firing. • Whether one acts in accordance with the ethical values should be directly tied to the firm's compensation/reward system.	• *Good*: The firm "Veritas" (Latin for truth) fired their CFO when it was discovered that he had lied years earlier about having an MBA on his resume. • *Bad*: Enron's performance appraisal system ("rank and yank" process of dismissing the bottom 10% performers) appears to have contributed to pressures to cut ethical corners.

(*continued*)

Table 6.1 (Continued)

	Recommendations	Examples
(1)(c) Core ethical values: practice	• All firm level and managerial level decision making should be based on and explicitly refer to the core ethical values whenever possible.	• Good: Drugstore retail chain CVS dropped the sale of cigarettes from their stores despite losing $2 billion in annual sales partly based on their core value of promoting health services.[161] • Bad: Enron's complete disregard for their explicit values as indicated in their code of ethics including respect and integrity (e.g., honesty).
(2)(a) Formal ethics program: code of ethics	• Ensure employee involvement in code creation or revision to help achieve buy-in and ensure realism and relevancy. • The code should apply to all of the firm's agents including contractors and suppliers.	• Good: Walmart's "Statement of Ethics" applies to all relevant stakeholders including the firm's suppliers, consultants, law firms, public relations firms, contractors, and other service providers. • Bad: WorldCom lacked a code of ethics based on CEO Bernie Ebber's view that having a code was a "colossal waste of time."
(2)(b) Formal ethics program: implementation	• Annual sign-off of the code should take place. • Relevant examples should be used during ethics training. • Managers should conduct ethics training whenever possible.	• Good: Johnson & Johnson periodically surveys its employees to evaluate how well the company lives up to its Credo responsibilities. The firm ensures that the Credo remains at the heart of the corporate culture by training its managers in the Credo-based Johnson & Johnson "Standards of Leadership". • Bad: Enron's training video "Vision and Values" includes CEO Jeffrey Skilling's statement: "Out there...there's a desire to cut corners, but we can't have that at Enron".

(2)(c) Formal ethics program: administration	- A whistleblowing channel should be established that is well communicated with protections against retaliation provided. - Best to refer to the whistle-blowing channel as a "helpline" and not a "hotline". - Annual audit of the ethics program's effectiveness should take place with modifications made if necessary.	- *Good:* Following their bribery scandal, Siemens created an ethics and risk compliance department with hundreds of employees, developed a training program, and changed the reporting system at the highest levels to try to prevent future misconduct.[162] - *Bad:* BP's alleged failure to protect their employees who raised safety complaints, in part leading to the Gulf of Mexico oil spill.
(3) Ethical leadership	- All actions and decisions at all levels throughout the organization should exemplify ethical leadership, up to and including the board of directors. - Managers should ensure that their personal behavior does not conflict with their ethical reputation at work.	- *Good:* J&J's CEO James Burke's decision to recall Tylenol nationwide based on their Credo despite the financial cost. - *Bad:* HP CEO Mark Hurd's concealed relationship with a marketing consultant and his submission of inaccurate expense reports.

recommendations and provides better known corporate examples of the "good" and the "bad" for each of the three pillars of an ethical corporate culture.

With significant corporate scandals taking place such as Toyota's recall troubles (leading to $1.2 billion in fines and billions of dollars in recall expenses),[163] Goldman Sachs betting against a sub-prime mortgage product while at the same time recommending the product to its own clients leading to a $550 million settlement,[164] along with BP's massive oil spill in the Gulf of Mexico leading to fines and settlement payments of $54 billion,[165] one might question whether these firms had *all* three elements of an ethical corporate culture clearly present.

Without all three of these elements firmly in place, each of these firms may have developed corporate cultures that emphasized financial considerations over the health, safety, or general well-being of other stakeholders. For example, Toyota has been referred to as having a "secretive corporate culture" in Japan which may have clashed with disclosing safety defects.[166] Goldman Sach's corporate culture focus on revenue generation, egos, and bonuses may have contributed to their clients being misled.[167] BP has been referred to by a US government commission as possessing a "culture of complacency" with profits taking priority over safety leading to the Gulf oil spill.[168]

Based on the above examples, firms that suffer ethical scandals are either deficient in having their ethical values infused throughout the organization, possess a weak ethics program, and/or lack ethical leadership. Firms that face an ethical scandal might initially respond by developing a stronger ethical corporate culture, but whether this is only temporary in nature depends on whether steps are taken to sustain it through the continuous presence of the three core elements we have just discussed.

While all three elements are distinct, they also reinforce and support each other. For example, ethical values become the basis for ethics programs, which in turn can enhance ethical leadership. Ethical leadership as discussed above is critical for the infusion of ethical values throughout the organization and the potential effectiveness of ethics programs. Nevertheless, due to human nature, crime, corruption, and other illegal or unethical activity will never be completely eliminated for a certain percentage of the workforce, regardless of whatever efforts are undertaken. However, business firms, and in particular the firm's board of directors, senior executives, and managers, all have an ethical obligation to make reasonable attempts to minimize the presence of crime and unethical activity, for the good of all society.

Chapter Summary

This chapter looked at the key ways in which an ethical corporate culture can be developed and sustained. This included the existence of a set of *core ethical values* infused throughout the organization in its policies, processes, and practices; the establishment of a *formal ethics program* (e.g., code of ethics, ethics training, reporting hotline, ethics officer); and the continuous presence of *ethical leadership*. In summary, with a strong ethical corporate culture in place, the extent of unethical activity can be reduced, thereby diminishing the need to face and resolve ethical dilemmas in the first place.

Chapter 7 will now provide a series of common ethical dilemmas faced in the workplace providing an opportunity to apply the various theories and concepts discussed throughout the entire book.

Notes

1. See: Greg Smith, "Why I am Leaving Goldman Sachs," *The New York Times*, March 14, 2012, http://www.nytimes.com/2012/03/14/opinion/why-i-am-leaving-goldman-sachs.html?_r=0&pagewanted=print (accessed 13 September 2016).
2. Treviño and Nelson (2011, p. 151). Corporate culture has also been defined as: "…a property of an organization constituted by (1) its members' taken-for granted beliefs regarding the nature of reality, called assumptions; (2) a set of normative, moral, and functional guidelines or criteria for making decisions, called values; and (3) the practices or ways of working together that follow from the aforementioned assumptions and values, called artifacts" (Jones *et al.*, 2007, p. 142). For other definitions of *corporate culture*, see: Geertz (1973); Pettigrew (1979); Schein (1985); Hatch (1993).
3. Treviño and Nelson (2011, p. 153).
4. Treviño and Nelson (2011).
5. There is a degree of confusion in the literature regarding the differences if any between *ethical culture* versus *ethical climate*. Ethical culture overlaps to a large degree with the notion of *ethical climate*, which is a sub-set of an organizational climate (Treviño *et al.*, 1998). Ethical climate can be defined as the prevailing perceptions of typical organizational procedures and practices that have ethical content (Victor and Cullen, 1988, p. 101). Collectively, both the dimensions of *ethical corporate culture* and *ethical climate* establish a firm's "ethical context," "ethical environment," or "ethical infrastructure" for managers and employees (Treviño *et al.*, 1998). For our purposes, however, the concept of *ethical corporate culture* will be referred to, as being considered more pertinent from a normative perspective when it comes to guiding and shaping ethical behavior, as opposed to *ethical climate* which appears to be more associated with a descriptive characterization of the attitudes held by those working within a firm (Treviño *et al.*, 1998). Many continue to stress the importance of additional research on organizational ethical context (i.e., including ethical culture and ethical climate) in relation to ethical decision making and behavior. See: Martin and Cullen (2006); Dean *et al.* (2010); Pimentel *et al.* (2010).
6. See: Hess and Dunfee (2000, 2003); Schwartz (2005a).
7. For example, see: Ferrell and Gresham (1985); Treviño (1986); Brass *et al.* (1998).

8. Ethics Resource Center (2012, p. 35). In reviewing the academic literature, one researcher states that: "[T]he results highlight the important role that organisational culture plays in ethical decision making…" See: Mcdonald (2009, p. 357).

9. See: Brooks and Dunn (2010, p. 256).

10. O'Fallon and Butterfield (2005).

11. Schwartz (2001).

12. Goldmann (2009, p. 11).

13. Treviño and Nelson (2011, p. 153).

14. Treviño and Nelson (2011).

15. Hunt *et al.* (1989, p. 79).

16. One conclusion after an extensive literature review on ethical decision making was that the research generally supports the view that ethical climates and cultures have a positive influence on ethical decision making. See: O'Fallon and Butterfield (2005, p. 397).

17. Covey (2004).

18. In a sense, universal ethical values might be considered as being similar to *hypernorms*, which have been described as "deep moral values" (Donaldson and Dunfee, 1999, p. 27) representing "… a convergence of religious, political, and philosophical thought" (Donaldson and Dunfee, 1999, p. 44). Hypernorms are considered "…so fundamental that, by definition, they serve to evaluate lower-order norms [while]…reaching to the root of what is ethical for humanity" (Donaldson and Dunfee, 1999, p. 44). On a practical level, it is assumed that the core ethical values by being universal in nature will have the greatest potential for both normative acceptance and actual adherence by a diverse group of managers and employees anywhere in the world.

19. Schwartz (2005b).

20. See: Schwartz (2005b). The objective of the study was to identify a set of moral values which both emerge from and recur within a number of different sources, and can thus be classified as being potentially *universal* in nature. An additional goal was to identify moral values which are not only mutually exclusive, but also sufficiently comprehensive so as to incorporate a wider range of values.

21. See: Scotiabank, "Guidelines for Business Conduct: A Message from our CEO," January 2014 (p. 3), http://www.scotiabank.com/ca/en/files/11/09/Guidelines_for_Business_Conduct.pdf (accessed 13 September 2016).

22. See: Johnson & Johnson website, "Our Credo Values," http://www.jnj.com/about-jnj/jnj-credo (accessed 13 September 2016).

23. For examples of how better to integrate values into a firm's corporate culture, see: Driscoll and Hoffman (1999).

24. Argandoña (2003).

25. See: Canary and Jennings (2008, p. 266).

26. Hum (2008).

27. See: Susan Todd, "Johnson & Johnson New CEO Emphasizes Company Credo at Shareholder's Meeting," April 26, 2012, *The Star-Ledger*, http://www.nj.com/business/index.ssf/2012/04/johnson_johnsons_new_ceo_empha.html (accessed 13 September 2016).

28. See: Johnson & Jonhson website, "Our Credo Values," http://www.jnj.com/about-jnj/jnj-credo (accessed 13 September 2016).

29. See: Pitt and Groskaufmanis (1990); Verschoor (2010).

30. Sims and Brinkmann (2003).

31. Stevens (2008).

32. Paine (1994).

33. Treviño and Nelson (2011, p. 166).

34. Schwartz (2009).

35. See: Woods and Savino (2007).

36. Morse (2004, p. 20).

37. See: Schwartz (2009).

38. See: Schwartz (2009).

39. Treviño and Nelson (2011, pp. 171–172).

40. Treviño and Nelson (2011, p. 172).

41. Paine (1994).

42. Pech and Slade (2007).

43. Treviño and Nelson (2011).

44. Messmer (2003, p. 13); Gibbs (2003, p. 41).

45. See: Schwartz *et al.* (2005).

46. Treviño and Nelson (2011, pp. 183–185).

47. This example is based on an employee's experience as indicated during an executive training session.

48. See: Southwest Airlines website, "Culture: Values," https://www.southwest.com/html/about-southwest/careers/culture.html (accessed 13 September 2016).

49. Southwest Airlines did, however, offer the passenger a full refund on her ticket. See: ABC7News, "Woman Says Southwest Flight Crew Wouldn't Let Her Call Suicidal Husband," May 17, 2015, http://abc7news.com/news/woman-says-flight-crew-wouldnt-let-her-call-suicidal-husband/727387/ (accessed 13 September 2016).

50. See: Paine (1994).

51. See: US Sentencing Commission, *US Federal Sentencing Guidelines for Organizations* (section 8B2.1), http://www.ussc.gov/guidelines-manual/2014/2014-chapter-8 (accessed 13 September 2016).

52. In a similar fashion, the US *Sarbanes-Oxley Act* or SOX, also requires firms to ensure the presence of certain elements of an ethics program. Not only are public firms essentially required to possess a code of conduct (or ethics), but SOX also suggests certain minimum content for the code, while requiring that firms have established appropriate whistleblowing channels. See: US Senate, *Sarbanes-Oxley Act 2002*, http://www.sec.gov/about/laws/soa2002.pdf (accessed 13 September 2016).

53. See: Messikomer and Cirka (2010); Schwartz (2001; 2004). My own research study on ethical programs involved 57 interviews of employees, managers, and ethics officers at four large North American business firms to determine their views on which elements are important in leading to an effective ethics program.

54. See: SCCE and NYSE Governance Services, *2014 Compliance and Ethics Program Environment Survey* (p. 31), http://m1.corpedia.com/resource_database/CEPEReport.pdf (accessed 13 September 2016).

55. See: Kaptein and Schwartz (2008).

56. Schwartz (2001).

57. In addition, the *Sarbanes Oxley Act* (2002, s. 406) indicates several provisions that should be included in any code of ethics: (1) honest and ethical conduct, including the ethical handling of actual or apparent conflicts of interest between personal and professional relationships; (2) full, fair, accurate, timely and understandable disclosure in reports and documents; and (3) compliance with applicable governmental laws, rules and regulations. See: US Senate, *Sarbanes-Oxley Act 2002*, http://www.sec.gov/about/laws/soa2002.pdf (accessed 13 September 2016).

58. Weber and Wasieleski (2013).

59. Erwin (2011, p. 545).

60. Brooks (1989, p. 124); Ethics Resource Center (1990, p. III–1); Pitt and Groskaufmanis (1990, p. 1649); Raiborn and Payne (1990, p. 883).

61. Sanderson and Varner (1984, pp. 28–31); Gibbs (2003, p. 40).

62. Murphy (1995, p. 731); Gibbs (2003, p. 40).

63. Austin (1961); Harris (1978, p. 315); Ethics Resource Center (1990, p. III–2); Raiborn and Payne (1990, p. 883).

64. Pitt and Groskaufmanis (1990, p. 1639); Brandl and Maguire (2002).

65. Raiborn and Payne (1990, p. 884).

66. Messmer (2003, p. 14); Messikomer and Cirka (2010, p. 68).

67. Molander (1987, p. 628); Ethics Resource Center (1990, p. II–3); Sweeney and Siers (1990, p. 34); Montoya and Richard (1994, p. 714).

68. Schwartz (2004).

69. Ethics Resource Center (1990, p. II-1); Montoya and Richard (1994, p. 714); Brandl and Maguire (2002); Mcdonald (2009). For example, "[T]he single most important task in ensuring an effective, successful code of conduct is garnering the full, enthusiastic support of the company's board of directors and senior management." See: Jordan (1995, p. 305).

70. Schwartz *et al.* (2005).

71. For example, in one study all respondents believed that it was a good idea to see a letter from the CEO: "[The CEO] is endorsing it. [The CEO] is saying that yeah, I buy into this concept … I am bound by the same rules you are." See: Schwartz (2004, p. 332).

72. Benson (1989, p. 318); Pitt and Groskaufmanis (1990, pp. 1649–1650).

73. Webley (1988, p. 15). Fortunately, electronic distribution and posting of codes of ethics now reduces the burden of communicating codes to multiple stakeholders.

74. Pitt and Groskaufmanis (1990, p. 1650); Lane (1991, p. 31); Gibbs (2003, p. 41).

75. See: SCCE and NYSE Governance Services, *2014 Compliance and Ethics Program Environment Survey* (p. 31), http://m1.corpedia.com/resource_database/CEPEReport.pdf (accessed 13 September 2016).

76. Schwartz (2004).
77. Schwartz (2004).
78. Benson (1989, p. 318); Gellerman (1989, p. 77); Pitt and Groskaufmanis (1990, p. 1650); Lane (1991, p. 31); Gibbs (2003, p. 40); Messmer (2003, p. 13).
79. Ethics Resource Center (1990).
80. Ethics training can lead to more "…positive perceptions of organizational ethics" (Valentine and Fleischman, 2004, p. 386) or "… can positively influence ethical behavior in the workplace" (Weber, 2007, p. 61). According to the commentary on the US Federal Sentencing Guidelines: "…compliance and ethics training [is] a requirement, and specifically extends the training requirement to the upper levels of an organization, including the governing authority [i.e., the board of directors] and high-level personnel, in addition to all of the organization's employees and agents, as appropriate." See: US Sentencing Commission, *US Federal Sentencing Guidelines for Organizations*, 2014.
81. See: SCCE and NYSE Governance Services, *2014 Compliance and Ethics Program Environment Survey*, http://m1.corpedia.com/resource_database/CEPEReport. pdf (p. 58) (accessed 13 September 2016).
82. Gellerman (1989, p. 77).
83. Lane (1991, p. 31).
84. Schwartz (2004).
85. Schwartz (2004, p. 333, emphasis added).
86. See: Arce and Gentile (2015, p. 537). The "Giving Voice to Values" approach can also be used to teach business ethics to students by focusing on action and behavior, rather than the more typical educational approach which focuses on teaching awareness and moral reasoning skills.
87. See: Gentile (2010, p. 230).
88. See: Gentile (2010, p. xiii).
89. Treviño and Nelson (2011, pp. 232–233).
90. Schwartz (2004).
91. Pitt and Groskaufmanis (1990, pp. 1649–1651); Treviño and Nelson (2011, pp. 220–221).
92. Schwartz (2004).
93. As one respondent noted in one study: "…it's just a document. A document doesn't change the culture, it doesn't change values, it doesn't change behavior…without everything else the document is just a document. You need the constant education, re-education, awareness, examples, and build that example base and present it on a regular basis." See: Schwartz (2004, p. 334).
94. The Sentencing Guidelines [Section §8B2.1 (b)(2)(c)] require firms to appoint an individual to be responsible for the firm's ethics program: "Specific individual(s) within the organization shall be delegated day-to-day operational responsibility for the compliance and ethics program." See: US Sentencing Commission, *US Federal Sentencing Guidelines for Organizations*, 2014.
95. See: NYSE Governance Services, "Compliance and Ethics Program Governance Report," (p. 8), 2014, http://m1.corpedia.com/resource_database/CEPEReport. pdf (accessed 13 September 2016).

96. Llopis, Gonzalez, and Gasco (2007).

97. See: Pitt and Groskaufmanis (1990, p. 1642). According to the Ethics Resource Center, chief ethics and compliance officers "…who are empowered to create and maintain strong ethics programs…contribute to the establishment of an enduring ethical culture." See: Ethics Resource Center (2007, p. 1).

98. The 2010 amendments to the US Federal Sentencing Guidelines adds the requirement that a direct channel of communication explicitly exists between ethics or compliance personnel and the firm's governing authority, meaning the board of directors or audit committee. See: Holly Gregory, "New Sentencing Guidelines for Corporate Defendants," July 15, 2010, http://corpgov.law. harvard.edu/2010/07/15/new-sentencing-guidelines-for-corporate-defendants/ (accessed 13 September 2016).

99. See: Institute of Business Ethics, *The Relationship Between the Board of Directors and the Compliance and Ethics Officer: Summary*," https://www.ibe.org.uk/ userassets/survey%20summaries/boards%20&%20eco%20relationship%20pdf. pdf (p. 2) (accessed 13 September 2016).

100. Hoffman and Rowe (2007).

101. Gellerman (1989, p. 78); Ethics Resource Center (1990, p. VII-1); Pitt and Groskaufmanis (1990, p. 1645). The US Federal Sentencing Guidelines require organizations: "… to have and publicize a system, which may include mechanisms that allow for anonymity or confidentiality, whereby the organization's employees and agents may report or seek guidance regarding potential or actual criminal conduct without fear of retaliation." See: US Sentencing Commission, *US Federal Sentencing Guidelines for Organizations* (section 8B2.1), 2014.

102. Jordan (1995, p. 312). Having a hotline serves an important purpose in providing an outlet for employees to voice concerns when speaking with co-workers or a manager is not an option. See: Schwartz (2004, p. 336).

103. Pitt and Groskaufmanis (1990, p. 1651); Sweeney and Siers (1990, p. 39); Gibbs (2003, p. 40); Messmer (2003, p. 14).

104. Schwartz (2004).

105. Treviño (1992, p. 647).

106. Molander (1987, p. 630); Raiborn and Payne (1990, p. 888).

107. This is now a requirement under the US Federal Sentencing Guidelines: "The organization shall take reasonable steps (A) to ensure that the organization's compliance and ethics program is followed, including monitoring and auditing to detect criminal conduct; [and] (B) to evaluate periodically the effectiveness of the organization's compliance and ethics program…" See: US Sentencing Commission, *US Federal Sentencing Guidelines for Organizations* (section 8B2.1), 2014.

108. See: SCCE and NYSE Governance Services, *2014 Compliance and Ethics Program Environment Survey* (p. 85), http://m1.corpedia.com/resource_database/ CEPEReport.pdf (accessed 13 September 2016).

109. See: Jordan (1995, p. 312).

110. Murphy (1988, p. 909); Pitt and Groskaufmanis (1990, p. 1650); Driscoll *et al.* (1996, p. 156).

111.   According to a Blue Ribbon Panel of the Ethics & Compliance Initiative, high-quality ethics and compliance programs have a purpose of "establishing and perpetuating a high standard of integrity that becomes part of the DNA of the organization." The report reveals five core principles that are shared by organizations with high quality programs: "(1) ethics and compliance is central to business strategy; (2): ethics and compliance risks are identified, owned, managed and mitigated; (3) leaders at all levels across the organization build and sustain a culture of integrity; (4) the organization encourages, protects, and values the reporting of concerns and suspected wrongdoing; (5) the organization takes action and holds itself accountable when wrongdoing occurs." See: Ethics & Compliance Initiative (ECI) website, *Principles & Practices of High-Quality Ethics & Compliance* Programs, 2016, https://www.ethics.org/eci/certification/blue-ribbon/brpreport-public (accessed 13 September 2016).

112.   These ethical crisis management examples are also discussed in Schwartz *et al.* (2012).

113.   See: BBC, "Bhopal Trial: Eight Convicted Over India Gas Disaster," June 10, 2010, http://news.bbc.co.uk/2/hi/south_asia/8725140.stm (accessed 13 September 2016).

114.   See: *The New York Times*, "Exxon Valdez Oil Spill (1989)," http://topics.nytimes.com/top/reference/timestopics/subjects/e/exxon_valdez_oil_spill_1989/index.html (accessed 13 September 2016).

115.   See: Allison Linn, "Starbucks Apologizes for Charging NYC Rescue Workers for Water," Associate Press, September 26, 2011, http://www.berkeleydailyplanet.com/issue/2001-09-26/article/7040?headline=Starbucks-apologizes-for-charging-NYC-rescue-workers-for-water–By-Allison-Linn-AP-Business-Writer (accessed 13 September 2016).

116.   See: Judith Rehak, "Tylenol Made a Hero of Johnson & Johnson: The Recall That Started Them All," *The New York Times*, March 23, 2002, http://www.nytimes.com/2002/03/23/your-money/23iht-mjj_ed3_.html (accessed 13 September 2016).

117.   See: Mark Bitman, "Time to Boycott Tuna Again?" September 20, 2011, *The New York Times*, http://opinionator.blogs.nytimes.com/2011/09/20/time-to-boycott-tuna-again/?_r=0 (accessed 13 September 2016).

118.   Schwartz *et al.* (2005); Sheeder (2005); Weaver and Treviño (1999); Brown and Mitchell (2010); Darcy (2010).

119.   James (2000, p. 54).

120.   Brown *et al.* (2005, p. 117).

121.   Brown *et al.* (2005, p. 120).

122.   Northouse (2001, p. 255).

123.   Hitt (1990, p. 3).

124.   Treviño *et al.* (1999, p. 142).

125.   Ethics Resource Center (2009, pp. 8–9).

126.   Podolny (2009).

127.   See: Rebecca Riffkin, "Americans Rate Nurses Highest on Honesty, Ethical Standards," Gallup, December 18, 2014, http://www.gallup.com/poll/180260/

americans-rate-nurses-highest-honesty-ethical-standards.aspx (accessed 13 September 2016).

128. See: Ipsos Mori website. "Ipsos Mori Trust Poll," 2013, http://www.ipsos-mori. com/Assets/Docs/Polls/Feb2013_Trust_Topline.PDF (accessed 13 September 2016).

129. See: Daniel Tencer, "Canada's Most and Least Trusted Professions: Sorry, CEOs and Politicians," *Huffington Post*, January 20, 2015, http://www.huffingtonpost. ca/2015/01/20/most-least-trusted-professions-canada_n_6510232.html (accessed 13 September 2016).

130. Treviño *et al.* (2003).

131. Treviño and Nelson (2011, p. 159).

132. Treviño and Nelson (2011, p. 159).

133. Treviño *et al.* (2000).

134. Toffler and Reingold (2003).

135. Treviño and Nelson (2011, p. 130).

136. Treviño and Nelson (2011, p. 160).

137. Adam and Schwartz (2009).

138. Gini (2004).

139. Brown and Mitchell (2010, pp. 588–599).

140. Watkins (2003). See also: Beenen and Pinto (2009, p. 279).

141. See: Jyoti Thottam, "Family Business: Lay's Sister Had a Sweet Deal Too," February 11, 2002, http://www.time.com/time/magazine/article/0,9171,1001781,00. html (accessed 13 September 2016).

142. Duska (2009).

143. Toor and Ofori (2009, p. 533).

144. See: Tom Bergin, "BP CEO Apologizes for Thoughtless Oil Spill Comment," *Reuters*, June 2, 2010, http://www.reuters.com/article/2010/06/02/us-oil-spill-bp-apology-idUSTRE6515NQ20100602 (accessed 13 September 2016).

145. See: Tom Bergin, "BP CEO Apologizes for Thoughtless Oil Spill Comment."

146. See: Tony Hayward, Facebook website, June 2, 2010, http://www.facebook.com/ notes/bp-america/bp-ceo-tony-hayward-issues-an-apology-for-remarks/43151 2288412 (accessed 13 September 2016).

147. See: Raphael Satter, "Gulf Oil Spill: Tony Hayward Attends Glitzy Yacht Race as Oil Spews into Gulf," *Huffington Post*, June 19, 2010, http://www.huffington post.com/2010/06/19/gulf-oil-spill-tony-haywa_n_618332.html (accessed 13 September 2016).

148. See: Renae Merle, "Boeing CEO Resigns Over Affair with Subordinate," *Washington Post*, March 8, 2005, http://www.washingtonpost.com/wp-dyn/ articles/A13173-2005Mar7.html (accessed 13 September 2016).

149. See: Ben Worthen and Pui-Wing Tam, "H-P Chief Quits in Scandal," *The Wall Street Journal*, August 7, 2010, http://www.wsj.com/articles/SB100014240 52748703309704575413663370670900 (accessed 13 September 2016).

150. See: Chron, "Veritas CFO Fired Over Education Lie," October 4, 2002, http://www.chron.com/business/article/Veritas-CFO-fired-over-education-lie-2100302.php (accessed 13 September 2016).

151. Schwartz *et al.* (2005).

152. See: "Enron: Vision and Values," January 11, 2009, *YouTube* video, https://www.youtube.com/watch?v=Bl6uF80FWzs (accessed 13 September 2016).

153. See: Aaron Smith, "Ex-Enron CEO Skilling Has 10 years Lopped Off Sentence," *CNN Money*, June 21, 2013, http://money.cnn.com/2013/06/21/news/companies/skilling-enron-resentencing/ (accessed 13 September 2016).

154. Schwartz *et al.* (2005); Treviño and Nelson (2011).

155. Donaldson (1996).

156. Wood (2004).

157. Sims and Brinkmann (2003).

158. Ethics Resource Center (2009).

159. Shleifer (2004).

160. See: Kate Linebaugh, Dionne Searcey, and Norihiko Shirouzu, "Secretive Culture Led Toyota Astray," *Wall Street Journal*, February 8, 2010, http://online.wsj.com/article/SB10001424052748704820904575055733096312238.html (accessed 13 September 2016).

161. See: Phil Wahba and Julie Steenhuysen, "CVS Becomes First Big US Drugstore Chain to Drop Tobacco," *Reuters*, February 5, 2014, http://www.reuters.com/article/2014/02/05/us-cvscaremark-cigarettes-idUSBREA140RP20140205 (accessed 13 September 2016).

162. See: Peter Löscher, "The CEO of Siemens on Using a Scandal to Drive Change," *Harvard Business Review*, November, 2012, https://hbr.org/2012/11/the-ceo-of-siemens-on-using-a-scandal-to-drive-change/ar/ (accessed 13 September 2016).

163. See: Bill Vlasic and Matt Apuzzo, "Toyota is Fined $1.2 Billion for Concealing Safety Defects," *The New York Times*, http://www.nytimes.com/2014/03/20/business/toyota-reaches-1-2-billion-settlement-in-criminal-inquiry.html (accessed 13 September 2016).

164. See: Sewell Chan and Louise Story, "Goldman Pays $550 Million to Settle Fraud Case," *New York Times*, July 15, 2010, http://www.nytimes.com/2010/07/16/business/16goldman.html?_r=0 (accessed 13 September 2016).

165. See: Chris Isidore, Charles Riley, and Terry Frieden, "BP to Pay Record Penalty for Gulf Oil Spill," *CNN Money*, November 15, 2012, http://money.cnn.com/2012/11/15/news/bp-oil-spill-settlement/index.html (accessed 13 September 2016). There may be additional payments in the future as well. See also: Tom Huddleston, Jr, "BP May Have Billions More to Pay, Even After Its $19 Billion Settlement," *Time*, July 13, 2015, http://time.com/3955864/bp-billions-compensation-claims/ (accessed 13 September 2016).

166. See: Kate Linebaugh, Dionne Searcey, and Norihiko Shirouzu, "Secretive Culture Led Toyota Astray."

167. See: Gretchen Morganson and Louise Story, "Clients Worried About Goldman's Dueling Goals," *The New York Times*, May 18, 2010, http://www.nytimes.com/2010/05/19/business/19client.html?dbk (accessed 13 September 2016).

168. See: Ed Crooks, "Bad Calls Preceded Gulf of Mexico Blast," *Financial Times*, November 9, 2010, http://www.ft.com/cms/s/0/a51cfcbc-ec0c-11df-b50f-00144feab49a.html#axzz19IZxMqx5 (accessed 13 September 2016).

References

Adam, A. and Schwartz, M.S. 2009. Corporate governance, ethics, and the backdating of stock options. *Journal of Business Ethics*, 85: 225–237.

Arce, D.G. and Gentile, M.C. 2015. *Giving Voice to Values* as a leverage point in business ethics education. *Journal of Business Ethics*, 131: 535–542.

Argandoña, A. 2003. Fostering values in organizations. *Journal of Business Ethics*, 45: 15–28.

Austin, R.W. 1961. Code of conduct for executives. *Harvard Business Review*, September/October: 53.

Beenen, G. and Pinto, J. 2009. Resisting organizational-level corruption: an interview with Sherron Watkins. *Academy of Management Learning & Education*, 8: 275–289.

Benson, G.C.S. 1989. Codes of ethics. *Journal of Business Ethics*, 8: 305–319.

Brandl, P. and Maguire, M. 2002. Codes of ethics: a primer on their purpose, development, and use. *The Journal for Quality and Participation*, 25: 8–12.

Brass, D.J., Butterfield, K.D., and Skaggs, B.C. 1998. Relationships and unethical behavior: a social network perspective. *Academy of Management Review*, 23: 14–31.

Brooks, L.J. 1989. Corporate codes of ethics. *Journal of Business Ethics*, 8: 117–129.

Brooks, L.J. and Dunn, P. 2010. *Business and Professional Ethics* (5th edn). Mason, OH: South Western Cengage Learning.

Brown, M.E. and Mitchell, M.S. 2010. Ethical and unethical leadership: exploring new avenues for future leadership. *Business Ethics Quarterly*, 20: 583–616.

Brown, M.E., Treviño, M.S., and Harrison, D.A. 2005. Ethical leadership: a social learning perspective for construct development and testing. *Organizational Behavior and Human Decision Processes*, 97: 117–134.

Canary, H.E. and Jennings, M.M. 2008. Principles and influence in codes of ethics: a centering resonance analysis comparing pre-Sarbanes-Oxley codes of ethics. *Journal of Business Ethics*, 80: 263–278.

Covey, S. 2004. *The 8th Habit*. New York: Free Press.

Darcy, K. 2010. Ethical leadership: the past, present, and future. *International Journal of Disclosure and Governance*, 7: 198–212.

Dean, K.L., Beggs, J.M., and Keane, T.P. 2010. Mid-level managers, organizational context, and (un)ethical encounters. *Journal of Business Ethics*, 97: 51–69.

Donaldson, T. 1996. Values in tension: ethics away from home. *Harvard Business Review*, September–October: 5–12.

Donaldson, T. and Dunfee, T.W. 1999. *Ties That Bind: A Social Contracts Approach to Business Ethics*. Boston, MA: Harvard Business School Press.

Driscoll, D.M. and Hoffman, W.M. 1999. *Ethics Matters: How to Implement Values-Driven Management*. Waltham, MA: Bentley College Center for Business Ethics.

Driscoll, D.M., Hoffman, W.M., and Petry, E.S. 1996. NYNEX regains moral footing. *Personnel Journal*, June: 147–156.

Duska, R.F. 2009. Corruption, financial crisis, and the financial planner. *Journal of Financial Services Professionals*, 63: 14–16.

Erwin, P.M. 2011. Corporate codes of conduct: the effects of code content and quality on ethical performance. *Journal of Business Ethics*, 99: 535–548.

Ethics Resource Center 1990. *Creating a Workable Company Code of Ethics*. Arlington, VA.

Ethics Resource Center 2007. *Leading Corporate Integrity: Defining the Role of the Chief Ethics & Compliance Officer*. Arlington, VA.

Ethics Resource Center 2009. The importance of ethical culture: increasing trust and driving down risks. *Supplemental Research Brief: 2009 National Business Ethics Survey*. Arlington, VA.

Ethics Resource Center 2012. *2011 National Business Ethics Survey*. Arlington, VA.

Ferrell, O.C. and Gresham, L. 1985. A contingency framework for understanding ethical decision making in marketing. *Journal of Marketing*, 49: 87–96.

Geertz, C. 1973. *The Interpretation of Cultures: Selected Essays*. New York: Basic Books.

Gellerman, S.W. 1989. Managing ethics from the top down. *Sloan Managing Review*, Winter: 73–79.

Gentile, M.C. 2010. *Giving Voice to Values: How to Speak Your Mind When You Know What's Right*. New Haven, CT: Yale University Press.

Gibbs, E. 2003. Developing an effective code of conduct. *Financial Executive*, 19: 40–41.

Gini, A. 2004. Business, ethics, and leadership in a post Enron era. *Journal of Leadership & Organizational Studies*, 11: 9–16.

Goldmann, P. 2009. *Anti-Fraud Risk and Control Workbook*. Hoboken, NJ: John Wiley & Sons, Inc.

Harris, C.E. 1978. Structuring a workable business code of ethics. *University of Florida Law Review*, 30: 310–382.

Hatch, M.J. 1993. The dynamics of organizational culture. *Academy of Management Review*, 18: 657–693.

Hess, D. and Dunfee, T.W. 2000. Fighting corruption, a principled approach. The C^2 principles (combating corruption). *Cornell International Law Journal*, 33: 595–628.

Hess, D. and Dunfee, T.W. 2003. Taking responsibility for bribery: the multinational's role in combating corruption. In *Business and Human Rights: Dilemmas and Solutions* (R. Sullivan, ed.). Sheffield, UK: Greenleaf Publishing, pp. 260–271.

Hitt, W.D. 1990. *Ethics and Leadership: Putting Theory into Practice*. Columbus, OH: Battelle Press.

Hoffman, W.M. and Rowe, M. 2007. Ethics officer as agent of the board. *Business and Society Review*, 112: 553–572.

Hum, B.J. 2008. Ethics in international business. *Industrial and Commercial Training*, 40: 347–354.

Hunt, S.D., Wood, V.R., and Chonko, L.B. 1989. Corporate ethical values and organizational commitment in marketing. *Journal of Marketing*, 53: 79–90.

James, H.S. Jr 2000. Reinforcing ethical decision making through organizational structure. *Journal of Business Ethics*, 28: 43–58.

Jones, T.M., Felps, W., and Bigley, G.A. 2007. Ethical theory and stakeholder-related decisions: the role of stakeholder. *The Academy of Management Review*, 32: 137–155.

Jordan, K.S. 1995. Designing and implementing a corporate code of conduct in the context of an effective compliance program. In *Corporate Counsel's Guide to Business Ethics Policies*. Chesterland, OH: Business Laws, pp. 301–314.

Kaptein, M. and Schwartz, M.S. 2008. The effectiveness of business codes: a critical examination of existing studies and the development of an integrated research model. *Journal of Business Ethics*, 77: 111–127.

Lane, M.R. 1991. Improving American business ethics in three steps. *CPA Journal*, February: 30–34.

Llopis, J., Gonzalez, M.R., and Gasco, J.L. 2007. Corporate governance and organizational culture: the role of ethics officers. *International Journal of Disclosure and Governance*, 4: 96–105.

Martin, K.D. and Cullen, J.B. 2006. Continuities and extensions of ethical climate theory: a meta-analytic review. *Journal of Business Ethics*, 69: 175–194.

Mcdonald, G. 2009. An anthology of codes of ethics. *European Business Review*, 21: 344–372.

Messikomer, C.M. and Cirka, C.C. 2010. Constructing a code of ethics: an experiential case of a national professional organization. *Journal of Business Ethics*, 95: 55–71.

Messmer, M. 2003. Does your company have a code of ethics? *Strategic Finance*, 84: 13–14.

Molander, E.A. 1987. A paradigm for design, promulgation and enforcement of ethical codes. *Journal of Business Ethics*, 6: 619–631.

Montoya, I.D. and Richard, A.J. 1994. A comparative study of codes of ethics in health care facilities and energy companies. *Journal of Business Ethics*, 13: 713–717.

Morse, G. 2004. Executive psychopaths. *Harvard Business Review*, October: 20–22.

Murphy, P.E. 1988. Implementing business ethics. *Journal of Business Ethics*, 7: 907–915.

Murphy, P.E. 1995. Corporate ethics statements: current status and future prospects. *Journal of Business Ethics*, 14: 727–740.

Northouse, P.G. 2001. *Leadership Theory and Practice* (2nd edn). London: Sage Publications.

O'Fallon, M.J. and Butterfield, K.D. 2005. A review of the empirical ethical decision-making literature: 1996–2003. *Journal of Business Ethics*, 59: 375–413.

Paine, L.S. 1994. Managing for organizational integrity. *Harvard Business Review* March/April: 106–117.

Pech, R.J. and Slade, B.W. 2007. Organisational sociopaths: rarely challenged, often promoted. Why? *Society and Business Review*, 2: 254–269.

Pettigrew, A.M. 1979. On studying organizational cultures. *Administrative Science Quarterly*, 24: 570–581.

Pimental, J.R.C., Kuntz, J.R., and Elenkov, D.S. 2010. Ethical decision-making: an integrative model for business practice. *European Business Review*, 22: 359–376.

Pitt, H.L. and Groskaufmanis, K.A. 1990. Minimizing corporate civil and criminal liability: a second look at corporate codes of conduct. *The Georgetown Law Journal*, 78: 1559–1654.

Podolny, J.M. 2009. The buck stops (and starts) at business school. *Harvard Business Review*, 87: 62–67.

Raiborn, C.A. and Payne, D. 1990. Corporate codes of conduct: a collective conscience and continuum. *Journal of Business Ethics*, 9: 879–889.

Sanderson, G.R. and Varner, I.I. 1984. What's wrong with corporate codes of conduct? *Management Accounting*, July: 28–31.

Schein, E.H. 1985. *Organizational Culture and Leadership*. San Francisco: Jossey-Bass.

Schwartz, M.S. 2001. The nature of the relationship between corporate codes of ethics and behaviour. *Journal of Business Ethics*, 32: 247–262.

Schwartz, M.S. 2004. Effective corporate codes of ethics: perceptions of code users. *Journal of Business Ethics*, 55: 321–341.

Schwartz, M.S. 2005a. Legally mandated self-regulation: the potential of sentencing guidelines. In *Ethics Codes, Corporations and the Challenge of Globalization* (W. Cragg, ed.). Cheltenham, UK: Edward Elgar Publishing, pp. 290–320.

Schwartz, M.S. 2005b. Universal moral values for corporate codes of ethics. *Journal of Business Ethics*, 59: 27–44.

Schwartz, M.S. 2009. Ethical leadership training: an Aristotelian approach. *Conference Proceedings*, European Business Ethics Network, Athens, Greece.

Schwartz, M.S. 2013. Developing and sustaining an ethical corporate culture: the core elements. *Business Horizons*, 56: 39–50.

Schwartz, M.S., Dunfee, T., and Kline, M. 2005. Tone at the top: an ethics code for directors? *Journal of Business Ethics*, 58: 79–100.

Schwartz, M.S., Hoffman, W.M., and Cragg, W. 2012. An ethical approach to crisis management. *IESE Insight*, 15: 36–43.

Sheeder, F. 2005. What exactly is 'tone at the top' and is it really that big a deal? *Journal of Health Care Compliance*, 7: 35–38.

Shleifer, A. 2004. Does competition destroy ethical behavior? *American Economic Review*, 94: 414–418.

Sims, R.R. and Brinkmann, J. 2003. Enron ethics (or culture matters more than codes). *Journal of Business Ethics*, 45: 243–256.

Stevens, B. 2008. Corporate ethical codes: effective instruments for influencing behavior. *Journal of Business Ethics*, 78: 601–609.

Sweeney, R.B. and Siers, H.L. 1990. Survey: ethics in America. *Management Accounting*, June: 34–40.

Toffler, B.L. and Reingold, J. 2003. *Final Accounting: Ambition, Greed, and the Fall of Arthur Andersen*. New York: Broadway Books.

Toor, S.R. and Ofori, G. 2009. Ethical leadership: examining the relationships with full range leadership model, employee outcomes, and organizational culture. *Journal of Business Ethics*, 90: 533–547.

Treviño, L.K. 1986. Ethical decision making in organizations: a person-situation interactionist model. *Academy of Management Review*, 11: 601–617.

Treviño, L.K. 1992. The social effects of punishment in organizations: a justice perspective. *The Academy of Management Review*, 17: 647–676.

Treviño, L.K., Brown, M., and Pincus-Hartman, L. 2003. A quantitative investigation of perceived executive ethical leadership: perceptions from inside and outside the executive suite. *Human Relations*, 56: 5–37.

Treviño, L.K., Butterfield, K.D., and McCabe, D.L. 1998. The ethical context in organizations: influences on employee attitudes and behaviors. *Business Ethics Quarterly*, 8: 447–476.

Treviño, L.K., Hartman, L.P., and Brown, M. 2000. Moral person and moral manager: how executives develop a reputation for ethical leadership. *California Management Review*, 42: 128–142.

Treviño, L.K. and Nelson, K.A. 2011. *Managing Business Ethics: Straight Talk About How To Do It Right* (5th edn). Hoboken, NJ: John Wiley & Sons, Inc.

Treviño, L.K., Weaver, G.R., Gibson, D.G., and Toffler, B.L. 1999. Managing ethics and legal compliance: what works and what hurts. *California Management Review*, 41: 131–151.

Valentine, S. and Fleischman, G. 2004. Ethics training and businesspersons: perceptions of organizational ethics. *Journal of Business Ethics*, 52: 381–390.

Verschoor, C.C. 2010. BP still hasn't learned ethical lessons. *Strategic Finance*, August: 13–15.

Victor, B. and Cullen, J.B. 1988. The organizational bases of ethical work climates. *Administrative Science Quarterly*, 33: 101–125.

Watkins, S. 2003. Pristine ethics: who do you trust? *Vital Speeches of the Day*, 69: 435–440.

Weaver, G.R. and Treviño, L.K. 1999. Compliance and values oriented ethics programs: influences on employees' attitudes and behavior. *Business Ethics Quarterly*, 9: 315–336.

Weber, J.A. 2007. Business ethics training: insights from learning theory. *Journal of Business Ethics*, 70: 61–85.

Weber, J. and Wasieleski, D.M. 2013. Corporate ethics and compliance programs: a report, analysis and critique. *Journal of Business Ethics*, 112: 609–626.

Webley, S. 1988. *Company Philosophies and Codes of Business Ethics: A Guide to their Drafting and Use*. London, UK: Institute of Business Ethics.

Wood, G. 2004. The relevance to international mergers of the ethical perspectives of participants. *Corporate Governance*, 5: 39–50.

Woods, D.R. and Savino, D.M. 2007. Do you blush often? Questions on integrity and personality tests that legally embarrass employers. *Employee Relations Law Journal*, 33: 3–31.

Chapter Seven

What Would You Do? Common Workplace Dilemmas

As we move into the final chapter, let's do a quick review of what we've covered so far. The first three chapters of this book explained through the Integrated-EDM model how ethical decision making takes place or is impeded. Chapter 4 laid out a set of normative criteria for determining ethical behavior through the Multifaceted-EDM model, while Chapter 5 set out criteria for when it is permissible or even obligatory to blow the whistle on misconduct. Chapter 6 indicated the key pillars leading to an ethical corporate culture. Now that we have covered the foundations of ethical decision making, let's continue with a more practical *application* of the descriptive and normative theory of ethical decision making covered throughout this book.

We'll begin with a very simple problem for illustration purposes. Suppose you buy something in a store, and you receive too much change. Would you tell the cashier? For the purposes of this example, let's assume the following:

- The amount of extra change is neither significant nor insignificant;
- You noticed the extra change shortly after leaving the store; and
- You are not sure whether the cashier will be held responsible for the missing change.

Based on the above assumptions, how would the normative Multifaceted-EDM framework apply? The first step is to realize in terms of *proper framing* that this is in fact an ethical dilemma. There are no legal issues; you would not be breaking the law, nor could you be sued for keeping the extra change. While this could be considered an economic dilemma related to your self-interest, if for example the amount of the extra change was significant, here this is not the case. Does the decision whether to return the change nonetheless have a potential impact on others? The answer is yes in terms of the cashier or the

Business Ethics: An Ethical Decision-Making Approach, First Edition. Mark S. Schwartz.
© 2017 John Wiley & Sons, Inc. Published 2017 by John Wiley & Sons, Inc.

owners of the store and if you realized this, you would possess *moral aware-ness* potentially leading to an automatic initial moral *intuition* that the extra change should be returned. Or you might immediately feel the *emotion* of sym-pathy for the cashier's mistake, especially if you were previously a cashier and made a few mistakes yourself in the past. You might also experience feelings of guilt if you kept the extra change. Experiencing either of these emotions would likely push you towards a moral judgment that you should return the change and motivate you to actually return it. On the other hand, if the cashier was rude, your feelings of anger towards the cashier might lead you to keep the extra change.

In conjunction with intuition and emotion, you might also reflect upon the various *moral standards* in deciding what the right thing to do is. A core moral standard is trustworthiness. Trustworthiness includes honesty. While it does not involve a direct lie, it does appear dishonest to keep the money. Avoiding unnecessary harm in terms of caring would require disclosure, since either the cashier or the owners would be directly or indirectly harmed. Utilitarianism would support giving back the change only if the benefit to you of keeping it does not outweigh the negative impact on the cashier or the store owners. Kantianism, based on reversibility (how would you feel if you were in the shoes of the cashier?) would require returning the change. The store owner's moral property rights would be infringed if you kept the change since the change really belongs to someone else and was given away only due to a mistake. But the most directly relevant moral standard of justice would require you to return the change. Is it fair to keep the change? Under distributive justice, what did you do to deserve it? Does the cashier or store owner deserve to lose income simply because they made an innocent mistake?

Other moral standards, however, would tend to push you toward keeping the change. Relativism would support keeping the change, but only if you assume that most other people would do so as well. Egoism might take into account how much money is involved, how much you need the extra change at that time, and how much time and inconvenience would be involved in returning it.

Assuming you have framed the dilemma properly and then applied all the moral standards, the moral judgment, other than one based on relativism or egoism, should be that you should return the money. But does this necessarily mean that you will actually return the money? This is where the *impediments* or barriers to executing moral judgment might kick in. For example, if the cashier was extremely rude, you might *rationalize* that it is acceptable to keep the money since the cashier is unworthy of concern and deserves to be punished due to the rude behavior (*denial of victim*). You might also conclude that no one will really be hurt if you don't return the extra change especially if the store is part of a big retail chain rather than a mom-and-pop store (*denial of injury*). If you don't notice the discrepancy until you get home, the inconvenience and difficulty you would face doing the right thing might prevent you from returning the money (*self-interest*). Each of these rationalizations combined with your self-interest can make it easy for you to believe that your *moral identity* has remained intact when you don't return the change, even if you came to an initial moral judgment that it is wrong to keep the extra change.

An application of the 3P Filter can help identify and illuminate the rationalization process taking place or emotions that are subconsciously affecting the moral reasoning process. You would probably not want to see the story of how you kept the change and that the cashier was fired as a result in the newspaper. As a parent, you would probably tell your child to return the change as part of maintaining intact your (or your child's) moral identity.[1] Finally, you would probably sleep better at night and avoid any possible guilt knowing you gave back money that did not belong to you, even if you felt angry or upset with the cashier's rude behavior.

While this dilemma referred to receiving too much change, it might also apply to other similar workplace dilemmas, including being paid too much by your employer or your customer, or discovering that you have not paid enough to your supplier. Would you inform the employer, customer, or the supplier, if you were certain they otherwise would not notice? To resolve the dilemma, the moral standards applied to being given too much change would similarly be applied to these situations as well.

The remainder of this chapter presents several examples of other ethical dilemmas actually faced by employees in the workplace and how they were resolved.[2] If you were faced with such dilemmas, what would you do? What did the employee do? Do you agree with how the employee responded? Refer back to Chapter 1 to determine which individual or situational factors would have the greatest influence in your decision. Chapter 2 can assist in understanding the process stages to work through leading from awareness to behavior. Consider the biases, psychological tendencies, rationalizations, and impact of self-interest referred to in Chapter 3 that might prevent you from acting on your moral judgment and doing what you know to be right. As you reflect on these questions, also try to apply the moral standards and the ethical decision-making tests (3P Filter) discussed in Chapter 4 to determine the most appropriate alternative. But before discussing the dilemmas, it can be helpful to realize that there are different categories or types of ethical situations or issues we might face, in other words, not all types of ethical issues are the same.[3] Let's now consider the main types of ethical situations.

Different Types of Ethical Situations

In my view, there are three major types of ethical situations or issues that we typically experience in the workplace: (i) *moral temptations*; (ii) *stand up for ethics*; and (iii) *ethical trade-offs*. Each type of ethical situation is distinguished primarily on the basis of whether the decision maker is affected by the decision and in what respect. For example, in many situations, the decision maker can directly benefit or avoid a loss by choosing a particular alternative, but must then compromise his or her *moral identity*. These sorts of ethical situations can be referred to as issues of (i) *moral temptation*.[4] There can be varying degrees of personal benefit, from minor conveniences like saving some time at work, all the way to receiving a significant bribe payment or kickback, getting a promotion, or avoiding getting fired. In these situations, our *moral willpower* discussed in Chapter 1 usually dictates what we end up deciding to do and whether we will cave in to our wants and desires.

In other cases, the decision maker will potentially suffer negative consequences by acting or not acting a certain way. These are known as (ii) *stand up for ethics* situations. There are several types of *stand up for ethics* situations, including resisting authority by refusing a command such as fudging a budget, resisting peer pressure from colleagues such as padding expenses, or reporting misconduct such as the fraudulent activity of a manager as discussed in Chapter 5. In each of these situations our level of *moral courage* tends to dictate whether we stand up for our core moral values despite the risks to ourselves in doing so.

In some cases, the decision maker is not directly affected in any way, but the decision necessarily means that some people or stakeholders will suffer, while others will benefit from our decisions and actions. These issues can be referred to as (iii) *ethical trade-off* situations. Sometimes in trade-off situations the victims are more easily identified, while in other cases they are unknown or less easily identified. Many refer to *trade-off* dilemmas as "true" or real ethical dilemmas, since they involve "right versus right" or "wrong versus wrong" alternatives such as deciding not to fire one person but as a result needing to fire someone else. For these types of ethical situations, our *moral character* (including our *moral value system* and level of *moral competence*) tends to dictate the sort of moral reasoning process we will engage in to find the optimal ethical solution. Figure 7.1 depicts a typology of the dominant ethical situations or issues we can face in the workplace.

On many occasions, the ethical situation might involve an overlap with the various types of issues indicated, such as refusing a command from an authority figure (e.g., manager) to cheat the customer or client, while at the same time deciding whether to report the manager's wrongdoing. I might also believe I can benefit financially or get someone into trouble I do not particularly like (*moral temptation*) by reporting misconduct while at the same time believe I am *standing up for ethics* by reporting the misconduct. For all types of ethical issues faced by employees, there are typically at least three basic alternatives including: (i) do nothing/status quo; (ii) do something; or (iii) quit. The use of

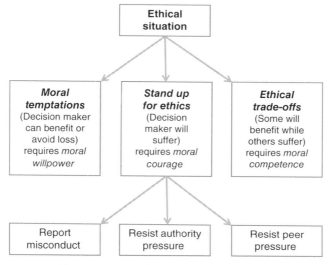

Figure 7.1   Typology of ethical situations.

moral imagination discussed in Chapter 1 can often lead to additional alternatives being perceived as well.

Let's now look at a number of different ethical situations. Each dilemma will be set out in four parts: (i) a *description* of the problem the employee faced; (ii) a brief *commentary* on which moral standards, 3P Filters, or impediments are related to the potential resolution of the dilemma; (iii) a *description* of how the situation was actually resolved ("what happened?") and (iv) my own *conclusion*. For a heightened learning experience, try to avoid the temptation (a dilemma in itself) and decide what you would do if you were the employee *before* reading the commentary. The dilemmas are presented in no particular order.

Pretending to be a Student to Get Competitive Information?

Bill is an employee working at a consulting firm. Often Bill is required to make phone calls to external parties such as customers and industry experts for research purposes for particular clients. Bill's experience working at a previous firm dictated that he should identify himself, his organization, and the purpose of the call. If the client did not want to be named, Bill would state that the client's name is confidential and let the interviewee decide whether to answer his questions. Bill, after having difficulty receiving information on a particular client's file, is then asked by his manager to make calls indicating that he is a business school student conducting research. Doing this would most likely make it much easier for Bill to obtain valuable competitive information for his firm's client. Should Bill now use this strategy, since it appears to have the blessing of a superior at the firm, refuse, or raise the issue directly with a more senior manager or someone else? Try to decide what you would do and why before reading on. Do you know what you would do? Okay, now let's examine the possible considerations.

Commentary

- *Framing*: at first glance this dilemma appears to fall within the economic frame, and perhaps the legal frame if there is a slight possibility of legal liability to the firm by pretending to be a student. But it should also be seen as falling into the *ethical frame* as well, since others could be harmed by the outcome.
- *Trustworthiness*: the ethical value of trustworthiness suggests that based on honesty and transparency, a person asking for information should disclose his or her identity and reason for the request. In this case, the practice clearly violates this value.
- *Kantianism*: Kant would not support treating others, including competitors of a client, with disrespect by using them merely as a means to an end (getting the information by whatever means necessary).
- *Public/Parent tests*: Bill might ask, how would he feel if this practice was reported in the newspaper? Would he tell his own child to do this? These tests might counter any possible rationalizations or biases he might experience that we will now consider.
- *Impediments*: Bill can rationalize based on *obedience to authority* that he is not responsible for his actions of pretending to be a student, rather his manager is responsible. In this situation, the firm's as well as Bill's self-interest is clearly served, because this helps the firm obtain valuable information and demonstrates Bill's value as an employee (*self-serving bias*). Bill could also rationalize based on an *appeal to higher authorities* that this is in the best interest of his firm, rather than his own self-interest. Ultimately, Bill may go through a process of *moral disengagement* and convince himself that the moral standards do not apply.

What happened?

Bill refused to pretend to be a student and *stood up for his ethics*, and discussed the issue directly with a senior manager. Bill also indicated to the senior manager that all employees could use some further guidance on this issue.

Conclusion

Bill did the right thing by refusing primarily based on trustworthiness, but it's not clear many others would have done the same. Bill demonstrated strong *moral courage* by raising the matter with a senior manager. The fact that Bill's manager made this request to Bill suggests that improvements to the firm's *ethical corporate culture* are in order.

Disclose Leaving Firm for Graduate School?

Jean is working for a prominent investment bank. Jean decides to apply for an MBA at several business schools, and she needs time off from work for interviews. If Jean tells her boss the truth about her plans to leave the company, she is at risk of being immediately unemployed for up to a year. Jean would also risk giving up important benefits such as health insurance and this year's bonus. Also, if she doesn't lie and winds up getting fired, the graduate schools might reject her. If Jean lies to her boss and says that she was sick or had a family obligation, she would most likely preserve her job security and health benefits as well as her bonus but compromise her moral identity. What should Jean say to her boss?

Commentary

- *Framing*: this dilemma involves both the economic (Jean's self-interest) and ethical frames (possible impact on the firm).
- *Trustworthiness*: this core ethical value is clearly at play. If Jean lies to her boss she is acting dishonestly with a lack of transparency.
- *Kantianism*: Kant's universalizability would never permit lying, since the purpose of making a statement would become self-defeating if everyone lied. If Jean places herself into her manager's shoes, and wants to treat him with respect and not merely as a means to an end, Jean would provide full disclosure of her real plans to her boss.
- *Pillow test*: the pillow test and the inability to sleep at night would likely make Jean feel guilty through her conscience for lying.
- *Intuition:* it is likely that Jean's intuition or gut reaction would tell her that flat out lying to a manager is wrong. But this is where the rationalization process can kick in providing a justification for acting in what would normally be considered to be an unethical manner.
- *Impediments*: Jean might believe that the relatively small cost to the firm of needing to replace her meant that no one was really harmed (*denial*

of injury). Jean clearly should lie in order to protect her short-term and long-term interests assuming there is a low risk of getting caught in her lie (*self-interest*).

What happened?

In the end, when faced with this *moral temptation* situation, Jean lied and first told her boss she was sick. Jean then said after her "recovery" from her illness that she needed to check out wedding venues, as well as needing to travel for her fiancée's family reunion. She ultimately was prepared to sacrifice the loss of trust by her boss (and a future reference letter) in order to ensure being accepted into a prestigious MBA program. While it was a relief when Jean finally disclosed that she was leaving her firm, she knew her boss would never trust her again.

Conclusion

Jean acted unethically by lying, although we might understand why she would be prepared to do so under the personal circumstances she was facing. Her "need for personal gain" was quite strong, the opportunity was there, and the risk of sanctions was slight. We might wonder whether Jean could have first spoken to her boss to discuss the situation, or whether it would represent too great a risk. For Jean to have told the truth to her boss and risk the consequences would have required a very strong *moral character*, which Jean appears not to have possessed. This dilemma often appears for MBA students, who sometimes receive MBA tuition from their firms even though they know they will not return to their firms after completing their degrees.

Sending Emails to Boss's Personal Account?

Mike works for a firm which has a strict policy against employees sending work-related emails to their personal email accounts. The concern is over client confidentiality and information security risks, and the policy applies to all employees and managers at all levels. Mike discovers that other analysts do not always follow the rule. They email spreadsheet models to their personal email accounts on Fridays so they can work on them from home over the weekend. Although employees have firm-owned laptops, taking them home is inconvenient, and employees cannot log into the company's network from home computers. While working with his boss on a project, Mike is asked to send several files to his boss's personal email account so she can review them at her country home over the weekend. Mike's boss would play a significant role in writing his end-of-year review. Should Mike comply with his boss's request, or refuse?

Commentary

- *Framing*: this situation might be perceived by Mike only as a legal (breach of confidentiality) dilemma. But there are ethical implications as well that may or may not be perceived by Mike.
- *Trustworthiness*: based on loyalty to the client and his firm, this core ethical value would require Mike to follow the firm's policy of not sending the work-related emails to ensure confidentiality of the client's information. Mike might, however, feel a degree of conflicting loyalty to his boss to assist in her request.
- *Kantianism*: under universalizability, the purpose of maintaining strict confidentiality would be defeated if all emails could be sent to personal accounts.
- *Public test*: this test would likely help identify sending the emails as ethically problematic since we would not want this activity to be publicly broadcast.
- *Impediments*: the pressure from Mike's boss could lead to *obedience to authority* by Mike as well as a possible rationalization that the rule does not always need to be followed (*prohibition unjustified*). Mike might also believe it is in the best interest of the firm for his boss to work from home on weekends (*appeal to higher authorities*). Since other analysts are not following the rule, it may be seen as being ethically justified given the group norm (*everyone else is doing it*). In terms of *self-interest*, Mike may believe it is in his best interest in terms of keeping his job or avoiding a poor performance review to send the emails to his boss's personal email account.

What happened?

Mike sent the files to his boss's home email account when faced with pressure from his manager. Mike was never reprimanded, and he wonders how his boss would have reacted if he had refused to send the files.

Conclusion

Mike acted unethically by sending the files and did not *stand up for his ethics* when faced with this ethical dilemma by breaching loyalty to the client. His own self interest and concern over his performance review took priority over any other ethical concerns. Clearly there are issues in the firm's ethical corporate culture in terms of ethics training and ethical leadership that need to be addressed.

Take Advantage of Firm's $25 Dinner Policy?

As an analyst working one summer at a prominent Wall Street investment bank before graduating from college, Samantha discovers that she is somewhere beneath the bottom of the totem pole. She also discovers that it is common practice for analysts to work very long days, typically to support the senior analysts and associates. As one possible fringe benefit, however, the bank provides dinner for employees who work past 7:00 p.m. Each employee is permitted to charge up to $25 for dinner. An employee can order the dinner to arrive at the office just past 7:00 p.m., and then take the dinner home with them. Dinner charges are then consolidated into expenses and billed to the client. In principle, "free" dinners are intended to compensate duty-bound employees who are required to work late for clients. Samantha discovers, however, that junior bankers stay just a few minutes past 7:00 p.m. to receive their free dinners and then leave. Samantha is concerned that the dinner policy is being abused and clients being unfairly charged. On the other hand, the aggregate dollars involved are small relative to the total transaction values, and Samantha believes that the junior bankers, including Samantha herself, generally work hard for the firm. Samantha also considers taking advantage of the dinner policy. What should Samantha do?

Commentary

- *Framing*: this might initially not be seen by Samantha as raising any ethical or even legal concerns, and thus any ethical implications might be ignored.
- *Kantianism*: while free food can be a powerful motivator, this practice would be prohibited by Kant due to reversibility and respect towards the firm and its clients.
- *Trustworthiness*: trustworthiness would be violated by this practice in terms of being honest and loyal towards the firm's clients.
- *Moral rights*: this practice can be considered a form of theft as an infringement of the moral property rights of clients.
- *Justice*: distributive justice or fairness supports taking the meals if Samantha is working harder than what was expected and there is a relatively small cost for the meals.
- *Impediments*: if there is a perceived negligible or "intangible" impact on the clients, it is easy to rationalize taking the food (the *abstract versus the tangible* tendency combined with the *denial of the injury* rationalization). The actions of other junior bankers would support charging the client for the dinners since this is the work group norm (*everyone else is doing it*). If Samantha believes she has worked harder than others, she might

rationalize that she deserves the free meals (*claim to entitlement*). It's also possible Samantha might engage in *moral equilibrium* by believing she has built up enough ethical credits that she can deviate slightly in this particular case. Samantha's *self-interest* supports taking the free meal if there is little chance of getting caught or suffering any major consequences.

What happened?

Samantha initially began to *stand up for her ethics* by cautiously raising the issue with a few junior bankers. They did not seem too concerned, and Samantha noticed that they continued to take advantage of the dinner policy. As a result, Samantha when faced with this *moral temptation* situation also then decided to take advantage of the dinner policy as well, but only occasionally.

Conclusion

Taking the food is unethical due to a breach of the moral property rights of clients (technically a form of theft), but since the practice is so pervasive, it needs to be addressed by Samantha's organization. In other words, the "free" food really should simply be explicitly considered part of an employee's compensation package as a fringe benefit. The lack of monitoring (opportunity), the fact everyone else was taking advantage of the dinner policy, and the perceived insignificant harm to clients appear to have allowed this practice to be rationalized and continue to take place. Samantha could argue that although the "spirit" of the policy might be infringed, the "letter" of the policy is still being complied with, and the firm has the responsibility to modify its free food policy if they will not accept technical compliance. This might, however, lead to a "slippery slope" *incrementalism* situation for these employees including Samantha where an initial minor ethical violation makes it easier to later engage in much more serious ethical violations. In this case, Samantha's *moral consultation* with her colleagues only reinforced the view that it was acceptable to take advantage of the dinner policy. In addition, Samantha's *moral character* was not strong enough for her to realize that what she was doing was wrong.

Disclose Impending Layoffs?

Steven works for a firm for several years and makes several very good friends, even outside of the department he works in. Steven discovers in his new role reporting directly to a senior executive that his firm's performance has been lagging and that there is a need for a significant cut in the number of employees from each division. Steven is tasked with discussing head count cuts with other senior level executives and compiling the final list of employees to be let go. This places Steven in a difficult situation as he knows the financial and personal situations of many of the employees on the list. Steven knows that most employees are unaware of the cuts and as a result Steven would like to warn his friends. Steven also has the ability to leverage his position to get rid of the people he does not like, despite being competent at their jobs. What should Steven do?

Commentary

- *Emotions:* anticipating the emotion of guilt by not telling his friends or acting upon the emotion of anger or resentment towards others might influence Steven's decision making and actions in an inappropriate manner.
- *Trustworthiness/loyalty:* Steven would want to remain loyal to his friends and warn them of the impending layoffs, but Steven also has conflicting obligations of loyalty to his firm and his management to keep the information confidential.
- *Caring:* Steven would want to take into account the harm that will be caused due to the firings, and might want to take steps to avoid this harm by warning his friends.
- *Kantianism:* Kant would require confidentiality to be maintained, since breaching confidentiality cannot be universalized.
- *Impediments:* Steven has received a directive from his superiors (*obedience to authority*) and can then deny any moral responsibility for the decision to fire employees, including his friends. Steven's desire to maintain his friendships or to get rid of colleagues he dislikes or who pose a threat might affect his decision of how to act (*self-interest*).

What happened?

Steven did not disclose the potential layoffs to anyone, and did not give any special treatment to his friends or enemies. All recommendations were based solely upon performance metrics and input from senior executives. In the end, the layoffs were not required when the CEO cancelled the plan. Steven then suffered from strained personal relationships with several friends due to his unwillingness to disclose the confidential information and lost the trust of several of his team members.

Conclusion

Steven acted ethically when faced with this combined *moral temptation* and *ethical trade-offs* (friends versus the firm) situation, despite having his *moral character* tested. Loyalty to his managers, the firm, and its owners took precedence over loyalty to his friends. While Steven might have tried to explain to his friends when telling them they would be fired that the information must not be disclosed to anyone else, the fact that Steven would be prepared to breach confidentiality might suggest that his friends would likely do the same and disclose to their friends as well.

Let Manager Take Credit for Your Analysis?

Barbara's manager asks her if he can speak to her for a moment. It was the first week for Barbara on a new project at her consulting firm. Barbara has just completed an analysis for her new manager, whom she has never worked with before. Barbara assumes her manager wanted to review her work, but she is mistaken. Instead, the manager explains to Barbara that he is up for a critical performance review, and was under pressure to demonstrate stronger analytics. He "asks" Barbara if he could take credit for her analysis. The manager acknowledges that it was an inappropriate request, but reiterates the pressure he is under, and indicates that there would be many other opportunities to build Barbara's reputation at the firm. Barbara is not sure how to respond. Should Barbara clearly and strongly object, risking her personal career development? Should Barbara identify a more appropriate way to help her manager, who was obviously distressed about his career? Should Barbara say nothing, and try to distance herself from the situation? Should Barbara ask a teammate to intervene and try to help resolve the situation? Should Barbara inform her manager's manager about this request?

Commentary

- *Trustworthiness*: the manager would be acting in an untrustworthy manner by being dishonest in taking credit for Barbara's work. But Barbara also would be contributing to the dishonesty by not saying anything. This would conflict with possible feelings of loyalty, however, towards her manager.
- *Caring*: this might be a situation where Barbara can feel she is doing a lot of good for her manager at relatively little cost to herself. Her action could be seen by the manager as Barbara being a team player by allowing him to take credit for her work.
- *Kantianism*: Kant would never support the practice of taking credit for someone else's work, or even letting someone else take credit for your own work. The practice cannot be universalized since the purpose of being rewarded for your own performance would become self-defeating. Kant

would indicate that Barbara's manager is using Barbara as merely a means to an end in terms of the manager's forthcoming performance review.

- *Justice*: letting the manager take credit would clearly violate distributive justice since the manager does not deserve to unfairly benefit from work he did not complete.
- *Impediments*: if not too important, it can be easier to rationalize saying nothing, especially if the manager's performance review is important to Barbara's career advancement (*self-interest*). *Obedience to authority* would also play a potential role in Barbara saying nothing to anyone due to her manager's request.

What happened?

Barbara said nothing and did not *stand up for her ethics*, giving tacit permission to her manager to take credit for her work. The result was disastrous for the manager. While reviewing the analysis with the partners, the manager could neither explain what had been done nor handle their objections. The manager was reassigned within one week, and left the firm at the end of the month. Unfortunately, the manager was not able to find another management position at another company. Barbara wonders if she would have said anything further if the analysis had received rave reviews from the partners.

Conclusion

While Barbara did not act unethically by not saying anything, there was nothing morally praiseworthy in her actions despite an appearance of humbleness and being a team player. Attempting to work out a different solution with the manager that did not involve plagiarism such as co-authorship, with the manager actually contributing to the report, would have addressed the key ethical concerns, but Barbara did not have the *moral courage* to take this route.

Disclose Mistake to Manager and Client?

Robert is working for a consulting company on a marketing project for a client. Robert has been with his consulting firm for less than six months. Robert's responsibilities on the project include measuring the financial impact of a new marketing promotion that his firm has created for the client. To measure the impact, Robert developed a methodology to measure the likely results. This was a relatively sophisticated analysis that the clients did not fully understand. However, the client was happy since over the first three months the promotion had increased profits by a significant amount. Three months into the promotion, Robert goes through the data and realizes that unfortunately there is an error in one of the spreadsheet cells. Although it was only an error in one cell of a six tab spreadsheet, Robert knows it could have serious ramifications for the results that have been reported to the client for the first three months. Robert updates the spreadsheet, and realizes that instead of the original reported amount of profits, the profits had only improved by half the amount. Robert fixes the error, but must now decide how to handle it. Robert, being new to his firm, is still in his probationary period. If Robert discloses the error to his manager, he believes he will look incompetent and would likely be let go. Since Robert is the only one who truly understands the spreadsheet, it is very unlikely anyone else would figure out the error. If it wasn't mentioned, everyone would just think the promotion was losing its positive impact. Should Robert tell his manager about the error? Should the client be informed of the mistake?

Commentary

- *Framing*: this dilemma might not even appear on the radar screen for many as an ethical dilemma, due to *ethical blindness*. It might instead at best be seen as possibly legal in nature if there is any concern about being sued by the client for the mistake, or economic in terms of Robert keeping his job or the firm losing its client.
- *Trustworthiness*: transparency and honesty would require full disclosure of the mistake to the manager and the client.
- *Responsibility*: taking full responsibility and being accountable for his actions including the mistake would require Robert to fully disclose, apologize, and fix the mistake.
- *Utilitarianism*: if there is little likelihood of any future harm to the client resulting from this mistake, then overall the tendency would be to do nothing in terms of net consequences to all those affected.
- *Compensatory justice*: fair compensation would need to be provided to the client if the mistake caused any loss, but this does not appear to be the case here.
- *Impediments*: since we tend to have strong ethical perceptions of ourselves (*overconfidence*), there is an incentive to rationalize doing nothing and simply hope no one will notice or really care if the mistake is discovered (*overoptimism*). The *self-interest* of Robert and the impact on his firm of possibly losing the client would also suggest not reporting the mistake, since there was little chance of it being detected and Robert presumably wants to keep his job.

What happened?

Robert informed his manager of the mistake despite the *moral temptation* not to. His manager fortunately took it in his stride and consoled Robert that small errors can be a common part of the job. This was a form of *moral consultation* with his manager. There was a concern, however, regarding full disclosure to the client and maintaining the client's trust. Since the client did not really understand the measurement methodology, Robert's manager announced at the next meeting with the client the reduced benefit of the promotion and explained it as a "refinement" to their methodology to take additional factors into account and more accurately measure the program. This was partially true but also masked the error. At the announcement, the clients barely noticed and accepted the refinement since the promotion was still providing significant benefits. The meeting quickly went on to other topics and the issue did not resurface again. Robert did not *stand up for ethics* and press the issue further.

Conclusion

It's always difficult and challenging to admit mistakes, whether to our superiors or clients or even to our loved ones. Taking responsibility, however, with Robert disclosing his mistake, in this case to his manager and the client as well, would have been the ethical action to take but would have required significant *moral courage*. Fortunately, discussing the matter with the manager worked out overall for Robert, but complete honesty with the client was not achieved.

Say Something When Boss Exaggerates Your Resume?

Lori works in advertising account management, where the motto is to "keep the client happy at all times". This occasionally calls for a certain degree of spinning the truth. For example, if a deadline is not met for the client, Lori's firm would respond that the work wasn't quite at a level that met the client's needs, even though the reality was that the creative team had not yet had a chance to work on the project. This was considered part of the job and was even encouraged by Lori's supervisors. One day Lori discovers that her manager sent her resume to a client. Lori reads the resume and realizes that her work experience and knowledge have been exaggerated to the point where it is completely fabricated. She also discovers after talking with her friends that also work in the industry that this is apparently the norm. Lori needs to decide whether to say anything, confront her boss and demand the client be told the truth about her experience, talk to the client directly herself, or go over her boss's head to discuss with more senior managers the blatant misrepresentation of her record. What should Lori do?

Commentary

- *Trustworthiness*: based on honesty and loyalty towards the client, Lori should ensure that the client is aware of her actual work experience and is not misled.
- *Utilitarianism*: if the expected outcomes will be met for the client and no one will really be hurt by the deception, then this would support the exaggeration in terms of overall consequences.
- *Sleep test*: telling her manager she is uncomfortable with the situation and letting him decide whether to inform the client might be sufficient to allow Lori to sleep peacefully at night.
- *Impediments*: the fact that the manager condones the practice (*obedience to authority*) means that Lori can rationalize that she is no longer morally responsible for the outcome (*denial of responsibility*). Lori might also rationalize that she is merely acting in the best interests of the firm (*appeal to higher authorities*). There is also no tangible harm to the client (*the tangible versus the abstract* and *denial of injury*) if Lori believes in the end she can do the work in a manner acceptable to the client. Since the norm in the advertising industry is for employees to exaggerate their experience, it is morally acceptable for Lori to do so as well (*everyone else is doing it*). Exaggerating her work experience to the client may be in the best interests of Lori and her relationship with her boss assuming this will not be realized by the client with any further implications (*self-interest*).

What happened?

Lori initially *stood up for her ethics* and spoke with her boss and indicated she felt uncomfortable about lying to the client. The boss explained that the client wanted someone working on the project with more experience than Lori possessed, so they were enhancing Lori's accomplishments and skills merely in order to appease the client and give them what they wanted. Lori did nothing further and rationalized that agencies had a habit of spinning the truth to clients, and that this was no different. The client was happy and remained pleased with the agency.

Conclusion

The ethical action, despite the challenges, would have been to confront the manager and then inform the client in a delicate way what Lori's actual experience and skills were. However, it appears Lori was able to rationalize, based on industry norms and acting in the best interest of the firm, that this was not necessary. Such practices might also lead to *incrementalism*, with bigger lies and misrepresentations to clients also becoming considered to be an acceptable practice.

Report Friend with Substance Abuse Problems?

Peter works for an equity research department of a leading global firm. Peter is one of several analysts on the team. Peter has built a strong personal relationship with Steve, the senior analyst on the team. Peter works closely together with Steve and Steve becomes Peter's mentor. Steve spends countless hours training Peter, and never hesitates to stay late when Peter needs help with intricate challenging analyses. Steve and Peter become close friends, and often socialize outside of work. Unfortunately, Steve's work ethic and professional behavior deteriorate. Steve's presence at work becomes sporadic, and he becomes irritable when dealing with clients and colleagues. Steve begins to ask Peter to cover for him and lie about his whereabouts. Peter's integrity has now been put at risk, and his productivity is suffering as he takes on a significant portion of Steve's work. After nearly a month, Peter confronts Steve and Steve confesses that he has a substance abuse problem but promises to get help. Peter soon realizes that Steve has not taken any concrete steps to address his addiction. Should Peter report Steve's situation?

Commentary

- *Emotions*: emotions such as empathy towards Steve might play a role in affecting the decision-making process.
- *Trustworthiness*: trustworthiness in terms of honesty would require not lying about Steve's whereabouts. Loyalty to Steve as a mentor and friend would mean Peter should do nothing. This dilemma highlights the challenges of conflicting loyalties in the workplace.
- *Utilitarianism*: a determination would have to take place of the likely outcome of reporting Steve on Peter himself, on Steve, and on others. If Steve's substance abuse problem was putting anyone in physical risk or serious financial harm, then Peter would be required to report Steve, regardless of the consequences to Steve.
- *Justice*: if Peter was to report Steve, there might be an option of warning him first based on procedural fairness and transparency to give him one last chance to address his substance abuse problem.
- *Impediments*: the self-interest of Peter is mixed, with friendship and gratitude to Steve being pitted against Peter's job performance and workload (*self-interest*) along with loyalty towards his firm, its owners, and the firm's clients (*appeal to higher authorities*).

What happened?

Despite Peter's awareness that reporting Steve was theoretically the right action, Peter did not report his friend Steve's situation, despite Peter's own workload becoming unmanageable, and client relationships being affected. Steve ultimately left the firm six months later, although the departure was on his own terms.

Conclusion

Rather than immediately report Steve, based on loyalty to the firm and its clients, as well as procedural justice, Peter should have warned Steve he must take steps to address his addiction or action will unfortunately need to be taken. If nothing changed, Peter should then have reported Steve's situation to his manager if he was unaware of what was going on. There may have been an opportunity that was not realized for Peter to work with Steve to get him the addiction assistance he needed, or to do this with the firm's assistance. This is an example of an *ethical trade-off situation* where someone will necessarily likely get hurt no matter what action (or inaction) is taken.

Hire Son of Important Client?

Janice is looking for a student to hire for an intern position at a fund she is running. Janice interviews several highly motivated students from top schools each possessing stellar grades and qualifications, and is about to hire one particular candidate that clearly stands out above the rest. Just before making the final decision, an important business client calls Janice to suggest that his son be hired for the job. Janice interviews the client's son and realizes that he is not nearly as impressive as the other front-running intern candidate. The problem is that turning down the son could risk losing the client. Should Janice hire the son to preserve the client?

Commentary

- *Trustworthiness:* loyalty towards the client and possibly to the firm would suggest Janice hire the client's son.
- *Justice:* according to distributive justice, it would clearly not be fair to hire the son of the client, since he does not deserve the position based on his capabilities and prospective contribution when compared with the other candidate. Procedural justice would also be violated, given the bias that Janice would be exhibiting due to the candidate's father being a client.

- *Impediments*: in this case, Janice could easily rationalize hiring the son, in terms of denial of any real harm taking place to the firm or even to the other candidate whom Janice might presume is well suited to find another position elsewhere (*denial of injury*). Hiring the client's son might also be perceived as the decision that will overall be most beneficial to the firm, given the relatively negligible negative impact of hiring a less qualified candidate for an intern position (*appeal to higher authorities*). This might be considered an ethical norm within the firm or industry in that favoritism often takes place when making decisions about interns (*everyone else is doing it*). It would likely be in the best interest of Janice to heed the client's request, given that this is an important client and there might be a risk of losing the client if she refuses to hire the son (*self-interest*).

What happened?

Janice explained to the client that while the son had an impressive resume, he had not yet acquired the requisite experience for the position. Janice was able through her contacts to find another better suited internship for the client's son, however.

Conclusion

These sorts of favoritism dilemmas occur frequently. Often the relative of a senior executive is looking for a position, and unofficial pressures are exerted to ensure the hiring takes place. By speaking with the client, Janice *stood up for her ethics* and demonstrated strong *moral courage*. The exercise of *moral imagination* might have led to one other option, such as attempting if possible to recuse herself from the hiring decision, although this would have simply passed the same dilemma onto someone else.

Post Rave Reviews for Product on Internet?

Lorne works on a team that creates a health care valuation software product. The team has spent approximately $1 million building and marketing the online product. At one of the marketing meetings, a colleague proposes that everyone pretend to be customers and visit online product review sites, discussion boards, and blogs and write "rave reviews" for the product. Everyone seems to think this is a good idea, and no one including the team leader expresses any disapproval of the suggestion. There is also a suggestion that Lorne write a Wikipedia page with some marketing content, although Wikipedia has policies against such practices. As far as Lorne was aware, it was legal to post reviews anonymously or under a false name. Lorne knows that most people do not use their real names online anyway. No one seemed to understand how Wikipedia's unenforceable policies had any bearing on behavior. The product designers were familiar with the tool and believed it was worth raving about. Every client who used Lorne's firm's product would save thousands of dollars. If Lorne's firm does not get the word out, other potential clients might not find out about it. On the other hand, was this too devious a marketing technique, which might make people angry at Lorne's firm if it was discovered? What should Lorne do?

Commentary

- *Trustworthiness*: honesty and transparency if upheld would play a direct role in resolving this dilemma by avoiding the posting of false reviews.
- *Kantianism*: Kant's universalizability would also prohibit such practices since the purpose of posting reviews would be self-defeating if everyone posted bogus or biased reviews. In terms of reversibility, if Lorne were in the shoes of his competitors, he would not want them to post fake reviews.
- *Utilitarianism*: Lorne could try to argue utilitarianism to support the deceptive behavior, if he truly believes the firm's product would benefit everyone overall.
- *Justice*: it would be unfair to the competition according to procedural justice if Lorne posted fake reviews of the product.
- *Impediments*: there may be a rationalization process whereby Lorne can deny that anyone really suffers, including the competitors, since the product really is a good product (*denial of injury*). In addition, if everyone else is believed to engage in this behavior, then Lorne can easily justify doing so as well (*conformity bias*).

What happened?

Lorne did not *stand up for his ethics* when faced with peer pressure from his colleagues and went into an online discussion board and posted several comments about how wonderful the product was. A few days later, Lorne was barred from the site and his posts were removed. Lorne's boss then chastised him, and asked his staff that any comments be posted only after identifying themselves as employees. An objective Wikipedia page was created with a link to the firm's website in the "helpful links" section. It was eventually removed from Wikipedia by competitors who instead put a link to their own software products.

Conclusion

The false reviews should not have been posted by Lorne as this is clearly dishonest, regardless of the low risk of any punishment and the opportunity for additional revenues through increased interest in his firm's product. Lorne's *moral character* was apparently not strong enough to come to a proper moral judgment and then resist engaging in the misconduct.

Summary of the Ethical Dilemmas

To help compare the ethical dilemmas discussed, Table 7.1 provides a summary of the various aspects of the ethical issues across several dimensions covered throughout the book. These dimensions include the key individual and situational factors affecting the decision-making process (Chapter 1), the process stages that take place from awareness to behavior (Chapter 2), the potential impediments (Chapter 3), the relevant moral standards and ethical tests that can be applied during the moral judgment stage that might affect the moral reasoning process (Chapter 4), as well as the type of issue (Chapter 7).

Chapter Summary

The above ethical dilemmas help to demonstrate the potential conflict between the moral standards or between competing stakeholder interests. There are three primary types of ethical issues: *moral temptations*, where we must choose between our own interests and those of others, *stand up for ethics*, where we may suffer negative consequences for sticking to what we believe in, and *ethical trade-offs*, where no matter what we choose to do someone will suffer. The most common ethical dilemmas I have seen from business students which involve all three types of ethical situations include issues related to possible theft, conflicts of interests (gifts and entertainment), whistleblowing, taking advantage of or being dishonest to clients/customers, confidentiality, discrimination, harassment, favoritism, bribery/corruption, and anti-competitive activities. As noted in Chapter 1, employees with strong moral character *capability* (moral maturity, moral value system, and moral competence) will be better equipped to handle "ethical trade-off" situations. Employees with strong moral character *commitment* will be most capable of surviving "moral temptation" situations and doing the right thing or "standing up for ethics" despite any possible negative repercussions.

The first step in ethical decision making is to identify and sort out the economic, legal, and ethical implications of the dilemma, hopefully enhancing the potential for *moral awareness*. The *Integrated Ethical Decision-Making* model discussed in Chapter 2 can assist in becoming aware of the various factors (individual and situational) that might be influencing each stage of the decision-making process, along with the potential impediments discussed in

Table 7.1 Summary of dimensions of ethical issues.

Ethical situation	Key factors (Chapter 1)	Process stages (Chapter 2)	Impediments (Chapter 3)	Moral standards/tests (Chapter 4)	Type of issue (Chapter 7)
Pretend to be a student to obtain competitive information?	Individual (moral character) Ethical corporate culture	Awareness Judgment Intention Ethical behavior	Obedience to authority Self-interest Appeal to higher authorities Moral disengagement	Trustworthiness (honesty; transparency) Kantianism (universalizability; reversibility)	Stand up for ethics
Disclose leaving firm?	Individual (moral character)	Lack of awareness Intuitive judgment Unethical behavior	Improper framing Denial of injury Self-interest	Trustworthiness (honesty) Kantianism (universalizability; reversibility) Pillow test	Moral temptation
Send emails to boss's personal email account?	Individual (moral character)	Lack of awareness Unethical behavior	Improper framing Obedience to authority Prohibition unjustified Self-interest Appeal to higher authorities Everyone else doing it	Trustworthiness (loyalty) Kantianism (universalizability) Public test	Stand up for ethics

(continued)

Table 7.1 (Continued)

Ethical situation	Key factors (Chapter 1)	Process stages (Chapter 2)	Impediments (Chapter 3)	Moral standards/tests (Chapter 4)	Type of issue (Chapter 7)
Abuse after 7 p.m. $25 dinner policy?	Organizational (ethical corporate culture, opportunity sanctions) Lack of moral courage	Awareness Moral consultation Judgment Unethical behavior	Improper framing Abstract versus intangible Moral equilibrium Incrementalism Claim to entitlement Everyone else doing it Self-interest	Kantianism (reversibility and respect) Moral rights	Moral temptation
Disclose impending layoffs?	Individual (moral character)	Awareness Judgment Intention Ethical behavior	Obedience to authority Self-interest	Trustworthiness (loyalty) Caring Kantianism (universalizability)	Moral temptation Ethical trade-offs
Give manager credit for work?	Individual (moral courage)	Awareness Unethical behavior	Self-interest Obedience to authority	Trustworthiness (honesty) Caring Kantianism (universalizability; respect)	Stand up for ethics
Disclose mistake to manager and client?	Individual (moral courage)	Awareness Judgment Moral consultation Intention Ethical behavior (partial)	Framing Overconfidence Self-interest Over-optimism	Trustworthiness (honesty; transparency) Responsibility Utilitarianism Compensatory justice	Moral temptation Stand up for ethics

Say something when CV exaggerated by boss?	Individual (moral character) Ethical corporate culture	Awareness Judgment Intention Ethical behavior (partial)	Denial of responsibility Obedience to authority Appeal to higher authorities Tangible versus the abstract Denial of injury Self-interest	Trustworthiness (honesty; loyalty) Utilitarianism Sleep test	Stand up for ethics
Report friend with substance abuse problems?	Individual (moral character)	Awareness Judgment Unethical behavior	Denial of responsibility Self-interest Appeal to higher authorities	Trustworthiness (honesty; loyalty) Utilitarianism Procedural justice	Ethical trade-offs
Hire son of client?	Individual (moral character)	Awareness Judgment Intention Ethical behavior	Denial of injury Appeal to higher authorities Everyone else doing it Self-interest	Trustworthiness (loyalty) Distributive justice Procedural justice	Stand up for ethics
Post fake rave reviews?	Individual (moral character) Organizational (peer pressure)	Lack of awareness Unethical behavior	Denial of injury Conformity bias	Trustworthiness (honesty) Kantianism (reversibility) Procedural justice	Stand up for ethics

Chapter 3. In this respect, the *Integrated Ethical Decision-Making* model at the very least provides a means to identify the various issues that can arise in coming to a moral judgment leading to ethical behavior.

The *Multifaceted Ethical Decision-Making* model *(Multifaceted-EDM)* discussed in Chapter 4 can provide *prescriptive* (actions to undertake) or *proscriptive* (actions to avoid) assistance by incorporating the dominant moral standards and key ethical decision-making tests into the moral judgment stage of the ethical decision-making process. For the most challenging dilemmas where all outcomes are negative, the ability to use moral imagination (i.e., imagine other possible alternatives) can also potentially lead to less ethically offensive outcomes. Did the employees make the same decisions you would have made? For those who want to work through more complex ethical issues or dilemmas taking place in a business context, you can review the list of Hollywood movies indicated in Appendix D, many of which are based on true events.

Now that we have worked through a series of dilemmas, we can move on to the Conclusion of the book which provides a series of key recommendations to help improve our ethical decision making and behavior.

Notes

1. To check this, I asked my 8-year-old son this question after we watched together the original 1971 movie "Willy Wonka & the Chocolate Factory." We had just watched the concluding scene (spoiler alert!) when the poverty stricken Charlie returns to Willy Wonka the "Everlasting Gobstopper" candy rather than selling it to a supposed Wonka competitor (Slugworth) for a large sum of money (even after Charlie's Grandpa Joe suggests he give the candy to Slugworth). It appears that on the basis of this ethical act, demonstrating his strong moral character and ability to overcome moral temptations, Charlie is deemed worthy by Willy Wonka of being gifted the entire chocolate factory. Wonka says "So shines a good deed in a weary world" and reminds us (at least in a movie) that acting ethically doesn't always necessarily cost, but can also pay. My son (fortunately) said he would also return any extra change he was given.

2. These dilemmas were presented to me by MBA students over the years as part of a class exercise. The dilemmas have been modified from their original versions.

3. In a study by Mudrack and Mason (2013), a review of the various ethical decision-making research instruments revealed six different categories of ethical dilemmas: (1) dilemma (there are two possibilities, neither of which is practically acceptable); (2) classic (a dilemma – however, the decision maker has complete freedom of action and the victims are identified); (3) conspiracy (agreement between at least two persons to break the law or commit an ethical violation in the future); (4) Sophie's choice (based on the book and movie where there are two equally undesirable alternatives); (5) runaway trolley (helping one person creates harm for

another, similar to the decision whether to switch the trolley onto different tracks in order to save additional lives); and (6) whistleblowing (inform someone about inappropriate activities). These categories are based on three different dimensions upon which each dilemma can be categorized including: (i) whether the protagonist (decision-maker) possesses free choice (i.e., not being ordered to act a certain way); (ii) whether the protagonist benefits (self-interest); and (iii) whether there is victim salience (a specific victim is harmed).

4. See: Kidder (1995).

References

Kidder, R.M. 1995. *How Good People Make Tough Choices: Resolving the Dilemmas of Ethical Living.* New York: Simon & Schuster.

Mudrack, P.E. and Mason, E.S. 2013. Dilemmas, conspiracies, and Sophie's choice: vignette themes and ethical judgments. *Journal of Business Ethics*, 118: 639–653.

Conclusion

Navigating the Moral High Road

This book is intended to provide both a *descriptive* and *normative* approach to ethical decision making in a general yet also *practical* manner. Let's look how each of these approaches come together in order to navigate the moral high road.

Part One explored *descriptively* why people decide to act ethically or unethically. Chapter 1 outlined the individual and situational approaches to explaining ethical decision making. Chapter 2 proposed a new ethical decision-making model that attempts to integrate the literature through a new approach called "Integrated Ethical Decision Making." Chapter 3 discussed the major impediments to ethical decision making, including biases, psychological tendencies, moral rationalizations, and self-interest.

Part Two used a *normative* lens to address how we should resolve ethical dilemmas through appropriate moral judgment. Chapter 4 presented a "Multifaceted Ethical Decision-Making" model which included reflection on several moral standards as well as the "3P Filter" to arrive at an ethically justified decision. Chapter 5 offered a normative framework for answering the question when it is morally permissible or even obligatory to report misconduct.

Part Three applied the theory in a *practical* manner and provided recommendations for reducing the extent of unethical activity within organizations. To assist in diminishing the occurrence of ethical dilemmas arising in the first place, Chapter 6 suggested three pillars to developing and sustaining an ethical corporate culture including a set of core ethical values, a comprehensive ethics program, and ethical leadership. A set of ethical dilemmas faced by employees were analyzed in Chapter 7 using the previous tools and frameworks set out in the first six chapters of the book.

Business Ethics: An Ethical Decision-Making Approach, First Edition. Mark S. Schwartz.
© 2017 John Wiley & Sons, Inc. Published 2017 by John Wiley & Sons, Inc.

Implications for the *Integrated* and *Multifaceted* Ethical Decision-Making Models

So what are some of the implications of the ethical decision-making models presented in this book? The *Integrated Ethical Decision-Making* (Integrated-EDM) model described in the first three chapters of the book has a number of important potential *implications* for both *academic* and *business* communities. In terms of teaching implications, despite a history of major corporate scandals, a debate continues over the utility of business ethics education.[1] For those like me who teach business ethics, many still argue over what the proper teaching objectives for a business ethics course should be.[2] The Integrated-EDM model suggests that the focus of business ethics education should be on two particular stages of ethical decision making, the *moral awareness* stage and the *moral judgment* stage. Enhancing moral awareness requires students to be exposed to an array of relevant ethical dilemmas. This sensitizes students to the existence of ethical dilemmas and the challenges of their resolution.

By explaining the tools of moral reasoning through the *Multifaceted Ethical-Decision Making* model, including the seven moral standards, students may be better prepared and better able to engage in moral reasoning enhancing their level of *moral competence*. The dangers of egoism in the form of greed along with the deficiencies of solely relying on relativism need to be pointed out to students. Students should also be exposed to the impediments of ethical decision making, so that they will be more alert to when they are in effect and can better guard against their occurrence. Role-playing in class using actual ethical dilemmas faced by employees can assist in the transition from intentions to actual behavior. Ultimately, business students need to possess the analytical tools to be able to determine and actualize what might be considered ethical versus unethical behavior.

Academic research that focuses on the relationship and interaction between moral reasoning, intuition, emotions, and moral consultation needs to be further pursued. It's not clear for example the extent to which intuition and emotions improve ethical decision making or hinder it. It would be valuable if more research is conducted on the particular aspects and types of ethical issues in relation to ethical behavior, beyond issue intensity such as issue importance and issue complexity. New scientific methods and studies of brain activity should assist in this endeavor. Given that the current ethical decision-making models have only partially explained the causes and processes of ethical behavior, clearly more work needs to be done to revise ethical decision-making theory leading to more fruitful empirical examination.

It would also be highly beneficial if future ethical decision-making research continues to consider whether certain individual and/or situational constructs and variables play a more significant causal or moderating role depending on which stage of ethical decision making is taking place. For example, it may be that during the awareness and judgment stages, our moral maturity, moral value system, and moral competence, along with issue intensity, issue importance, and issue complexity, are more important. On the other hand, during the intention to behavior stage, moral identity, moral willpower, and moral courage along with perceived "need for personal gain" might play more important roles. The role of biases, psychological tendencies, rationalizations, and self-interest should also continue to be examined in relation to ethical decision making during each of the stages of decision making.

In terms of managerial considerations, the Integrated-EDM model suggests that ethical corporate culture and moral consultation play important roles in ethical decision making, with formal elements such as codes and training potentially being more important for awareness and judgment. The model also suggests that hiring practices based on seeking individuals with strong moral character should continue to be pursued, especially for managers and senior executives. For managers and employees, the Integrated-EDM model may have possible *normative* implications as well, such as avoiding the sole use of intuition and emotion whenever possible, taking steps to improve our ethical awareness potential, and to always be cognizant of biases, rationalizations, and self-interest affecting the ethical decision-making process.

Key Recommendations and Takeaways

So what can we ultimately learn from our discussion on ethical decision making? The following are suggested as the most important potential *recommendations* or key *takeaways* with respect to ethical decision making resulting from the book.

Gather sufficient facts and use moral imagination

Sometimes lacking sufficient information regarding the situation and our options can make the difference between selecting the most morally appropriate decision. Always take the time whenever possible to properly research the facts and morally consult with others before determining what to do. The process of moral imagination, or realizing there are other possible alternatives to consider, can often be the most important step of the ethical decision-making process, sometimes leading to initial moral awareness in the first place. At the same time the process of gathering information can't go on forever. Remember that although we always want more information, at some point there may be a need to "pull the trigger," make a decision, and then act on that decision.

Be morally aware

Try to be aware of the process of ethical decision making and the factors that might influence our ethical judgment and behavior. Through proper *moral framing* of the situations we face we can become more aware and more sensitive to the fact that we are facing an ethical dilemma in the first place. Steps to recognize and avoid the processes of ethical fading and ethical blindness should be undertaken. Ethical awareness requires effort, and often does not happen automatically.

Avoid bias

Psychological tendencies such as obedience to authority, conformity bias, and incrementalism can all make people of good moral character act in unethical ways they could never have initially predicted. We need to constantly strive to minimize our biases and psychological tendencies through training and getting critical feedback from our trusted friends and colleagues on our intended courses of action through moral consultation.[3]

Avoid making decisions while in an emotional state

Decisions which involve ethical implications can be affected by our emotional state such as empathy, envy, anger, fear, or resentment. Intuitive or gut reaction moral judgments can then ensue, leading to non-rational decisions. If we are able to self-regulate our emotions and pause for a moment before acting, potentially more rational decisions will be made. So how can emotions be self-regulated or controlled? As just one example, avoid the temptation to send an email at work while in an emotional state, particularly while in a state of anger or frustration. While emails should be responded to promptly, it may be necessary to reflect for a period of time before responding. Creating a draft email and letting it sit for a while can be helpful in this respect. Another important technique is giving the other person the benefit of the doubt. We often come to judgments of how we should act based on what we see or perceive, which can trigger automatic emotions. If we give the other person the benefit of the doubt, however, we may not become so emotional. Maybe the other person is just having a bad day? Maybe there are reasons for the other person's behavior, which if we understood, we would be less angry or frustrated? The key is to always ask ourselves if our decisions and actions are emotionally-based, and if so, to try to take out the emotion from affecting our decisions and actions in an improper manner.

Further develop your moral character

Since we will always find ourselves facing challenging ethical dilemmas, we need always to continue to work on further developing and refining our moral character. Remember from Chapter 1 that our moral character includes two dimensions: (i) our moral character *capability* (moral maturity, moral value system, and moral competence); and (ii) our moral character *commitment* (moral identity, moral willpower, and moral courage). A strong moral character can make the difference when facing moral temptations or properly controlling our emotions. While situational factors are not always in our control, the development of our moral character is much more in our control. Ethics education and training is one possibility. Through training we potentially become more aware of the range of ethical dilemmas that might arise or that we are even currently facing but framing only as a business and/or legal concern. Through training, we can improve our level of moral reasoning skills and thus our moral character, including the speed by which we work through difficult ethical issues for ourselves or for others, and our motivation to follow through on our moral judgments. Understanding and engaging in the moral reasoning process involving consideration of all of the moral standards and 3P Filter's ethical decision-making tests is also important. Remember that while considering your own self-interest in deciding how to act is certainly ethically justified, your self-interest should not always take priority when the interests of others are negatively affected as a result.

Strive to be an ethical role model at home and at work

While we can't always change our upbringing or our situational context, we can play an important role for our immediate family members (especially our children) in terms of developing proper moral character. Will we act as moral role models that they will then hopefully emulate later in life? Spouses also play a big role. Will we support our spouse when they decide to take the moral "high road" despite any potential financial hit to our families? We can also play an important role in influencing the ethical behavior of our colleagues, when we are asked for advice or in terms of others emulating our own behavior. As leaders of business firms, whether as manager, senior executive, CEO, or member of the board, our ethical behavior becomes even more significant in terms of impacting the behavior of others as well as affecting the ethical culture of the firm.

Conduct due diligence

Whenever possible, conduct due diligence on the firm for which you are thinking of working. The goal is to try to avoid getting into those situations or working in firm environments where you may be more ethically vulnerable. Sometimes even a simple Google search will reveal legal or ethical issues faced by particular companies. But even better is to try to find someone working in the company who might share some general information on the corporate culture.[4] Questions to ask might include: In general, is the emphasis at the firm on the bottom line or short-term results? Have you been pressured to do things you were not comfortable doing? Is there support at the firm for doing the "right thing?" Most students I ask do not engage in any degree of due diligence on the firms for which they are about to work. Instead, the main concern when seeking employment appears to be compensation/salary.

Don't take personal financial risks

While obviously everyone generally wants to avoid being subject to personal financial difficulties, many are nonetheless willing to take big financial risks for the opportunity for even bigger financial rewards. When we are young and do not have any dependents, this can be considered a reasonable strategy to take if "making it big" is an important goal. But once we have a family to provide for, taking big risks to improve our financial situation can lead to severe financial pressures. If it doesn't work out, the odds are only increased that we will engage in misconduct when the opportunity and potential rewards are there. One way to avoid problems is to save and build up a "walk away" bank account if at all practical and as early in life as possible to reduce ethical vulnerability. Since financial pressures often drive unethical decision making, it can be important to have sufficient financial resources that allow us to walk away from our job as a last resort if necessary rather than cede to the pressures of acting unethically in order to keep our job.[5]

Be content with your "lot" in life

Building on the previous point, we always seem to want more material possessions: a bigger house, a nicer car, or maybe an expensive watch. We often assess our accomplishments in life based on our net worth compared with our neighbors and friends, rather than the relationships we build or our impact on others. This appears to have become the norm for many living in our consumerist society. The problem is that this can only enhance our continuous perception that we always need more. As discussed in Chapter 1, this perceived "need for personal gain" can often drive unethical decision making. How can this be addressed? I believe the key is achieving basic contentment with our current "lot" in life. Studies show that levels of happiness basically plateau at a certain amount of income.[6] This doesn't necessarily mean that we shouldn't strive to gain more wealth or material possessions. It simply means that hopefully we can be grateful and content for whatever we have at a particular point in time. Reduce the size of your glass so that it will always be "full" with whatever wealth we currently have in our possession. If we are able to diminish our perceived "need for personal gain" or material "wants," then we will always be content with our current financial situation. Easier said than done. But if we do feel content with our "lot," we will no longer have the same desire to cut ethical corners in order to fill our "big gulp" size cup that can never be filled.

Reflect carefully before reporting misconduct

If you witness illegal or serious unethical activity at work, you have several options. If approaching and discussing the matter with the perpetrator or blowing the whistle internally or externally as discussed in Chapter 5 will likely lead to personal repercussions, then quitting may be the only viable option, presuming there is another place you can work. If you are working with an unethical or psychopathic manager, figuring out how to move if at all possible to another department within the company would probably be best.

Ensure an ethical corporate culture exists

As a board member, executive, or manager, ensure that the three pillars of developing and sustaining an ethical corporate culture discussed in Chapter 6 are always in effect. Infuse a set of core ethical values throughout the organization's policies, practices, and processes, implement a comprehensive ethics program, and maintain ethical leadership. Everyone at the firm can play a key role in terms of whether their own behavior contributes to an ethical corporate culture continuing to flourish, or is overtaken by unethical norms.

Pre-commit yourself to ethical action

Based on the idea of "Giving Voice to Values" referred to in Chapter 6, by pre-committing to action through rehearsing or forming behavioral "prescripts" if faced with a particular ethical dilemma, we can increase the likelihood of following words or intentions with consistent actions.[7] This is also known as decreasing the influence of the "want" self so that the "should" self can take priority in decision making.[8]

Respond to and learn from ethical mistakes

As much as we would like to avoid doing so, we need to respond to and learn from our ethical mistakes. We all make mistakes, including ethical mistakes, for a variety of reasons. No one is perfectly ethical in all of their actions, although we hopefully strive to "do the right thing" to the extent this is determinable, whenever possible. Maybe we don't have all the information we need or would like to have before making a decision. Maybe we rushed our decisions, or based them on emotion, biases, or rationalizations rather than carefully reflecting on them. Maybe we face "no-win" situations, and have had to make difficult decisions that have a negative impact on others, including our friends and family members. Accepting this reality, the question then becomes, how do we respond to our mistakes, and what do we learn from them? Do we base our response to our mistakes on the core ethical value of responsibility, by admitting fault, taking reasonable steps to ensure it won't happen again, apologizing, and avoiding blaming others?

Do good for others as well

Remember that acting ethically is not just avoiding unnecessary harm, respecting the rights of others, or acting fairly. Acting ethically is not just sidestepping acting unethically, but doing good for others as well, often referred to as being a "good Samaritan." Most business ethics dilemmas we looked at tended to focus on making decisions that involve selecting the alternative that causes the least harm to others. Moral awareness includes not just realizing when you face a decision-making situation with possible impacts on others, but realizing when you have opportunities to do something good for others as well, even when they don't ask for your help.[9] When we start to live our lives seeking not only to pay back the people who have helped us, but to "pay it forward" to others as well, our workplace and our world will become a better place, both for ourselves and for our children.[10] This can be as simple as holding the door open a little bit longer for someone pushing a stroller or carrying things, to helping someone find a job, to mentoring a colleague at work, to volunteering, or to making a phone call to a family member you haven't spoken to for a long time.

Consider working in other less "profit-oriented" organizational environments

As a final consideration for those who remain concerned, deciding to work outside of the traditional for-profit business world might alleviate some, but certainly not all, of the common pressures that can lead to ethical dilemmas or misconduct in the workplace. For example, working for a social enterprise[11] or "benefit corporation"[12] that attempts to merge together financial returns with societal benefits may diminish some of the pressures many managers and their subordinates face to cut ethical corners or "make more money," rather than do what is considered the morally right thing to do.[13]

Final Thoughts

One important note of caution is necessary. While avoiding legal and ethical scandals and impropriety can certainly save thousands if not millions of dollars in fines or lawsuits to firms and individuals, or indirectly through avoiding loss of image and reputation to the firm and the resultant negative impact for customers/clients, employees, suppliers, and the government, this is not the only reason or even the primary reason for firms and their agents to behave ethically. The reason being advocated is that behaving ethically, however defined, is an obligation in and of itself for each of us operating within society. If upon acting ethically, we take pleasure in knowing that we have "done the right thing," or avoid feelings of guilt, this should be considered only as an additional benefit, rather than being the core reason to behave ethically. While "good ethics" is often "good business," especially in the long term, this is not always the case, and ethics and the bottom line or our self-interest can and do come into conflict. To put it another way, our "should" self *must* always take priority over our "want" self, if our goal is to live a truly ethical life.

Finally, behaving ethically on a consistent basis every day might be considered one of the greatest challenges we face in both our personal and professional working lives. In fact, resolving ethical dilemmas in the workplace has even been referred to as navigating through a "minefield of ethical hotspots."[14] As indicated earlier, it does not matter if we are a religious leader, the leader of a country, a judge, a government prosecutor, a police officer, a doctor, a CEO, or even a business ethics professor. We all slip up, make mistakes, break rules, lie a little bit, violate the law, and even harm others, all the while convincing ourselves through a rationalization process that we are still basically good ethical people. But the degree of difficulty to act consistently in an ethical manner does not mean that it should not be confronted. The contents of this book are just one small part of a learning process or tool, a business ethics "moral compass" of sorts. Hopefully, the book provides a degree of assistance in keeping us on the "moral high road." But at the end of the day, whether we stay on the right path, take minor unethical detours, or get completely lost, is ultimately up to each of us.[15]

Notes

1. See: Bosco *et al.* (2010).
2. See: Sims and Felton (2006).
3. See: Bazerman and Tenbrunsel (2011, p. 159).
4. Of course, confidentiality should still be maintained.
5. Prentice (2014, p. 363) refers to this as "screw you" funds which provides us with a degree of financial freedom to do the right thing when necessary.
6. The suggested threshold level of income whereby happiness does not increase much more is around $75,000. See: Kahneman and Deaton (2010).
7. Gentile (2010).
8. Bazerman and Tenbrunsel (2011); Prentice (2014, p. 363).
9. Grant (2013) provides abundant evidence that "givers," with certain caveats, often succeed much more than "takers."
10. See: Pay It Forward Foundation website, http://www.payitforwardfoundation .org/ (accessed 16 September 2016).
11. A "social enterprise" can be defined as an organization or venture that achieves its primary social or environmental mission using business methods. See: Nemetz (2013, p. 476).
12. A "benefit corporation" can be defined as a corporation that allows a modification of shareholder primacy/shareholder wealth maximization principles to include other objectives such as social impact on the community or environment. See: Nemetz (2013, p. 478).
13. Of course, moral temptations or ethical dilemmas due to performance pressures will arise while working in any organization, including government, academic, non-governmental, and charitable organizations as well.
14. Warren and Smith-Crowe (2008, p. 82).
15. At the end of the day, being truly ethical means doing what you should do even when no one else is watching and no one will ever know except yourself what you actually did. This is the real challenge for each of us to overcome when we are faced with moral temptations or ethical dilemmas.

References

Bazerman, M.H. and Tenbrunsel, A.E. 2011. *Blind Spots: Why We Fail to Do What's Right and What to Do About It*. Princeton, NJ: Princeton University Press.

Bosco, S.M., Melchar, D.E., Beauvais, L.L., and Desplaces, D.E. 2010. Teaching business ethics: the effectiveness of common pedagogical practices in developing students' moral judgment competence. *Ethics and Education*, 5: 263–280.

Gentile, M.C. 2010. *Giving Voice to Values: How to Speak Your Mind When You Know What's Right*. New Haven, CT: Yale University Press.

Grant, A. 2013. *Give and Take*. New York: Viking.

Kahneman, D. and Deaton, A. 2010. High income improves evaluation of life but not emotional well-being. *Proceedings of the National Academy of Sciences of the United States of America*, 107: 16489–16493.

Nemetz, P.N. 2013. *Business and the Sustainability Challenge: An Integrated Perspective*. New York: Routledge.

Prentice, R.A. 2014. Teaching behavioral ethics. *Journal of Legal Studies Education*, 31: 325–365.

Sims, R.R. and Felton, E.L. 2006. Designing and delivering business ethics teaching and learning. *Journal of Business Ethics*, 63: 297–312.

Warren, D.E. and Smith-Crowe, K. 2008. Deciding what's right: the role of external sanctions and embarrassment in shaping moral judgments in the workplace. *Research in Organizational Behavior*, 28: 81–105.

Appendix A

Factors Affecting Moral Character

Which factors affect an individual's *moral character* potentially leading to more ethical decision making? In Chapter 1, the theoretical meaning of moral character is examined, including the dimensions of *moral capability* and *moral commitment*. But we also need to understand why some people end up with a strong moral character, while others do not. When you look at the empirical research on the various factors or variables that might influence or moderate ethical decision making, you quickly discover that impacts have not yet been clearly established.[1] Studies tend to assert that ethical decision making is primarily affected by factors such as your gender, age, education, work experience, or personality. While I agree that there might be some degree of indirect impact due to these factors, I remain skeptical of the value of much of this research to date.

In terms of demographic factors, would a person's *gender* really make a difference in terms of how they behave ethically? Studies have found mixed results,[2] and when any differences have been observed, females tend to be more ethical than males.[3] For example, women seem more inclined to judge questionable activities as less appropriate than men.[4] In my view, while there may be some generalized differences in how men or women recognize, approach, or analyze dilemmas, whether that leads to differences in behavior seems to be a large leap. *Age* has also been examined in many studies, and has also been found to generate mixed results.[5] This may suggest that there is a more complex relationship between age and ethical decision making.[6] Age for example might relate to personal or work experience, which might then relate to generalized differences in how a person analyzes or responds to ethical dilemmas. It has also been suggested that *nationality* or *culture* might impact ethical decision making, with a number of studies finding a degree of influence. What isn't clear, however, is the extent of that influence.[7] In my view, while there may be

Business Ethics: An Ethical Decision-Making Approach, First Edition. Mark S. Schwartz.
© 2017 John Wiley & Sons, Inc. Published 2017 by John Wiley & Sons, Inc.

national or cultural dimensions that can be generalized,[8] the global and often multicultural nature of the workforce would make this feature more difficult to isolate and assess in terms of its impact on ethical decision making.

Another series of demographic factors that have been examined are a person's level of *education*, type of *employment*, and years of *work experience*.[9] The majority of studies have found a positive relationship between these factors and ethical decision making. For example, higher levels of professional affiliation appear to lead to stronger ethical decision making with well trained professionals being more likely to make ethical decisions.[10] It seems though that the type of education a person has acquired, such as being a business or non-business major, leads to little or no effect on the ethical decision-making process.[11]

Personality or psychological factors have also been examined to see if they play a role in ethical decision making. The more heavily studied factors include: level of cognitive development, locus of control, Machiavellianism, religiosity, and philosophy/value orientation. The first factor, a person's *level of cognitive development*, is described in Chapter 1. Would a person who tends to focus on punishments (stage one), rewards (stage two), or the views of others (stage three) in deciding how to act, rather than the law (stage four), societal concern for the welfare of others (stage five), or universal moral principles (stage six), be more or less ethical? For this factor, research has found, with few exceptions, that higher levels of a person's cognitive moral development lead to better ethical judgments and ethical decision making.[12]

Locus of control is another personality dimension that has been examined. Locus of control is defined as a person's perceived control over the outcomes of their own behavior.[13] There are two types of locus of control: internal and external. *Internal* locus of control means the person believes outcomes are the result of their own efforts, while *external* locus of control means the person believes outcomes are determined by fate, luck, or powerful others.[14] So far, research studies on the impact of locus of control on ethical decision making have been mixed, with several studies reporting no significant differences. The studies that have found differences report that individuals with an *internal* locus of control lead to more ethical decision making, while those with an *external* locus of control tend to engage in unethical decision making.[15] Based on the student ethical dilemmas I have seen over the years, quite often, students who believe that they would have little influence over the outcome or expect to leave their positions in the near future, tend to ignore or walk away from situations which might involve unethical activity. Why get involved if you likely won't have any impact and put your own interests at risk?

Another personality factor is called *Machiavellianism*, named after Niccolò Machiavelli, the author of *The Prince*. Machiavellianism is defined as acting in a self-interested, opportunistic, deceptive, and manipulative manner to win no matter what the cost or how it affects other people.[16] It appears that this personality factor does impact ethical decision making, in that those who are Machiavellian tend to make more unethical decisions.[17] *Religiosity* has also been examined to see if it impacts ethical decision making. Religiosity includes the different religious activities, levels of dedication, and beliefs of a person associated with particular religious principles.[18] Studies have found that religiosity tends to have a positive relationship with ethical decision making.[19]

Other studies have examined a person's *philosophy* or *value orientation*. For example, studies have found that people who tend towards *idealism*, meaning they make decisions that maximize the benefits of other parties, are generally more ethical. Those who base their decisions on duty-based principles and are thus considered to be *deontologists* also tend to be more ethical. Those who are more *relativist*, however, by believing that ethics is based on context and situation, who are more *utilitarian* by basing their decisions on consequences, or have more *economic* orientations, tend to be generally less ethical in their decision making.[20]

So overall, which individual factors have been considered relevant for ethical decision making? One of the meta-studies on empirical ethical decision making concludes the following in terms of the individual factors:[21] "The most consistent findings appear in the studies that test for the direct effects of gender, ethical philosophies (i.e., idealism and relativism), cognitive moral development, locus of control, Machiavellianism, and religion. On the other hand, mixed findings were commonly found with regard to education level, work experience, nationality, and age." The bottom line appears to be that overall, there are very few individual variables for which one can say with confidence, based on research conducted to date, that a clear relationship with ethical decision making exists.

Rather than directly affecting the ethical decision-making process as suggested in much research, the key individual variables found in ethical decision-making literature instead appear to potentially affect a person's *moral character* (e.g., *moral maturity* and *moral competence*) which then potentially affects the various ethical decision-making stages. These include *demographic* variables such as gender, age, nationality, education, and work experience, *personality* or *psychological* variables such as cognitive moral development, Machiavellianism, locus of control, or value orientation, and variables more directly related to one's *ethical experience* such as religion/religiosity, ethics training, professional education, and previous ethical dilemma experience.[22] Figure A.1 depicts the groups of factors that are proposed to affect an individual's *moral character* as discussed in Chapter 1.

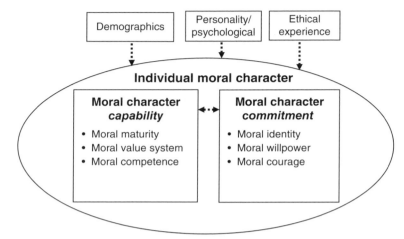

Figure A.1   Individual moral character. *Source*: Schwartz, M.S. 2016. Reproduced with the permission of Springer.

Notes

1. Based on the meta-studies conducted so far including: Ford and Richardson (1994); Loe *et al.* (2000); O'Fallon and Butterfield (2005); Craft (2013); Lehnert *et al.* (2015).
2. See: Craft (2013, p. 230).
3. O'Fallon and Butterfield (2005, p. 379).
4. Mudrack and Mason (2013, p. 582).
5. Craft (2013, p. 239).
6. O'Fallon and Butterfield (2005, p. 392).
7. See: O'Fallon and Butterfield (2005, p. 391). According to Mudrack and Mason (2013, p. 588): "Different groups of respondents sometimes, but not always, differ in their judgments of the appropriateness of ethically questionable activities. More research is needed before any firm, or even tentative, conclusions can emerge regarding relevant differences between and among different groups."
8. For example, see Hofstede's (1980) dimensions of national culture including individualism/collectivism; power distance; uncertainty avoidance; masculinity/femininity; and long-term/short-term orientation.
9. Craft (2013, p. 238).
10. See: Lehnert *et al.* (2015, pp. 200–202).
11. O'Fallon and Butterfield (2005, p. 387). One study on gender and business ethics education found the following in terms of the differences between the genders (Wang and Calvano, 2015, p. 591): "Our results indicate that women are generally more inclined to act ethically than men, but paradoxically women who have

had business ethics instruction are less likely to respond ethically to business situations. In addition, men may be more responsive to business ethics education than women. Finally, women's personal ethical orientations may become more relativistic after taking a business ethics class."

12. O'Fallon and Butterfield (2005, p. 392). Mudrack and Mason (2013, p. 584), however, find that: "There is little evidence that ethical judgments relate systematically to respondent moral reasoning."
13. See: Treviño and Nelson (2011, p. 84).
14. See: Treviño and Nelson (2011, pp. 84–85).
15. See: O'Fallon and Butterfield (2005, p. 392); Mudrack and Mason (2013, p. 584).
16. See: Treviño and Nelson (2011, p. 85).
17. See: O'Fallon and Butterfield (2005, p. 392). Another meta-study found, however, the following: "There is little evidence that ethical judgments relate systematically to respondent Machiavellianism" (Mudrack and Mason, 2013, p. 584).
18. See: Craft (2013, p. 239).
19. O'Fallon and Butterfield (2005, p. 392). Another meta-study, however, came to the opposite conclusion: "There is little evidence that ethical judgments relate systematically with respondent religiosity" (Mudrack and Mason, 2013, p. 582).
20. See: O'Fallon and Butterfield (2005, p. 379). Mudrack and Mason (2013, p. 583) found, however, that: "Ethical idealists tend to regard many, but not all, ethically questionable activities as wrong…but there is little evidence that ethical judgments relate systematically with respondent relativism."
21. O'Fallon and Butterfield (2005, p. 396).
22. See: O'Fallon and Butterfield (2005) and Craft (2013) for a complete list of ethical decision-making individual-related variables that would potentially fall into these categories.

References

Craft, J.L. 2013. A review of the empirical ethical decision-making literature: 2004–2011. *Journal of Business Ethics*, 177: 221–259.

Ford, R.C. and Richardson, W.D. 1994. Ethical decision making: a review of the empirical literature. *Journal of Business Ethics*, 13: 205–221.

Hofstede, G. 1980. *Culture's Consequences: International Difference in Work Related Values*. Beverly Hills, California: Sage.

Loe, T.W., Ferrell, L., and Mansfield, P. 2000. A review of empirical studies assessing ethical decision making in business. *Journal of Business Ethics*, 25: 185–204.

Lehnert, K., Park. Y., and Singh, N. 2015. Research note and review of the empirical ethical decision-making literature: boundary conditions and extensions. *Journal of Business Ethics*, 129: 195–219.

Mudrack, P.E. and Mason, E.S. 2013. Ethical judgments: what do we know, where do we go? *Journal of Business Ethics*, 115: 575–597.

O'Fallon, M.J. and Butterfield, K.D. 2005. A review of the empirical ethical decision-making literature: 1996–2003. *Journal of Business Ethics*, 59: 375–413.

Schwartz, M.S. 2016. Ethical decision-making theory: an integrated approach. *Journal of Business Ethics*, 139: 755–776.

Treviño, L.K. and Nelson, K.A. 2011. *Managing Business Ethics: Straight Talk About How to Do It Right* (5th edn). Hoboken, NJ: John Wiley & Sons, Inc.

Wang, L.C. and Calvano, L. 2015. Is business ethics education effective? An analysis of gender, personal ethical perspectives, and moral judgment. *Journal of Business Ethics*, 126: 591–602.

Appendix B

Descriptive Ethical Decision-Making Models

In order to understand better the academic theoretical basis for the Integrated Ethical Decision-Making (I-EDM) model described in Chapters 1, 2, and 3, this appendix will summarize the dominant ethical decision-making models that have been proposed, along with their graphic depictions. The models described include: (i) the *four-component* model;[1] (ii) the *person–situation interactionist* model;[2] (iii) the *synthesis integrated model*;[3] (iv) an *issue-contingent model*;[4] and (v) the *social intuitionist model*.[5] Several ethical decision-making models contain the same four elements including a *decision process*, modified by *internal* and *external* factors, leading to ethical or unethical *behavior*.[6] The dominant models in the ethical decision making literature will now be described.[7]

The *four-component model* by James Rest is considered to be the dominant *rationalist* model of ethical decision making in that moral reasoning, rather than intuition or emotion, is the essential process that leads to moral judgment.[8] The four components also form the basis for most other ethical decision-making models. The four-component model suggests that there are four distinct and typically sequential process components or stages of ethical decision making:[9]

1. *Moral awareness (or sensitivity)*: moral awareness means becoming *aware* or realizing that there is a moral issue or ethical problem or that the situation has ethical implications.[10] This component has also been referred to as interpreting or recognizing the situation as having a moral nature.[11]
2. *Moral judgment*: if you are potentially aware you are facing an ethical issue, then you can engage in the next stage of the ethical decision-making process, that of moral judgment. Moral judgment has also been referred to as "moral evaluation", "moral reasoning," or as "ethical decision making".[12]

Business Ethics: An Ethical Decision-Making Approach, First Edition. Mark S. Schwartz.
© 2017 John Wiley & Sons, Inc. Published 2017 by John Wiley & Sons, Inc.

Moral judgment is more specifically defined as figuring out what you should do by applying moral standards to the situation to determine the moral course of action.[13]

3. *Moral intention (or motivation)*: your moral judgment may then be converted into a moral *intention* to act which is also referred to as moral "motivation," "decision," or "determination."[14] Moral intent is more specifically defined as giving priority to moral values above other personal values such that a decision is made to intend to do what is morally right.[15]

4. *Action or implementation*:[16] if you have the intention to act, this may not be sufficient. The intentions still need to be acted upon through our *behavior*, which is also referred to as "implementation" or "action." Moral action is more specifically defined as implementing and executing a plan of action based on having sufficient perseverance, strength of conviction, and implementation skills to be able to follow through on your intention to behave morally, to "withstand fatigue and flagging will," and to overcome any obstacles.[17]

Figure B.1 depicts the *four-component model* of ethical decision making.[18]

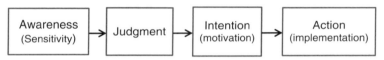

Figure B.1   The four-component model of ethical decision making (adapted from Rest, 1986; Narváez and Rest, 1995).

One of the first comprehensive ethical decision-making models was called a *person–situation interactionist* model by Linda Treviño and included both the "apples" (the individual's moral character) and the "barrels" (the situational environment) in the ethical decision-making process.[19] This model begins by suggesting that the ethical dilemma is analyzed by the individual decision maker via Kohlberg's moral development stages. The moral judgment is then moderated by individual factors including ego strength (strength of conviction or self-regulating skills), field dependence (dependence on external social referents such as work colleagues), and locus of control (perception of how much control one exerts over the events in life). Situational factors also moderate behavior such as immediate job context (reinforcement contingencies such as rewards and punishment for ethical/unethical behavior) and other external pressures (including personal costs, scarce resources, or competition). Organizational culture (normative structure, referent others, obedience to authority, and responsibility for consequences) and characteristics of the work also

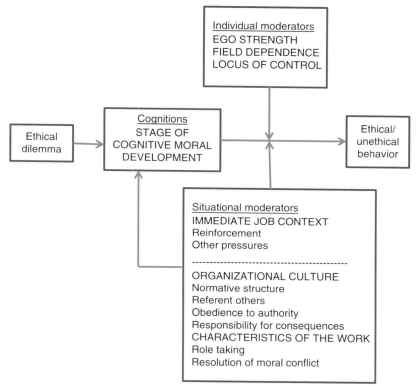

Figure B.2   Person–Situation interactionist model of ethical decision making in organizations (Treviño, 1986).

moderate behavior. Figure B.2 depicts the *person–situation interactionist model* of ethical decision making.

Another approach that builds on and combines several ethical decision-making models is referred to as a *synthesis integrated model* of ethical decision making by O.C. Ferrell, L.G. Gresham, and J. Fraedrich.[20] The model incorporates Kohlberg's moral development theory and also works through different stages of decision making. First, an ethical dilemma arises from the social and economic environment. The decision maker then moves through various stages, including awareness of ethical issues, cognitions (which take into account a person's cognitive stage of moral development based on Kohlberg), moral evaluations (deontological/duties and teleological/consequences), determination/intentions, and then action/behavior. Consequences and behavioral evaluation then follow as a feedback loop back to the

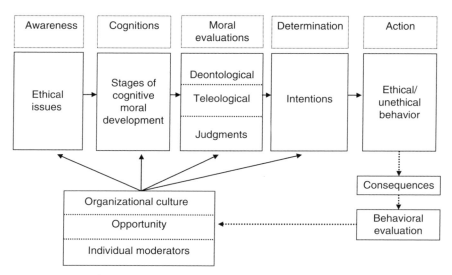

Figure B.3   Synthesis integrated model of ethical decision making. *Source:* Ferrell, O.C., Gresham, L.G., and Fraedrich, J. 1989. Reproduced with the permission of Sage Publications.

moderating variables. Throughout each stage of the ethical decision-making process, various contingency factors such as organizational culture, opportunity, and individual moderators play a moderating role.[21] Figure B.3 depicts the *synthesis integrated model* of ethical decision making.

Another important contribution to ethical decision-making theory was an approach that formally introduced an important new factor, that of the *moral intensity* of the ethical issue. This approach was proposed by Thomas Jones and is referred to as an *issue-contingent model* in that the characteristics of the moral issue itself are also considered.[22] The moral intensity of the issue is proposed to affect Rest's four stages of ethical decision making and can act as both an independent and moderating variable. Another important contribution of the model is that it consolidated several other models.[23] The model begins with the "environment" (social, cultural, economic, and organizational), works through the four stages (recognize moral issue; make a moral judgment; establish moral intent; and engage in moral behavior) and depicts the influence of "significant others," "individual moderators," "situational moderators," and "opportunity." Figure B.4 below depicts the *issue-contingent model*.

The final dominant ethical decision-making model differs from the others by challenging the dominance of moral reasoning being at the core of ethical

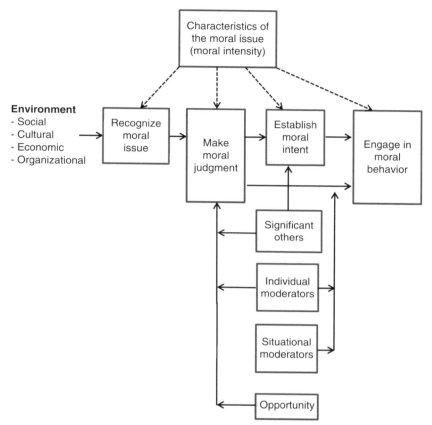

Figure B.4 Issue-contingent model of ethical decision making (Jones, 1991).

decision making. This *non-rationalist approach* is referred to as the *social intuitionist model* of moral judgment by Jonathan Haidt in 2001.[24] First an "eliciting situation" triggers valence-based intuitions. From these moral intuitions, moral judgments appear in our consciousness automatically and effortlessly leading to a moral judgment. Once a moral judgment is made, post hoc moral reasoning can take place to find arguments that will support the already-made judgment. Discussions with others can trigger new intuitions. If others, such as friends and acquaintances, have made a moral judgment, this can also influence the decision-maker. Figure B.5 below depicts the *social intuitionist model* of moral judgment.

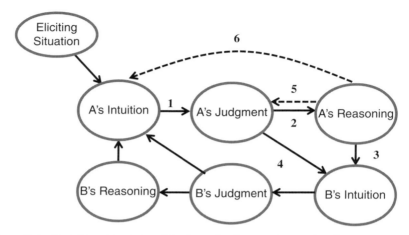

Figure B.5   Social intuitionist model of moral judgment. *Source*: Haidt, J. 2001. Reproduced with the permission of the American Psychological Association. The numbered links, for person A only, are (1) intuitive judgment link; (2) the post hoc reasoning link; (3) the reasoned persuasion link; (4) the social persuasion link; (5) the reasoned judgment link; and (6) the private reflection link.

Notes

1. Rest (1984; 1986).
2. Treviño (1986).
3. Ferrell *et al.* (1989).
4. Jones (1991).
5. Haidt (2001). Other ethical decision-making models not depicted include a *behavior model* (Bommer *et al.*, 1987), a *general theory model* (Hunt and Vitell, 1986), an *integrative model* (Stead *et al.*, 1990), and a *reasoned action* model (Dubinsky and Loken, 1989).
6. See: Brady and Hatch (1992). The four models with the same elements are: Ferrell and Gresham (1985); Hunt and Vitell (1986); Treviño (1986); Bommer *et al.* (1987).
7. There are several other *rationalist* models that focus on the moral reasoning process. For example, in the *general theory model* (Hunt and Vitell, 1986), four factors moderate decision making, including three environmental factors (cultural, industrial, and organizational) and personal experiences. These four factors affect perceptions of the existence of an ethical problem, perceived alternatives, and perceived consequences. Such perceptions along with consideration of deontological norms and evaluation of the consequences lead to deontological and teleological evaluations. These evaluations lead to an ethical judgment. The judgment affects intentions which in addition to situational constraints lead to behavior.

The *integrative model* combines individual and organizational factors (Stead *et al.*, 1990). A person's personality (ego strength, Machiavellianism, and locus of control) and socialization (sex roles, religion, age, work experience, and significant others) influence our ethical system (ethical philosophy and ethical decision ideology). Past decisions affect current and future decisions via the creation of an ethical decision history. A second set of factors exists in the organizational context being composed of managerial philosophy, managerial behavior, reinforcement systems, and characteristics of the job. Our ethical decision history and the organizational forces lead to our ethical behavior. Work experience with its reinforcement and significant influence by management become critical socialization forces influencing the individual.

Another model (Brass *et al.*, 1998) attempts to summarize the various models and concludes that there are three sets of factors influencing decision making: (i) organizational factors (climate, reward systems, norms, and codes of conduct); (ii) individual factors (locus of control, cognitive moral development, and Machiavellianism); and (iii) issue-related factors (magnitude of consequences, social consensus, probability of effect, and proximity). The types and structure of relationships (i.e., social network) then work to influence how these factors affect unethical behavior.

8. Rest (1986).

9. Rest makes it clear that there may be additional stages to the four stages he proposed (1984, p. 28): "Down the road it may seem useful to distinguish five processes, or seven, or whatever." Rest also states that each of the four stages may operate in an order other than moving from awareness to action: (1986, p. 5): "I do not intend to create the impression that the four components depict a linear sequence in real time…In fact, there is research that suggests complicated interactions among the components." Rest also states: "…each component influences the other components through feedback and feed-forward loops" (1984, p. 34). According to Valentine and Hollingworth, the four stages are connected (2012, p. 510): "Previous empirical research demonstrates that these steps are positively interrelated either directly or indirectly."

10. Rest (1986, p. 3). Rest seems to equate "awareness" with a preliminary moral reasoning process prior to a person's moral judgment taking place. This raises the question whether moral awareness precludes the advent of intuitions and emotions. One answer may be that intuition/emotion can also arise after an initial or partial moral reasoning process (e.g., as a "dual process"). In other words, only after we have begun to realize the potential consequences of our potential actions are our gut instincts or emotions triggered.

11. The awareness stage is also referred to as "heightened ethical concern" (De Cremer *et al.*, 2010, p. 3) or "recognizing the moral/ethical issue" (Elm and Radin, 2012, p. 315). Sonenshein (2007, p. 1029) refers to the moral awareness phase as involving "issue construction," i.e., "how individuals create their own meaning from a set of stimuli in the environment…."

12. See: Mencl and May (2009, p. 204): "This phase has been conceptualized as moral reasoning, moral judgment, and moral evaluation."

13. Rest (1984, p. 26).
14. For "determination," see: Ferrell *et al.* (1989, p. 60). Moral intention might be considered synonymous with moral motivation. This stage has been distinguished from moral judgment as follows (Jones, 1991, p. 386): "Once a person has made a moral judgment, a process that is dependent on his or her cognitive moral development…he or she must decide what to do. A decision about what is morally 'correct', a moral judgment, is not the same as a decision to act on that judgement, that is, to establish moral intent." This stage implies placing "ethical" motivations before economic (or self-interested) motivations.
15. Rest (1986, p. 3). In Chapter 1, the process of moving from intent to behavior can be referred to as "moral conation." See: Hannah *et al.* (2011).
16. Narváez and Rest (1995) refer to the fourth stage as "implementation" rather than as action or behavior. This stage has also been referred to as "moral character" (see: Rest *et al.*, 1999, p. 10; Morales-Sánchez and Cabello-Medina, 2013, p. 718).
17. Rest (1986, pp. 4–5).
18. See: Rest (1986, p. 3); Narváez and Rest (1995, p. 386). Rest (1984, p. 35) provides a list of situational factors that can influence each of the stages. He mentions factors such as *moral blindness* that can affect moral awareness ("…presuppositions and prior expectations that blind a person to notice or think about certain aspects") as well as rationalizations that can affect our moral intent ("…defensively reinterpreting the situation by blaming the victim, denying need or deservingness"). The impediments to ethical judgments are discussed further in Chapter 3.
19. Treviño (1986).
20. Ferrell *et al.* (1989).
21. The original model was referred to as a *multistage contingency model* of ethical decision making (Ferrell and Gresham, 1985). Later, Ferrell *et al.* (1989) proposed their revised *synthesis model* which incorporates into their original model (1985) Kohlberg's stages of moral development. Their *synthesis model* also incorporates into their original model (1985) the deontological and teleological moral evaluation process taken from Hunt and Vitell's (1986) ethical decision-making model.
22. See: Jones (1991).
23. The ethical decision-making models integrated by Jones (1991) include: Ferrell and Gresham (1985); Hunt and Vitell (1986); Rest (1986); Treviño (1986); and Dubinsky and Loken (1989).
24. Haidt (2001).

References

Bommer, M.C., Gratto, J., Gravender, J., and Tuttle, M. 1987. A behavioral model of ethical and unethical decision making. *Journal of Business Ethics*, 6: 265–280.

Brady, F.N. and Hatch, M.J. 1992. General causal models in business ethics: an essay on colliding research traditions. *Journal of Business Ethics*, 11: 307–315.

Brass, D.J., Butterfield, K.D., and Skaggs, B.C. 1998. Relationships and unethical behavior: a social network perspective. *Academy of Management Review*, 23: 14–31.

De Cremer, D., Mayer, D.M., and Schminke, M. 2010. Guest Editors' introduction on understanding ethical behavior and decision making: a behavioral ethics approach. *Business Ethics Quarterly*, 20: 1–6.

Dubinsky, A.J. and Loken, B. 1989. Analyzing ethical decision making in marketing. *Journal of Business Research*, 19: 83–107.

Elm, D.R. and Radin, T.J. (2012). Ethical decision making: special or no different? *Journal of Business Ethics*, 107: 313–329.

Ferrell, O.C. and Gresham, L. 1985. A contingency framework for understanding ethical decision making in marketing. *Journal of Marketing*, 49: 87–96.

Ferrell, O.C., Gresham, L.G., and Fraedrich, J. 1989. A synthesis of ethical decision models for marketing. *Journal of Macromarketing*, 9: 55–64.

Haidt, J. 2001. The emotional dog and its rational tail: a social intuitionist approach to moral judgment. *Psychological Review*, 4: 814–834.

Hannah, S.T., Avolio, B.J., and May, D.R. 2011. Moral maturation and moral conation: a capacity approach to explaining moral thought and action. *Academy of Management Review*, 36: 663–685.

Hunt, S.D. and Vitell, S. 1986. A general theory of marketing ethics. *Journal of Macromarketing*, 6: 5–16.

Jones, T.M. 1991. Ethical decision making by individuals in organizations: an issue-contingent model. *The Academy of Management Review*, 16: 366–395.

Mencl, J. and May, D.R. 2009. The effects of proximity and empathy on ethical decision-making: an exploratory investigation. *Journal of Business Ethics*, 85: 201–226.

Morales-Sánchez, R. and Cabello-Medina, C. 2013. The role of four universal moral competencies in ethical decision-making. *Journal of Business Ethics*, 116: 717–734.

Narváez, D. and Rest, J. 1995. The four components of acting morally. In *Moral Development: An Introduction* (M. Kurtines and J. L. Gewirtz, eds). Boston: Allyn and Bacon, pp. 385–399.

Rest, J.R. 1984. The major components of morality. In *Morality, Moral Behavior, and Moral Development* (W. M. Kurtines and J. L. Gewirtz, eds). New York: John Wiley & Sons, Inc., pp. 24–38.

Rest, J.R. 1986. *Moral Development: Advances in Research and Theory*. New York: Praeger.

Rest, J., Narvaez, D., Bebeau, M.J., and Shoma, S.J. 1999. *Postconventional Thinking: A New-Kohlbergian Approach*. Mahwah, NJ: Lawrence Erlbaum Associates.

Sonenshein, S. 2007. The role of construction, intuition, and justification in responding to ethical issues at work: the sensemaking-intuition model. *Academy of Management Review*, 32: 1022–1040.

Stead, W.E., Worrell, D.L., and Stead, J.G. 1990. An integrative model for understanding and managing ethical behavior in business organizations. *Journal of Business Ethics*, 9: 233–242.

Treviño, L.K. 1986. Ethical decision making in organizations: a person–situation interactionist model. *Academy of Management Review*, 11: 601–617.

Valentine, S. and Hollingworth, D. 2012. Moral intensity, issue importance, and ethical reasoning in operations situations. *Journal of Business Ethics*, 108: 509–523.

Appendix C

Normative Ethical Decision-Making Models

The use of simplified ethical decision-making questions, similar to the "3P Filter" described in Chapter 4, has been referred to as an *ethical test* approach.[1] These tests tend to incorporate the moral standards described in Chapter 4 while being more simplified and requiring less cognitive effort to reflect upon.[2] The following will outline several other ethical tests or models that have been proposed.

One commonly referred to example of a series of ethical tests is provided by Nash:[3]

1. Have you defined the problem accurately?
2. How would you define the problem if you stood on the other side of the fence?
3. How did this situation occur in the first place?
4. To whom and what do you give your loyalties as a person and as a member of the corporation?
5. What is your intention in making this decision?
6. How does this intention compare with the likely results?
7. Whom could your decision or action injure?
8. Can you engage the affected parties in a discussion of the problem before you make your decision?
9. Are you confident that your position will be as valid over a long period of time as it seems now?
10. Could you disclose without qualms your decision or action to your boss, your CEO, the board of directors, your family, or society as a whole?
11. What is the symbolic potential of your action if understood? If misunderstood?
12. Under what conditions would you allow exceptions to your stand?

Business Ethics: An Ethical Decision-Making Approach, First Edition. Mark S. Schwartz.
© 2017 John Wiley & Sons, Inc. Published 2017 by John Wiley & Sons, Inc.

Another test was prepared by the Center for Business Ethics at Bentley University and consists of the following:[4]

1. Is it right?
2. Is it fair?
3. Who gets hurt?
4. Would you be comfortable if the details of your decision were reported on the front page of your local newspaper?
5. What would you tell your child to do?
6. How does it smell? (How does it feel?)

A similar model is proposed by Blanchard and Peale:[5]

1. Is it legal? Will I be violating either civil law or company policy?
2. Is it balanced? Is it fair to all concerned in the short term as well as the long term? Does it promote win–win relationships?
3. How will it make me feel about myself? Will it make me proud? Would I feel good if my decision was published in the newspaper? Would I feel good if my family knew about it?

Carroll and Buchholtz present another set of ethical tests:[6]

1. Common sense test: does the action I am getting ready to take really make sense?
2. One's best self test: is this action or decision I'm getting ready to take compatible with my concept of myself at my best?
3. Making something public test: how would I feel if others knew I was doing this? How would I feel if I knew that my decisions or actions were going to be featured on the national evening news tonight for all the world to see?
4. Ventilation test: expose your proposed action to others to get their thoughts on it.
5. Purified idea test: am I thinking this action or decision is right just because someone with appropriate authority or knowledge says it is right?
6. The gag test: the action is going too far if you would simply gag at the prospect of carrying it out.

Another model proposed by Saul focuses on an employee's relationship with his or her company:[7]

1. Can I affirm that I am subordinating my personal interests to the interests of the company?

2. Am I placing my duty to society above my duty to the company and above my personal interests?
3. Have I revealed the facts of any situation where my private interests conflict with those of the company, or the company's with those of society?

The Markkula Center for Applied Ethics has proposed a template to work through in order to make an ethical decision involving a series of steps.[8]

Recognize an ethical issue
1. Could this decision or situation be damaging to someone or to some group? Does this decision involve a choice between a good and bad alternative, or perhaps between two "goods" or between two "bads"?
2. Is this issue about more than what is legal or what is most efficient? If so, how?

Get the facts
3. What are the relevant facts of the case? What facts are not known? Can I learn more about the situation? Do I know enough to make a decision?
4. What individuals and groups have an important stake in the outcome? Are some concerns more important? Why?
5. What are the options for acting? Have all the relevant persons and groups been consulted? Have I identified creative options?

Evaluate alternative actions
6. Evaluate the options by asking the following questions:
   • Which option will produce the most good and do the least harm? (The Utilitarian Approach.)
   • Which option best respects the rights of all who have a stake? (The Rights Approach.)
   • Which option treats people equally or proportionately? (The Justice Approach.)
   • Which option best serves the community as a whole, not just some members? (The Common Good Approach.)
   • Which option leads me to act as the sort of person I want to be? (The Virtue Approach.)

Make a decision and test it
7. Considering all these approaches, which option best addresses the situation?
8. If I told someone I respect, or told a television audience which option I have chosen, what would they say?

Act and reflect on the outcome

9. How can my decision be implemented with the greatest care and attention to the concerns of all stakeholders?
10. How did my decision turn out and what have I learned from this specific situation?

Many companies have also developed their own ethical decision-making tests for their employees that are typically found in their codes of ethics.[9] As one example, Texas Instruments has a "TI Ethics Quick Test" which is provided on a business-card size mini-pamphlet and asks the following questions:[10]

- Is the action legal?
- Does it comply with our values?
- If you do it, will you feel bad?
- How will it look in the newspaper?
- If you know it's wrong, don't do it!
- If you're not sure, ask.
- Keep asking until you get an answer.

Each of the normative models attempts to provide a series of steps for people to determine the ethically appropriate course of action. A number of additional normative decision making models have also been suggested.[11]

Notes

1. Carroll and Buchholtz (2012).
2. Many of these ethical decision-making tests are referred to in Barr *et al.* (2011).
3. Nash (1981).
4. Weiss (1994, p. 80).
5. Blanchard and Peale (1988).
6. Carroll and Buchholtz (2012).
7. Saul (1981, p. 271).
8. See: Markkula Center for Applied Ethics, "A Framework for Ethical Decision Making," August 1, 2015, http://www.scu.edu/ethics/ethics-resources/ethical-decision-making/a-framework-for-ethical-decision-making/ (accessed 17 September 2016).
9. See: Barr, Campbell, and Dando (2011).
10. Texas Instruments website, "Corporate Social Responsibility," http://www.ti.com/corp/docs/company/citizen/ethics/quicktest.shtml (accessed 17 September 2016).
11. For other normative ethical decision-making models see the list compiled by Alex Wellington, "Sample Decision Making Models," 2009, http://www.ryerson.ca/content/dam/ethicsnetwork/downloads/list_of_decision-making_models.pdf (accessed 17 September 2016).

References

Barr, D., Campbell, C., and Dando, N. 2011. *Ethics in Decision-making*. London: Institute of Business Ethics.

Blanchard, K. and Peale, N.V. 1988. *The Power of Ethical Management*. New York: Fawcett Crest.

Carroll, A.B. and Buchholtz, A.K. 2012. *Business and Society: Ethics, Sustainability, and Stakeholder Management* (8th edn). Mason, OH: South-Western Cengage Learning.

Nash, L.L. 1981. Ethics without the sermon. *Harvard Business Review*, 59: 79–89.

Saul, G.K. 1981. Business ethics: where are we going? *Academy of Management Review*, 6: 269–276.

Weiss, J.W. 1994. *Business Ethics: A Managerial, Stakeholder Approach*. Belmont CA: Wadsworth Publishing.

Appendix D

Business Ethics in Hollywood Movies

For those who want to engage more fully in working through difficult moral temptations or ethical dilemmas within a business context, you might consider watching the following Hollywood movies or documentaries. Several of the movies are based on true events. For illustration purposes, only the key ethical issue or dilemma will be mentioned below. The movies are listed in reverse chronological order.[1]

- *Deepwater Horizon* (2016). Inspired by true events, visiting executives from the BP oil company put pressure on the employees of the offshore drilling rig compromising its safety. http://www.imdb.com/title/tt1860357/.
- *The Big Short* (2015). Inspired by real events, several individuals bet against the housing market prior to its collapse and take on the big banks for their lack of foresight and greed. http://www.imdb.com/title/tt1596363/.
- *The Wolf of Wall Street* (2013). Based on true events involving Jordan Belfort, a penny stockbroker who engages in a massive 'pump and dump' securities scheme leading to money laundering and bribery. http://www.imdb.com/title/tt0993846/.
- *Promised Land* (2012). A salesman for a natural gas company must attempt to convince farmers of the benefits of selling drilling rights to the company despite the environmental concerns. http://www.imdb.com/title/tt2091473/.
- *Arbitrage* (2012). A manager of a hedge fund cooks the books in order to cover up a loss and result in a potential highly profitable sale of his company. Should the manager admit the fraud and go to jail? http://www.imdb.com/title/tt1764183.
- *Margin Call* (2011). After discovering it is headed towards a financial disaster, should the investment bank attempt to dump its mortgage-backed

Business Ethics: An Ethical Decision-Making Approach, First Edition. Mark S. Schwartz.
© 2017 John Wiley & Sons, Inc. Published 2017 by John Wiley & Sons, Inc.

securities to its clients which have become toxic assets in order to avoid bankruptcy? http://www.imdb.com/title/tt1615147/.

- *Inside Job* (2010). A documentary that analyzes the changes in the financial industry leading to the global financial crisis of 2008, which caused millions of people to lose their homes and jobs, nearly resulting in a global financial collapse. http://www.imdb.com/title/tt1645089/.
- *Money Never Sleeps* (2010). In the sequel to the movie *Wall Street*, Gordon Gekko, after being released from prison for insider trading and securities fraud, attempts to rebuild his empire. http://www.imdb.com/title/tt1027718/.
- *Unstoppable* (2010). Inspired by an incident which took place in 2001, a train company must decide whether to intentionally derail a runaway train carrying toxic chemicals in a rural area before it heads towards more populated areas. http://www.imdb.com/title/tt0477080/.
- *The Informant!* (2009). Based on a true story, vice president Mark Whitacre blows the whistle on the price-fixing activities of his agro-business firm Archer Daniels Midland. http://www.imdb.com/title/tt1130080/.
- *Up in the Air* (2009). A corporate downsizer travels around the world firing employees. How should employees be fired? What should be said to them? Is it okay to fire employees via video conferencing? http://www.imdb.com/title/tt1193138/.
- *Avatar* (2009). Do you help your company remove the indigenous alien population on another planet in order to extract a valuable mineral resource needed on Earth? http://www.imdb.com/title/tt0499549/.
- *The Box* (2009). A financially desperate couple must decide whether to push a button in a box and earn $1 million but knowing that one person somewhere will die as a result. http://www.imdb.com/title/tt0362478/.
- *Michael Clayton* (2007). A lawyer must decide to what extent he will try to prevent a colleague from blowing the whistle on a chemical company client he knows is guilty. http://www.imdb.com/title/tt0465538/.
- *Enron: The Smartest Guys in the Room* (2005). A documentary showing the extent of greed and corrupt practices rampant at Enron leading to its downfall. http://www.imdb.com/title/tt1016268/.
- *Lord of War* (2005). Should an arms dealer continue to earn a fortune in an amoral manner by selling weapons to an African warlord? http://www.imdb.com/title/tt0399295/.
- *Thank You for Smoking* (2005). The chief spokesperson for Big Tobacco speaks on behalf of cigarettes while trying to remain a role model for his 12-year-old son. Should one argue on behalf of a business that makes money selling a product that when used as intended harms its customers? http://www.imdb.com/title/tt0427944/.
- *The Constant Gardener* (2005). While searching for the reasons for his wife's murder, the husband discovers that the pharmaceutical industry is

prepared to engage in dubious drug testing on the local Kenyan population. http://www.imdb.com/title/tt0387131/.

- *Hotel Rwanda* (2005). Based on real life events taking place in 1994, a hotel manager must decide whether to try to save over one thousand Rwandan refugees by giving them shelter in the hotel after civil war erupts. http://www.imdb.com/title/tt0395169/.

- *The Corporation* (2003). A documentary critiquing the practices of corporations and comparing the way companies behave with the symptoms of psychopathy. http://www.imdb.com/title/tt0379225/.

- *John Q.* (2002). A father discovers that his son is diagnosed with a serious heart condition and that his health insurance will not pay for a life-saving heart transplant. Do we blame the father for taking hostages in the hospital until his son is placed on the recipient list? http://www.imdb.com/title/tt0251160/.

- *Monsters, Inc.* (2001). Monsters scare children in order to generate power for their city, but one of the monsters must decide what to do when he discovers the lengths his CEO will go in order to deal with a child who has entered into their world. http://www.imdb.com/title/tt0198781/.

- *Erin Brockovich* (2000). Based on a true story, a legal assistant takes on a class-action lawsuit against energy giant Pacific Gas Company that has covered up polluting the water supply. http://www.imdb.com/title/tt0195685/.

- *Boiler Room* (2000). A college dropout begins to work as a broker for an investment firm. Should he follow instructions and take advantage of his clients in order to gain financial success? http://www.imdb.com/title/tt0181984/.

- *Rogue Trader* (1999). Based on a true story, Nick Leeson is a British trader working in Singapore for Barings Bank. Leeson must initially decide whether to disclose a subordinate's trading error, or gamble with the client's money to make up for the loss. http://www.imdb.com/title/tt0131566/.

- *The Insider* (1999). Based on the true story of Dr Jeffrey Wigand, a tobacco executive must decide whether to blow the whistle on his firm Brown & Williamson which he discovers is selling an even more addictive and dangerous cigarette. Should Wigand blow the whistle despite signing a comprehensive confidentiality agreement at a time when he is relying on corporate health benefits for his ill child? http://www.imdb.com/title/tt0140352.

- *The Truman Show* (1998). Is it acceptable to manipulate the life of a person from birth in order to achieve substantial television ratings? Is it acceptable to watch such a show? http://www.imdb.com/title/tt0120382/.

- *Rainmaker* (1997). A young lawyer takes on an insurance company that has a strategy of refusing the claims of its policy holders. http://www.imdb.com/title/tt0119978/.

- *Gattaca* (1997). In order to fulfill one's life goal and become an astronaut, do you assume the identity of a genetically superior person in order to get through the company's training program? http://www.imdb.com/title/tt0119177/.

- *Jerry Maguire* (1996). Should a successful sports agent change from the dishonest way he currently takes care of his clients? http://www.imdb.com/title/tt0116695/.
- *Quiz Show* (1994). Based on real events, Charles van Doren must decide whether to give the correct answer on a game show when he knows that the producers know that he already knows the answers. Should he give the correct answer and become the new champion? http://www.imdb.com/title/tt0110932/.
- *Schindler's List* (1993). Based on a true story, Oscar Schindler must decide whether to risk his own life and engage in bribery in order to save over one thousand of his Polish-Jewish workers from Nazi persecution during the Holocaust. http://www.imdb.com/title/tt0108052/.
- *Barbarians at the Gate* (1993). Based on the actual takeover of RJR Nabisco in 1988, the firm's CEO attempts a leveraged buyout of the company but a bidding war ensues raising the share price substantially. http://www.imdb.com/title/tt0106356/.
- *Glengarry Glen Ross* (1992). Four Chicago real estate salesmen and their supervisor work to sell real estate at inflated prices. A competition takes place where the two worst performing salesmen will be fired. What is one willing to do to get the firm's best leads on potential buyers and make the sale? http://www.imdb.com/title/tt0104348/.
- *Other People's Money* (1991). A corporate raider buys companies and then sells off the assets. As the target company and the main employer in a small town, what would you be willing to do to convince the raider to go away and prevent the hostile takeover? http://www.imdb.com/title/tt0102609/.
- *Class Action* (1991). Roughly based on the Ford Pinto, a lawyer represents a client suing an auto manufacturer for injuries caused by a defective automobile. Should the number of future driver deaths be compared with the cost of fixing the cars? http://www.imdb.com/title/tt0101590/.
- *Wall Street* (1987). During the high flying 1980s on Wall Street, a young stockbroker engages in insider trading under the mentorship of a ruthless and greedy corporate raider. Would you pass on confidential information to finally make it to the big leagues? http://www.imdb.com/title/tt0094291/.
- *Silkwood* (1983). Based on the true story of Karen Silkwood and her attempts to expose worker safety violations at the plutonium fuel facility where she worked. Would you attempt to report the wrongdoing? http://www.imdb.com/title/tt0086312/.
- *The China Syndrome* (1979). After a near nuclear meltdown, a shift supervisor discovers there is a safety hazard at the plant. The plant superintendent is determined, however, to start up the reactor again. Should the

technician blow the whistle and ensure the facility remains shut down until it is safe to operate? http://www.imdb.com/title/tt0078966/.

- *On the Waterfront* (1954). An ex-boxer who has become a longshoreman struggles with his conscience whether to stand up to his corrupt union bosses. http://www.imdb.com/title/tt0047296/.

Note

1. For those interested in greater discussion on the use of movies for teaching business ethics, there are now several writings on the topic. See: Teays (2015) who provides in-depth discussion of business ethics through movies, or Boyle and Sandonà (2014) who discuss their own experiential approach to using movies to teach business ethics.

References

Boyle, E.J. and Sandonà, L. 2014. Teaching business ethics through popular feature films: an experiential approach. *Journal of Business Ethics*, 121: 329–340.

Teays, W. 2015. *Business Ethics Through Movies: A Case Study Approach*. Oxford: Wiley-Blackwell.

Index

Page numbers in *italics* refer to Figures; page numbers in **bold** refer to Tables.
EDM stands for Ethical Decision Making.

Business Ethics: An Ethical Decision-Making Approach, First Edition. Mark S. Schwartz.
© 2017 John Wiley & Sons, Inc. Published 2017 by John Wiley & Sons, Inc.